ELUL 5775

To KESHET —
with gratitude
for all that you have
done to heal our
broken world and
bring justice to all —
with love and
respect —

[signature]

Jeff / Rachel,

Gratitude - for
all that you
have done for
all will miss
you but I am
glad

Eric 9745

קהילה קדושה בית שמחת תורה

CONGREGATION
BEIT
SIMCHAT
TORAH

# CONGREGATION BEIT SIMCHAT TORAH

קהילה קדושה בית שמחת תורה

CONGREGATION BEIT SIMCHAT TORAH
NEW YORK, NY

# CHANGING LIVES, MAKING HISTORY: CONGREGATION BEIT SIMCHAT TORAH

## THE FIRST FORTY YEARS

RABBI AYELET S. COHEN
FOREWORD BY RABBI SHARON KLEINBAUM

Copyright © 2014 by
Congregation Beit Simchat Torah

All rights reserved. No part of this book may be reproduced or utilized in any form or by any means, electronic, or mechanical, including photocopying, recording, or by any information storage or retrieval system, without permission in writing from the publisher.

For information, address all inquiries
to office @ cbst.org
www.cbst.org

The photo credits that appear on page 320 constitute an extension of this copyright page. Every effort has been made to obtain permission to reproduce material protected by copyright. Where omissions or errors have occurred, the publisher will provide correct credit in future printings.

PROJECT EDITORS: Susan E. Meyer, Marsha Melnick
ADMINISTRATIVE AND RESEARCH ASSISTANT: Tasha Calhoun
ART DIRECTION: Jon Glick, mouse+tiger
DESIGN PRODUCTION: Michaelis/Carpelis Design
COPYEDITOR: Susan Pensak
PROOFREADER: Jack Greenberg
PRODUCTION: Bill Rose Production
INDEXER: Vered Meir
LEGAL CONSULTANT: Nancy J. Mertzel

ISBN: 978-0-9794009-1-9

Printed and bound in China
by Oceanic Graphic International

FRONTISPIECE: Janet Pavloff sounding the shofar

10 9 8 7 6 5 4 3 2 1

וְעָשׂוּ לִי מִקְדָּשׁ וְשָׁכַנְתִּי בְּתוֹכָם

שמות כ"ה: ח

*Make for Me a holy place so that I may dwell among you.*

*Exodus 25:8*

CONGREGATION BEIT SIMCHAT TORAH is grateful to the following individuals for their generosity as underwriters of this historic publication:

    Erika Karp & Sari Kessler
    Heymi Kuriel
    Susan E. Meyer & Marsha Melnick

THE COMMUNITY also offers thanks to the following supporters for their substantial contributions:

    William H. Fern
    Barbara Gaines & Aari Ludvidgsen
    William J. Hibsher & Richard Orient
    Rabbi Sharon Kleinbaum & Randi Weingarten
    Rosanne Leipzig & Ora Chaikin
    Regina Linder & Leah Trachten
    Jonathan Sheffer
    Rabbi Rachel Weiss

# CONTENTS

| | |
|---|---|
| FOREWORD BY RABBI SHARON KLEINBAUM | 9 |
| INTRODUCTION AND ACKNOWLEDGMENTS | 10 |

## THE EARLY YEARS

| | |
|---|---|
| 1. FROM SHOPPING BAG TO SANCTUARY | 14 |
| 2. LAYING THE CORNERSTONE | 40 |
| 3. THE IMPACT OF AIDS | 56 |
| 4. A RABBI FOR CBST | 84 |

## BUILDING THE SANCTUARY

| | |
|---|---|
| 5. SPIRITUAL AND LAY LEADERSHIP | 108 |
| 6. INSCRIBING THE TEXT | 132 |
| 7. DAYS OF CELEBRATION AND AWE | 152 |
| 8. SINGING A NEW SONG | 180 |

## ENLARGING THE TENT

| | |
|---|---|
| 9. A SACRED COMMUNITY | 200 |
| 10. COME OUT AND LEARN | 224 |
| 11. TRANSFORMING OUR WORLD | 246 |
| 12. BUILDING FOR THE FUTURE | 286 |
| GLOSSARY | 310 |
| ABBREVIATIONS | 313 |
| INDEX | 314 |
| PHOTO CREDITS | 320 |

אֶבֶן מָאֲסוּ הַבּוֹנִים הָיְתָה לְרֹאשׁ פִּנָּה

תהלים קי"ח:כב

*The stone that the builders rejected has become the cornerstone.*

Psalm 118:22

# FOREWORD

IF THIS BOOK told only the story of the first forty years of a remarkable, quirky, irreverent, profound LGBTQS (Lesbian, Gay, Bisexual, Transgender, Queer, Straight) synagogue community—*dayeynu*—that would have been enough. But there is so much more.

The story, or rather the stories in *Changing Lives, Making History: Congregation Beit Simchat Torah* illuminate forty revolutionary and transformative years in the life of New York City, the nation, and the Middle East—in the gay liberation movement; progressive Jewish religious movements; in the rise of feminism; the explosion of the politicized religious right, and in the ongoing Israeli/Palestinian struggles to achieve lasting peace. These past forty years have witnessed, among other things, the impact of AIDS; breakthroughs in reproductive technologies and the gay baby boom; the emergence of the queer and trans movements; and major Supreme Court decisions in support of equal rights.

Through it all, CBST has been at the epicenter. Our members and clergy have been the authors, the activists, the leaders, the foot soldiers, the victims, the protagonists, the lawyers, the board members, the executive directors, the staff, the demonstrators, the litigants, the litigators, the lovers, the parents, the children, the grandparents, and the teachers. At the same time and in the midst of these profound changes, CBST has created a spiritual sanctuary where so many individuals have been nourished and transformed on the deepest level of their souls. Prayer, Shabbat, music, and community have always been at the core, providing strength for the work to be done in the world and connecting us to the One who has created us all.

When CBST celebrated its first service that cold night in February 1973, no Jewish organization or synagogue in the world accepted us. The world outside asked, "why a gay synagogue?" And now that so many claim gay people are welcome in their synagogues, they ask, "why a GLBT synagogue?"

And I ask: Why do 4,000 people from all over the world—young and old, gay, queer, and straight, with widely differing backgrounds and beliefs—attend CBST's High Holidays services each year? I believe CBST has created a paradigm for living a meaningful Jewish life in challenging times that resonates across religious boundaries, ages, races, sexual, and gender identities. Our unique history contains many of the answers and our present community and vision for the future holds the promise.

Rabbi Ayelet Cohen brilliantly explores the stories, the history, and the individuals whose personal narratives woven together create a magnificently textured, moving, and inspiring fabric. Rabbi Cohen served CBST for ten years—first as a Cooperberg-Rittmaster Rabbinical Intern and then as my rabbinic partner. In this volume, she paints a profound portrait of a community sometimes under attack from the outside, sometimes struggling under the weight of internal debates and pressures, and at other times rejoicing in the dignity of their lives. Thank you to all who contributed to making this forty-year celebration a reality. We often say we stand on the shoulders of those who came before us and here we can truly remember and see why. We hope that those who follow us will read this book with affection, forgiveness, and love. We are doing all that we do for you who might be reading these words on CBST's eightieth.

*Tov l'hodot*, with deep gratitude to the One who has brought us to this day, we pray that the work of our hands and the prayers of our hearts will bring blessings to all who enter our open doors.

RABBI SHARON KLEINBAUM, 2013

# INTRODUCTION

CBST HAS UNDERGONE REMARKABLE TRANSFORMATION in its first four decades. What began as a bold experiment of barely a minyan of gay men in 1973 unquestionably has changed the fabric of American Judaism. The synagogue has consciously expanded its mission to serve the constituencies of lesbians, transgender, and straight members who quickly followed, and the bisexual, intersex, queer, questioning, and label-defying members who help make the community what it is today.

I had been to CBST several times before I began my Cooperberg-Rittmaster Rabbinical Internship in 2000. The community was entering a period of stability and optimism after a tumultuous few years. Right away I was drawn in by its ritual diversity, its deep and joyful *Yiddishkeit*, its brave spirit, and its sense of history. Rabbi Sharon Kleinbaum taught my fellow intern David Dunn Bauer and me not only the skills we would need to become rabbis, but the stories that would make us fall in love with CBST. Still reeling from the devastating AIDS deaths that had rocked the community in the previous several years, she described those who had come before with humor and love and introduced us to the people who would continue building the community into the next century.

The decade I spent at CBST was a time of profound transition for LGBT people in Jewish and American life. Almost every significant Jewish LGBT leader at some point passed through CBST, spent formative moments there, or turned to it for support. Some younger activists may not even know the ways in which CBST paved the road for them to perform the radical and inspiring work they do today. It is my great hope that the accounts of the people and the community contained in these pages will claim their rightful place within the annals of LGBTQ Jewish history.

It is a tremendous challenge to tell the story of a living community, whose members' lives are so deeply entwined with its history. For as many stories as are told on these pages, there are countless others that may feel to some readers equally as significant, as poignant, as dramatic, which constraints of time and space made impossible to include. It is also a singular challenge (and great honor) to try to recount the history of a community to which I am so deeply connected. I have attempted to chronicle events that place CBST in the broader context of other changes in LGBT and Jewish history: revealing how those changes played out at CBST and how CBST helped advance those changes. I have done my best to paint an honest portrait of these four decades at CBST, recording both painful, as well as triumphant episodes. Ultimately, this community and its history are worthy of great celebration, and I hope my telling captures the great affection and deep respect I have for its protagonists.

The process of researching this book was something of a treasure hunt, which entailed wading through boxes of unmarked photographs, piles of dusty flyers, and stacks of files which were the result of several unfinished attempts to organize the CBST archives through the years. That a fledgling synagogue kept such copious troves of letters, drafts of liturgies, and artifacts attests either to an astounding prescience as to its own historic import or is evidence of a deep nostalgia that set in almost as soon as events occurred in real time. I believe both to be at play, and to all of the collectors, the packrats and freelance archivists, I offer my gratitude.

This book could not have been completed without the work of many people. Almost without exception, anyone who was approached to help stepped forward, searching their memories and files until they found what we were looking for. I am very grateful to everyone who responded to calls for interviews and invitations to share photos and other artifacts.

*Mikol melamdai hiskalti.* I have learned from all of my teachers. Jack Greenberg, Art Leonard, and Regina Linder were stalwart research partners, providing steady and essential assistance; I relied on their remarkable memories and personal records as they answered countless questions, read and fact-checked chapters (and in Jack's case, proofread and fact-checked the entire book). Along with Yehuda Berger, Bill Fern, Bruce Friedman, Hanna Gafni, Rosanne Leipzig, Michael Levine, Annette Miller *z"l*, Yolanda Potasinski, Lou Rittmaster, and Saul Zalkin they made themselves available for additional interviews, identified photographs, sorted through the archives, shared personal mementos, or introduced me to former CBST members now far afield whose stories were essential to record. Despite health challenges, Reb Pinchas ben Aharon generously pored over old images and shared his recollections of CBST's formative history.

Richard Howe's careful research and meticulous files provided a valuable foundation for this book. The CBST StoryCorps project, initiated by Harriet Beckman, helped create an essential core of recorded interviews. Nancy Mertzel provided important legal advice. Rich Wandel guided us through the LGBT Center Archives. For the evocative photos in this book I thank all of CBST's official and unofficial photographers, past and present, in particular Barbara Gaines and Aari Ludvigsen, whose online photo archive proved invaluable.

The CBST staff excelled as research assistants and personal detectives, shlepping boxes, locating materials and reaching out to members. I am grateful to all of them, especially Chet Roijce, Gabriel Blau, Gustavo Cecilio, Ariel Kates-Harris, and Rabbi Rachel Weiss. Almost every former Cooperberg-Rittmaster Rabbinical Intern, Cantorial Intern, and board president contributed to this book, taking care to recall the transformative moments they spent at CBST. Tasha Calhoun's patience, sensitivity and dedication, which have earned the trust of CBST congregants and staff for many years, were essential beyond measure.

I was blessed to have the opportunity to work with such careful and caring editors as Susan Meyer and Marsha Melnick, who guided me through the uncharted waters of this vast project and steered it home. My friend and colleague Rabbi Sharon Kleinbaum has championed this project and has supported it steadfastly at every turn.

My friends and family provided much advice and encouragement, especially Jeff Waller, who consistently provided both as well as a place to write. Tamara Cohen, my lifelong writing coach, first brought me to CBST and in so doing changed the course of my life; Maya Orli Cohen, one-time CBST photo archivist and source of unending love and support who shares my love of this community; Gwynn Kessler who understands the power of sacred text; Elaine Shizgal Cohen and Stephen P. Cohen taught me how a deep understanding of history can propel us forward; and most of all, Rabbi Marc Margolius, a keen editor, a beautiful writer, and my partner in all things, who carried the weight of this project alongside me to its fruition. I am constantly inspired by our children, Max and Sammy who are already engaged in the work of transforming their generation for good, and by Galia, Meital, and Ziv who, forty years after the founding of CBST, are growing up in a world with infinitely more possibility, freedom, and justice.

*Vehigad'ta l'vincha* וְהִגַּדְתָּ לְבִנְךָ
*You shall tell this story to the generation to come.* Exodus 13:8

דור הבונים

THE EARLY YEARS

# 1. FROM SHOPPING BAG TO SANCTUARY

On a cold February evening in 1973, a small group of gay men gathered in New York City to celebrate Shabbat. They came together in the belief that it was possible to be both deeply Jewish and proudly gay, an idea truly radical for its time. The prayers they uttered had been spoken millions of times before over thousands of years. But this particular *Kabbalat Shabbat* would change the lives of countless lesbian, gay, bisexual, transgender, and straight Jews of all ages and Jewish experiences for generations to come. The founders had hoped simply to create a community in which they could integrate and celebrate their Jewish and gay identities. The synagogue born that night has become Congregation Beit Simchat Torah—a spiritual home for its members that has redefined the relationship between Judaism and sexuality and continues to transform the religious and political landscape throughout the world.

## In the Beginning

The ad Jacob Gubbay placed in the *Village Voice* announced simply, "Gay Synagogue, Friday Night Service and Oneg Shabbat, Feb. 9, 8:00 PM"

The truth was Jacob—an Indian Jew living in New York—didn't really know how to lead a Friday night service, not to mention how to create a synagogue. But he sensed the time had come. So, on that first Friday night in 1973, he packed candlesticks and *kippot*, kiddush wine, and challah in two paper shopping bags and waited to see who would come.

ABOVE: Jacob Gubbay moved to Australia not long after founding CBST.

LEFT: Ad in the *Village Voice*, February 1973

Between ten and fifteen people showed up at that first service, held in the annex of the Church of the Holy Apostles. Within a year the number grew to one hundred. By 1975, only two years later, the annex could no longer accommodate the Friday night service. Some came to those early services because they had seen the ads in the *Village Voice* or the *New York Times*. Others had picked up a flyer at a bar or read a skeptical article in the local Jewish press. Many came at the urging of a friend. Michael Levine attended his first High Holiday service in 1974

> **HOW I GOT TO CBST**
>
> I'm one of the founding members of CBST. I saw a very small article in the Jewish newspaper of Northern New Jersey about a group of gay people who were having a synagogue service somewhere in Manhattan. I called up a very good friend of mine, Irving Cooperberg, who is now deceased, and I said, "Irv, I just read about this group; we've got to go there." I was leaving for Europe a few days after that, so he said to me, "Well, when you get back from Europe in six weeks, we'll go together." And I said, "That's fine." Well, I came back from Europe six weeks later and I said "Irv, I'm ready to go to meet with this group," and he said, "Bill, I couldn't wait. I had to go without you. I had to see what it was. And I'm telling you, although we have been friends for years, if you don't like these people I don't think I can ever be friends with you at all." I said, "Give me a chance and let me meet them!" We met at the church on 28th Street, and of course I fell in love with them right away, and that was how I began.
>
> BILL FERN, MEMBER SINCE 1973

Bill Fern making announcements at the second International Conference of Gay Jews, held at CBST, April 1977

after a friend described a flyer hanging in the pornography shop on Christopher and Hudson Streets.

While many more than fifteen people claimed to have attended the first service, Dick Radvon, who arrived at CBST within its first six weeks and quickly became a mainstay, modestly took care not to describe himself as a founder. "CBST was right for me. I saw the ad: Gay Synagogue. And I thought, hey, I'm gay, I'm Jewish. Why don't I go there? I came and never left." Like many others, Dick discovered his Jewish identity on Friday night as he perched on a children's desk in the Church of the Holy Apostles annex. "I thought, 'this feels like home. And this is what I should have been doing all my life.'"

In 1973, and still today, for many people, venturing into the service for the first time was terrifying and exciting. Yehuda Berger recalls carrying the ad folded up in his wallet for weeks before summoning the courage to come for the first time. In 1980 Jack Greenberg walked around the block three times before he felt brave enough to make his first trip up the ramp and into the shul. Yolanda Potasinski felt a similar fear and exhilaration at her first service in 1987. For them and many others, entering that sanctuary was a transformative act of claiming a joyful, prayerful, Jewish gay life.

A flyer for the synagogue from 1974 or 1975 explained the mission of the synagogue as understood by its founders:

The Gay Synagogue is more than a house of worship. Rather it is dedicated to a total immersion in Jewishness and enjoyment of the many facets of rich Jewish heritage . . . .

Why a separate synagogue for gays? Probably there are as many reasons as there are people in attendance. Some find it difficult to relate to Establishment congregations in which they are shunned unless they conceal their predilections. Others have lost interest in a religious life altogether but find a special rapport with this group. Still others, with no religious background whatsoever, are eager to establish a Jewish identity within their own special framework. Perhaps the greatest attraction of all is the opportunity openly to enjoy one's Jewishness and one's gayness.

When Yehuda finally walked through the door into the church annex, he saw a classroom crowded with twenty or thirty men. He took a seat near the door to facilitate an easy escape. At the bimah stood Pinchas ben Aharon, described by member Elenore Lester as "a tall, heavyish man of about thirty with luminous gray eyes, dark hair, and a trim dark beard framing a yeshiva pale face." Reb Pinchas, who came from a Chasidic background, had quickly emerged as the volunteer spiritual leader of the community. The room echoed with familiar Shabbat songs and prayers. Yehuda didn't need his early exit. He said to himself, "I'm home. I've really found a place where I can be myself."

## The Institutional Landscape

The climate for gay men and lesbians in the Jewish community during the early 1970s mirrored that of secular society: at best silence, but frequently outright derision and discrimination. "For me to practice being gay was very difficult," Michael Levine remembers. "I had to hide everything, from family, friends, school, and I was dating girls at the same time. It made me feel terrible. I would have trouble breathing sometimes when I thought of the difficulty of leading this lifestyle. But how could I ever tell my family? A Jewish household, they expected me to get married and have lots of children. How could I tell them that I am 'homosexual?' I hid the truth for all of those years."

In the wake of the Stonewall riots of 1969, change was in the air. The gay and lesbian community in New York had begun to organize. Newly free from the culture of the closet, activists founded a proliferation of advocacy and affinity groups. Many of the organizations founded then no longer exist, like the Gay Activists Alliance, which emerged as the political center of the gay liberation movement. Others continue to thrive, pursuing LGBT civil rights and social transformation. Along with CBST, Lambda Legal and the National Gay Task Force (now NGLTF) were founded in New York in 1973.

"At that time, a lot of gay groups were forming around all different kinds of

Early CBST flyer c. 1974

### A Homosexual Temple Holds Rites on West Side

**By MARCIA CHAMBERS**

The men took seats on wooden folding chairs in a semicircle in a room at a West Side church community center they call their synagogue.

The lights dimmed. A young man with a maroon velvet yarmulke on his head stood be-

American Hebrew Congregations, the congregational arm of Reform Judaism—which has more than 700 synagogue affiliates and more than one million members—for membership.

If approved, the Los Angeles congregation would receive fu

true identity for fear of professional retaliation. All those interviewed asked to be called by their first name or by a fictitious first name.

"This is the first time I have felt at ease in a synagogue," David said. "It is the first time the two very different parts of

In 1970s New York, the existence of a gay synagogue was newsworthy as reported in the *New York Times*, December 23, 1973.

The Christopher Street Liberation Day March, 1970s

identities," recalls Regina Linder. "Learning that there was any kind of group that melded Jewish and gay identities was a tremendous attraction for me."

Some progressive rabbis were beginning to take on gay civil rights as an issue of social justice. In a 1974 article in *Present Tense*, a Jewish magazine, Elenore Lester noted that "a number of rabbis joined last spring with clergymen of other faiths and social agencies in taking a strong stand on the civil rights issue, supporting Intro 2, the twice defeated New York City bill banning discrimination against homosexuals in jobs and housing." The American Jewish Committee joined the coalition supporting the measure. Ultimately, the bill was defeated, in no small part because of the Chasidic cooperation with the Catholic opposition, an unlikely coalition that was just beginning. The measure was not to pass until 1986.

Synagogue life in general revolved around the constant assumption and celebration of heterosexuality. Synagogues across the spectrum of affiliation deferred to the ancient Levitical prohibitions. Many gay men and lesbians could

not find their place in any synagogue. "I needed the tie to a shul," Michael Levine recalled. "I missed it dreadfully in my life. Whenever I went to a synagogue, the first thing I would hear on a Friday night, was, 'Do we have a girl for you!' That was not what I was looking for. That's why I left Brooklyn."

At the same time, it was apparent that LGBT people of faith were beginning to assert their existence. In 1968 the Reverend Troy Perry had founded Metropolitan Community Church in his living room in a Los Angeles suburb; by 1973 the denomination had expanded to churches in other major cities, including New York. MCC resonated deeply for many gay Jews who had grown alienated from Judaism after coming out. It allowed them to imagine a Judaism that didn't insist on heterosexuality as a prerequisite. In Los Angeles, Reverend Perry encouraged Jews seeking a gay spiritual life at MCC to create a gay synagogue; they founded Beth Chayim Chadashim (BCC) in May 1972.

The Episcopal Church of the Holy Apostles in Chelsea had become the temporary home for numerous fledgling New York City gay and lesbian organizations, including MCC, the Catholic Church of the Beloved Disciple, and the Westside Discussion Group. Holy Apostles had a long history of social justice activism dating back to its founding as an outreach church for immigrants working on the Hudson River waterfront. It is also rumored to have been a stop on the Underground Railroad. (In 1977 two of the first women priests—one being the first openly lesbian priest—in the Diocese of New York—were ordained at Holy Apostles.) Father Weeks, the rector of Holy Apostles, welcomed the gay Jews who attended church services and, like the Reverend Perry in Los Angeles, encouraged them to create their own synagogue. In fact, it is rumored that the idea for the shul was born at an interfaith Passover seder at Holy Apostles. When Jacob Gubbay took the bold step of announcing the advent of the new gay synagogue, he knew where it would meet. The question was whether anyone would come.

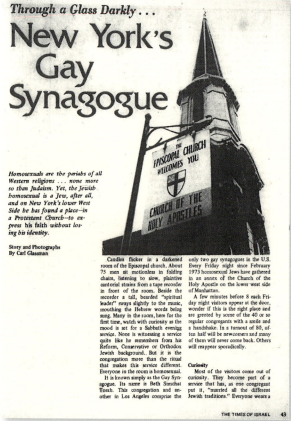

The Church of the Holy Apostles on Ninth Avenue and 28th Street, 1975

### Becoming CBST

For its first few months, the "gay synagogue" had no name and no formal membership structure. Bill Fern recalls that after services attendees would contribute a dollar or two to cover costs. After the Yom Kippur War broke out in October 1973, New York's gay and lesbian Jews, like

> Bill Fern recalls that after services attendees would contribute a dollar or two to cover costs.

other Jews across the country, sought a Jewish community. Attendance surged, as did expenses. The members decided to incorporate as a synagogue.

The 1970s were a time of great innovation in the American Jewish community. Many young Jews advocated abandoning the organized synagogue structure in favor of lay-led, participatory *chavurot*. The founders of CBST sought a more traditional structure. They wanted to be a synagogue and felt validated by the presence of their traditionally oriented rebbe. Although CBST was pushing boundaries in terms of sexual orientation, the group viewed itself as fully within Jewish norms in practically every other way. Its major concerns were Israel, Soviet Jewry, and gay civil rights. The language of CBST's early documents and newsletters expresses the desire for the legitimacy and authenticity of a "real" synagogue combined with the pioneering spirit present in the post-1967 Zionism of American Jews.

CBST was incorporated on November 2, 1973. The incorporation certificate

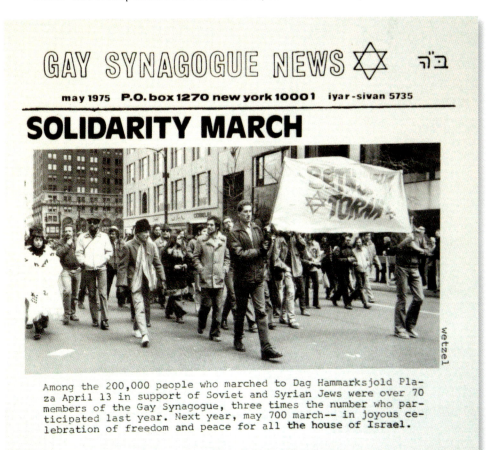

March for Soviet Jewry, 1975

7. The names of the persons elected as trustees, and the terms of office for which they were respectively elected are as follows: Jerome Cunningham, Jacob Gubbay, Nancy Lowe, Arnold Mandelbaum, Henry Mendelson, Paul ———, Saul Mizrahi, Elliot Terr, and Fred Weber, all of whom to hold office until the first annual election of trustees, at which time one third of the trustees shall be elected to hold office until the first annual election thereafter, one third to hold office until the second annual election thereafter, and one third to hold office until the third annual election thereafter.

8. The principal place of worship of said congregation is located in the City of New York, County of New York and State of New York.

IN WITNESS WHEREOF, we have executed and acknowledged this certificate this 30th day of November, 1973.

*[Signatures: Murray Lichtenstein, Jerome Cunningham, Jacob Gubbay, Nancy Lowe, Henry Mendelson, Saul Mizrahi, Elliot Terr]*

*[Stamp: State of New York, County of New York, No. 075237, DEC 5 1973, Norman Goodman, County Clerk]*

CBST's certificate of incorporation, dated December 5, 1973

names nine members present at the meeting. The members of the appointed interim Board of Trustees included Jerome Cunningham, Jacob Gubbay, Nancy Lowe, Arnold Mandelbaum, Henry Mendelson, Pinchas ben Aharon, Saul Mizrahi, Elliot Terr, and Fred Weber.

The name of the congregation, was the subject of significant debate. Bill Fern recalls, "Initially, we agreed on the name 'Congregation Beth Torah v'Simchah' which means 'congregation of Jewish learning and joy.' But the fellow who was delegated to file the legal papers was not especially well educated in Judaism and thought we had mixed it up. He was familiar with the holiday Simchat Torah but not with the expression 'Torah v'Simchah,' so he switched it around. And we became CBST instead of CBTS."

After years of ambivalence, the synagogue spent twelve months between 1977 and 1978 debating the issue, putting the name change up for a board resolution and a membership vote. Determined to position CBST as a serious and authentic synagogue in the Jewish landscape, these decisions felt extremely significant to the founders. In March 1977, a letter signed by Elenore Lester on behalf of the board went out to the entire membership, calling on the congregation to reconsider the name.

> Most of you are aware that Beth Simchat Torah is not a suitable name for a synagogue.
> Simchat Torah is the name of a holiday and shuls are not normally named after holidays. Many individuals, both within our group and outside of it, have questioned the name, laughed about it, and finally put it down to our ignorance of, or lack of concern for, Jewish learning and Jewish tradition. In fact, the name was chosen hastily as an expedient to get incorporation papers so that the synagogue could start functioning. It was planned that there would be a change at a later date.

## "Simchat Torah is the name of a holiday and shuls are not normally named after holidays." ELENORE LESTER, 1977

The very earliest of Simchat Torah celebrations at CBST

> From a public relations point of view, it is very poor policy for us to continue with a name that misrepresents our point of view and the caliber of our group. Our message to the Jewish community and to the world at large is that we are both gay and deeply, fully Jewish. Our spiritual and educational leadership is made up of individuals profoundly versed in Hebrew and devoted to our Jewish heritage. We do not want anyone to get the idea that gay Jews are ignorant Jews or Jews who are disdainful in their approach to Judaism.

A committee vetted alternative names, seventeen of which were proposed by eight members. The call for suggestions specified that "names should have some meaningful association with our congregation, be easy to pronounce, and have a pleasing sound. Other criteria might be conformity with tradition, or similarity with our current name for recognition purposes." Front-runners included Shirah Hadashah (New Song), Orah v'Simchah (Light and Joy), or Torah v'Simchah, (Torah and Joy). Finally on February 13, 1978 the congregation voted on the name change. The headline in the March issue of *Gay Synagogue News* announced the results, "BST to stay BST."

> No news was big news last month, as the congregation voted overwhelmingly to retain our name—Congregation Beth Simchat Torah. . . . After a year of thought and discussion, some of those who at first favored a change decided that the concept of "gladness in the Torah" (translation of Simchat Torah) was appropriate after all, and that the negative reaction in the community had never been widespread, as far as we knew. Our inability to choose from among the excellent alternative names suggested by different members also helped decide the issue.

Ad in the inaugural issue of *Gay Synagogue News*, November 1974, for a loft to accommodate the expanding membership

## Moving to Westbeth

Almost from its inception, CBST began to search for a permanent home. The community room at Holy Apostles was increasingly crowded and unavailable to CBST during the week. The first issue of *Gay Synagogue News*, published in November 1974, includes an advertisement for a loft space to accommodate the expanding congregation. The next six months of the *Gay Synagogue News* chronicle the rapidly intensifying search for a new location. In December, the membership voted to find space for "full-time exclusive use" by CBST and approved an annual budget of $10,000 for rent and utilities. Soon there was an added degree of urgency: the Church of the Holy Apostles informed the congregation that the room would no longer be available. A housing committee, led by Joe Freitag, was established to explore options.

Allan Masur (left), counsel to the board, and Herman Barkan

Lyn Knieter, one of the first women on the board, chaired the new fund-raising committee, supported by Allan Masur, counsel to the board. By April 1975 the fund-raising efforts, spearheaded by an unnamed "gay Jewish brother who is a prominent volunteer fund-raiser for the big-time Jewish organizations" had exceeded expectations. Pledges from thirty-eight members totaling $25,475 had been secured, exceeding the budget that had been approved to cover the costs associated with a new space.

The July 1975 newsletter joyfully announced the move to Westbeth at 151 Bank Street. The initial sixteen-month contract, at a rent of $600 per month, was unanimously approved by the eighty members present at the June 12 membership meeting.

> During the meeting, it was conceded that Westbeth constitutes a frontier between a fashionable residential area and a notorious cruising ground. Some members complained that they found the location inaccessible (though others lived nearby). All agreed that the short term of the contract would be, in effect, a good trial period. The space will be turned over July 1, though the first Shabbat service cannot be held until the chairs are delivered a few weeks later. We welcome all Israel, and gay people everywhere, to rejoice with us. Blessed are you Lord, our God, King of the Universe, who has kept us alive and preserved us and enabled us to reach this season!

The first service in the new space was held on August 8, 1975. Acknowledging the sanctuary's remote location, members were directed to "the second floor of the 'L' building in the Westbeth complex, between West and Washington Streets. First door to the right in the Bank Street courtyard—through the rainbow door." A brief dedication service was held after the first membership meeting at Westbeth, at which the major business was approving the purchase of an air-conditioning system. Those queasy about the $3,500 expense were reassured that the suppliers had thrown in a free refrigerator with a huge ice cube capacity. A more formal dedication was held on February 9, 1976, during CBST's third anniversary celebration.

The space at 151 Bank Street space was short-lived. When the theater from which CBST was subletting moved, the Westbeth management asked CBST to vacate the space. In January 1977 CBST signed a long-term lease on what was originally intended as an interim space in Westbeth, at 57 Bethune Street. The February *Gay Synagogue News* instructed, "TIME TO UNPACK!"

> After forty years of wandering, the children of Israel reached the Promised Land. After only four years of wandering, our congregation has found a home. It is not yet the Promised Land, but with a little work and spirit it will do nicely for the next five years. At the January 5 general membership meeting, the members voted by a more than 2–1 margin to accept Westbeth's offer of a 5-year lease on the space we have been occupying since August.

They could not have imagined that CBST would make its home at Westbeth for more than thirty-five years.

The rainbow entrance to CBST's first home in Westbeth, 1975

TOP: When Irving Cooperberg ordered 400 folding chairs for the move into Westbeth, many in the synagogue were outraged. Why would we spend the money on 400 chairs when we have nowhere near that many members? Irving insisted that getting fewer chairs was shortsighted, "Believe me," he promised, "the people will come." It wasn't long before every chair was filled.

TOP RIGHT: Many members recall their first walk up the ramp to CBST's 57 Bethune Street sanctuary.

### The First Women

Regina Linder first attended CBST in 1974 and never left, despite being one of very few women present. "My experience growing up in an Orthodox Hebrew school in the Bronx was not so terribly different," she remembers, laughing ruefully, "so I wasn't discomforted. And yet I was very motivated to attract other women. I did that by working the bars, handing out printed flyers, which we did, not too successfully." Regina regarded the gender disparity at CBST as an extension of the separatism prevalent in gay life at the time, when lesbians were trying to establish a distinct identity. Being in a primarily male space and affiliating with a primarily male organization was neither comfortable nor politically acceptable for many women. Regina grew close with Elenore Lester and Ros Regelson, two of the first woman members who became essential organizers of the *oneg*, the cultural hour after services. The May 1976 newsletter announced the creation of a women's outreach committee, chaired by Nancy Lowe, the only woman on the original board.

Although it wasn't until the arrival of Rabbi Sharon Kleinbaum that the population of women began to equal that of men, the attempts at outreach and programming for women in the late 1970s started to have an impact. Before Rosh Hashanah in 1977, Elenore, Ros, Regina, and her partner at the time went on WBAI's *The Real Live Lesbian Show* to make the case for CBST. "Our members explained that women participated fully in all aspects of our synagogue life. They regretted that the number of women at services remained small, a fact they attributed largely to a vicious cycle—a woman joining us for the first time sees a preponderance of men and may conclude that the congregation is a 'male' congregation and not congenial to women. The panelists ended by inviting all listeners to participate with them in High Holiday services at shul."

CBST's commitment to ritual egalitarianism, still fairly novel in Jewish life, was significant to women like Annette Miller, who felt at home at CBST when she first came in 1977, despite the few women in attendance. "When I walked in, my first impression was that it was a male-oriented place, but I was treated equally. I felt it was much better than where I came from, and I knew it was gay."

Like the other founding members, the first women at CBST made it the spiritual home they may not have even known they were seeking. "I think I understood from the first service that this was going to be a lasting addition to my life," recalls Regina. "The Friday evening services were a tremendous draw. The rebbe and the music and the prayers were quite magnetic. It was a tremendously exciting phenomenon."

## Women

A Women's Outreach Committee has been formed and has received a mandate from the Bd. of Trustees. Its purpose is to reach out into the lesbian community of New York, to inform sisters of the activities of the synagogue, and to encourage them to join in our celebration of our Jewish heritage and identity.

The committee invites all members of the synagogue to contribute their ideas and efforts toward these ends.

Committee members have already begun to spread the word at meetings and social gatherings of gay women's groups. A flyer has been prepared to be distributed at these times; copies will be posted on the bulletin board.

Sisters in the community are being informed of the unique, full participation of women in religious services, classes, and social events at our shul, despite the problems that women have often faced in other synagogues. This participation will be even further developed as more women find out about our shul, lend us their talents, and share in our Jewish re-education.

All synagogue members are invited to attend meetings of the committee, held at member's homes. Chairperson Nancy Lowe will be glad to give you details.

### The Friday Night Service

Regina Linder's feelings about CBST's Friday night services were widely shared. From the community's very first gathering, Shabbat has been the center of its life, and the Friday night service remains CBST's central experience of prayer

# CLOSEUP: ROS REGELSON AND ELENORE LESTER

Ros Regelson and Elenore Lester were role models and leaders in the early years of CBST. "They taught us we could be gay and successful professionals," Regina Linder remembers. A generation older than many of the early leaders of CBST, they were out as lesbians, acknowledged as a couple, and recognized in their professions while many of the younger members were still struggling to find themselves. Ros and Elenore, both significant writers and cultural critics, set the intellectual and cultural tone for the synagogue. They ran the *oneg* after Friday night services, a major feature of CBST life for many years, which extended Friday night services into a full evening of gay Jewish life, encouraging members to explore various facets of their Jewish identities. Just as they were unapologetic about being gay, Elenore and Ros confidently asserted CBST's right to participate in every aspect of mainstream Jewish culture. One program, a reading of Isaac Bashevis Singer's "Yentl the Yeshiva Boy," led to a visit by the author to CBST's Yiddish class.

"Ros and Elenore had an instinct for building community that was not gender bound," Regina reflects. "Their presence in the inner leadership circle of CBST made a strong statement about the synagogue not being a male institution."

They were at the core of a small group of women present at the start, who also worked to encourage more women to join CBST. They had close friendships with many gay men as well, sharing a house on Fire Island with a group of them. Elenore and Ros were also close with Reb Pinchas, who held them in high regard. He was proud when Elenore began to observe Shabbat and considered her an important influence in his own return to observant Judaism.

Elenore and Ros met as undergraduates at Hunter College in the 1940s. Elenore grew up in the Bronx with very little Jewish connection. The Six-Day War in 1967 informed her Jewish sensibility, and her involvement at CBST mirrored the increasingly Jewish focus of her journalism. Her *New York Times Magazine* article about Raoul Wallenberg and her subsequent book, *Wallenberg: The Man in the Iron Web*, brought his story to international attention. Another major article she wrote for the magazine focused on the resurgence of Yiddish. She became arts editor of the *Jewish Week*, a position she held until her death from lymphoma in 1990.

Ros was an out lesbian decades before Stonewall. She had close friends among lesbian activists, such as Barbara Gittings and Kay Tobin Lahusen; she knew Bayard Rustin; she taught courses on homosexuality at NYU long before the field of lesbian and gay studies existed. An advocate for "queer" sensibility before its time, Ros included transgender people in her classroom and in the life of CBST.

Ros also merged CBST with her literary work. Yehuda Berger and others appeared in *Secret Space*, the movie she wrote that aired on PBS in 1976. When deadlines loomed at the *SoHo News*, where she was a book editor, more than one CBST member contributed a last-minute book review.

Elenore Lester (left) and Ros Regelson were accustomed to being the only women in the room.

> "My goal is to make each Jew look forward to *shabbes* all week long."
>
> REB PINCHAS

and community, fulfilling Reb Pinchas ben Aharon's vision: "My goal is to make each Jew look forward to *shabbes* all week long."

Reb Pinchas shared the leadership of Friday night services with Murray Lichtenstein, a scholar of the Ancient Near East. They alternated delivering the *drash*, and were soon joined by Carl Bennett, who was working on his doctorate in Classics. The three formed an unlikely yet serendipitous leadership troika. As Murray recalls, "Here you could come to the gay synagogue and hunger for a fundamentalist, literalist kind of approach, and you would get it. If you didn't like it, the next week you would get an academic rationalist approach. You didn't like that, the next week there was a mystical approach. And it worked." Yehuda Berger describes the scene, "Every week Reb Pinchas would lead the services: just before candle lighting, he asked that the lights be dimmed, the candles lit, and then he delivered a midrashic meditation based on a *pasuk* from *Shir hashirim*. It was always very tender, very dramatic, very emotional. The lights came up again and the *Kabbalat Shabbat* part of the service ensued."

Members gathered for a Rosh Hashanah dinner, mid 1970s.

LEFT: Chairs in the community room at Holy Apostles, used for Friday night services, August 1975

At first twenty or thirty men and a few women gathered, sitting on children's chairs or folding chairs. Before long, that number grew to forty, growing at times to one hundred. The davening was joyful and spirited, with members leaping to their feet and dancing to recorded music after *L'chah dodi*. Many recall being moved to tears, overwhelmed with emotion and wonder.

Shabbat at CBST offered a joyful respite from a week of navigating the closet. It was a rare experience of integration, a reprieve from fragmented and hidden lives. The music evoked childhood memories for those who had grown up steeped in Judaism. But, unlike the Jewish communities so many had fled, this gathering did not demand or expect heterosexuality. It offered a Judaism without shame or judgment. For many, this was the only place where members could openly be their full Jewish and gay selves. Saul Mizrahi, a member since 1973, recalls coming to CBST after work and a hurried Friday night dinner with his mother in Brooklyn, "You do your job all day, keep your mouth shut. Then you see your family. Then you run to CBST and then you can be who you really are in all the fullness of your dimension. Not just half a person."

For some, the social time provided by the kiddush and the *oneg* was as meaningful as the service. After kiddush, congregants would stay for singing, Israeli dancing, a lecture or a discussion. This chance to socialize with other gay people was an experience members like Bill Fern had rarely encountered outside the bars. Some felt much more comfortable at CBST than in the bar scene. Bill found it transforming to meet a community of gay people with whom he connected intellectually and Jewishly.

> "You do your job all day, keep your mouth shut... run to CBST and then you can be who you really are... Not just half a person." SAUL MIZRAHI

At that time I compartmentalized. I had a gay life, I had a Jewish life, and one had absolutely nothing to do with the other. . . . The division between being gay and the rest of my life was an impermeable wall. We linked arms that Friday night and sang *Shalom aleichem*, which harkened back to my Hebrew school days when I was a kid. It brought forth all of those warm memories of friends of mine even before my bar mitzvah. And it was a very Jewish thing to do. Here I was with my arms linked around all of these other people who were gay. As I sang that song, there were times when I simply had to stop singing to choke back the tears. I felt that wall melt. For the first time in my life, I was able to decompartmentalize, to see the possibility of integrating all of the pieces of me. It was one of the most profound experiences I have had. It made an enormous difference in my life.

## HOW I GOT TO CBST

The first time I saw an ad for the synagogue in the *New York Times*, I was totally incredulous. I thought, it's a flash in the pan—I'll wait until next week and see if the ad is still there. And it was there the next week and the next. So I went. That became one of my early jobs, to bring the money to the *New York Times* so the ad would run.

Jacob Gubbay wasn't a citizen and didn't have a green card. His knowledge of Judaism was limited. He had a very simple service. I said to him, "Jacob, you don't have a *Sh'moneh esreh* here anywhere. You've got to add something so it has the *matbeya* of a service." It didn't take long before he asked me to take over altogether. He said, "I have to keep a very low profile. It isn't good for people to see me." (In those days, homosexuality was grounds for deportation.) He was soft-spoken, had a small physique, not a commanding presence. But he was the gutsiest person.

I grew up Conservative, at Temple Emanuel in Newton, Massachusetts, where they had a choir, a great rabbi, and a magnificent *chazzan*. I'm not musically trained but the music was in my head. I loved it, but, I wasn't a shul goer until I was twenty-eight, when I came out, or at least understood that I was gay. There was a need for me to do what Jacob wanted to do, but he didn't have the tools. That's what kept me in shul for the next thirty-seven years. I sang the *Musaf* on *yontif* at CBST for twenty of those years.

People say that if you're gay it drives you away from Judaism. Au contraire! It changed my life. Before CBST, I wouldn't have been in a shul on a Friday night. After, I wouldn't have been anywhere else.

MURRAY LICHTENSTEIN, MEMBER SINCE 1973

Murray leading services in the 1990s

**Reb Pinchas**

The combination of intense joy and deep *Yiddishkeit* that Reb Pinchas brought to CBST made him the ideal spiritual leader for the fledgling synagogue. Those who came to CBST wanted to live Jewish lives based not in shame but in celebration. They sought to connect with their Jewish souls on their own terms. In 1974 Reb Pinchas reflected, "At the time I finally decided to accept myself, I remembered that there is a Chasidic belief that each man has a unique task to perform in life. Perhaps this is mine—to help the straight world understand us and to help gays feel better about themselves."

Pinchas ben Aharon grew up in Brooklyn, descended from what he described as "generations of very passionate Chasidic Jews." He received ordination from a prestigious American yeshiva. In a 1974 interview with Elenore Lester in *Present Tense*, he described his journey out of the closet:

> As far back as I can remember I intended to make the rabbinate my life, but at nineteen I realized my sexual inclinations were making it impossible. I wrote anonymously to the Lubavitcher Chasid for help. He told me to see a doctor and said he would pray for me. I followed his advice and went into psychotherapy for five years, throughout the time I was involved in rabbinical studies. I wound up with aversion therapy—they give you electric shocks when they show you pictures of attractive members of your own sex. I almost had a breakdown before I decided to accept myself and recognize that God must have wanted to make me as I am.
>
> I gave up the idea of serving as a rabbi and went into teaching in a religious school, but the pressure in the Jewish community, especially my kind of community, to get married is unbearable. You must constantly lie and conceal. So I finally went into social work, helping drug addicts.

Like many people, Pinchas had drifted away from observant Judaism when he came out. By the time CBST was founded, he had left Brooklyn and was living with a non-Jewish partner. But despite his lapsed Orthodox observance, he remained deeply religious. Years later, he recalled:

Pinchas ben Aharon at the Christopher Street Liberation Day March, 1975

> I had come out of the closet a very short time before the synagogue started. I met a lot of Jewish people. I had gone to the Firehouse, to the Gay Alliance of Brooklyn. But when you met Jews they were the kind of Jews who were really not interested in Judaism or were really opposed to it. When I heard about a gay synagogue I thought, "Oh my God, what would that look like with these anti-Semites?" I saw the ad in the *Village Voice* and I went down one week. I talked to some of the people who were running things there. Someone said, "Why don't you lead the davening." And I said OK.

Most early members cannot talk about Pinchas without recalling his lover at that time. Michael Levine remembers, "We said, 'the *chasidishe rebbe* is married to the son of a black Baptist minister.' And it was a perfect marriage in many ways. Because they both had that heavy, spiritual flavor. It was wonderful. They would both go into a trance over Chasidic music or revivalist music. It touched them each the same way." Murray Lichtenstein remembers first seeing Pinchas at CBST:

> Pinchas ben Aharon arrived with his partner at the time, a beautiful black man named Jerry Cunningham. He was a marvelous presence and very self-confident in the leadership role. They came in with a tape recorder and set it up. He played the most wonderful stuff. [*Niggunim* called *ga'aguim*.] I had never heard anything like it. It captivated me. No one had ever seen anything like this guy. It galvanized the place. He was away for a couple of weeks and then he came back. He wanted to see if it took.

## CBST's Religious Sensibility

Ritually, CBST had a far more traditional orientation than the other gay synagogues that began to appear across the country, most of which sought affiliation with the Reform Movement. Jack Greenberg reflects on what made CBST different: "New York had so many people who had some kind of upbringing that perhaps prepared them for running a synagogue. The people who came are the ones who had the influence. If Pinchas hadn't shown up, how different the shul might have been . . . ." Like Pinchas, many of CBST's early ritual leaders came from Orthodox and traditional Conservative movement backgrounds. The Judaism they sought to inhabit was ritually similar, in feeling if not in rigidity of practice, to their childhood synagogues. "I think that we felt that we are *or lagoyim* and that we should maintain a certain standard, a high standard of *Yiddishkeit*," recalls Yehuda Berger. "That was an undercurrent throughout the early days. We are gay, we're Jewish, and we're proud of both."

Jerry Cunningham (left) and Pinchas ben Aharon

Members varied greatly in their personal religious observance. Those who had not grown up in traditional Jewish communities were equally drawn to the charisma and authenticity of Reb Pinchas and CBST. Pinchas was proud of the Chasidic elements he introduced, correctly believing they gave CBST its unique flavor. "At the heart," he said, "it is all about our relationships with God." The combination of traditionalism and flexibility, *Yiddishkeit* and out gayness, created a distinct CBST sensibility.

## Diversity and Contradiction

The Jewish diversity of its members became another one of CBST's hallmarks. Elenore Lester described the phenomenon in her 1974 article. (She referred to Pinchas by the pseudonym "Rabbi Aaron.")

Carl Bennett carrying the Torah on Hoshanah Rabbah, 1975

> Unlike ordinary congregations, Beth Simchat Torah is made up of individuals representing a broad spectrum of beliefs from secularists experiencing a flare of religious affirmation to Rabbi Aaron's mutant Chasidic-tinged Orthodoxy. The rationalists find the services too religious and the traditionalists find them not religious enough. But all the congregants seem to be able to bury their differences in their accord on the central issue of affirmation of a dual identification—Jewishness and homosexuality.

The religious and philosophical diversity of the community was reflected on the bimah through the *drashot* of Pinchas, Murray Lichtenstein, and Carl Bennett. CBST's commitment to diversity was also reflected in its policy of egalitarianism. From the outset, women and men were permitted equal participation in service leadership. Regina Linder remembers with pride and admiration that, despite his Orthodox background, Pinchas encouraged women to participate actively.

> It was stunning to be in a community that was led by this incredibly charismatic guy who came from a tradition that ought to in a way have made him narrow and suspicious. And he was none of those things. He was quite a remarkable person and still is. He was open to the participation of women from the jump. In fact, he really encouraged women to participate in service leadership. Pinchas was determined to engage the very few women who were there.

At first, the commitment to egalitarianism existed more in theory than in practice. Most of the early service leaders were men. There were few women members of CBST and, as was the case throughout the Jewish world in the 1970s, even fewer with experience leading services. Not all the men shared Reb Pinchas's enthusiasm for women's ritual engagement, but he set the tone.

Perhaps the contradictions that Reb Pinchas seemed to embody helped make CBST members feel their own conflicted lives were possible. Elenore wrote:

> During one of our conversations, Rabbi Aaron made a vital point. "I feel that we, as gays, have something special to say to the Jewish community, some important message for our time. The very fact that they reject us gives us a special significance." He turned to his friend Frank. "What is that psalm I'm thinking of—you know, the one about the stone builders reject?" "Psalm 118, verse 22," promptly replied Frank.

"Ah yes, here it is," said Aaron riffling through the Bible. "The stone the builders refused has become the cornerstone."

### Pinchas Returns to Orthodoxy

CBST reignited Pinchas's intense Jewish spirit, and he began to return to strict ritual observance. Initially Pinchas tried to bring CBST with him on his journey back to *frumkeit*. He tried to expand and deepen the Shabbat and prayer experience at CBST, creating a Shabbat afternoon class and *Minchah* service and later a monthly Shabbat morning minyan. Some members were open to connecting or reconnecting with traditional observant Judaism. For others, who loved attending Friday night and holiday services, CBST was their community, an essential, even daily part of their lives, but they didn't aspire to a more stringent personal observance.

> "From the long range, at least from my perspective, we did a good thing in the world. We came at a time when people really needed it."
>
> REB PINCHAS

Eventually Pinchas could no longer tolerate the religious compromises that had been a part of his out gay life. He didn't want to continue traveling to CBST on Shabbat. "As time was going on, I was interested in more and more traditional Judaism," he recalls. "Eventually it wasn't my place anymore. I just wasn't comfortable." Ultimately Pinchas returned to an Orthodox life. He separated from his non-Jewish partner and stopped davening at CBST. In the Orthodox synagogues and *yeshivot* where he spent most of his time, he was no longer public about his sexual orientation or his past involvement with CBST. He retained his connection with CBST through certain friendships, but primarily with those in the Talmud class, which he founded in CBST's first year and was still teaching in 2013. He remains proud of the influence he had on CBST and proud of the ways in which CBST made it possible for other Orthodox gay people to return to Judaism. "From the long range, at least from my perspective, we did a good thing in the world. We came at a time when people really needed it."

Pinchas's joyful spirit and his love for God and Shabbat remain at CBST, as does the profound teaching that living a gay life is not in contradiction to closeness to God, a deep connection to Judaism, and the synagogue as an integral, daily part of life.

## CBST After Pinchas

Reb Pinchas's departure was a traumatic break for some, a necessary evolution for others. It was certainly the most significant transition CBST had experienced in its history up to that point. The shul was trying to evolve, along with its growing membership, to meet the needs of an increasingly out and sophisticated gay community, often with conflicting visions of what the synagogue should be. Many members felt that Pinchas perfectly embodied the spirit of the synagogue. Others worried that his old world affect would alienate less traditional potential members. Michael Levine, who was elected chair of the board in 1978, remembers going to Pinchas's Upper West Side apartment to discuss his impending departure. "Many people came to me and said, 'I'm not coming back unless you get rid of that Orthodox rabbi.' On the other hand, I had people who said, 'If he leaves, I'm leaving too.'" The January 1979 newsletter announced the news:

> After over five years of serving as our dedicated (and unpaid) spiritual leader, Pinchas ben Aharon has relinquished some of his responsibilities for religious and ritual affairs. However, he will continue to be active in Shabbat and Holiday services and celebrations, and in other synagogue activities as his time permits.
>
> It is difficult in a few words to adequately express our thanks to Pinchas for all that he has done for the synagogue. We know that he feels our appreciation and love for him.

The board created a Religious Committee. Michael chose Mark Bicber, who had already assumed some of the administrative duties for Pinchas, as its first chair. Its earliest members included Yehuda (then known as Howard) Berger, David Krause, and Jonathan Stowe. Yehuda recalls, "When Pinchas left, there was a vacuum that had to be filled." But no other lay person would ascend to the role of charismatic religious leader that Pinchas held.

## The Religious Committee

This transition to lay leadership signaled a dramatic power shift in the synagogue. With no spiritual leader, the board, and particularly the chair of the board, became extremely powerful. Eager to cultivate that control, the board determined to create a committee rather than appoint another individual to make ritual decisions. Still,

Saul Zalkin at an anniversary dinner in the 1980s

> **HOW I GOT TO CBST**
>
> I grew up in Brooklyn in a Conservative observant household. For me, personally, religion was important. I moved to the Upper West Side, to the apartment where I still live. I went to several services at a Conservative synagogue not two blocks away. The service was familiar—there was no problem with that. And then one day, after I had been there for three weeks in a row, some guy came up to me and said, "So, nu, are you married?" And since I couldn't say—I wasn't able to say—something as facile as "no, is your son available?" or anything else like that, I stopped going. Because I refused to put myself back into that position.
>
> At that time I was a regular at a piano bar on Barrow Street called Marie's Crisis. Many people from CBST were regulars. They said, "You have to come, you have to come, you have to come." So I had to be part of the shul. I *had* to be part of the shul. I went to CBST on Simchat Torah. The shul was packed. I already knew a lot of people there. I didn't feel like a stranger. Nobody had to bring me. I arrived all by myself.
>
> SAUL ZALKIN, MEMBER SINCE 1978

once it was established, the Religious Committee had an authority and a gravitas that no other committee attained. While it was responsible to the board, the committee functioned independently of the board's supervision, a complicated relationship that led to significant autonomy with a few notable clashes over the years. The Religious Committee had a board liaison, but, as Michael Levine discovered when he tried to drop in on a meeting, the board chair was not welcome to attend meetings uninvited.

Carl Bennett and Murray Lichtenstein, who had most frequently shared the bimah with Pinchas, never served on the Religious Committee. Carl remained a frequent presence on the bimah on Friday nights. Saul Zalkin joined the committee soon after his own arrival at CBST, while it was still in formation, and eventually served as its chair. He remembers that Mark Bieber insisted on running ritual decisions past Carl and Murray, whom he considered arbiters of the ritual sensibility of CBST. "They were the *éminences grises*," Saul reflects. "We couldn't just make policy for the synagogue. Anything that we wanted to decide according to halachah had to be passed by Yehuda or Carl or somebody else." Still, he doesn't remember them ever overruling committee decisions "because Mark was there. Mark knew what the synagogue was."

# CLOSEUP: MARK BIEBER

Anyone who encountered Mark Bieber—whether presiding at the board table or at the Religious Committee or in his pink tutu as Queen Esther on Purim—was unlikely to forget the experience. Mark was an outsize person with an outsize personality, as Michael Levine described in his eulogy for Mark.

> Mark was a founder of our shul, and he never let anyone forget that. He came to CBST in 1974 during our formative years and immediately put his stamp on everything he touched. He selected liturgy; he conducted services; he delivered *drashot*; he served as *ba'al tefillah*; he even cooked potato latkes for hundreds at Chanukah. And he made sure that everyone knew the way he did things was not just the best way but also the only way. So often, and so aggravatingly, he was right.

Mark also used his forcefulness as a leader to create (or impose) compromise. Saul Zalkin, who served on the Religious Committee, of which Mark was founding chair, recalls that "Mark would go for consensus because he didn't want someone to feel like they lost." To create the 1981 CBST siddur, a project he spearheaded, Mark worked closely with Yehuda Berger and David Krause, navigating the many conflicts that arose between the two in the course of the project. Yehuda remembers, "Mark was an extraordinary mediator and kept us in balance."

Mark grew up in Cleveland in a Jewishly involved family. After earning a PhD in biochemistry, he came to New York as an NIH postdoctoral fellow at Columbia University in nutritional science and made his career at Best Foods. The American Heart Association Industry Nutrition Advisory Panel established an award in his memory, honoring his contributions to the field. He worked, he said, to support his family: CBST. In his 1985 *Kol Nidrei* talk, Mark reflected on the role of CBST in his life:

"This Synagogue has shown me the riches I receive when I am part of a true community, a community that I feel most at home with, Lesbian and Gay Jews. This Synagogue and the people who make it real give me the strength to do things I never had thought imaginable years ago. The greatest one was that of being a whole person, especially with my family. When we published the current Shabbat prayer book in 1981, my mother happened to be visiting that week. With great pride, I gave her a copy of the new siddur. I asked her where she was going to put it. She told me, "In the bookcase of the living room." I asked if she and my father would really want it there in their home, then in Cleveland, and she looked back at me and said, 'And where should I put it, in the closet?'"

In the 1970s Mark was one of the first members to bring his parents to CBST. "Ethel Bieber became everyone's mother," Rabbi Sharon Kleinbaum reflected in her eulogy for Mark, "mothering the young men at CBST who could not come out to their own mothers. His 'CBST brothers,' close friends Jonathan Stowe and Ian Lobel, who both died in the 1980s, traveled with him, listened to his jokes, told him to lose weight, stop smoking, argued with him, sat in cars tolerating his unique personality, and sat on committees with him." Mark loved all things Jewish and enjoyed getting pleasure out of life. He had a world of close friends with whom he embarked on adventures and misadventures, celebrating the first seder at Irving Cooperberg and Lou Rittmaster's home, looking up from a table of CBST members gambling at a Las Vegas casino horrorfied when he suddenly remembered it was Tish'ah B'av.

Mark sat on seven CBST boards and served as chair in 1987–1988. He was president of the World Congress of Gay and Lesbian Jewish Organizations in 1987. Along with his partner, Bill Amplo (above), he became active in the New Jersey Lesbian and Gay Havurah. Mark died in 2001 while traveling to Germany for business. He was buried in the CBST cemetery just weeks after its dedication.

FROM LEFT TO RIGHT: Jerry Ganz, Jack Greenberg, Ron Weiss, Steve Siegel, and Murray Karger in the entry to CBST, January 1981

## HOW I GOT TO CBST

When I started to really come out, I experimented with not being Orthodox. Almost the first thing I did was go to CBST. I'd never gone before, because I didn't travel on Shabbat. I had seen the ads in the *Village Voice* and I was so tempted to go.

Going to CBST was the first healthy thing I did to meet gay people. Here I went as myself. I used my own name. I walked in and I met people and cared who they were and what their names were.

I walked around the block over and over. To get to that front door on Bethune Street you had to walk through this "narrow place," as we call it. God knows what's on the other side. Then you saw this endless ramp. And at the front door…I thought, "What if I can't go in? I'm going to have to go all the way back down." It was very frightening. I didn't know what I would find. I didn't know what a homosexual was like.

When I walked in, Murray Karger was sitting at the front door. I said, "I'm here for the first time." He made this big deal. It was scary but also very welcoming that somebody cared that I walked through the door.

I came back. I started becoming a person that people knew, and it became a comfortable place for me. I felt like I was with my people.

JACK GREENBERG, MEMBER SINCE 1980

Saul Zalkin recalls the tensions that occasionally arose as the committee endeavored to chart the religious course of CBST, "We all brought our various backgrounds. We had fights on the Religious Committee—I would say, 'What I think is right is right,' and someone else would say, 'The way I think is right is right.' Eventually, through Mark's insistence, we would work out an agreement on how things would go."

Most members of the committee were from traditional Conservative or Orthodox backgrounds with varying degrees of formal Jewish education. Jack Greenberg became active in what later became the Ritual Committee soon after his arrival at CBST in 1980 and was its longest serving chair. A graduate of Yeshivah of Flatbush, he recalls, "I got so involved because CBST was respectful of where I was coming from. Not that it was exactly the way that I was before I came. I had to adapt a lot." That ability to adapt characterized most members of the committee, who considered it their role to serve the needs of the congregation, even if those needs were different from their personal traditions. "We might make a decision that we were comfortable with, but if somebody came along and the committee decided it's a great idea, why not?" Saul reflects. "Nobody was beholden to halachah purely for halachah's sake. The needs of the congregation had to be met."

The shared decision-making among an educated laity became a fierce point of pride for those involved, as did the new democratization of service leadership. It also opened up new debates: How much autonomy was granted to service leaders and *darshanim*? How would the value of democratic access to the bimah be balanced with the desire to have high-quality services and *drashot*? These considerations fell to the Religious Committee.

**A New Chapter**
For almost thirteen years, the Religious Committee ably led the ritual life of the synagogue, struggling through shaky services, too much innovation and not enough. Chairing the committee, a position held by only three people in the history of the synagogue—Mark Bieber, Saul Zalkin, and Jack Greenberg—was an immense and often thankless task. From the time Pinchas ben Aharon left until Rabbi Sharon Kleinbaum was hired, they were the religious leadership of CBST, establishing a powerful identity for the synagogue as a lay-led institution. They carried the synagogue through crucial years of development, growth, and tragedy, until the community determined the time had come to hire a rabbi.

# 2. LAYING THE CORNERSTONE

Nearly from the outset in the '70s, CBST began to develop its infrastructure, system of governance, and fund-raising apparatus in order to sustain its growth.

Reb Pinchas recalls that the influx of members after the Yom Kippur War first brought in people with a more sophisticated understanding of organizational development and the resources to build a synagogue. "Before, we did a lot of good things, but we were shleppers. With Irving Cooperberg, Bill Fern, Allan Masur, suddenly we got people who knew how to run things." In CBST's twentieth year, Irving reflected on those early years, "We started in the church in the kindergarten room, and we sat in little chairs and played shul. The first year we played shul, because we had a lot of mock services, a mock seder on a different day, and so on. Then we decided we could do everything *al pi din*, according to law. We decided that we would find a permanent home."

The first board was assembled hastily to incorporate the synagogue. Saul Mizrahi recalls, "We all elected ourselves. We said, 'Who wants to be on the board?' and nine people raised their hands. That was the election." One woman served on the first board; no board in the first decade exceeded that number, and half had no women at all. By 1974 the election process and board structure was more formal, and the process was progressively streamlined. Michael Levine recalls that Arnold Mandlebaum, the first elected chair, was a reluctant leader who would say he just wanted to be helpful—he needed a shul, and he didn't feel comfortable anywhere else.

### *Im ein kemach ein Torah:*
### Dues and Fund-raising

Between 1974 and 1975, CBST's membership jumped from 65 to 180. Annual dues were $18, payable in up to three installments. Michael Levine recalls that soon after arriving at CBST he joined a fund-raising committee, chaired by one of the few women, Lyn Kneiter. "I've always been a joiner," says Michael, "so I volunteered to work on fund-raising, which I don't even like to do, but it was one place where they said they needed help." Allan Masur, an attorney who had founded Congregation B'nai Olam, the gay synagogue

The January 1975 newsletter encouraged readers to join at the $18 annual membership rate.

> **MEMBERSHIP DRIVE CONTINUES**
>
> Over 60 people have signed up for 1975 membership so far, with almost no prompting from the committee. Another 40 would make it more feasible for us to pay the rent at our new place, when we find one. Annual dues: $18, payable in up to three installments, the last of which must be in by January 30 to qualify for a vote in elections for the new board. A few members have given us checks for $30, which was last year's dues figure, and we accepted them gratefully. Get membership forms from and give checks to Jeff Katz.

A crowd assembled in Bill Fern's living room, 1980.

Michael Levine painstakingly recorded the synagogue's business: board members, bank accounts, committees, events, all on stacks of yellow cards.

Fire Island, served as CBST's counsel. He steered the fund-raising committee from raffles and bake sales to more substantial fund-raising efforts, filed for CBST's incorporation and nonprofit status, and helped secure the Westbeth space. Allan's guidance was straight-forward: "Gather people in a room, give them good food, and ask them for money." The initial fund-raising meetings were at Irving Cooperberg's or Bill Fern's home.

Fund-raising has often been controversial at CBST, which strives to balance its foundational values of open access and egalitarianism with the consistent need to cover costs and grow. At a membership meeting in March 1975, some members complained that large donations made at the fund-raising brunches might intimidate small givers. Michael Levine recalls that board member Herbert Honig objected to the expectation that he was obliged to donate money. "Herbert had joined CBST because he was a gay activist and made it clear to me from the beginning that he was not going to fulfill his pledge to the synagogue." From those who did fulfill their pledges, the shul was able to raise enough money to fund the expanded $25,000 budget to cover the lease on the new space and operating expenses for the next year. In spring 1975, to allay some of the anxieties, the board determined that no donations could be earmarked for a particular purpose. All donations would go to the building fund account, used for premises or related expenses, and no donated ritual objects could bear a donor's name.

Michael Levine served as board secretary beginning in 1975, overseeing the new rules governing committees. As chair, he continued the work of reorganizing and developing the committee structure, relishing the role of administrator so much, that after his term expired he became CBST's "parliamentarian," moderating annual meetings and overseeing changes to the bylaws. Irving Cooperberg—known more for his strong personality and skilled and charismatic fund-raising than for his affection for process—was happy to cede the role to Michael.

## Service Leadership

For many members in the early days, being tapped to lead services was a path to becoming known in the synagogue and integrated into the community. A service structure had developed that called for three roles to be filled on the bimah every Friday night: in CBST parlance, *a ba'al or ba'alat tefillah* to sing the Hebrew liturgy; a service leader to prepare English supplementary readings and set the tone of the service; and *darshan* or *darshanit* who delivered the sermon. The structure of the service, and eventually the service outlines developed by the Religious Committee, were intended to encourage multiple voices on the bimah and facilitate a certain amount of flexibility. In this way, the services could accommodate the religious diversity of the community, while maintaining a recognizable CBST style.

> **No Photos, Please!**
> In the interests of good taste and discretion, the Board has approved the following policies:
> No photographs may be taken on synagogue premises, at any time, without written approval from the Board.
> No photograph of any person, taken on synagogue premises or at a synagogue function, may be used without the person's written approval. Release forms will be prepared for this purpose.

David Asch (center) prepared to sing with the CBST chorus on the first night of Chanukah, 1979

Art Leonard recalls that a short-lived affair with David Asch led the way for Art, then a newcomer, to become a service leader at CBST. In the fall of 1978, David—a social work student who had begun vocal training—was a regular *ba'al tefillah*; he later became a member of the chorus of the Metropolitan Opera. Art remembers, "David invited me to lead services with him. We were no longer dating each other, but we remained friendly. He said, 'You should lead services—you're a lawyer, you know how to speak in public.' I ended up leading services two or three times a year, until the time we had a rabbi."

Yehuda Berger recalls that years earlier, when Pinchas ben Aharon led services at CBST, he made a copy of a new English reading to include in each Shabbat service. The proliferation of handouts became a running joke at CBST. At the insistence of member George Mooy, the handouts were finally organized in a filing cabinet. After Pinchas left, service leaders followed his format. According to Saul Zalkin, "In the days of the *Blue Shmatte*, the original prayer book, there were guidelines. You had to go into the file drawers and pick out two readings to add to the service." Yehuda remembers first introducing a reading he had authored. "I wanted to test out a reading of my own. I chose *Magen avot*, and made it gender neutral. I asked David Asch to sing it and I wanted a translation for the *kahal*. It worked well."

Once the CBST siddur was introduced in 1981, and the circle of leaders widened, the committee developed more systematic guidelines for service leaders. Saul recalls early Religious Committee meetings that felt like a re-creation of ancient rabbinic debates. "Here we were, brand new, creating a service: 'Do you stand or do you sit for the *Sh'ma*?'" Under the guidance of the Religious Committee, more experienced members coached the newcomers. "We taught each other," Rosanne

## HOW I GOT TO CBST

I came to New York after law school. I didn't have a synagogue and I wasn't interested in one, really. But one morning while reading the *New York Times*, I saw an article, "Homosexuals in New York Find New Pride." It was October 25, 1977. I had only been in town for about a month and a half. The lead paragraph read, "It was Yom Kippur at Congregation Beth Simchat Torah, Manhattan's four-year-old self-proclaimed 'gay synagogue' and the temple facilities in Westbeth apartments in Greenwich Village were overflowing with more than 350 worshippers." Now that really knocked me for a loop. The idea of a gay synagogue was totally new for me. I had never heard of any such thing. I was immediately curious. I wasn't sure where Westbeth was—somewhere in Greenwich Village. I called the gay switchboard and asked for directions.

My parents, who had grown up in New York, had said, "Don't take the subway, it's not safe." So I was taking buses everywhere. I took the Second Avenue bus from East 83rd all the way down to the Village and walked across town. I left much too much time. I walked into the space, and there were exactly two people: Mark Bieber and Alfred Deibach. They were cutting cake. I told Mark that I was looking for Congregation Beth Simchat Torah and he said, "You found the place; do you want to help us cut some cake?" I was immediately put to work. The moment I arrived at CBST, I became a volunteer. And I came to know two people right away.

When the service started, I had my next shock: a woman was on the bimah. I had never seen a woman leading a service. When it was time for the sermon, which I later learned everyone called the *drash*, someone got up from the front row. It was Pinchas ben Aharon. He had been sitting with his eyes closed for most of the service, swaying back and forth. Earlier in the service, after we sang *L'chah dodi*, music broke out from an overhead sound system, and people started dancing around the congregation. They formed a long line, circling around the congregation. I had never heard of anything like this in a service; it blitzed me away.

I resolved I would come back. Those early services were really exciting to me.

ART LEONARD, MEMBER SINCE 1977

Chasidic and Israeli music and dancing were a highlight of the service and the *oneg*.

## FIVE YEAR ANNIVERSARY

We have nearly completed the first five years of our synagogue's history. Let us enter the second five-year phase with a strong united voice. There will be lots of work to do to make our sanctuary more attractive, and our kitchen and bathrooms more efficient. If we start off with the right spirit, we can't fail.

**OCTOBER 1979 NEWSLETTER**

Leipzig recalls. "I love to sing. When I first began to lead services I learned the music from someone singing into my answering machine. I'd take the cassette tape out, put it onto my tape recorder, and study the music that way. It was a nice mentoring relationship. I think Saul Zalkin taught me the music for the first service I led. With time, I became a regular and served as a lay cantor for many years."

To democratize the service leading, the Religious Committee invited members, regardless of religious education or experience, to construct and lead services, pairing inexperienced service leaders with veteran *ba'alei tefillah* and supervising the *drashot* of members new to the role. "Anyone could lead a service," Jack remembers. "Anybody could give a *drash*." Interested members requested a slot from the Religious Committee. Sometimes committee members approached newcomers. Saul remembers, "You're sitting in the *kahal* and you hear a person sing. You say, 'Listen, would you like to lead services? Would you like to give a *drash*?'" The results were mixed: some pairs worked frequently together and planned their services carefully. Others did not coordinate or were less skillful; those services felt awkward and disjointed. The Religious Committee evaluated every Friday night service, a time-consuming and contentious task. Jack recalls, "People who were really good could lead more often. People who were just getting by, once a year." Only if there was a major problem would someone not be invited to return to the bimah. Saul remembers, "We would tell the *darshanim*, 'You have twelve minutes.'" At one infamous

Bruce Friedman prepares to lead a Friday night service, 1977.

The ritual calendar was created by the Religious Committee.

service I was leading, somebody spoke and couldn't stop. So I got up and I said, 'You're done.' We didn't invite him to speak again." Disgruntled congregants were not shy in voicing their disappointment if a service leader or *darshan* did not pass muster.

## Shabbat Morning Services

If Friday night offered a service for the wider CBST community, Shabbat morning was always a more intimate affair. CBST held morning services on festivals, but few members attended synagogue on Saturday mornings with frequency. Since CBST members lived all over New York and its surrounding areas, those who regularly attended Saturday morning services often maintained a membership at another synagogue closer to home.

Pinchas tried to create a Shabbat morning service as early as 1974, but it never became as popular as he had hoped. In 1976, he tried to establish a monthly Saturday *Minchah* service, perhaps hoping a late start would be more appealing for a population that rarely left CBST before 11:00 PM on Friday nights before heading off to the bars. To increase the appeal, Pinchas tried to pair the Shabbat day services with meals or other programs. Yet, after initial excitement, this effort also foundered. In a final attempt, Pinchas reintroduced the Shabbat morning and afternoon minyanim in the fall of 1977, again without success. Ultimately, the failure to institute a regular Shabbat day davening experience was one of the reasons Pinchas came to feel that CBST could no longer be his spiritual home.

A few years later, a monthly Shabbat day minyan did take root, meeting on *Shabbat mevarchim*, the Shabbat preceding the beginning of the new Jewish month. As Saul Zalkin remembers, the Religious Committee initially established it as a *Minchah* service, with Carl Bennett frequently teaching between *Minchah* and *Havdalah*. After some time, the committee shifted the service to Shabbat morning, using the Orthodox de Sola Poole siddur or, for a time, using a photocopied liturgy that Yehuda Berger created.

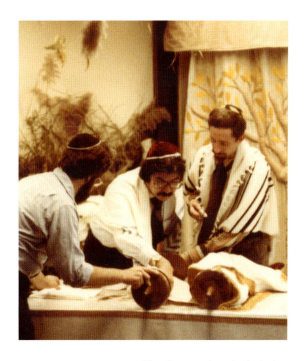

Morning services included a Torah service. Saul Mizrahi (center) is called to the Torah as David Alter (right) prepares to chant.

### FALL AND WINTER SATURDAY PROGRAMS

Starting in November, the shul will begin a new program of Shabbat activities on Saturday mornings and afternoons.

The first Saturday in each month, Shabbat services will be held at 10:30 AM. The tone will be intimate and joyous, similar to our Yom Tov morning services, with singing, readings, and a Torah Service. At 12:00 noon, we will share a Shabbat kiddush.

On the third Saturday of the month, an afternoon discussion group will be held, on topics of lively interest to all. The discussions beginning at 1:30 PM will be informal, lasting for approximately two hours. A shaleshudis (Sabbath meal) will follow. The afternoons will end with Havdallah at around 5:00.

The first Shabbat morning service will take place *Saturday, November 5, at 10:30 AM*.
The first discussion session will be held *Saturday, November 19, at 1:30 PM*. The topic will be that old favorite, Gay Morality. All views will be entertained.

The November 1977 newsletter announced a monthly program that would extend the Shabbat experience throughout the day.

Having a regular Shabbat morning minyan prompted new opportunities for community members to challenge their assumptions about Jewish identity. Penny Dachinger, whose reflections on growing up as an Orthodox lesbian appear in the 1981 anthology *Nice Jewish Girls*, was a regular at the Shabbat morning service. "Penny taught me that it was too easy for me, as a man who grew up in a Conservative community, to make assumptions that simply are not true," Saul reflects. "Month after month, I would offer her an *aliyah*, and she'd refuse. Once, I glibly remarked, 'So tell me, Penny, what's the matter? We're not good enough?' And she responded by saying, 'Saul, you have no idea what it's like to be a woman who is told her entire life she's not good enough to go up to the Torah for an *aliyah* and then have somebody just come and say "Here, have one." I have all this childhood upbringing to overcome.'"

The Mevarchim Minyan filled an important void for some members who came from more traditional backgrounds. Comfortable in that setting, but always seeking ritual innovation, Yehuda Berger initiated a second Shabbat morning service in October 1988, with "an emphasis on alternative readings and prayers, lots of music, and new traditions." Yehuda, whose strength lay more in creating new initiatives than in maintaining them, sought others to share in the leadership of the Innovative Minyan's, also known as Minyan Chadash" (the New Minyan). The minyan was mandated to be created anew each month, so its leadership required a great deal of effort. Some members, including Rosanne Leipzig and Ora Chaikin (then known as Judy Mable), agreed to lead services. The minyan met fairly regularly for about a year and a half, but, lacking a core group of leaders, failed to take root.

### Growing Pains

CBST's members have always identified with the synagogue deeply and personally. Bill Fern believes that "the organization played an extraordinarily important part in the lives of the people who were members of the synagogue, because it provided so much satisfaction in their personal lives. People became highly identified with the community, deeply invested in what happened there. It wasn't just a synagogue: it was family, and family felt in a very intense way." Rafaela Anshel felt that way when she first attended services in 1982, "I remember saying to myself, 'This is going to be my adult family. I am creating a new family.'" This familial sentiment fuels the remarkable dedication of CBST's volunteers, and also generates greater intensity among members when conflicts arise.

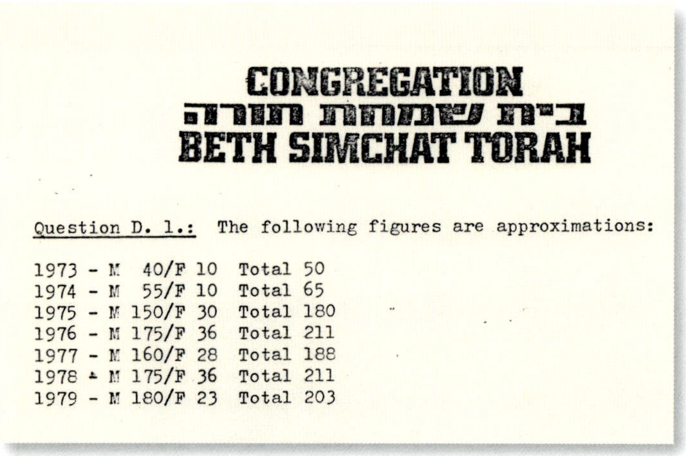

Membership numbers broken down by gender from 1973–1979

**CONGREGATION**
**בית שמחת תורה**
**BETH SIMCHAT TORAH**

Question D. 1.: The following figures are approximations:

```
1973 - M  40/F 10  Total  50
1974 - M  55/F 10  Total  65
1975 - M 150/F 30  Total 180
1976 - M 175/F 36  Total 211
1977 - M 160/F 28  Total 188
1978 - M 175/F 36  Total 211
1979 - M 180/F 23  Total 203
```

Because of CBST's great personal significance to them, some members' initial perception of the synagogue was indelibly inscribed in their memories, and often they experienced any changes as a profound loss. The nostalgia for "CBST as it used to be" was powerful—even if the "golden days" had in fact been brief or less than ideal. Murray Lichtenstein reminisces, "We didn't have membership. People put money in the *pushke*. After the service we had modest cakes and cookies and coffee. And challah, of course, as well as *neirot* and wine. You needed those simple things, and there was no bureaucratic structure, no dues structure. It was wonderful. It was just a group of people who all wanted the same thing. I remember when all that changed because a structure was needed. It felt like something in me died." Murray presided at the synagogue's incorporation meeting in November 1973 at which the board structure was created.

By 1982 membership had swelled to over three hundred, and the volunteer structure designed for a much smaller shul was fraying. Personality and leadership disputes erupted as lay leaders tried to recapture the intimacy of the 1970s and steer the congregation forward at the same time.

When the board created a community development committee in April 1982, Bill Fern engaged Dr. Peter Beebe, a psychologist and consultant specializing in church and nonprofit organizational development, to help the shul recreate a sense of warmth while broadening its leadership base, and to engage a wider swath of the community in envisioning the future. Saul Zalkin recalls the sometimes complex process, "Like any good therapy, we were honest with our feelings about each other, so there were some painful sessions." He recalls Irving Cooperberg likening CBST to Israel. "In the 1920s and 1930s, everybody did everything, and when the state was first founded everyone still did everything, but, as the generations changed, people were no longer willing to pick up the garbage. The same thing was happening at CBST. The founders were willing to sweep the floor, put out and fold up chairs, serve and clean up the food, change the light bulbs—everything. It was still like that when I joined in the synagogue's seventh year. The idea of hiring somebody to sweep the floors was foreign; we took care of it. But as the generations

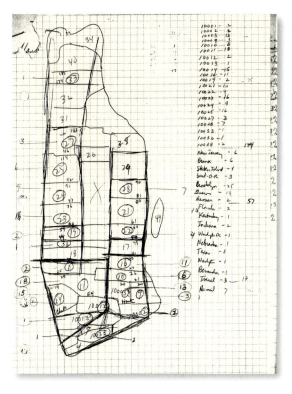

A map illustrating the distribution of newsletters by zip code

> **NEW ONEG MIXER**
>
> How many times have you said or heard: "This place is too cliquish," or "I can't meet anyone here (who I find interesting)" or "I can only speak to my crowd," or "This place is cold. I feel alone here," or "I have a great group of friends here, and I wish others could find the same."
>
> When we were a fledgling group of twenty to fifty in our early years, including new people came easily. Now, with 150–250 mingling on a typical Friday night, meeting others, and overcoming those perceptions take certain commitment and skills.
>
> **DAVID KRAUSE, MARCH 1992**

changed, the people who used to do the shlepping and carrying stopped."

Although the process helped revamp the leadership and volunteer structure, not everyone adjusted easily to the culture of a maturing organization. The community continued to struggle with civility and productive discourse. Harriet Beckman joined the board in November 1983 to fill a vacancy and quickly became involved in the work of the Community Development Committee. In an upset, she was elected chair of the board in April 1984, earning the rancor of the longer-serving board members who had believed they would be chair. She was the first woman to hold the post. Harriet recalls her own shock at being elected and the struggle of leading a contentious board, some of whose members tried to undermine her at every turn. When Harriet resigned after a difficult year, Art Strickler was elected chair, serving for two years, followed by Mark Bieber, who served for a year.

> ### THE FIRST WOMAN PRESIDENT
>
> CBST has been a major part of my life. My vision was to make it more democratic and open, where people could feel involved and express how they felt and enjoy the fruits of the religion without feeling like it's So-and-So's synagogue. It may not have succeeded then, but I feel as if I planted the seed. Over time, I think that's come to pass. Whether people remember that I did that is unimportant to me. What's important to me is that it happened.
>
> Being the first woman to serve as board president was a major experience. As time goes on, I think I appreciate that even more. It's given me a center in terms of my Judaism, in terms of being gay, in terms of my relationship. It's given me a community. I have friends from other places but not like I do here. This is a place where I can totally be myself. Even with all of the difficulty, pain, and struggle of those early years, CBST is just wonderful.
>
> **HARRIET BECKMAN, PRESIDENT 1984-1985**

### Diversity on the Bimah: Women at CBST

As the centerpiece of CBST's life, the Friday night service became a reflection of the identity issues unfolding within the community. Some service leaders introduced new readings. A few *ba'alei tefillah* incorporated musical instruments into the service. Each variation was noted and debated among CBST members, some of whom resented innovation, while others wanted more. Under the watchful eye of the Religious Committee the bimah became the stage on which to play out issues of ideological diversity and compromise. Having the people on the bimah reflect the ethos of the congregation was important. Finding the right balance—eclectic and diverse, but not overly polarizing or painful to sit through—was always complicated.

The Friday night service was an opportunity to assert the community's commitment to the presence of women at the synagogue, but also belied its anxiety about it. Ruth Plave was thrilled when Mark Bieber invited her to serve as *ba'alat tefillah* in the early 1980s, after having sat on the sidelines in Orthodox and nonegalitarian Conservative synagogues throughout her life. After every service, an older man at CBST would inevitably tell her, "You have a very lovely voice, but I will never get adjusted to hearing a woman lead services." She believed they were trying to be nice, but eventually she tired of feeling like a "token" woman on the bimah and stepped away from the *ba'alat tefillah* role. "You couldn't have two women on the bimah at the same time," Rosanne Leipzig recalls of the late 1980s. "It wasn't written anywhere, but it was very clear that many congregants were uncomfortable if the service leader and *ba'alat tefillah* were both women."

Many CBST traditionalists were deeply uncomfortable with women in roles of religious leadership and did not welcome the increasing visibility of women on the bimah. A "CBST traditionalist" was not necessarily Orthodox in practice or personal observance, although some were. The traditionalist was someone who wanted things done as they were done in the times of Pinchas, or at least as they *remembered* things were done. Ironically, some of the most devout traditionalists were equally uncomfortable when Pinchas tried to move the service closer to Orthodoxy. These members greeted any change with suspicion and were vocal in their disapproval. The traditionalists were a powerful force, and they defended their nostalgia with the force of religious fervor.

Judith Tax (left) and Rabbi Nancy Wiener leading services in the early 1990s

## Innovation and Preservation

In the mid-1980s, as more knowledgeable liberal Jews became active in the synagogue, the Religious Committee underwent what Jack Greenberg calls "a renaissance of thought. New people were coming to the synagogue with more modern ideas. Now not only the members who grew up Orthodox wanted to be on the committee, but others, who were living in the modern world and observing a more progressive Judaism, wanted to influence what the synagogue was doing." The Religious Committee expanded to include Diane Burhenne, Rosanne Leipzig, Harry Lutrin, and Victor Appel, who later became a Reform rabbi. "We started to let the creative juices flow," Jack recalls. "We felt the synagogue was changing, that the people coming onto the committee represented a new energy." The committee created a more liberal service outline allowing the leader more choices. "We allowed for meditation as an alternative to a reading. Many more things were optional, including when to sit and stand at different places in the service. So you knew far less what to expect when a service leader got up there."

In an effort to counteract its male-dominated image, by 1974 CBST's newspaper ads specified that the synagogue was for women as well as men (The *New York Times*, April 4, 1975).

To the relief of CBST's traditionalists, few service leaders took advantage of these opportunities for innovation. But one notorious service, led by longtime member David Alter, pushed the synagogue, and even the Religious Committee, far beyond its comfort level: David set the *Hashkiveinu* prayer to the tune of "Amazing Grace." "That was horrendous," remembers Yehuda Berger, still offended as he recalled the service more than two decades later. Instead of standing for the silent *Amidah*, David led a seated guided meditation. As Bruce Friedman recalls, "a group of about twenty outraged people, led by Harvey Israelton, got up and went into the other room to pray a silent *Amidah*." Jack reflects on the immediate fallout. "When Bruce made the announcements that night, he said, 'The Religious Committee is meeting next week, and you should all come down to voice your disapproval about tonight's service.' Normally it was hard to get all the members of the Religious Committee to come to meetings, but that night we had forty or fifty angry people—not committee members—at that meeting. 'What are you doing to the shul?' 'You're tearing us apart.' David was there to defend his choices, and for a while we were more cautious with services." That uproar, instigated by a few traditionalist members, was part of a larger backlash against change, which also played out on the board. Jack reflects, "The Religious Committee had always been this holy group of people you trusted no matter what they did. Suddenly people stopped trusting us. They felt threatened by the changes we were making." In 1988, as Jack became chair of the committee, a slate of people came on the board hoping to preserve ritual life as it had been.

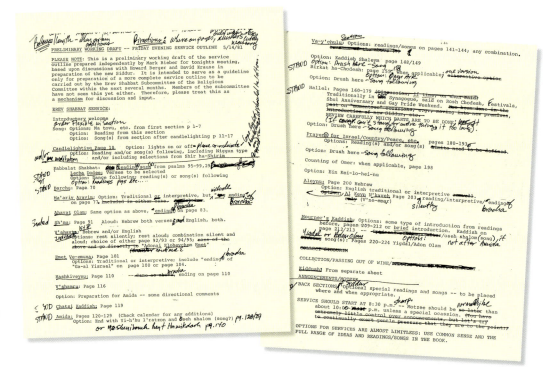

Service leaders and *ba'alei* or *ba'a lot tefillah* worked together to construct a service.

Diane Burhenne (left) and Judy Ribnick in 1988

### HOW I GOT TO CBST

I learned about CBST though some JTS friends. I was intrigued. I graduated from the JTS dual masters program and I was curious and excited about finding a community of committed Jews who were gay and lesbian. I went to a Friday night service and was thrilled to find something that brought together so many parts of my life that were so important to me. I grew up deeply immersed and rooted in my Conservative Jewish community in Minneapolis and I had a lot of background and experience leading Shabbat *tefillot* and High Holiday services there. I felt very welcome at CBST and very much at ease to bring what I wanted to bring. At CBST, I was thrilled to be among so many Jews without having to hide.

As a new *ba'alat tefillah* I was paired with Diane, a veteran service leader, who had been involved since the late 70s. (Little did I know that she had requested me.) We led a service; it ended up in a relationship, and we have been together ever since.

JUDY RIBNICK, MEMBER SINCE 1985

### Turning Points

As board chair from 1988–1990, Bill Wahler oversaw a major renovation of the Bethune Street interior and initiated an extensive board process to investigate the hiring of paid staff and of either an executive director or a rabbi. He also created a committee to explore affiliation and encouraged a review of dues structure, to broaden the fund-raising base and reduce reliance on the High Holiday Appeal. Bill appointed Mark Bieber to chair the committee to explore hiring full-time staff. Mel Rosen and Jordan Barbakoff produced an extensive report with the rabbi exploratory committee's findings.

As chair, Mel Rosen continued where Bill Wahler left off. He too leaned on the support of past chairs to explore controversial changes and new ideas. Mel created the committee of past chairs, led by Mark Bieber, to investigate other venues for Yom Kippur services.

By 1991 CBST membership once again had nearly doubled. At a time when many leaders had been lost to AIDS and others were burnt out, Mel Rosen tried to rejuvenate volunteer energy, recruiting new board members, including three women (the most to date), and initiated another process to restructure the board and committees. In August 1991, he warned that "the current structure has become dysfunctional due to our tremendous growth in a short span of time. The day-to-day operations of the synagogue falls to our small Board of Trustees. The board acts on day-to-day operations rather than policy issues, fund-raising, and long-term

CBST board presidents (standing from left to right) Irving Cooperberg, Bill Wahler, Arthur Strickler; (seated) Harriet Beckman, Michael Levine, and Mel Rosen, 1992

planning. This becomes so time- and energy-consuming that most of our brightest, most respected, and talented members refuse to run for the board. We must be at least in the process of changing this situation as we bring in our rabbi." Mel also wanted high-level board members to be comfortable with being publicly out of the closet so that they could represent CBST in the larger Jewish community.

### New Ritual Initiatives

In late 1990 and early 1991, CBST was staggering under the impact of AIDS and in the throes of the debate about hiring a rabbi. Many members mourned the intimacy that had been lost as the congregation grew. At the same time, real questions were emerging about the ability of a single Friday night service to meet the spiritual needs of its hundreds of members from diverse Jewish backgrounds. CBST members had high expectations of their community. They did not succumb to dissatisfaction or disaffection quietly. Walking away from the community felt extreme; waiting for a rabbi to resolve the issue would have been out of character. Instead, members tried to create what they felt the community lacked. Some of these efforts became part of the fabric of the community; others were not sustainable as the community evolved. Each initiative helped determine what CBST could and would not become, leading the congregation into its next decade and beyond.

As the Friday night service could no longer accommodate everyone's various spiritual needs, the Religious Committee began to approve the creation of alternative minyanim. Saul Zalkin recalls, "The Religious Committee didn't say no. We said, 'You want it? We'll help you.' We used to joke, 'you want to start a shul in Brooklyn? We'll help you. We'll give you siddurim.' And of course somebody actually tried to do just that." The committee saw its role as facilitating these initiatives, but left it to the various constituencies to organize them. "We'll give you whatever support you need for what you want to do, but we're not going to run it," Saul remembers saying. "If you want it, you have to put it together on your own."

There were a few conditions: All services had to be open to all members. No other event could meet at the same time as the 8:30 PM Friday night service. Participating in a minyan would not prevent anyone from attending the main service, enabling the Religious Committee to reassure those who feared the new minyanim would fracture the community. The committee insisted that allowing members to meet their particular needs would actually enhance the community as a whole.

## IS CBST TOO TRADITIONAL?

I often felt frustrated at the conservatism of the synagogue. As a person who studies Jewish texts for a living, I feel strongly that rabbinical (traditional) Judaism is in many ways an oppressive system, profoundly sexist and homophobic.

As a modern Jew, I believe that we must be looking for ways of radically transforming Judaism to incorporate feminist and gay experience and spirituality, and it was my hope that at a gay and lesbian synagogue I would find a large group of like-minded people. Instead, I have found a pervasive attitude of nostalgia for traditional Judaism and for the notion that the more traditional a service is, the more authentic it is.

I do not understand why we vest so much authority in a system that has denied us for so long. Why do we treat our gayness as a private matter that should in no way interfere with our Judaism? Why do we fool ourselves that, with the exception of certain attitudes about homosexuals and women, traditional Judaism is fine and deserves our devotion? These questions have consistently frustrated me and prevented me from feeling comfortable as part of the CBST community.

I have tremendous admiration for the amount of learning and knowledge that exists at CBST. I would challenge any synagogue in New York to equal our commitment to and participation in Jewish life. For me, it was wonderful to have a „safe space" in which I did not have to justify myself, and I want to thank the synagogue for all the support they gave me and for the beautiful shofar that was given to me as an ordination gift.

But, I would love for the synagogue to begin a serious exploration of what it means to be gay and lesbian in terms of spirituality and God-imaging, and see if we can't use our commitment and knowledge to place ourselves at the creative forefront of creating a Judaism that is both Jewish and gay. We must make our experience as gays and lesbians an integral, not incidental, component of our Judaism.

DAVID EDELSON,
newsletter, December 1990

## IS THIS CONGREGATION REALLY TOO TRADITIONAL?

Anyone who has been around CBST for a while is bound to meet people who do not relate to the "traditional" flavor of many of our services. But when I read Rabbi Edelson's article in the December newsletter, with his criticism of our supposed "nostalgia" and "conservatism," I realized that some people believe that only a lack of courage or insight keeps us from seeing things in their "radical" way. They are mistaken. In fact, many of us have arrived at our traditional viewpoint via a long, conscious growth process . . .

Women have been reading from the Torah at CBST from the very beginning; but so do their sisters at hundreds of Reform and Conservative congregations and even a few Orthodox minyanim. Here and there, we have gone further. We have added one clause to the first blessing of the Amidah--we say: "God of Sarah, Rebecca, Leah, and Rachel. Me, I'd rather not blue-pencil the siddur. I don't take its words in their most literal sense anyway. But if some women want to say, in effect, "make no mistake, this is my God too!" more power to them!

In short, we have not felt the need to concoct a "radical" new gay religion. But isn't that word a bit tarnished these days? OK, it's a free country. You want a new religion, go make one up . . . But why assume that lesbians and gays are a natural constituency for such experiments? Outside of a narrow circle of "politically correct" activists, there are few radicals in our diverse community. Anyway, as Jewish gays and lesbians, we're fortunate to belong to a community that is responding more thoughtfully to our needs than most religious or ethnic groups.

There is a sense of the word "radical," however, that may be relevant here--getting to the root of the matter. I have learned from my lover Jeff, that for modern Jews like us traditional prayer and observance can be a very radical experience. It can draw us past the obsessions of the moment in our personal or communal lives, and allow us to see the forest beyond the trees . . .

This might not work for you. But for myself, spare me your modern, relevant, and topical readings, please! When it comes to prayer, what was good enough for my forebears in the shtetl is, by a miracle, still good enough for me.

BARRY YOUNGERMAN,
newsletter, February, 1991

## New Friday Evening Services

In January 1991, the board approved an additional monthly 6:30 Friday night service for a provisional six-month period. Chair Mel Rosen, confident that the synagogue could sustain the additional service, declared in the newsletter, "The diversity of our congregation has always given us cause for celebration… We've tried to accommodate this diversity with a more traditional yet flexible Shabbat service. Obviously, this service doesn't and can't serve everyone's needs. It's our hope that this additional service will respond to the needs of some of our members who have voiced dissatisfaction, attend other synagogues, or have stopped coming to our Friday 8:30 night services, or are new to CBST." Mel described the new early service as "more participatory and feminist oriented than our regular 8:30 PM services." For its first few months, the 6:30 service, with Rosanne Leipzig as its contact, was cautiously called the Additional Service. It soon became known as the Feminist Minyan and marked the focal point of a growing series of monthly feminist programming initially coordinated by Yolanda Potasinski and Catherine Sull. In May 1991, another early Friday evening minyan began to meet for *Minchah* and *Ma'ariv*, calling itself the Orthopractic Minyan, which they explained meant "doing it the 'right way.'" Jeff Katz, Larry Kay, and

Yehuda Berger were listed as the contacts. The first announcement specified that the minyan would use the Orthodox de Sola Poole siddur and that women as well as men would be counted in the minyan. Including women in service participation and leadership was obligatory according to the requirements set out by the Religious Committee but was uncomfortable for many of the men participating in the minyan. They agreed to compromise anyway, because they felt that creating the minyan was, in itself, momentous. Many members of the Orthopractic Minyan (sometimes called the Early Minyan or the Traditional Minyan) believed that they were carrying on the true legacy of Reb Pinchas, preserving a corner of CBST as it was meant to be, safe from the winds of change. To their delight, along with other former regulars who no longer traveled on Shabbat, Pinchas himself was occasionally able to attend when the service, followed by Shabbat dinner, began and ended before nightfall. Barry Youngerman expressed his excitement in the December 1991 *Gay and Lesbian Synagogue News*.

> Some two dozen women and men have been quietly making history at CBST over the past seven months. For the first time, a fully traditional Jewish prayer service by and for gay men and lesbians has been established on a regular basis. . . Each month brings new worshippers, some of them new to CBST, some of them old friends who have not davened with us for years . . . .

In August 1991 the newsletter began to feature a full page of feminist programming.

## Challenging a Tradition of Inclusion

Both the Feminist and Orthopractic minyanim challenged CBST's long-standing practice against holding events where any person was excluded from participation because of sex, financial ability, or any other consideration. Certainly members had always self-selected when joining particular classes or affinity groups, and for many years most CBST events and services were de facto all male, but the shul consistently stated that women were welcome. Feminist programming emerged as a response from women who expressed the need for a safe women-only space in the predominantly male congregation. Many of the men who davened at the Orthopractic Minyan were more comfortable in prayer environments with exclusively male leadership and a *mechitzah* separating them from the women. While the impetus for these minyanim came from markedly different motivations, the Religious Committee felt that permitting any exclusively separate groups would create a dangerous precedent. Jack Greenberg

> ### MECHITZAH
>
> A young man called the office and wanted to know if we have a *mechitzah*. The answer was no, we do not. Why do you ask? And he said, "Well, I couldn't possibly come if there is no *mechitzah,* because I can only sit with the women so that I won't be distracted by looking at the men." That is not legend; it's fact.
>
> DICK RADVON

recalls, "There was a tension: we would not grant permission for women to meet exclusively. Of course they could publicize the minyan in a way that would make it clear the service was designed for women. Mostly women came to it, but not exclusively. We had a similar issue with the Orthopractic Friday night service. They were just the opposite: not friendly to women. If a woman came, they would want her to sit behind a *mechitzah,* and we were not going to allow that. Some of the men hid behind the pillars or did what they needed to do." But the Religious Committee would not allow ritual separation of women and men.

The board was relieved that the new minyanim had not, as some had feared, proved increasingly divisive or eroded attendance of the main Friday night service. On the contrary, Mel Rosen reported to the congregation that "these services have brought back many disaffected people and brought in many new people. On the Shabbat of these additional services we still fill the sanctuary for our main service." In fact, some minyan attendees stayed on for the main service as well. The experiment seemed to be a success. As Mel liked to say, "Diversity is our strength, not our weakness." By the early 1990s, after many years of adaptive lay leadership, CBST felt proud of its ability to encourage ritual experimentation and create new minyanim to support and sustain disparate members of the congregation.

> "Diversity is our strength, not our weakness." MEL ROSEN

# 3. THE IMPACT OF AIDS

FOR YEARS THE RELIGIOUS COMMITTEE managed not only the ritual life of the synagogue but its lifecycle needs as well. At first, the pastoral demands were modest. The congregation was fairly young, with most members in their twenties, thirties, and forties. As such, there were few funerals. When Pinchas served as CBST's rebbe, if there was a need for someone to officiate at a funeral or, in rare cases, at a wedding, he served in that role. There were almost no children, so there were few baby namings or b'nai mitzvah.

Later the Religious Committee developed a stable of knowledgeable congregants who could lead services and who could officiate when a lifecycle need arose. "Mostly we as a committee handled everything that needed to be handled," Jack Greenberg recalls. "As a lay person, you could do a funeral, and sometimes that was OK. But there were some things where you really needed a rabbi. People often didn't want just any congregant, no matter how competent. They wanted a rabbi." As chairs of the Religious Committee, Saul Zalkin and, later, Jack Greenberg developed an extensive referral process to help members find friendly local rabbis.

No one anticipated how the need for rabbinical support would increase as the 1980s progressed.

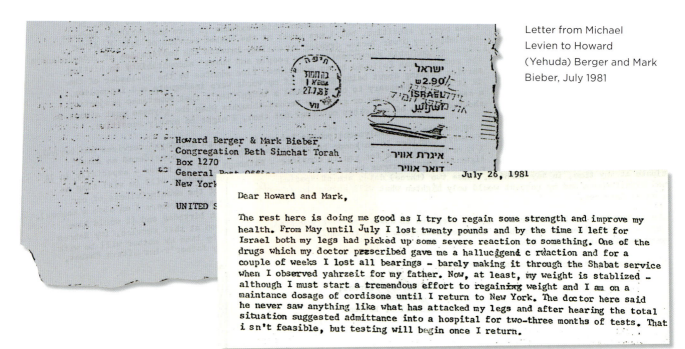

Letter from Michael Levien to Howard (Yehuda) Berger and Mark Bieber, July 1981

## FEBRUARY 1982

### IN MEMORIAM

It is our sad duty to inform the congregation of the death of a valuable, beloved member, **MICHAEL S. LEVIEN**, on December 28, 1981. Michael grew up in Seattle and was graduated from Columbia University. Michael had been a member of CBST for about three years, and had been active in the religious affairs of the shul by reading from the Torah, delivering *drashot*, and participating in many phases of religious policy and planning. He was instrumental in establishing West Side High School and served as teacher, Director and Assistant Director of the school. His total commitment to Judaism and to public education guided all his activities, including serving on the Boards of the ACLU and Stephen Wise Free Synagogue, and participating in Upper West Side Politics. He will be missed by all of us and his absence is indeed a diminishing of our congregation.

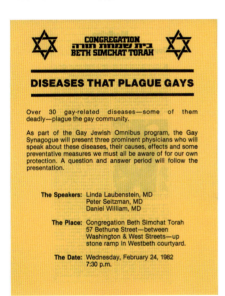

CBST's first AIDS-related program, in February 1982, was one of the earliest forums in the city.

### February 1982

The February 1982 issue of *Gay Synagogue News* includes a small article entitled "Diseases That Plague Gays." This was the first mention in the CBST newsletter of what would come to be known as AIDS. Just below that article is a death announcement for member Michael Levien, who died on December 28, 1981. He is thought to have been the first CBST member to die from AIDS. Sheldon Post was one of the earliest CBST members to understand the seriousness of the illnesses that had started affecting the community. Under the auspices of the education program, he organized the first CBST program on the topic. "More than 30 gay-related diseases, some of them deadly, plague the gay community," the newsletter announced. "The Gay Jewish Omnibus will present three prominent physicians who will speak about these diseases. They will discuss the causes and effects, and some preventative measures we must all be aware of for our own protection." The forum, featuring some of the doctors who would become the most prominent AIDS doctors in New York, drew 350 men, most from outside of CBST. Shelly Post, who would die of AIDS in 1988, wrote on the event, a report that highlights the tragic lack of knowledge at the time.

> We learned that most gay-related diseases are transmitted during sexual encounters, many of which are one-night stands and/or anonymous. One of the doctors suggested, for starters, that those who engage in those types of liaisons can halve their exposure to disease by seeing every one-nighter a second time. The object, of course, is to try to know your partners and minimize risk of infection. Regarding the new gay-related immuno-deficiencies (Kaposi's Sarcoma, Pneumocystis Carinii Pneumonia), while there are some causal theories—i.e., use of nitrates/poppers, other drugs, numerous sexual partners—none of these has yet been proven.

Nearly half of the men at CBST died from AIDS. (standing left to right) Ira Berger*, Jesse Goldman, Lou Rittmaster, Bill Fern, Irving Cooperberg* (seated left to right) Shelly Post*, Jeff Katz, Ya'akov Gladstone.
*Died from AIDS

Shelly urged members to become aware of the potential for exposure to disease and lobby for research funding. The term A.I.D.S (Aquired Immune Deficiency Syndrome) first appears in the CBST newsletter in October 1982 in a discussion of the proliferation of new organizations for AIDS research and support. CBST members founded many of them. Paul Rapoport was among the small group that gathered in Larry Kramer's living room in 1981 to launch the organization that became Gay Men's Health Crisis. Larry Kramer joined and resigned as a member of CBST on a few occasions over the years. Mel Rosen served as GMHC's first executive director, and Shelly Post was an early board president, as was CBST member Ira Berger, who was instrumental in the purchase and renovation of GMHC's first building on West 20th Street.

In the months that followed, awareness and anxiety of the disease began to grow. The synagogue saw itself as having a role in providing AIDS education and resources; CBST hosted community meetings with AIDS doctors and disseminated information about the developing network of AIDS support organizations, freely offering its sanctuary at a time when it was still a rarity for a gay organization to have a large physical space.

By 1983, AIDS is mentioned in almost every issue of the newsletter. CBST became active in raising money for GMHC, selling a block of tickets for the GMHC Circus fund-raiser that would fill the 17,000 seats of Madison Square Garden. Shelly Post, representing CBST

### NOVEMBER–DECEMBER 1982

**IN MEMORIAM**

CBST member **JEFFERY CROLAND** died on October 29 from AIDS (Acquired Immune Deficiency Syndrome). Anyone wishing to make a donation in his memory is asked to contribute to the National Gay Health Education Foundation, P. O. Box 834, Linden Hill, NY 11354. NGHEF is a not-for profit foundation concerned with gay and lesbian health care issues.

on the newly formed AIDS Network, wrote updates for the newsletter, publishing AIDS statistics and noting Mayor Koch's failure to acknowledge the epidemic in New York City, where by 1982 there were two hundred AIDS deaths and 540 new diagnoses, fully half of the cases reported nationally. Mel Rosen testified before Congress in the summer of 1983 about the severity of the crisis.

The September 1983 newsletter included an article by member Art Leonard about legal issues surrounding AIDS; a similar article about AIDS and Social Security appeared the following month. Members with professional expertise offered their services. Art, a law professor who has written on LGBT legal issues in law journals and the gay press for over three decades, recalls the significant role CBST members played as volunteers and professionals in the early days of AIDS.

Before acquiring its 20th Street building, GMHC operated from a rooming house at 318 West 22nd Street owned by Mel Cheren.

> As a new member of Lambda Legal Defense Fund's Board of Directors in 1983, Bill Hibsher and his law firm represented Dr. Joseph Sonnabend, a prominent NYC doctor who had many AIDS patients, in the first AIDS-related discrimination case that went to the New York state courts, perhaps in any court in the U.S. In 1983, when there was much panic and little information about AIDS, the co-op apartment building where Dr. Sonnabend had his office refused to renew his lease because they were unhappy having PWAs coming into the building. Bill's firm teamed with Attorney General Bob Abrams to persuade the court to order the co-op to allow Dr. Sonnabend to remain.

Another member, Peter Vogel, active in the New York State Democratic Party, became close to Governor Mario Cuomo. Art notes that Peter "played an important part in the legislative activities that led to the establishment of the New York State AIDS Institute, one of the first state agencies in the country devoted exclusively to dealing with AIDS. Peter also played an important role in lobbying for sane public health policies around confidentiality, contact tracing, and testing." State Senator Roy Goodman, an East Side Republican who was the leading Senate sponsor of the bill that established the AIDS Institute, attended Peter's memorial service at CBST.

As a member of the Legal Advisory Committee for Lambda Legal Defense in the early 1980s, Art Leonard volunteered as a cooperating attorney for Lambda to represent the first person to bring an AIDS-related discrimination claim

MAY 1982

IN MEMORIAM

We mourn the death on March 18, 1983, of our member, **MICHAEL CORTMAN**. Michael was a victim of AIDS. May his memory be a blessing.

before the New York City Human Rights Commission. The favorable settlement set a precedent for the handling of AIDS discrimination claims under the New York City Human Rights law. Art helped lay the groundwork for Lambda to provide training on AIDS issues for all the offices of the New York State Division of Human Rights. In 1983, after a faculty colleague at New York Law School died from AIDS, Art helped set up the first AIDS pro bono legal panel through the organization that became the LGBT Bar Association and helped persuade GMHC to create a legal services department to run it. Art wrote the first published law review article

## TESTIMONY OF MEL ROSEN, EXECUTIVE DIRECTOR, GMHC

House Committee on Government Operations, Federal Response to AIDS: Hearings before a Subcommittee of the Committee on Government Operations, House of Representatives, 98th Cong., 1st Sess.,

When a person is told he or she has AIDS it is not like hearing that they have cancer. When you have cancer you are told what the diagnosis, prognosis, and treatments are. When you are told that you have AIDS you are hearing that you have a time bomb inside of you, that any day you will get an opportunistic infection and one of these infections would kill you, usually within three years.

The Federal Government has not done its share. You must appropriate massive sums of money for research into this disease. You must appropriate money to the States so they can distribute moneys to local self-help organizations or set up their own programs. If you are not motivated to help disenfranchised groups, let me tell you something as a professional social worker.

Since most researchers and health officials have determined that this disease is sexually transmitted, it is probably the long incubation period that has kept the disease for the most part confined to certain groups. This will change shortly. There is a steaming locomotive roaring down the tracks at the general population. The people of this country depend on your God-given wisdom to ascertain the eventuality of certain events and to protect them.

I call upon you to not only appropriate the necessary funds but to create an office inside the Department of Health and Human Services that does two things: one, establishes a national effort that coordinates services to affected individuals and a national educational effort to the public at large and, two, gives resources and technical assistance to States and self-help organizations in locations where the disease is spreading or likely to spread.

[The prepared statement of Mr. Rosen follows:] . . .

I sit before you a very changed man from a year ago when I called the CDC. I have discovered that medicine, research, and the so-called safeguards we have in place to warn us about pending disasters are political and do not work when disenfranchised minorities are involved. When toxic shock and Legionnaire's disease first came on the scene there was an immediate response by government and press. Why did hundreds of people have to die before anyone moved in this case? ...It is the American way for us to respect and care for the individual person who is in trouble in our country. I have become disillusioned about this in the past year in relation to our government. However, I take heart in the response of the community itself . . . .

Washington, DC: U.S. Government Printing Office, 1983

NEWSLETTER, 1984

on AIDS discrimination in 1985, based on a chapter he wrote for Lambda's 1984 *AIDS Legal Guide*. Two years later he collaborated in publishing the first law school textbook about AIDS.

## Controversy and Silence

There were few mentions of AIDS in the newsletter in 1984, reflecting the "AIDS fatigue" that many organizations experienced after the initial period of fear and organizing in 1982 and 1983. Many felt the gay community was finally reaping the rewards of the gay rights movement and that political and social equality were within reach. The community was ambivalent about how much attention to give AIDS. While advocacy for funding and resources clearly were needed, some in the community were terrified of being re-stigmatized and re-marginalized by focusing too much on AIDS. Some worried that so much attention on AIDS was a thinly veiled anti-sex campaign. Many feared that the fear and stigma of AIDS would reverse the modest achievements of gay liberation.

Active volunteers at GMHC, such as Ron Weiss and Penny Dachinger, encouraged other CBST members to become involved. "This is OUR crisis, they are OUR brothers, OUR friends, and OUR lovers," they wrote in 1984. An AIDS update from Penny later that year highlights a new controversy emerging as the earliest AIDS antibody tests were becoming available. While the benefits of testing were unclear, the dangers of being known to have AIDS loomed large. Confidentiality was paramount:

> Dr. Steve Caiazza, President of NY Physicians for Human Rights, states unequivocally that Gay men should not be tested for the AIDS virus at this time. The test that is being developed is to test for antibodies only. In Caiazza's view, as many as 80% of all Gay men may have been exposed to the active AIDS virus and have antibodies in their blood streams. This does not necessarily mean that they are carrying the virus (this will require an antigen test which will not be available for at least another year), that they have AIDS, that they will get AIDS, or that they are carriers of AIDS. In short, all the test will do is tell you that you have been exposed and perhaps raise your anxiety level to the point that you become more susceptible to disease, and any disease may compromise your immune system.

> **DECEMBER 1984**
>
> IN MEMORIAM
>
> Memorial services at CBST are a means of finding consolation through tributes to members of our community who have passed away. Many of us attended recent services for **HARVE PRESS**.

Many worried that their names would be collected and that all gay men would be considered AIDS carriers and thus denied jobs or housing. Most agreed that "this is certainly a gray area in which we have to be as concerned about politics as we are about staying well."

JANUARY 1985

> **IN MEMORIAM**
>
> We regret to announce the passing of our friend and member, **JEFFRY KLOTZ**, a victim of A.I.D.S., on December 7, 1984. CBST will hold a memorial service on Sunday, January 13, at 11 am. Many remember his fine piano playing at CBST and his participation in our musical *onegs* and Holiday services. We will all miss him.

## The Toll Rises

CBST had yet to define a unique role in the AIDS crisis. There had been no real conversation of what CBST as a synagogue could offer in the face of the epidemic, nor any discussion of the spiritual or pastoral implications of AIDS. Likely the first AIDS service in which CBST participated, and one of the first AIDS services held in New York, was an interfaith candlelight prayer vigil for people with AIDS on Sunday, June 17, 1984. Representing CBST, Ron Weiss recited the Mourner's Kaddish. In 1984, the notion of Jewish Healing Services had barely emerged. At CBST, the traditionally rooted members of the Religious Committee were more likely to use ancient Jewish liturgy for new applications than create new liturgy and new rituals. CBST would eagerly participate in services like the interfaith vigil, offering prayers and texts from the Jewish liturgical canon—Kaddish or Psalms. That fall, David Bank composed a prayer for his friend Jeffry Klotz, who was sick with AIDS in a Pennsylvania hospital. It began, "Dear G-d, Our community is afflicted and we know not why." This was probably the first new AIDS prayer included in a CBST Friday night service. Although the prayer does not mention AIDS by name, it was clearly composed as a prayer of healing and strength in the face of AIDS.

As the AIDS deaths at CBST accelerated in 1985, the community continued to host events and disseminate updates on AIDS research. The newsletter reported without taking positions on the controversies surrounding the testing and closing of the bathhouses. That November, CBST featured Dr. David Axelrod, the New York State Health Commissioner, for a Friday night lecture and discussion. The talk, which came only weeks after the New York State decision allowing local health departments to close down bathhouses, was Axelrod's first to a gay organization.

Axelrod, who davened with CBST that night, praised the gay community's efforts at safe-sex education. *Gay Synagogue News* reported:

> In a lively question and answer period that followed, Dr. Axelrod was put to task with some incisive probing about how the state's emergency health measure discriminated against Gays. One vocal questioner claimed that labeling Gay male sex acts as dangerous promoted the idea that Gays were meant to feel "shame for expressing love and carrying out sexual relationships with loved ones." Someone in the audience aptly remarked that if the larger heterosexual community were denied their primary mode of expressing affection and love, the uproar that would ensue would be unfathomable. In relating these statements to the media-hyped closing of the bathhouses, the doctor stated that despite the efforts of many of the bathhouses to advocate safe sexual practices, it would be unthinkable to check that everyone there observed these recommendations.

The following month CBST hosted its first consciously Jewish program targeted toward people with AIDS; seventy-five people attended. The event, a brunch including Chanukah candle-lighting and dancing, was intended to be the first in a series of programs for people with AIDS, with the proceeds benefiting AIDS research. But while lighting Chanukah candles among PWAs was a significant community-building event, it didn't address the spiritual dimension of the AIDS crisis itself: CBST needed to take a more active, and more Jewish, role in the crisis.

**A Jewish Response**

Michael Levine recalls that, like most gay men, he lived in terror during the 1980s. "Every Friday night we would come to shul and we would say, 'Oh no, someone else.' The thin face, the marks on the skin from the cancers. The pneumonia. And in a year or two they would be gone." Saul Zalkin, then a board member and Religious Committee chair, recalls that with members newly diagnosed every week, the CBST board sought ways to help beyond fund-raising for AIDS organizations, but they struggled to identify exactly what they could do. As the only gay synagogue in New York, CBST was uniquely poised to make a religious Jewish contribution. The board, with Arthur Strickler as chair, asked Saul to explore the possibilities. "I was instructed not to re-create what was already being done by GMHC or God's Love We Deliver. I sent out inquiries to various rabbis, and the result was the creation of the Bikkur Cholim Committee, to visit people with AIDS."

Interestingly, the Chevra Bikkur Cholim, established in January 1986 wasn't focused on the needs of CBST members living with AIDS. Rather, CBST established the committee as the synagogue's contribution to and a Jewish extension of the overburdened AIDS social services agencies. It became a crucial Jewish resource at a time when most of the organized Jewish community was still refusing contact with people with AIDS. Many people with AIDS had been treated terribly by Jewish community institutions, including Jewish funeral homes refusing to perform the ritual of *taharah* for people who had died from AIDS. Marc Blumenthal and Rabbi Isaac Trainin, founder of the new Coordinating Council on Bikkur Cholim, trained the volunteers. Rabbi Trainin had created the coordinating council to facilitate

> **FEBRUARY 1985**
>
> IN MEMORIAM
>
> With increasing sadness, we report the loss of another member of the CBST community to the relentless scourge AIDS. **DOV WERTHEIM**, a CBST member in years past and a friend to many, passed away on January 7, 1985.

> MAY 1985
>
> **IN MEMORIAM**
>
> In the past month, two more friends of CBST have succumbed to AIDS. Both were members of the Shul in its formative years. A memorial service was scheduled for **HAROLD JAFFE** on April 21. The family of the second victim requested that his name not be published. We all grieve together and pray for a better future.

> NOVEMBER 1985
>
> **IN MEMORIAM**
>
> We are saddened by the death of our member, **DR. STUART SCHWARTZ**, from AIDS complications. We offer condolences to his family and friends.

the development of synagogue-sponsored *bikkur cholim* groups. It was an ideal model for a community that had no rabbi of its own and that few, if any, rabbis were willing to visit. Saul recalls:

> Members of the committee understood that their participation was on a confidential basis. Articles were written for the newsletter, and we expected people to call to let us know they would appreciate a visit. We began to contact rabbis at St. Vincent's, Beth Israel, and Cabrini Hospitals to let them know we were available to visit. The board then expanded the program to create gift packages for Jewish holidays: Rosh Hashanah, Chanukah, Purim, and Gay Pride. We had a budget, we created the packages, and then, if someone in the hospital wanted one, we delivered them to the bedside. Sometimes we delivered them to the rabbi who then delivered them on our behalf.

While CBST encouraged members to contact the committee for visits, few did. Many members sought AIDS services away from CBST, without disclosing their AIDS status at the synagogue until it was too late to hide it or until they died. As such, most *bikkur cholim* visits were arranged by the various hospital chaplains. "We served anyone who requested a visit; they didn't have to be Jewish. Certainly, the hospital chaplains did not ask if someone was a member of CBST," remembers Saul. In fact, Saul recalls an awkward moment when he and the person he was visiting in the hospital recognized each other from the synagogue. "I went to deliver a package and recognized the person, not the name. Though he was embarrassed, he did say the chaplain had already told him we were coming from CBST, so we wound up having a pleasant visit."

> FEBRUARY 1986
>
> **IN MEMORIAM**
>
> With much sadness, we announce the passing of **LOUIS BLAKE**, our member, on December 27, 1985, yet another casualty of AIDS. May his family and friends find comfort in his memory as we pray for a speedy end to this plague which is decimating our community.

Art Leonard recalls that in 1987 when Governor Cuomo attended the installation of a plaque honoring Peter Vogel's contributions to the Center, Irving Cooperberg, who had been bedridden and unable to walk, had a "miraculous" remission and was able to greet the governor there.

## APRIL 1986

### IN MEMORIAM

Our member **PETER VOGEL** died of AIDS on February 21. Peter was chair of Governor Cuomo's Gay Task Force and vice-chair of the AIDS Advisory Council at the time of his death. He was a also a founder and president of Brooklyn's Lambda Independent Democrats, head of the National Association of Gay and Lesbian Democratic Clubs, and a founding Board member of the Lesbian and Gay Community Services Center. The California State Assembly adjourned in his honor upon his death. His funeral at CBST drew over 500 mourners. The warmest condolences are offered to his father, Adolph, his life partner of 20 years, Don Castellanos, and to all who knew him and were touched by his courage and compassion.

On Friday, March 7, it was announced at services that CBST lost two of its long-time members. **DR. LAWRENCE LERCHER** was active in the Synagogue's early years and could always be counted on to provide for the shul anonymously. **MARK TURKEL** was involved in many worthy causes, notably Lambda Legal Defense Fund. We share in the sorrow of their friends and families.

JUNE-JULY 1986

### IN MEMORIAM

**IRWIN "IAN" LOEBEL**, a faithful member of our Synagogue community for over 12 years, passed away on April 17. Though an outspoken individual, he always gave of his time, energy, and artistic talents, designing among other things our letter-heads, Chai cards, and the calendar insert for this newsletter. Beneath his feisty manner, he had heart, warmth, and humanity. Tears were never far when he sensed pain in others. Blessed with a sharp wit and a winning smile, Ian was a real presence in the Shul, with his own sense of style. He will be sorely missed by all those who knew and worked with him all these years.

Ian Loebel, 1977

At a spring 1986 AIDS planning session, thirty CBST members gathered to help define CBST's role in the AIDS crisis. "As of now the shul has a Chaverim Committee, chaired by Pam Plastock and David Spegal, dedicated to helping any member of the shul in time of need. Saul Zalkin, chair of the Religious Committee, now coordinates the Chevra Bikkur Cholim, which provides religious counseling to Jewish AIDS patients. And Michael Hirsch is chair of the NY AIDS Action Committee, which provided meals at the Shul on Friday afternoons to any persons with AIDS (PWAs) who request them." Some of the many AIDS-related *oneg* programs included "The Body and Its Dangers," by AIDS educator and writer Allen Barnett and pianist Gary Knox with a program of "healing and meditation music."

CBST members participated in many emerging AIDS initiatives—including GMHC's new AIDS Walk, a bold act of visibility in New York City in 1986—and the new National Jewish AIDS Project with Art Strickler representing CBST. Thanks to the advocacy of a few devoted activists, the Jewish community was trying to repair its track record of treating people with AIDS. Mel Rosen worked tirelessly to get the organized Jewish community involved with AIDS, as Art Leonard recalls, "cajoling the Jewish Board of Family and Children's Services to establish services for people with AIDS, modeled on the buddy system he had devised for GMHC, and later helping to plan the establishment of the first day treatment program for people with AIDS."

In early 1987, Mel and later Art Leonard served on the advisory committee of the JBFCS AIDS Project, which received a grant from the Philadelphia Federation

From the April 1988 newsletter

```
PWA
We challenge the label "victim"
which implies defeat, and we are
   only occasionally "patients."
     We are people with AIDS.
```

"ACT UP knew how to manipulate the media and it was exciting," recalls Gary Adler (center). "In ACT UP there was no constitution, so it was every person for themselves. If you wanted to rip up a sign in front of St. Patricks at Gay Pride, you could. It was against the philosophy of ACT UP but not against its policies."

to expand its AIDS services. Pinchas Berger, coordinator of the JBFCS AIDS Project, spoke at CBST on several occasions.

With a history in the militant non-violent Gay Activists Alliance, Gary Adler felt frustrated with many members of GMHC. "They weren't political enough for me." Gary found his way to another meeting at Larry Kramer's apartment. "I was in on the founding of ACT UP. Ten years into the AIDS epidemic and the Reagan silence was deafening." He recalls the early involvement of women in ACT UP. "They had a better sense of the gravity of the situation and how needed they were. They patiently educated men about sexism. There were painful confrontations sometimes, but the women patiently kept on. To some extent, they were the brains of ACT UP, the proponents of non-violence.

### The Controversy on Testing

The first AIDS test had become available in 1985, but it was still new and controversial. With an epidemic of fear escalating as quickly as the AIDS crisis itself, discrimination was rampant, and no effective treatments had been discovered.

MAY 1986

**TURKEL SERVICE**

A memorial was held at the Shul on May 4 for **MARK D. TURKEL**, who died of AIDS in March. A lawyer active in civil rights campaigns, Mark was on the national board of Lambda Legal Defense Fund and was a founder of FAIRPAC, a political action committee that worked toward the passage of legislation for Lesbian and Gay civil rights. He was free with his time for any organization that needed his help.

Without a system of confidential testing, many worried that a positive test would only cause despair and discrimination. This fear, as well as misinformation and misunderstandings about transmission, delayed the widespread adoption of AIDS testing.

CBST held a public AIDS forum in January 1986 exploring these issues, featuring Steven Caiazza of NY Physicians for Human Rights, Dixie Beckham, a social worker at Memorial Sloan-Kettering, Art Leonard offering the legal perspective, and Mel Rosen, by then the executive director of the New York State AIDS Institute. The newsletter continued to highlight the testing debate, as well as the advent, potential availability, and efficacy of AZT, an early AIDS treatment.

Both Mel Rosen and Irving Cooperberg became passionate advocates for testing and made a point of being open about their HIV status, pleading with the congregation to be tested. In his 1989 Yom Kippur Yizkor *drash*, Irving spoke on the death toll from AIDS at CBST: about 3.4 percent of the men of CBST had died that year.

After telling stories about members who had died and were suffering from AIDS, he told his own story of testing positive three years earlier. "It is not enough to remember the dead at Yizkor. We have to work on the living." Irving called on the congregation to be tested for HIV, saying that his early detection had given him at least three more years. (He would survive until 1997.) "There's no reason to be surprised by pneumonia. We don't have to sit like sheep to be slaughtered." Mel Rosen declared in the April 1990 newsletter, "Everyone at risk for AIDS in our shul should be tested. Whatever your immune status, through monitoring and drugs you can continue a quality of life and diminish your risk of getting sick."

**Filling the Spiritual Void**

With so many deaths, the synagogue needed to provide some ritual resources the congregation had not considered before this crisis. Mark Bieber convened a Yahrzeit Plaque Committee that designed a memorial board, dedicated on Shemini Atseret 1986. Saul Zalkin, on behalf of the Religious Committee, researched purchasing a CBST cemetery plot and establishing a relationship with funeral parlors. The shul made its sanctuary available for anyone who wanted to hold a memorial service regardless of membership or Jewish status.

In 1986 there were 4,224 AIDS diagnoses and 2,720 deaths in New York city—and 6,523 deaths since the beginning of the crisis. It had become increasingly clear that CBST's needs around AIDS were greater than the informational resources, sanctuary space, *bikkur cholim* visits, and holiday food baskets the synagogue was providing. As more members struggled with physical and spiritual

## OCTOBER 1986

### IN MEMORIAM

Sadly we mourn the passing of two of our members this past August: **DR. GILBERT MILLER** and **JONATHAN SAND**. A memorial service for **GIL MILLER** was held at CBST on August 26. His family and friends spoke movingly of his activities in the Synagogue, his care and concern for all who knew him, and his love for Israel. May both men be long remembered in our extended CBST family.

## NOVEMBER 1986

### IN MEMORIAM

Sadly we report that our member **RONN CHARLES** died of AIDS complications this September at his family's home in San Francisco. Who can forget his rendition of "Sam, You Made the Pants Too Long" at our cabarets and New Member socials? Ronn was an active force in the fashion industry's AIDS fundraiser last May, and we draw strength from his courage and determination as he attended our Bar/Bat Mitzvah celebration in June.

We must also announce the AIDS-related death of our member **MORT GINDI**. A friend to many of us, Mort served as an openly Gay Democratic district leader in Manhattan. A memorial service is planned at CBST for October 29.

## DECEMBER 1986

### IN MEMORIAM

We sadly note the passing of **IRA M. BERGER**, 46, who was a member of CBST for many years. Ira was Associate Dean for Public Affairs at New York Law School, and had devoted much time in recent years to Gay Men's Health Crisis as a board member and, briefly, as President. He was the primary mover for the purchase of a building by GMHC, which will be an important community asset. We extend our condolences to his lover, Ricardo Mercado, and the members of his family.

## MARCH 1987

### IN MEMORIAM

Our member **MICHAEL SABIN** passed away last December, a victim of AIDS. He was active in many Jewish/Zionist organizations. A board member and secretary of, the North American Conference of Ethiopian Jewry (NACOEJ), he traveled to Ethiopia to investigate conditions there. He was also involved in the Israel Bond Drive. He wrote plays and poetry, especially on the oppressed and the Holocaust. Among his works were a volume on Jewish history through poetry and "The Spirit Moves Me" about AIDS bereavement. We offer condolences to his many friends and family.

---

crises, they increasingly wanted to turn to a rabbi for their pastoral needs. Jack Greenberg recalls, "With AIDS, the rabbi referrals became a full-time occupation."

Yehuda Berger created the first AIDS healing services for CBST, announcing the first service, scheduled for February 1987, with this introduction:

> When times are hard, Jews traditionally go to shul and daven, that is, pray and petition for better times. These are assuredly hard times: for People with AIDS or AIDS-related Complex, for the worried well, and for those who try to help and support and love those who are ill. In our dedication to the living, and in memory of those who have passed away, the Synagogue is planning a service in which we may grieve and mourn, express our fear and pain, and seek solace and hope.

Jack Greenberg recalls that the service included "prayers and readings meaningful to all of us in the age of AIDS/HIV before there was any sort of medication or hope for survival, whether we were infected or not or didn't know." The Religious

---

The Jewish Week, Inc. February 13, 1987

## Solemn rites at gay synagogue for AIDS victims

By MARION KWARTLER

### 'Chicken soup brigade'

Yehuda Berger sobbed heavily into his hands last Sunday as the haunting strains of the memorial prayer *Eyl Malay Rachimim*, filled the sanctuary of Congregation Beth Simchat Torah, New York City's only gay synagogue. He,

The Board of Jewish Family Services has recently formed a volunteer program, dubbed the "chicken soup brigade" to bring hot meals to AIDS victims of all denominations who are too ill to cook for themselves. Financed by a $25,000 grant from the UJA-Federation, the brigade will be entirely staffed by specially trained volunteers supervised by a profes-

ish Appeal-Federation of Jewish Philanthropies allocated its first $25,000 in support of the community's AIDS victims through a project run by the Jewish Board of Family and Children's Services.

Yet, for Mel Rosen, director of the New York State Office of Public Health's AIDS Institute, satisfaction with the allocation is min-

The *Jewish Week*, February 13, 1987

Committee, propelled into a new inventiveness by the urgency of the situation and by Yehuda Berger's liturgical creativity, experimented with a few different formats before establishing the Service of Hope and Comfort as a monthly event. In April 1987 CBST held its first Passover seder for people with AIDS. The Religious Committee called a communal fast for AIDS in May of that year. Committee chair Saul Zalkin invited the larger Jewish community to join in a day of fasting, prayer, and study—a historical Jewish religious response in times of extreme communal crisis intended to focus the community's energies on the illness and to pray for God to intervene. In the newsletter, the synagogue struggled to address the theological and spiritual questions created by the crisis.

> But where is God when we think we choose life, and tragedy strikes? When someone contracts AIDS and dies of the disease? Where then is God?
>
> God is in the compassion we feel for the stricken.
>
> God is in our resolve to fight for more responsible governmental action.
>
> God is in the strength that we must all search for as we make our way through the shadow.

Rosanne Leipzig led High Holiday services during some of the most devastating AIDS years. She recalls the difficulty of approaching the High Holiday liturgy within the context of AIDS "and trying to understand how you could take the liturgy and make it meaningful and not painful. It was hard.

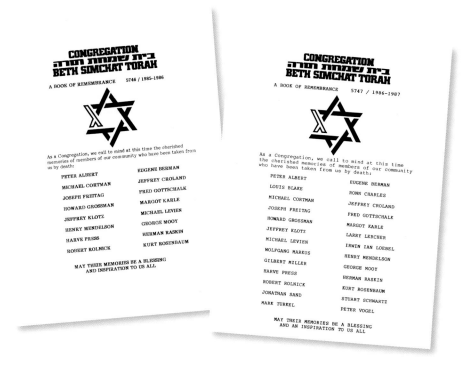

The CBST Yizkor list grew by ten names between Yom Kippur 1985 and 1986.

MAY 1987

IN MEMORIAM

Several weeks ago another of our members died after a long struggle with AIDS. Known to friends as either **ED** or **EVAN CLEIN**, he was a special person. He was a sometime actor and a sometime antiques salesman. He had a good heart, a sense of humor, and an interest in the unusual. He put up a strong fight against AIDS and came to CBST during most of his illness.

RON WEISS

JUNE 1987

IN MEMORIAM

**THEODORE KRULWICH**, 34 years old, died April 11. A long-time shul member, he was a partner at a midtown law firm. He was active in community affairs, most recently as a member of Manhattan Community Planning Board 8 and as Director of Community Concerns for Senior Citizens. We join in offering our sincerest condolences to Ted's family and friends.

### YIZKOR, 2006

I had a large family, all of whom were married, having children, or on their way to these typical signs of heterosexual adulthood. At least I could find refuge with my cousin Teddy Krulwich, who was also gay. He and his blond non-Jewish boyfriend would go to CBST every Friday night. Ted found out he had AIDS, and after a very brief struggle with the disease, he died. He was 34 and he had never really come out. He first introduced his lover to his family at the very end of his life. He didn't tell anyone at work that he was gay and he didn't tell any of his friends that he was sick. His death shocked all of his friends and associates, because in the end they realized that no one really knew who he was. When Ted died CBST had no rabbi, so Ted's parent's asked their Orthodox rabbi to officiate at his funeral. The service was unbelievably painful. The rabbi refused to mention that Ted was gay and made no mention of his lover Bruce. The service totally denied who Ted was and failed to honor his life. The worst was, Ted was buried by a man who hated that he was gay. But I guess Ted's death had one positive benefit. It propelled me out of the closet. I decided to change my future. I realized that everybody was hurt by Ted's refusal to be honest about his life. I learned that being closeted wasn't really a gift to anyone.

SARA KRULWICH, MEMBER SINCE 1992

Because there is so much in the *machzor* that makes it seem you are responsible for your own fate." These High Holiday services became another way in which lay leaders tried to adapt Jewish liturgy to face the crisis. A parallel *Kol Nidrei* service had been added in 1987 because of overcrowding, the overflow service tapping new service leaders. "I just couldn't say the words or think about the meaning of the holiday, ignoring what we as a community were going through," Rosanne reflects. Invoking a traditional theology of reward and punishment

The plaque in memory of Paul Rapoport that hangs in New York City's LGBT center

SEPTEMBER 1987

IN MEMORIAM

We sadly mourn the passing of our members:
**MARK LUTVAK ROBERT NACHEMIN PAUL RAPOPORT**
We offer condolences to their families and friends

would be destructive and traumatic for many people in a community in the throes of AIDS. Rosanne felt, as a service leader, she needed to adapt the liturgy in order to serve the spiritual needs of the community. She remembers this effort as the impetus for the parallel *Kol Nidrei* service evolving into an alternative, less traditional service. "We needed to be able to change things more than was customary at CBST. We began asking everyone to rise for Kaddish because we needed to be saying Kaddish for those people for whom no one was saying Kaddish. So we began having both a more liberal High Holiday service and a more traditional one."

The memorial board, dedicated in fall 1986, initially provided room for 340 names and included two plaques, one to commemorate the Holocaust and another, much debated, of equal size to memorialize those who had died from AIDS.

## The Quilt

A significant CBST delegation traveled to the October 1987 March on Washington. In the newsletter Lee Levin wrote an account of the march and of seeing the AIDS quilt, from the newly established Names Project, displayed on the Mall:

> How can any who participated forget the surge of people gathering on the Ellipse, or the seemingly never-ending wave of marchers along Pennsylvania Avenue swinging into the vast greenery of the Mall? How could we not be caught up in the spirit of all that Life? As I walked my way back though the crowds on the Mall, I reached a crossover—passing through an invisible curtain—into the stillness of the air hovering above an expanse of variegated tapestries, woven together into a gigantic patchwork quilt, which encompassed the length and breadth of two football fields. My God! the enormity of it—the thousands of names spread out like a carpet upon the lawn before me—engulfed me. The first vision of it—etched forever in my minds' eye. And in the silent stillness, as I walked along the paths, gazing upon the names—a whole generation of life—not totally fulfilled. I wept as I walked the field—trying to fathom the myriad tasks left incomplete by the departure of all these names—these human beings—representative of the thousands who had succumbed to AIDS.

BELOW: Many of the people who worked on the quilt sewed their names on scraps of fabric used to stuff the Torah scroll on the quilt. (standing) Rob Sinacore; (from left to right) Annette Miller, Dick Radvon, Yolanda Potasinksi, Carol Troum

BOTTOM: Annette Miller with the CBST AIDS quilt displayed as a part of the Names Project on the Mall, Washington DC, in 1987

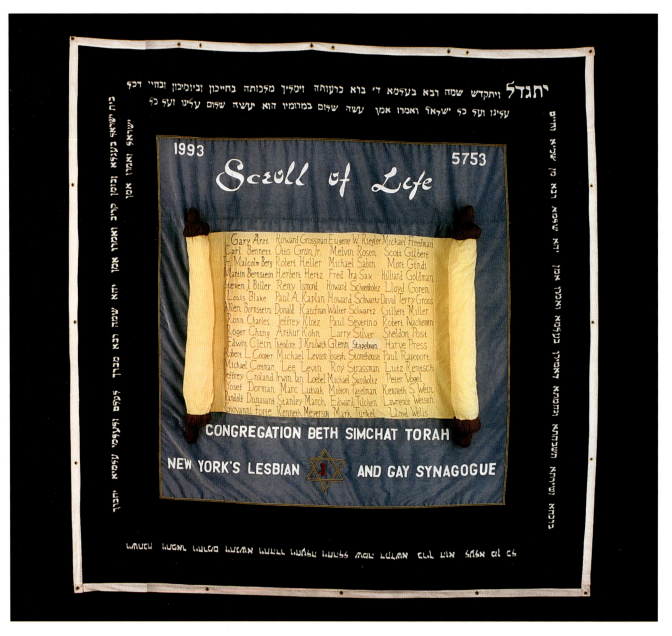

Pat Morgan had a dream in which she envisioned the design of the quilt. She and Yolanda Potasinski organized the first quilt in connection with the Names Project.

## JANUARY 1989

### IN MEMORIAM

**BOB HELLER** died Wednesday, December 14 of AIDS-related complications. He was a member of CBST for many years, and had helped at times with the production of this newsletter. He was 44 and lived in Jersey City. About 100 persons attended his funeral at the synagogue that Friday morning. Many in attendance were from the hearing and visually impaired communities, on whose behalf Bob had served both professionally and as a volunteer.

ABOVE: Members of the committee working on the second quilt, (left to right) Hanna Gafni, Annette Miller, Leslie Deutsch, Sydney Rosenberg, Liz Deutsch.

LEFT: The second quilt was displayed in the Chelsea sanctuary at Friday night services.

When the first CBST AIDS quilt was completed in 1993, Lee Levin's name was among the sixty-four names embroidered on it. The Scroll of Life quilt was created to be donated to the Names Project. A second quilt for permanent display at CBST, called the NuQuilt, by coordinators Leslie Deutsch and Elizabeth Deutsch, adding the names of those who had died since the completion of the Scroll of Life quilt, was completed in 1998. Member Larry Gifford, an accomplished quilter, initiated the creation of a third AIDS quilt in 2003—which would accommodate still more names—and taught a quilting class to interested volunteers.

## A Place of Refuge

By the late 1980s, service leaders regularly included some AIDS-related liturgy during Friday night services, most often prayers for healing and strength written by Ron Weiss. When a member died, on the Friday night following the burial, the community would stand and recite a memorial prayer based on an elegy by S. Y. Agnon, the Israeli writer and Nobel prize laureate. Member Sheila Michaels introduced a new prayer in memory of member Alfred Schwartz, who died in 1991. By the fall of 1991, there were so many deaths that the Religious Committee assembled a booklet for use during the frequent CBST memorial services.

A third quilt was created for people who died of AIDS. This one provided space to accommodate new names.

## MARCH 1989

### IN MEMORIAM

**ALLEN BORNSTEIN**, a CBST member who was also co-founder and the first president of our sibling congregation Beth Chai of Long Island, passed away on January 30 as a result of complications from AIDS. Allen's death came at a time when our friends on Long Island were just coming to grips with closing their congregation that same month. Friends of Allen and of Beth Chai request donations be made in his name to the Long Island Association for AIDS Care and to CBST.

Mel Rosen worried that CBST focused too much on death and dying and not enough on living with AIDS. In a 1990 newsletter article, he told of being first hospitalized with AIDS-related illness and receiving phone calls from other congregants who had kept their own illness a secret. "Shul people who know I'm sick treat me differently and I want to be treated like I always have been. People are afraid of me. The service doesn't comfort me; I'm living with AIDS and all I hear from the pulpit is 'death' and 'dread disease.' I'm trying to live a high quality life with AIDS and the shul's message contradicts this." Mel worked to sensitize the community as how to best welcome and embrace people living with AIDS. "We're dealing here with disease, death, pain, fear. We don't know how to act in these situations. We don't know what to say, how to comfort. And that's where we need to begin."

By 1991 there had been close to 32,000 recorded AIDS deaths in New York since the beginning of the epidemic, with 6,475 AIDS deaths in New York City that year alone. The synagogue continued to develop its healing liturgy and to expand its successful efforts of *bikkur cholim* visits and distributing holiday packages to PWAs. Still, many tried to conceal their illness, to protect themselves or respect the wishes of their families. They wanted CBST to be a respite from the disease, preferring not to be known there as sick. Why more people were not open about having AIDS at CBST was an ongoing question. Without a rabbi to provide spiritual and pastoral counseling, it wasn't clear what CBST had to offer people with AIDS.

## MAY 1989

### IN MEMORIAM

**LLOYD WELLS** was an accomplished and respected school administrator. Prior to his retirement, he served as principal of a high school near Nyack, NY, where he resided. The father of two, Lloyd had also been the devoted life partner of the Reverend Ron Balint, who died this past January. Friends report that while caring for Ron, Lloyd displayed great calm and an abidingly deep faith. They say that Lloyd met his own death with the same tranquility.

## MAY 1989

### MEMORIAL CONCERT

Saul Zalkin, a past member of the Board of Trustees, will show his virtuoso side in a benefit recital at the Shul on April 9 from 4:30–6 p.m. The concert is a benefit for the Caring Community and the Village Nursing Home. It is in memory of **SHELLY POST**, another past Board member who died last June. Shelly was our representative to the Caring Community, which helps the elderly of the Lower West Side. Every year in that capacity, he would organize some Synagogue event to raise money for it.

## MAY 1989

### IN MEMORIAM

A memorial service will be held at the synagogue on Sunday, June 11 at 2 PM for our member, **HOWARD SCHOENHOLTZ**. Howard died of AIDS-related illness May 14 at his home in the Bronx, and was laid to rest the following day. A fellow CBST member and friend remembered Howard as "understanding, fun, friendly, and a great voice." Howard, a frequent attendee of Friday night services, was a Physical Education instructor in a Bronx intermediate school. He had been a teacher in the City schools for about 25 years.

## JULY-AUGUST 1989

### IN MEMORIAM

**MICHAEL SUSSHOLTZ** 45, died May 26 of complications from AIDS. Michael was a psychologist employed by the State of New York and worked in a group home. He was also a member of the Gay Male S&M Activists. About 3 years ago, he and another GMSA representative presented a heavily-attended *oneg* program on sadomasochism. Among Michael's survivors is his lover of seven years, Jim Strassburger.

**JEFFREY A. SHUMAN**, 41, died from AIDS-related illness on June 5. Jeffrey was a partner in the law firm of Shuman and Wood-Smith. Among Jeffrey's survivors is his lover, Richard Coyne. Memorial contribution may be made to the Lambda Legal Defense Fund.

## SEPTEMBER 1989

### IN MEMORIAM

Our member **RENY ISMOND**, 35, died from a heart attack on August 12. Reny was a steady volunteer at the synagogue, always willing to help with whatever needed to be done. He is survived in part by his lover, past Board Vice-Chair Lee Levin. Our profound condolences go to Lee and all of Reny's friends and relatives.

## OCTOBER 1989

### IN MEMORIAM

**DON KAUFMAN** died September 1 at the age of 46 after a brief illness with PCP. He was actively involved with the synagogue's Theatre and Entertainment productions and outings. He was also strongly devoted to the cause of planting trees in Israel. He was the father of two boys and a girl.

**HAROLD SADOWSKY**, a real estate developer, died in late August. He is survived by his lover, Vincent Ruizio.

APRIL 1990

### IN MEMORIAM

**HOWARD SCHWARTZ**, 41, died on February 23 from AIDS. Howard was an unusually gentle, earnest, and caring man. During the Yom Kippur War, he went to Israel as a volunteer. His active participation at CBST included several years on the Religious Committee.

Howard was an environmental biologist employed by the U.S. Environmental Protection Agency. His main project involved exposing environmental violations along the Hudson River.... He felt a strong need to help people more directly, so he went back to school for a dental degree. Howard was determined to provide services to people with AIDS and was one of a handful of dentists in this city who accepted PWAs as clients without any special fuss and a no fee basis in many cases. In 1987, Howard developed tuberculosis and was diagnosed with AIDS. He was able to secure access to AZT and able to practice until this past fall. Howard is survived by his lover of nine years, Dr. Jose Sotolongo, who provided love and support during his illness, and by his parents and sister.

EDITED FROM ART LEONARD

> HOWARD SCHWARTZ, D.D.S.
> Comprehensive Care
>
> VILLAGE EAST DENTISTRY
> 158 East 7th Street, NY, NY 10009
> (212) 254-7459

Howard Schwartz regularly advertised his dental practice in the CBST newsletter. His ad last appeared in the December 1986 issue.

JUNE 1990

### IN MEMORIAM

We mourn the loss of our member **ROGER CHUNG**, who succumbed to AIDS in April at the age of 43. Roger came to the United State from Taiwan in 1973. Several years later he joined CBST as a result of a strong interest in Judaism. He learned Hebrew, including the ability to read the commentaries of Rashi. He was an active member of the Talmud class, and could often be found on Friday evenings studying Talmud with Carl Bennett in the library. Roger worked as a computer programmer for Chemical Bank, and enjoyed sailing.

JULY 1990

### IN MEMORIAM

**YOSEF DORMAN** (Naine Dorman, who after converting to Judaism preferred to be called Yosef), died from AIDS on June 10. Yosef volunteered in many ways, but will be remembered for chairing the Jewish Outreach Committee, which coordinated efforts on behalf of Soviet and Ethiopian Jewry. He worked as permissions editor for a publishing house. He is survived by his lover, Johnny Lopez.

## JULY-AUGUST 1990

### IN MEMORIAM

**STAN MARCH**, 49, a hard working member, died June 10 after a prolonged illness. Stan worked as a photo retoucher, computer graphic artist, and word processor. Before his illness, he had been an active member of the synagogue's Food Services and House committees. He was there when needed, ushering on High Holy Days, baking hamentaschen, helping run the antique sale. He is survived by his lover of six years, Ralph Julius.

**DR. LARRY SILVER**, 32, who joined CBST last year during the High Holy Days, died May 2 from meningitis. He attended Yeshiva University High School, NYU, and Downstate Medical College, and as a doctor worked for Beth Abraham hospital and HIP.

## SEPTEMBER 1990

### IN MEMORIAM

We mourn the loss of our member of several years, **HERBERT HERTZ**, who died from AIDS-related complications in early August. Herbert, a veterinarian, was a service leader for CBST's Service of Hope and Comfort series, a special outreach for PWAs.

## OCTOBER 1990

### IN MEMORIAM

Our member **PETER HRUSKA** died from AIDS on Friday, September 14 at the age of 53. Peter co-founded the Unexpected Company, an improvisation group. He also volunteered for the New York City Gay and Lesbian Anti-Violence Project, designing and supervising the renovation of its office space in the Community Center. Peter was a lifetime New Yorker, working nearly 30 years as a speech therapist for the Jericho, Long Island school system. Our sympathies go out to all Peter's friends and relatives, particularly Arthur Goodman, his beloved companion for seven years.

## DECEMBER 1990

### IN MEMORIAM

**ROBERT MARK DENNET**, who has been a member of the synagogue for many years, died from AIDS complications October 26. Former Board of Trustees Chair Mark Bieber delivered the eulogy at the funeral. Bob was very active with the Imperial Court of New York City, which every year stages a grand drag charity ball. Bob coordinated several synagogue events, including an anniversary party. He frequently drew on his talents as a professional decorator. For one party, he put up Japanese lanterns to cover up the lighting in the social hall. The room looked so much better that the lanterns remained in place for many years. Bob was born and raised in Queens, and got his degree in architecture. He devoted much of the last two years to his home on Fire Island. He is survived by his lover, Daniel Sager.

## JANUARY 1991

### IN MEMORIAM

**LEE LEVIN**, Vice-Chair of the CBST Board of Trustees from 1986–1987 and 1988–1989, died from pneumonia Tuesday, December 4. In addition to serving on the Board from 1985 through 1989, Lee led the Food Services Committee, which managed our Shabbat Kiddushes, Rosh Hashanah luncheons, Passover Seders, Gay and Lesbian Pride Dances, and countless other synagogue events. Hundreds of mourners crowded in to the synagogue sanctuary for the funeral on Thursday morning, December 6. Among those present were Lee's parents and siblings from Toronto, his three children, synagogue members, and volunteers from other community organizations with whom he worked. Rabbi J. B. Sacks and Cantor Jay Azneer officiated.

CBST Board of Trustees Chair Mel Rosen gave the first of four eulogies. Rosen recalled the many sermons Lee delivered on the High Holy Days and other occasions, always starting with words in Yiddish, and always with the purpose "to make us feel." Arlene Kochman, Senior Director of Volunteer Services for Senior Action in a Gay Environment, spoke of Lee's work with Group Activities Committee, including the monthly Saturday socials held at CBST. Lee and Charles Ching co-founded the Dance Committee, the first volunteer committee at the Gay and Lesbian Community Services Center. Charles recounted all the fundraising events Lee ran. "From set up to take down, Lee did it all."

Former Board Chair Art Strickler, who called Lee "a human dynamo," knew him both as a fellow Board member and as an employee. "He was so trusted and relied upon that he ran the store and allowed me to go to Israel for a month, saying, "don't worry, everything will be taken care of, and it was." The eulogies revealed Lee as a man of wide-ranging interests, accomplishments, and good works, even beyond what was generally known. Lee, known professionally as Dr. Leon Levine, graduated from Brandeis University, and went on to obtain two doctoral degrees, including one in Mid-Eastern Studies. Lee was Editor-in-Chief of *The CEO Club*, and helped run such prestigious places as the Harvard Club. As a volunteer, Lee devoted himself to Jewish causes as well, including Soviet and Ethiopian Jewry. He was the head usher for the annual gathering of Holocaust Survivors at Madison Square Garden. Rosen described how Lee sought out and took care of those in the final stage of AIDS, and how many people died in his arms. Just sixteen months earlier, Lee himself suffered the loss of his lover Reny Ismond, who died of a heart attack. Summarized Strickler, "A more sincere, caring, loving person cannot be found."

## JANUARY 1991

### IN MEMORIAM

Another member, **KENNETH MEYERSON**, died from complications of AIDS on November 24. Ken volunteered for many of our mailings.

## APRIL 1991

### IN MEMORIAM

We are saddened to learn of the death of our member **MICHAEL SILVER**, who died of AIDS-related complications on February 22.

## JUNE–JULY 1991

### IN MEMORIAM

**WALTER SCHWARTZ**, a member of CBST for many years, died on May 4. Walter was born and brought up in New York and received a BA from Marietta College in Ohio. After training for the Peace Corps, he worked as a caseworker for the NYC Welfare Departments. His true calling was in the world of art, however, and he worked as a free-lance artist for many years, specializing in hard-edge geometric painting. He was also the associate art director of Family Circle *Great Ideas*. But his masterpiece was the apartment he lived in on East 9th Street for over twenty years. Not only his artwork, but also the furniture he built and the total environment he created there made it a visually exciting as well as eminently livable ambience.

Having joined CBST back in the days when we were on Ninth Avenue, Walter became active in two areas where his skills allowed him to make great contributions to the synagogue. He did the layout for the newsletter for many years, bringing to it a professionalism that gave it the visual image he thought the synagogue deserved. His long-lasting creation in this regard is the "lambda-star" design he incorporated into the newsletter masthead (a Magen David composed of six lambdas) and made into a sign that still decorates the synagogue entrance. Walter's second great contribution to the look of the synagogue came about in the major renovations that were done in our current premises on Bethune Street, notably his graphic sunrise that dominated the eastern wall and the design of the lions and lionesses sculpture atop the Aron Kodesh. When it was decided to replace the eastern wall graphic last year, Walter was slightly amused that the committee asked his permission to do so, and freely granting it, showed how little his ego was involved in such things. But the greatest contribution Walter made to CBST was in his quiet strength, which showed itself for years in his hard-working and cheerful participation in all kinds of synagogue activities and then, during the years of his illness, when his bravery and optimism made him an example and source of inspiration to all, both those already ill and those not yet so. Not one to use a lot of words and preach his message, Walter taught, by example, how a positive attitude and love of G-d's creation could make a life cut short in number of years into a full and rich one.
CARL BENNETT

I will give, in my house and within my walls, a monument and a name. I will give them an everlasting name which shall not perish. ISAIAH 56:5

וְנָתַתִּי לָהֶם בְּבֵיתִי וּבְחוֹמֹתַי יָד וָשֵׁם שֵׁם עוֹלָם אֶתֶּן לוֹ אֲשֶׁר לֹא יִכָּרֵת

# 4. A RABBI FOR CBST

As the AIDS crisis intensified, CBST's lay leaders did all they could to address the spiritual needs of the congregation. "The need for pastoral care became extraordinary for the community, and especially because we were beginning to lose a lot of our leadership as well," Rosanne Leipzig recalls. The Religious Committee was stretched beyond its capacity. The rabbi referral system created by Saul Zalkin and Jack Greenberg was wholly overtaxed. CBST's laity, however skilled and educated, could no longer serve all the needs of the congregation.

### The Need Is Too Great

CBST tried bringing in a social worker/psychotherapist to lead a support group on AIDS-related issues for members. They invited Pinchas Berger, coordinator of the AIDS Program at the Jewish Board of Family and Children's Services that Mel Rosen had helped create. He came with four other JBFCS social workers for a lecture and discussion afternoon for PWAs and the "worried well." Rabbi Pesach Kraus, director of Jewish Rabbinical Counseling at Memorial Sloan Kettering Cancer Center, led a seminar on grief. The community consistently tried to publicize and expand its offerings to PWAs (People with AIDS). In the newsletter each month, Saul Zalkin listed his home phone number for those who sought Jewish AIDS counseling. One member, who identified himself as Israel ben Pinchas, described his experience in the CBST "self-help group" for people affected by AIDS, which Saul encouraged him to attend:

> My lover has AIDS, and I am dealing with it rather well, but I could have used some support and counseling. . . With so many of my friends sick or who have their own problems, I couldn't and didn't want to burden them with my situation . . . Coming from a strong Jewish background, I needed religious questions answered and dealt with. What prayer can/ought I say for my lover? How can I as a Jewish gay person come to terms with this crisis and my Jewishness? How can I relieve my anxiety and fear of the situation, be comforted, and *live*?

Through CBST's group, Israel ben Pinchas came to understand that his Jewishness could help him confront the situation with his lover. He summoned the courage to take an anonymous HIV test at the Board of Health, and discovered that he was positive. He was grateful to have "a few good people around whom he could tell, especially in the group."

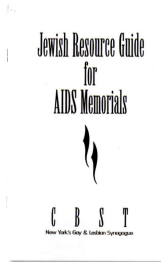

This CBST pamphlet is one of several resources created during the AIDS crisis.

While many of these lay-led initiatives had a significant impact on people affected by AIDS, these efforts often lacked the resources to sustain them over the long term. Even the groundbreaking Service of Hope and Comfort varied in attendance and gradually disappeared altogether from the synagogue calendar. Mel Rosen, then a board member and chair of the Education Committee, was convinced that without a rabbi CBST would be unable to provide the framework to maintain these programs or to adequately support PWAs with sufficient spiritual sustenance. In a newsletter article critical of the synagogue's response to AIDS, Mel compared CBST's volunteer efforts to that of the rabbinically led program for PWAs at Congregation B'nai Jeshurun on the Upper West Side. B'nai Jeshurun, he wrote, "with its two sensitive liberal rabbis, has attracted large numbers of PWAs, their families and friends to monthly Shabbat programs."

## Taking the First Steps

In May 1988, with membership approaching one thousand, the synagogue hired its first paid employee: Mark Roth—a CBST member who lived on the tenth floor of Westbeth—to work twenty hours a week as an administrative assistant. Many long-time members felt that hiring any paid staff was antithetical to the all-volunteer ethos of CBST, but the synagogue leadership understood that CBST had outgrown its volunteer structure. Anticipating the negative backlash, the newsletter ran a full-page cover story on the hire as well as a note from Rob Selden, board secretary, reassuring the congregation that the major share of the work of running CBST would remain in the hands of volunteers. By the time the article ran, Mark had quit. Saul Zalkin began working in the office several hours a week, which he did for a number of years.

Hiring a part-time office assistant was a tentative first step to developing a full-time professional staff, but the leadership differed on where to go from there: what staff position would best serve the synagogue's needs? Some leaders, including the chair, Bill Wahler, insisted that the synagogue most urgently needed an executive director. He understood that hiring an administrator would be much less controversial than hiring a rabbi and might ease the congregation's transition to a professional staff. Others felt that a social worker would serve the pastoral needs without upsetting the status quo. It was clear that the AIDS crisis had already begun to shift the synagogue's priorities toward hiring a rabbi. Jack Greenberg reflects, "If not for AIDS, maybe we would never have had a rabbi. Who knows, right? Maybe by now. But it would have taken a lot longer."

July/August 1988 Newsletter

In the summer of 1989, the board established a committee to explore the hiring of full-time staff. When, after months of extensive discussions, the committee returned to recommend the congregation hire a full-time rabbi, the board created a second, larger committee, intended to be more representative of the diverse synagogue membership, which would work for many more months to explore all the implications of that proposal.

At the same time, the synagogue was exploring the question of affiliating with a mainstream Jewish movement. In hopes of finding a movement that was a good fit both in terms of religious ideology and attitudes towards gay men and lesbians, the Affiliation Committee met with representatives of the Reform, Reconstructionist, and Conservative Movements. The Reconstructionist and Reform Movements

Report of the Rabbi Committee
Presented to the Board of Trustees
Cong. Beth Simchat Torah
February 22, 1990

Jordan Barbakoff & Mel Rosen
Co-Chairs

Each committee presented an extensive report to the board on hiring a rabbi.

## HOW I GOT TO CBST

I first came to CBST in 1983. I had heard about it before. I lived in Rochester prior to moving to New York, where I was part of a statewide "women in medicine" group. We had a meeting in New York in 1980 or '81, where I met Margot Karle. She told me there was a gay synagogue. I must have looked at her like she was out of her mind. I was totally shocked, but I kept it in the back of my mind.

I came to New York in July of 1983. My mom died the year before. I had been saying Kaddish in Rochester and shul shopping because there was no place that felt quite right. You go into the synagogues and they say, "Who are you; what do you do? A nice Jewish doctor, do I have a boy for you!" When I came to New York, I walked into CBST and it was an amazing experience. I remember walking in the first time. Murray Karger was giving out name tags as I walked into Bethune Street. I didn't know anyone. I just wore my name tag and sat in the back of the room. Shami Chaiken was the *ba'alat tefillah*. She was amazing. She had such soul and *Yiddishkeit* that I was transported to another world. Jewish music has always been my passion, so hearing her was incredible. I felt as if I had come home. And so, even though it was the end of the time to be saying Kaddish for my mother, I continued for a few more months anyway. That was my introduction to the city.

ROSANNE LEIPZIG, MEMBER SINCE 1983

invited CBST to affiliate. The Reconstructionist Movement had the longest standing policy of gay inclusion, but was by far the smallest of the movements. Most of the other gay synagogues were affiliated with the Reform Movement's Union of American Hebrew Congregations, which gave them access to the Reform Movement's extensive rabbinical placement system. The committee was divided on the issue of affiliation, recommending the decision be deferred until after a rabbinic search might be conducted.

In February 1990, just as Bill Wahler's term as chair was coming to an end, the rabbinical exploratory committee reported to the board recommending the need for a full-time rabbi. The board accepted the report, asking the committee to return with more information about the fiscal ramifications of hiring a rabbi and with a methodology and process to educate the entire congregation on these issues.

**Resistance and Change**

Mel Rosen wanted a rabbi for CBST. A lay leader and communal professional with an institutional perspective, he keenly understood the need for a rabbi. As a congregant and a person with AIDS, he needed one. When Mel was elected chair of the CBST Board of Trustees on March 28, 1990, his primary goal was to prepare the congregation for a rabbi. "Mel Rosen was a visionary," reflects Rosanne Leipzig. "He understood the need that we as a community had to take the next step. A lot of us went there kicking and screaming. . . . It was a real process to get us to the point of even *saying* we are going to hire a rabbi. And he got us there." Mel Rosen understood the community's resistance. In each of his early reports to the congregation, he focused on keeping the community informed about the intensive process already underway, stressing its natural and widespread evolution. Mel recounted the timeline, the length of the process, the multiple committees, the number and diversity of the members involved, and their trustworthy diligence. He reiterated that the initial committee was not established to explore hiring a rabbi specifically, but rather "assessing the need to hire an individual to help us in areas where we are falling short of congregational needs." Each committee in turn came to the same conclusion—the congregation needed to hire a full-time rabbi.

In May 1990, the Board of Trustees voted unanimously to hire a full-time rabbi, pending congregational discussions. At the same meeting, they voted not to affiliate with a movement, a decision that allowed the synagogue to move forward with the rabbinic search process, while simultaneously asserting its independence. The board declared that their vote to engage a rabbi was not a decision for the synagogue to become overly conventional or to adhere to anyone else's definitions of Jewish community.

Having convinced the board to hire a rabbi, Mel now had to convince the congregation. His report in the July/August 1990 newsletter, announcing the

# CBST AND THE AMERICAN JEWISH MOVEMENTS

CBST closely followed the internal denominational debates on issues regarding gay and lesbian Jews. Some members had strong feelings of connection to a particular movement; some believed that being unaffiliated was a matter of principle. Others felt betrayed by a particular movement after a synagogue, summer camp, or youth movement had rejected them. Still others were trying to replicate their childhood synagogue, minus the heterosexual bias. A number of CBST members were or would become rabbinical students at HUC, JTS, and RRC, in the closet to varying degrees depending on the policies of their schools and movements.

The Reconstructionist Movement was the first to adopt policies permitting the admission and ordination of lesbian and gay rabbinical students and rabbis. In 1984, the Reconstructionist Rabbinical College adopted an admissions policy prohibiting discrimination based on sexual orientation. The movement then set its sights on deepening its institution's commitment to the full integration of its gay and lesbian members, officially welcoming gay and lesbian congregations in 1985 and establishing a policy of nondiscrimination in rabbinic placement in 1990. As a rabbinical student, Sharon Kleinbaum was active in that process. Still, when Rabbi Kleinbaum was ordained in 1990, getting a job as an openly gay or lesbian congregational rabbi in a non-gay synagogue was unheard of.

The Reform Movement, in no small part because of the inquiries of gay synagogues, had begun to formally address the issues surrounding gay Jews and gay synagogues as early as 1973. Shortly after its founding, Congregation Beth Chayim Chadashim in Los Angeles appealed to the Union of American Hebrew Congregations, requesting affiliation. While the discussion sparked some heated and often ugly debate, BCC's membership in the UAHC was resoundingly approved in June 1974. In the subsequent years, more and more gay synagogues affiliated with the Reform Movement, and in 1979 San Francisco's Sha'ar Zahav was the first gay synagogue to use the Central Conference of American Rabbis placement process to hire a full-time rabbi.

Rabbi Joan Friedman, a CBST member, was one of the first women to be an active presence on the bimah. She was ordained at HUC in 1980, eight years before the school automatically stopped disqualifying applicants who were gay. In 1990, just when CBST members Nancy Wiener and David Edelson were ordained as rabbis, the CCAR voted to accept the recommendations of its Ad Hoc Committee on Homosexuality and the Rabbinate to admit openly gay and lesbian rabbis to the rabbinical organization. Established in response to a resolution on admissions policies and rabbinic placement proposed by Rabbi Margaret Moers Wenig of Beth Am, the People's Temple, and Margaret Holub, then a rabbinical student, the Ad Hoc Committee studied and debated the issue intensely for four years. Rabbi Wenig and Rabbi Yoel Kahn of Sha'ar Zahav served on the Ad Hoc Committee and were two of the most powerful advocates for change.

The Conservative Movement would have been, in many ways, the most natural fit for CBST if it weren't for its policies on homosexuality. A few young Conservative rabbis, including J. B. Sacks (Mel Rosen's partner) and straight allies Simkha Weintraub and Rolando Matalon, began to organize an attempt to change the movement's policies on lesbian

Judith Tax (left) and newly ordained Reform Rabbi Nancy Wiener at Pride in 1990, the year the CCAR voted to admit openly gay rabbis.

and gay Jews. In May 1990, with the support of a few senior colleagues, the Rabbinical Assembly voted almost unanimously to pass a resolution calling for full gay and lesbian civil rights. J. B. Sacks, who would be the first Conservative rabbi to come out as gay, helped author the resolution. (A similar resolution was passed by the Reform Movement's CCAR in 1977, nearly fifteen years earlier.) The RA resolution, passed the same year as the CCAR voted to admit gay and lesbian rabbis, made no mention of the religious aspects of gay and lesbian inclusion. A paper submitted by Rabbi Bradley Shavit Artson to the Law Committee, calling for lesbian and gay inclusion in religious life—and embracing the ordination of gay and lesbian rabbis as well—would be debated for two more years before it was finally rejected. The six papers it inspired, denying religious equality and rabbinical ordination to gay men and lesbians, all passed. So did a "Consensus Statement on Homosexuality," which became the movement's policy document on homosexuality and would remain in effect for fourteen years. It prohibited same sex-marriage, denied the admission of gay men and lesbians to rabbinical and cantorial schools and the Rabbinical and Cantor's Assemblies, and affirmed the right of Conservative rabbis and institutions to prohibit gay people from any positions of religious or communal participation or leadership, while rather weakly welcoming gay and lesbian congregants of those institutions. Rabbi Howard Handler submitted an impassioned dissent; shortly afterward he was outed as gay. Responding to his case the following year, the Law Committee debated the issue of allowing gay rabbis to use the placement services of the Conservative movement and established a commission to study the issue of homosexuality. Rabbi Kleinbaum and Art Leonard would testify during those debates. Meanwhile, an underground network of closeted rabbis and rabbinical students was developing within the Conservative Movement, many of whom used CBST as their anchor.

**HUC–JIR:** Hebrew Union College-Jewish Institute of Religion (Reform)

**JTS:** Jewish Theological Seminary of America (Conservative)

**RRC:** Reconstructionist Rabbinical College (Reconstructionist)

**UAHC:** Union of American Hebrew Congregations (Reform)

**CCAR:** Central Conference of American Rabbis (Reform)

**RA:** Rabbinical Assembly (Conservative)

**CA:** Cantors Assembly (Conservative)

CBST members with roots in the Conservative Movement proudly and defiantly gather in front of the headquarters of United Synagogue—Conservative Judaism's congregational arm— as they march down Fifth Avenue at Pride, 1991.

decision, firmly declared the victory while reminding the skeptics why such a move was necessary. "As the world, the community, and our congregation change around us, we too must change if we are to remain a relevant, vibrant, and responsible organization." Reasserting the need for a rabbi rather than an executive director, Mel reminded congregants of the need for *spiritual* leadership, also articulating a broader goal: "CBST's rabbi will take his or her place among the rabbinic leadership of the city, thereby representing our viewpoint and needs to the larger lay and rabbinic Jewish community. This is an enormously important step at a time when many of the major Jewish movements are reassessing their current view toward Lesbians and Gays."

> "I think a fairly large number of us felt that being lay led was something to be very proud of. We wanted to retain that and not surrender it to a rabbi." YEHUDA BERGER

As Mel promised, three congregational meetings were held that July to discuss members' concerns. About one hundred members attended the meetings; many expressing vehement opposition to the idea of hiring a rabbi.

Many CBST members feared that a rabbi would inexorably alter the character of the synagogue. They valued the uniqueness and independence of being led by a diverse and capable laity. "We took a lot of pride in our lay leadership and what we had accomplished," Rosanne Leipzig reflects on the intense and emotional opposition. "One of the things about being gay, particularly then, is that people wanted to be outside the mainstream in certain ways. A rabbi would make us more like everybody else." Jack Greenberg agrees, "We used to bring people to services who were amazed at what we could do as a totally lay-led congregation with no rabbinic help. People didn't want to lose that. If you have a rabbi, however great the rabbi may be, you are just one more synagogue with a rabbi. Then what's so special about you?"

Mel urged the community not to hold itself back because of its desire to remain unique. "There is no reason to deny ourselves the services of a rabbi. We are a large, complex, maturing congregation. We have congregants with problems and needs as in any other synagogue."

Religious leaders within the congregation feared losing their primacy on the bimah and ceding their power to control ritual decision-making. These members treasured the eclectic and painstakingly considered ritual process that allowed them to retain a traditional flavor while accommodating the religious diversity within the congregation at the same time. They worried that a rabbi would impose his or her ritual standards and practices on the congregation. "People were concerned that we would end up being a single denomination and that we would only fit one size.

People were concerned that there would be rules going on we didn't agree with," Rosanne remembers. Some recalled old fears of Pinchas ben Aharon imposing his intensifying Orthodoxy on CBST. Bruce Friedman told the *Jewish Week*, "I don't think we need a rabbi. The experiment of our first rabbi didn't work out. From it, we started a community-wide effort as far as leading services and establishing religious policies. I think a rabbi would cut into that." Sheila Michaels opposed hiring a rabbi because of her anti-establishment tendencies and because she feared that a male rabbi would keep women away. Feeling unheard by the synagogue leadership, she circulated a petition on *Kol Nidrei*, a move that infuriated many. For a significant minority, the idea of a part-time rabbi seemed more palatable than hiring someone for a full-time position. The board reopened the discussion on the feasibility of a part-time rabbi, an idea that had already been twice discounted by the exploratory committees. Their conclusion was the same. The more the vision of the rabbinic job description developed, the more it was unquestionably full-time. "Even without a rabbi, we currently receive calls for rabbinic help every day," wrote Mel. In arguing for a rabbi, he stressed the increased pastoral needs due to AIDS and other lifecycle events. He was more cautious in outlining how a rabbi would work in association with, but without overtaking, the Religious Committee to improve the quality and consistency of services or with the Education Committee to guide curriculum.

Mel believed the greatest point of resistance was simply "fear of change." "This is a most natural feeling for a congregation that has done it on its own for the past eighteen years," he reassured the members. Ultimately the majority felt ready to move forward. On August 13, 1990 the board voted, again unanimously, to hire a full-time rabbi.

**The Rabbi Search Committee**

The board instructed Mel to create a rabbinic selection committee. Mel invited Arthur Leonard to serve as its chair. "I thought it would be inappropriate to have a male be the sole chair of the committee," Art recalls. "For this congregation, we need co-chairs, one woman and one man, so that both points of view are represented." With that in mind, they recruited Rosanne Leipzig to be co-chair." As Mel, Rosanne, and Art assembled the committee, they took into account the major issues within the community at the time. "We tried to make a committee that was balanced—people who were more observant and less observant; men, women; people who had been members for a long time and those who had been members for a shorter time," Art remembers. It was essential to construct the committee carefully in order to establish credibility within the community, assuaging the congregation's fears. Bill Fern, who was invited to represent the longtime members, reflects, "They figured that if a member from each constituency were to say, 'This is a legitimate, worthwhile endeavor that's not

## CLOSEUP: MEL ROSEN

Mel Rosen helped chart the course of the national response to AIDS and left an indelible mark on the life of CBST. In 1983 Mel served as the first executive director of Gay Men's Health Crisis and became the director of the newly created New York State AIDS Institute. As Mel's *New York Times* obituary read, "Once he realized the severity and scope of the AIDS crisis, Mr. Rosen began to devote his life to combating the disease."

Roger McFarlane, who succeeded Mel at GMHC, recalled that Mel's background in social services made him invaluable there. "When AIDS came along, Mel was one of the few gay men who knew about Medicare and social services." Mel had been an executive at Wildcat, an agency providing social services to the formerly incarcerated. In 1982, while working toward an MSW in administration at Hunter College, he came to the year-old GMHC to fulfill his internship requirement, becoming volunteer executive director and creating GMHC's financial assistance program and "buddy" system.

Being all too familiar with the symptoms of AIDS, Mel diagnosed himself with the disease. He wrote, "In December 1988, a few days before my partner and I were having fifty people over for Chanukah, I began having difficulty breathing . . . I knew exactly what was wrong with me."

A traumatic visit from an Orthodox hospital rabbi during his first hospitalization with AIDS-related pneumonia galvanized Mel's activism in the Jewish world. When Mel told the rabbi he had AIDS, the rabbi couldn't get out of the room fast enough. Mel was enraged that rabbis funded by the New York Board of Rabbis were treating Jews with AIDS this way. In February 1989 he published an article in the *Jewish Week* excoriating the Jewish community for taking financial contributions from gay Jews while ignoring their suffering with AIDS. Mel was convinced that CBST members would continue to get substandard treatment unless they had a rabbi of their own.

Increasingly concerned with the Jewish community's response to AIDS, Mel became chair of the volunteer services program for people with AIDS at the Jewish Board of Family and Children's Services. By raising awareness and advocating for compassionate treatment and the development of AIDS services, Mel became the prime figure in changing

FROM LEFT TO RIGHT: Harris Rafael Goldstein, Mel Rosen, and Joel Schreck at Pride, 1990

the New York Jewish community's response to AIDS.

Rabbi Rolando Matalon of Congregation B'nai Jeshurun recalls that it was Mel's advocacy that spurred him and Rabbi Marshall Meyer to create a monthly outreach program for people with AIDS. "Mel told us, 'You can't just say that you're supportive, you have to do something.'" Mel's involvement in synagogue life was a natural extension of his Jewish upbringing. He felt moved to find a Conservative synagogue with progressive rabbis committed to social justice and was active at both B'nai Jeshurun and CBST. "He said we needed outreach to people with AIDS," Rabbi Matalon remembers. "We listened to him." In the autumn of 1989, B'nai Jeshurun established a monthly spiritual gathering for PWAs and their families. Mel shared his own story at the first meeting. Rabbi Matalon credits Mel's initiative with building B'nai Jeshurun's reputation as a gay-friendly congregation. "Once we started doing the program for PWAs, we sent the message that BJ is open and safe for anyone; the numbers of gay members started increasing."

Mel lived fully in the years following his AIDS diagnosis. He and his lover, J. B. Sacks, a Conservative rabbi, celebrated a *brit ahavah* ceremony in November 1991. Already sick with AIDS when he became chair of the CBST board, Mel felt that it was imperative that the synagogue be represented by a PWA and that as chair he could best realize his singular goal of bringing a rabbi to the synagogue. Mel was incredibly proud that he had accomplished his dream, giving newspaper interviews from his deathbed at NYU hospital about Rabbi Kleinbaum's arrival at CBST.

Mel Rosen and Marjorie Hill, then director of the Mayor's Office for the Lesbian and Gay Community, who became chief executive officer of GMHC in 2006, on the bimah, 1990

going to endanger the welfare of the synagogue,' the people who trusted that person would go along with it. That system worked very well." The committee of eight—Rosanne Leipzig, Art Leonard, Bill Fern, Jack Greenberg, Shayna Caul (then known as Janet Sonnenstein), Bill Wahler, Nancy Alpert, and Marvin Heldeman—made an initial commitment to work together for a year. "It was a great committee," recalls Jack, "the best committee I've ever been on. We got to know each other and we were a real team, even though we were picked from all these different factions within the synagogue."

Before beginning the search, the committee had to determine the procedure. "We did a lot of work before we interviewed anyone," Rosanne remembers. "We tried to think about the values. We weighed everything, ranging from concerns about attitudes over different lifestyles to how good a speaker they were. We decided early on that we didn't care if they were straight or gay and we didn't care if they were male or female. Everybody agreed: they needed to be the right person." Mel was often told that CBST would need to look for "a superhuman to do an impossible job." The committee, however, was convinced that finding the right rabbi was possible. They spent months designing the hiring process, creating the job description, and determining the acceptable personal, professional, and halachic qualifications for candidates, consulting with several rabbis for guidance. Art Leonard described the committee's principles to the congregation:

> We are open to a wide variety of people as potential rabbis for CBST. We will not exclude anyone from consideration on the basis of sex, sexual orientation, age, marital status, or past or present affiliations with CBST. Above all else, we are committed to finding the right rabbi for our congregation. If necessary, we will extend our search for as long as it takes to do that.

The rabbi search process was very intense and very exciting," Art remembers. The process helped the members of the committee better understand what hiring a rabbi would mean for CBST and gave the committee and the rest of the congregation time to adjust to the idea. "Some people only wanted a pastoral rabbi, somebody to do counseling and hospital visits, and maybe not even come to services. He or she would be the CBST rabbi but not interfere with what was already running so well," Jack Greenberg, then chair of the Religious Committee, recalls. "But, as part of the rabbinic search, we saw you couldn't get a rabbi just for that. Getting a rabbi was really a package. You were going to get somebody on the bimah, even though we felt we had all these wonderful service leaders and *ba'alei* and *ba'alot tefillah* and *darshanim*. You'd have to expect that a rabbi was going to be up there at least some of the time, and any rabbi worth hiring wanted more of a role in that area. So we would have to yield that part of ourselves to this new person." Bill Fern recalls his own trepidation about hiring a rabbi. "I personally and very deeply was not sure. We were independent for so long. We were wary of having some sort of authority figure placed over us, telling us what to do. But I thought, 'OK, if that's the way it's going and that's what we need, then I'll go along with that.' Other people felt the same way. My group said, 'Look, if Bill Fern says it's OK, then it's going to be all right with us.' Other groups said if so-and-so says it's OK, then it's OK with them too."

The Rabbi Search Committee walked a fine line between trying to maintain a level of transparency about their process, dispelling the many rumors that circulated, and maintaining strict confidentiality about the candidates. They published regular updates on the search in the newsletter and met with the Religious Committee and with invited congregational leaders. Each step in the process went before the Board of Trustees for approval. However, the board never learned the names of the applicants until the final candidates were chosen. All correspondence was to be sent to Art Leonard's office at New York Law School so that no mail could be seen by curious eyes at CBST. Lou Rittmaster recalls that his partner, Irving Cooperberg, was beside himself, disbelieving that even as past chair he couldn't get any inside information from his close friend, Bill Fern, or any other members of the committee.

Members of the search committee included (clockwise from left) Art Leonard, Rosanne Leipzig, Nancy Alpert, Shayna Caul, Bill Fern, Jack Greenberg, Marvin Heldeman, and Bill Wahler.

## The Search Is On

The search got off to a rocky start. While some initial press coverage in the *Jewish Week* generated excitement, it wasn't until March 1991 that the board accepted the committee's proposal to begin the search process and gave them approval to advertise the position. But few inquiries came in. When CBST declined to affiliate, the Reform Movement refused to circulate the opening, and their placement procedures precluded Reform rabbis from seeking positions in unaffiliated congregations. The much smaller Reconstructionist Movement had also hoped that CBST would choose to affiliate with them, but they nonetheless agreed to list the position. Initially, Mel Rosen, who himself felt most comfortable in the Conservative Movement, had secured a promise from the Rabbinical Assembly's placement director to list the position. But that decision was overruled. Mel was incensed. He contacted Ari Goldman, the religion reporter for the *New York Times*.

> **CONGREGATION BETH SIMCHAT TORAH**
> NEW YORK'S SYNAGOGUE SERVING THE GAY & LESBIAN JEWISH COMMUNITY
>
> **PRESS RELEASE**
>
> For Immediate Release
> March 9, 1991
> Contacts:   Rosanne Leipzig, 212-548-5760 (evening number)
>                    Arthur Leonard, 212-431-2156 (daytime number)
>
> **NEW YORK'S GAY AND LESBIAN SYNAGOGUE SEEKS TO HIRE ITS FIRST RABBI**
>
> Congregation Beth Simchat Torah (CBST), the egalitarian gay and lesbian synagogue serving the greater New York City area, has initiated a nationwide search to hire its first rabbi. Founded in 1973, the 1150-member congregation made the decision to hire a rabbi after more than a year of study and discussion by the congregants and the Board of Trustees.
>
> "Our continued growth, the diversity of our members and the increasing need for counseling and spiritual guidance in this time of the AIDS crisis have created the desire among the Board and the congregation for a full-time rabbi to provide pastoral care and spiritual leadership," explained Arthur Leonard, co-chair of the Rabbi Search Committee.
>
> "We believe that this position offers a unique opportunity to a progressive rabbi who would enjoy the challenges and rewards our synagogue has to offer," added Rosanne Leipzig, the Committee's other co-chair.
>
> Since CBST is an unaffiliated synagogue, the congregation welcomes applicants from all backgrounds. The congregation is seeking an ordained rabbi with a minimum of two years of pulpit experience and a willingness to share the pulpit with lay leaders. Until now, congregants at CBST have conducted all services, and men and women participate on an equal basis. The congregation has adapted traditional liturgy and a wide spectrum of religious and cultural observances in order to meet the diverse needs of its members.
>
> Interested candidates should submit a resume or an indication of interest no later than June 1, 1991, to:
>
> Professor Arthur Leonard
> New York Law School
> 57 Worth Street
> New York, N.Y. 10013-2960

The story ran on the front page of the Metro section. Goldman reported that the Conservative Movement's Rabbinical Assembly had reversed its position because of the movement's opposition to "homosexual activity." The moving article, which focused on the impact of AIDS at CBST, quoted both Mel Rosen and Art Leonard, appealing to the Conservative Movement and expressing the urgent need for a rabbi at CBST. Goldman also quoted Rabbi Gilbert M. Epstein, then head of the RA's Commission on Rabbinic Placement, "Our hands are tied until and unless our Law Committee reviews its position." The article, exposing the Rabbinical Assembly's refusal to serve a congregation whose members were suffering from AIDS, embarrassed the Conservative Movement. It could not have been better publicity for CBST's rabbinical search.

"The *New York Times* came to the rescue," recalls Art. "After the story ran, we received more than a hundred inquiries from all over the country, even including one or two Orthodox rabbis. We said, 'Do you really think you want to be the rabbi of a gay synagogue?' And they said, 'Well, we can't allow a synagogue to go without a rabbi.'" The committee devised an extensive questionnaire for the applicants to complete before they could be considered for a preliminary interview. The application process was rigorous.

Some chose not to apply. Many Reform and Conservative rabbis were afraid to risk the consequences of violating their movement's placement procedures or the Rabbinical Assembly position against serving a gay congregation. Some gay rabbis were afraid that applying would raise questions about their personal sexual orientation. In 1991 fewer than ten American rabbis were publically out as gay or lesbian. Other would-be candidates were dissuaded by the application process. "We were told some people decided not to apply because they were offended by the questionnaire, which asked for their views on a number of controversial issues," recalls Art. Others, aware of the dissent within the congregation about hiring a rabbi, thought it would be wiser to wait for the next rabbinic search. Art wryly remembers a conversation he had that year with the rabbi of a California gay synagogue. "The rabbi said, 'The word is out, and no one really wants your position. Everyone is sure that the first rabbi will be absolutely destroyed by all the dissension, backbiting, and politics in your congregation and will never last.'" Nevertheless, more than forty candidates applied for the position.

> "The *New York Times* came to the rescue. We received more than a hundred inquiries from all over the country."
>
> ART LEONARD

The committee moved forward with seventeen applicants, of whom only two were openly gay or lesbian. "We had some great candidates," recalls Rosanne. "The decisions were hard because different people had different strengths and potential weaknesses." The applicants were as diverse as the committee had hoped. Some were promising; others, including some highly credentialed rabbis, were not appropriate for CBST. "We got a mixture of men and women," Jack remembers. "They were straight and gay and from all different religious backgrounds. Some candidates were trying to work out their own sexuality as part of this process, which didn't feel like a good thing for us to get involved in. Sometimes you got people who clearly understood what they were getting into and applied for positive reasons. And sometimes you got people who thought they were being altruistic—they wanted to help the poor gays and lesbians." Some candidates had little experience with illness, a significant lack considering CBST's needs. Others had no previous interaction with lesbian and gay people. Some were simply not a good fit. Bill Fern recalls, "We interviewed a couple of zany people. There were rabbis who assumed that because we were gay we knew nothing; there were rabbis who were ready to retire and wanted one more year with a group of ignorant people; there were rabbis who were feeling very self-important but who were not competent. We certainly went through a lot of rabbis."

While Mel, whose health was declining, hoped the new rabbi would be in place by early 1992, the process took another six months. As the search committee did its work, the board made the financial and capital preparations for a rabbi. Some members feared that dues, which for years had been kept artificially low, would skyrocket to support a rabbi's salary. They worried about losing control, afraid that an authoritarian rabbi would quash CBST's religious diversity, impelling the synagogue to adhere to his or her singular religious vision. Mel continued to prepare the congregation emotionally and philosophically. "The rabbi we hire can never be everything to everybody," he wrote. "Our Rabbi Search Committee is, of course, looking for the best possible fit. But we have been doing things our way for nineteen years and we need to be prepared for change." He enlisted former chair Michael Levine to help. In a two-part series in the newsletter, Michael addressed the major anxieties as he saw them, promising the leadership would look to the congregation to "determine areas of policy over which the rabbi will have authority, areas in which the Board will retain full authority, and areas of mutual authority."

The committee also instructed the congregation on the proper treatment of a rabbi, a concern that would prove more difficult to enforce. "The energy generated by our members can drive outsiders—and insiders alike—to despair," Michael wrote. Mel tried a more diplomatic appeal, "Many of us can be quite acerbic when we don't like a fellow lay person's sermon. Our rabbi, however, must be treated with dignity and respect, no matter what he or she says from the pulpit." The rabbi would also have absolute freedom of the pulpit, a major shift from the Religious Committee's policy restricting *drashot* to Torah commentary, thereby prohibiting lay people from speaking politically from the bimah.

As search committee spokesperson, Art did his best to reassure the congregation:

> We are looking for a rabbi who can "fit in" to our present structure and embody the values and goals of our Congregation, and at the same time give us spiritual leadership and new directions. There is a difficult balance to achieve. A rabbi who preserves everything as it is without attempting to exert any influence for change would not be worth engaging, for everybody agrees that there are things we could be doing better than we are now, and things we are not doing that we should be doing (although not everybody would agree on what those things are!). On the other hand, we are not looking for a rabbi who will come with an agenda to make over the entire Congregation to suit her or his image. CBST must be an expression of the membership, not a flock of sheep to be herded by an all-powerful rabbi. We are seeking a candidate who will lead through education, example, and persuasion, not by fiat, somebody who will welcome sharing leadership with the Board, Religious Committee, and the other active members, who will take pleasure in seeing us grow as a Congregation and develop to our fullest as individuals, and not insist that all decisions be unilaterally made by the rabbi. This is a rare individual.

Conveying the committee's optimism that they would find the appropriate person, Art pledged that the ultimate decision would lie in the hands of the membership.

## CBST Finds Its Rabbi

The committee reached consensus on the candidates quickly. Those who made it past a phone interview were asked to meet the committee in person. Some were invited for second interviews. Anyone who hadn't recently attended a service at CBST was asked to do so surreptitiously, without disclosing that they were a candidate.

Rabbi Sharon Kleinbaum had not applied for the position when she delivered the keynote address at the Twelfth Annual International Conference of Gay and Lesbian Jews in May 1991. Several CBST members were there, some of whom attended the conference to hear her. Art recalls the general reaction to her talk. "'Wow.' Then someone who knew someone who knew her got back to her and urged her to apply for the CBST position."

By September 1991, the committee had narrowed the field to four candidates, with hopes of making a recommendation by the end of the year. Art recounts the process. "We narrowed the search down to four finalists: Two were gay; two were not. Two were men; two were women." Jack recalls, "One was a straight man; one was a straight woman; one was a lesbian, one was a gay man; one was Conservative, two were Reconstructionist, and one was Reform."

Rabbi Kleinbaum recalls that all eight members of the search committee came to "covertly" observe her giving a sermon at a West Hartford, Connecticut synagogue. "They didn't exactly blend in, eight gay people from New York City in a Connecticut Reform synagogue. It wasn't yet public that I was leaving my previous job, so I had asked them to be discreet. I watched from the bimah as each of them walked through the doors and took a seat in a different part of the sanctuary, dispersing themselves among the members of the congregation." Twenty years later, Bill Fern could still describe her sermon from that night. "It was brilliant. It became obvious that she was very talented." "Rabbi Kleinbaum had not done a lot of congregational work up to that time," Rosanne recalls, "but she impressed every one of us in terms of her intellect, her caring, and her ability to scope out the issues."

Rabbi Kleinbaum was the only candidate invited for a third interview, which was held on folding chairs in the still unfurnished living room of Art Leonard's new Upper West Side apartment. He recalls that in the strangeness of the echo in the nearly empty room, they understood they had found CBST's rabbi. "What really struck us is that she had a genuinely strong inner core, a real vision of what a synagogue could be: not just of a religious organization for its members but as a part of a larger community. One of the things to inspire us was that she seemed like someone who would be a great representative of us to the Jewish world, and a great representative of us to the gay world, and to the world in general. She was someone who would become an important spokesperson for the community."

The committee had completed its search. At a special meeting at the end of December, they recommended Rabbi Kleinbaum to the board. "The Board thought if we presented four candidates they would choose the best of the four," Bill recalls, "but by the time we got down to interviewing the others, it was apparent to us that there was just one worthwhile candidate: Sharon Kleinbaum. So we gave our report to the Board, and said, 'This is the one we've got.' They responded, 'We thought we were going to choose among two or three at least.' We said, 'This is the one.'"

After interviewing Rabbi Kleinbaum in January 1992, the board members present voted unanimously to recommend her to the congregation. The search committee organized an intensive weekend in February for the candidate to interact with every aspect of the congregation "religiously, educationally, and socially." The packed weekend schedule included meetings with three significant centers of CBST influence, the Orthopractic Minyan, the Feminist Minyan, and the Religious Committee.

Sharon Kleinbaum's eclectic background made her a persuasive fit for the Jewishly diverse congregation. Raised in a Conservative synagogue in New Jersey, she graduated from the Orthodox Frisch Yeshiva High School and was ordained by the Reconstructionist Rabbinical College. She came to CBST from the national staff of the Reform movement, serving as director of congregational relations for the Religious Action Center of Reform Judaism in Washington, D.C. As a rabbinical student, Rabbi Kleinbaum served as student rabbi at Bet Haverim, the synagogue serving Atlanta's gay and lesbian community, and she was a leader in the efforts to make RRC more hospitable for lesbian and gay students. She had been active in AIDS work for many years providing pastoral care and engaged in education and activism within the Jewish community.

While her yeshiva credentials appealed to traditionalists, Rabbi Kleinbaum's multi-movement Jewish life reassured the more liberal Jews. The more politically oriented among the community appreciated that Rabbi Kleinbaum was a natural activist, raised

---

**Special Candidate Weekend**
**February 21-23**

Friday, February 21
- 6:30 p.m.—Candidate attends Feminist Minyan
- 8:30 p.m.—Candidate attends Friday service
- 9:15 p.m.—Candidate delivers drush
- Oneg Program—Candidate talks with congregants

Saturday, February 22
- 2 p.m.—Candidate meets with past chairs
- 4 p.m.—Candidate leads Torah Study
- 5:20 p.m.—Candidate leads Havdalah
- 5:30 p.m.—Social hour

Sunday, February 23
- 9 a.m.—Candidate davens and meets with Orthopractic Minyan
- 11 a.m.—Buffet lunch & lecture on contemporary issues by Candidate; questions, answers, discussion
- 1 p.m.—Candidate meets Feminist Minyan
- 1:45 p.m.—Candidate meets with Religious Committee

Since CBST had not yet voted to hire Rabbi Kleinbaum, her name was not published in the newsletter.

in a family of social activists. Her father, a lifelong Jewish community professional, was a pacifist who had been a conscientious objector in World War II. While a student at Barnard College, Rabbi Kleinbaum led protests for the divestment from Apartheid South Africa and against nuclear proliferation. She appealed to the Yiddishists, having served as the assistant director of the National Yiddish Book Center. She had also traveled to the former Soviet Union to meet with Jewish activists, which resonated with CBST's long history of activism in the movement to free Soviet Jewry. Her time at the Religious Action Center helped develop her understanding of the political system and hone her sharp instincts for political theater. Already accustomed to the spotlight, Rabbi Kleinbaum was unafraid to put herself in the line of fire for her beliefs. Before rabbinical school, she served a month in a federal prison for her activism with Women's Pentagon Action. Shortly before she came to CBST, she officiated at the wedding of two Georgia women, an event that was at the center of one of the major gay rights cases of the 1990s.

On March 25, 1992, at the annual congregational meeting, the membership voted to approve Rabbi Kleinbaum as CBST's first rabbi. That meeting also marked

Rabbi Kleinbaum (third from left) at a 1980s protest; Grace Paley (second from right)

LEFT: Rabbi Kleinbaum on the cover of a National Yiddish Book Center pamphlet

the end of Mel Rosen's term as chair. He had accomplished his dream for CBST and his illness had advanced to the point where he was no longer well enough to serve another term. The leadership scrambled to identify his successor. So many of the most active men in the congregation were sick or had died from AIDS. Irving Cooperberg, who also had AIDS, but was doing well, stepped in to serve as chair to oversee the transition to the new rabbi. The very same day of CBST's announcement, the Conservative movement's Committee on Jewish Law and Standards voted on its papers on homosexuality, resoundingly rejecting equality for gay and lesbian Jews in religious life. The confluence of events was explosive and led to a media firestorm. Articles appeared in the *New York Times* and throughout the Jewish and gay press about these two seminal occurrences.

**New York Law School**
57 Worth Street
New York, New York
10013-2960

ARTHUR S. LEONARD
PROFESSOR OF LAW

(212) 431-2156
(212) 219-8141 FAX

December 3, 1991

Rabbi Sharon Kleinbaum
1731 S Street, N.W.
Apt. 6
Washington, D.C. 20009

Dear Rabbi Kleinbaum,

    I am pleased to inform you that the Search Committee intends to recommend to the Board of Trustees that the Congregation engage you as our first full-time Rabbi. We have scheduled a meeting with the Board for December 26, the earliest available date, formally to present your candidacy to the Board. We will be back in touch with you shortly to confirm dates for you to meet with the B---
of Trustees in January and for a w---
Congregation in F---
the Annual Member
that the Board au
your representati

CONGREGATION
BETH SIMCHAT TORAH

February 11, 1992

Dear CBST Member:

    Your Board of Trustees unanimously recommends that Rabbi Sharon Kleinbaum of Washington, D.C. be engaged by the Congregation as its first full-time rabbi, at the salary stated below. Rabbi Kleinbaum brings an unusual blend of experience to CBST, spanning all of the branches of organized Judaism. A charismatic speaker, Rabbi Kleinbaum will provide strong intellectual and spiritual leadership for CBST.

    Rabbi Kleinbaum was raised in a Conservative family, graduated from an Orthodox yeshiva high school, from Barnard College and from the Reconstructionist Rabbinical College. She is currently employed in a social action position by the Reform Movement. Her rabbinic experience as a student

> "There will be many days you will be very frustrated. There will be many times you want to tear your hair out. Don't despair. What counts are the people who will be sitting in these chairs. Always remember the big picture." IRVING COOPERBERG

Now that the work of the search committee was concluded, a new committee was created to help ease the transition of the new rabbi. Art Leonard was invited to chair the newly formed Rabbi Liaison Committee, which met monthly with Rabbi Kleinbaum for many years as a forum for open communication and discussion. Irving Cooperberg, Michael Levine, Nancy Alpert, Mel Rosen, Jack Greenberg, and Regina Linder were chosen to serve with Art on the first committee. In his final newsletter column, Mel continued preparing and educating the congregation for a rabbi, reiterating the rabbi's job description, and firmly asserting that she "will *always* have access to the pulpit and will enjoy total freedom of the pulpit."

Irving made sure the construction of the rabbi's office was completed just in time for her arrival on August 1. "On my first day of work at CBST, Irving Cooperberg and his beloved partner Lou Rittmaster met me at the door of the shul and walked me to the bimah. They stood on either side of me and Irving said, 'There will be many days you will be very frustrated. There will be many times you want to tear your hair out. Don't despair. What counts are the people who will be sitting in these chairs. Always remember the big picture.' They gave me a pen and we said the *Shehechiyanu.*"

Rabbi Alexander Schindler, president of the Union of American Hebrew Congregations, presided over Rabbi Kleinbaum's installation. "It was a huge deal for the synagogue that someone like Alexander Schindler would speak at CBST," Rabbi Kleinbaum remembers. He said to the congregation, "You are fortunate to have found Sharon Kleinbaum and to have her now as your spiritual leader . . . But then, she too is fortunate, for by all accounts this congregation is also a find, rare and remarkable in its complexion." In her installation address, Rabbi Kleinbaum laid out her vision for the future of CBST, words that became a template for the synagogue's growth over the next two decades.

Mel Rosen died of AIDS on September 1, 1992, just days before Rabbi Kleinbaum's formal installation. He was forty-two. He had achieved what he promised for CBST, and CBST's own Rabbi Sharon Kleinbaum was in place to officiate at his funeral.

### Conservative Branch Rejects Proposal to Allow Gay Rabbis

By coincidence, the Conservative Movement rejected equality for gay and lesbian Jews on the same day the news of Rabbi Kleinbaum's hiring was announced.

OPPOSITE: Rabbi Kleinbaum's hiring inspired a flurry of articles throughout the United States and Israel.

## NATIONAL

# Local rabbi to lead gay synagogue

### Rabbi Sharon Kleinbaum to leave Religious Action Center

By Debra Nussbaum Cohen
Jewish Telegraphic Agency

NEW YORK — Congregation Beth Simchat Torah, New York's gay and lesbian synagogue, has finally found a rabbi.

The search, which took two years, was neither easy nor typical, and it brought to light some of the challenges faced by gay and lesbian congregations and rabbis.

Rabbi Sharon Kleinbaum, who was ordained by the Reconstructionist Rabbinical College and is a member of the Reform rabbinical association, has been warned by col-

ordinary opportunity for me as a rabbi."

Kleinbaum has been working at the Reform movement Religious Action Center in Washington as director of congregational relations.

As a student rabbi, she worked at the gay and lesbian congregation in Atlanta where she officated at a now-famous ceremony of commitment for a lesbian couple last July.

One of the partners in that relationship, Robin Shahar, lost her job with the Georgia Attorney General's Office when her sexual orientation and the fact that she had been part of a commitment cere-

Rabbi Sharon Kleinbaum: 'I am not a rabbi for any sexual orientation. I am a rabbi.'

## VILLAGE CONGREGAT HIRES LESBIAN RABBI

# Top Gay Synagogue Invites Lesbian to Be First Rabbi

by Frederic Millen

Rabbi Sharon Kleinbaum, who gave the keynote address at the 11th International Conference of the World Congress of Gay and Lesbian Jewish Organizations (WCGLJO) in San Francisco last May, has been called to head the largest homosexual synagogue in the

bian rights."

Kahn was in Los Angeles March 28-29 to attend the western regional meeting of WCGLJO, which includes about 40 member groups. About half of them are full-fledged synagogues and the others are groups working toward becoming synagogues.

# EXCERPT FROM RABBI SHARON KLEINBAUM'S INSTALLATION DRASH

SEPTEMBER 11, 1992/14 ELUL 5752

When it is my turn, in the presence of the One, to tell of how I came to be honored by serving as the rabbi of Congregation Beth Simchat Torah, I will tell of the many from whom I have been blessed to learn—some living and others now dead—who have taught me with their lives, with their words, and with their wisdom. I do not stand alone tonight.

We all benefit from the many who have contributed the work of their hands and the work of their souls to this congregation for the last twenty years. For twenty years the visionaries who created, nurtured, supported, and nudged this sacred community of Congregation Beth Simchat Torah have been fulfilling Isaiah's charge in this week's *haftarah*:

Enlarge the site of your tent,
Extend the size of your dwelling.
Do not stint!
Lengthen the ropes and drive the pegs firm.

These last twenty years have seen heroism, courage, and imagination. We are here tonight, even while we mourn those who have not arrived with us, celebrating the past that has brought us to this day and glimpsing, tasting the future, which, with much hard work, awaits us.

It is in community that we Jews find God. Congregation Beth Simchat Torah represents much of what is best about American Judaism, even if America doesn't know it yet.

In the month since I have been rabbi, we have

buried four members, and a lesbian couple has given birth to twins. We celebrated the conversion and adoption of a four-week-old baby and the conversion of an active CBST member in the presence of her partner of thirteen years. And last week we buried the immediate past president, visionary extraordinaire, Mel Rosen, *alav hashalom*.

We are a community enriched by diverse families. And we will celebrate them, sanctify them within the Jewish community that we create.

For twenty years, CBST has enlarged the size of its dwelling. For twenty years CBST has risen to Isaiah's challenge. But that charge from Yeshayahu is as pressing today as it ever was. We must continue to enlarge the size of our dwelling and lengthen the rope even while we make sure that the pegs are firm. And we must not stint.

We must remain committed to a Judaism that insists social justice be an integral part of who we are. We must not say, "Enlarge the tent so big to bring us in, but close it tight behind us." We must take our knowledge, our skills, and our resources and ensure that the disenfranchised, the weak, the vulnerable, will never be abandoned by this congregation of Jews. God demands nothing less of us. We must not stint.

"Enlarge the site of your tent," Isaiah challenges us. Imagine a CBST that could educate our young to help build a world where the senseless hate of our day and time are only of historical interest. We want our children to be Jews.

"Enlarge the site of your tent." Imagine a CBST that is a training ground for rabbinical students from all the movements in the pastoral care of people with AIDS and their families.

"Extend the size of your dwelling." Imagine a CBST that is a center for Jewish arts. Our members are among the most talented artists in this city. Let us create a Jewish community where music, theater, literature flourish, and our souls are enriched.

FROM LEFT TO RIGHT: Irving Cooperberg, Rabbi Sharon Kleinbaum, Rabbi Alexander Schindler

The possibilities know no bounds. But our foundations must be strong. "Lengthen the ropes and drive the pegs firm." Our life and work together must be founded on our mutual sacred orientation: visiting the sick, comforting the bereaved, burying the dead, educating ourselves, observing Shabbat and *yamim tovim*, celebrating the events of our lives, being involved in the great social concerns of our day.

"Enlarge the site, the *makom* of your tent." *Makom* means "place." And it means "God." We must always have the wisdom to remember that this site, this place, this *makom* of ours, is a place of the Holy Ancient One of Old.

To Irving Cooperberg and Rabbi Schindler, May *Hakadosh baruch hu*, the One before whom we all stand, give me the strength, wisdom, and humor to fulfill your charge.

Standing before this ark, on this day of the Fourteenth of Elul 5752, in the presence of my teachers, mentors, family, friends, colleagues, and students, I accept the honor of serving as your rabbi.

*Hazak hazak v'nithazek*.

Let us go from strength to strength together.

# 5. RABBINIC AND LAY LEADERSHIP

Rabbi Kleinbaum's arrival at CBST did not immediately create the seismic shift that some members feared and others hoped for. In her first year at CBST, she took on the role of studying the synagogue rather than transforming it. She immersed herself in the community, scheduling parlor sessions with every demographic in the community—two a month for most of a year—getting to know the members and listening to their concerns. Jack Greenberg reflects, "Rabbi Kleinbaum sat back the whole first year. She came to events to observe, not to make changes." Naturally, her presence on the bimah was an immediate and visible change.

## A Rabbi on the Bimah

Initially Rabbi Kleinbaum attended five Shabbat services a month: three 8:30 PM services, one early minyan—alternating between the Feminist and Orthopractic minyanim—and one Shabbat morning service. Rabbi Kleinbaum also became part of the rotation on the bimah. Jack Greenberg, who continued to be responsible for the ritual calendar, scheduled her for two *drashot* and two service-leading slots each month. Members served as *darshanim* and service leaders for the rest of the month and lay people continued to serve as *ba'alei tefillah* every week. This schedule meant Rabbi Kleinbaum was present in the congregation at least once every month while a congregant was leading the service or giving the *drash*, reinforcing their status as lay leaders and communicating Rabbi Kleinbaum's respect for them.

Still, with Rabbi Kleinbaum regularly leading services and giving *drashot*, lay service leaders and *darshanim* had fewer opportunities on the bimah. Many members appreciated the increasing consistency of the quality of the services and *drashot*. Others mourned the change. Sheila Michaels is nostalgic about the service-leading and *drash* rotation prior to the rabbi's arrival, "There were good weeks and bad weeks, but I thought we were doing OK. I didn't think we needed a leader. After the rabbi started giving *drashot*, I gave only one *drash* a year instead of three or four." While many lay leaders may have expressed sadness at their own diminished frequency on the bimah, they also preferred attending services when the rabbi delivered the *drash*. When the service leaders and *darshan* were announced in advance, attendance would vary significantly on Friday nights depending on who was scheduled to be on the bimah. Even acknowledging this pattern, some longtime members continued to resent any presence of the rabbi, who in their view displaced congregants on the bimah. This duality increased as the clergy

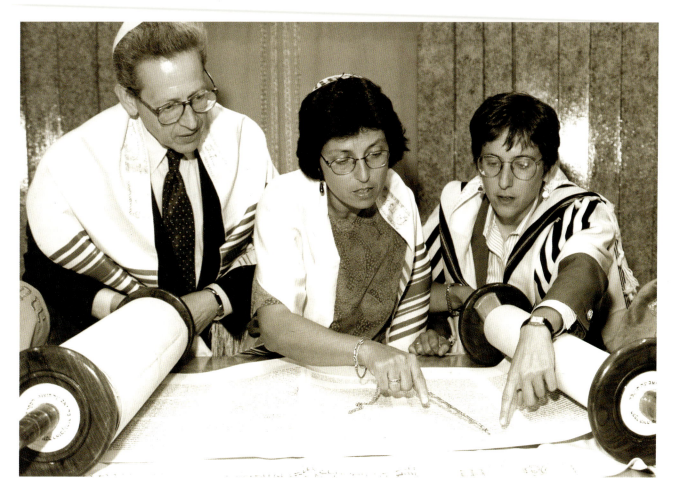

Rabbi Kleinbaum (right) shares the bimah with Michael Levine and Yolanda Potasinski.

staff expanded. Sandy Warshaw joined CBST in Rabbi Kleinbaum's first year. She recalls, "I began to realize this was a synagogue that had gone through quite a process to get a rabbi, and that they weren't quite sure they wanted a rabbi. They went through this process and hired a woman rabbi, but there were parts of the community that weren't sure they wanted a woman rabbi."

The discomfort of some CBST traditionalists with women as religious leaders, which had intensified along with the increased presence of women at CBST, became intolerable when Rabbi Kleinbaum arrived. Some of these men preferred to pray in Orthodox settings, with a *mechitzah* and services led exclusively by men. Some simply did not want to be around women at all. Regina Linder remembers the misogyny that surfaced around Rabbi Kleinbaum's arrival as "viciously monstrous." The split that occurred at the time was deeply upsetting. "After all, they were our friends, but they were very destructive," Regina recalls. "They also craved secrecy." Some men preferred the subterfuge of the closet and were uncomfortable as gay life became more open, and CBST became increasingly a place where members were more public about their lives. Ultimately, many of these men left CBST to attend Orthodox and Conservative synagogues. Some married women and raised Orthodox families.

Over time, the Friday night service began to change. Ironically, Rabbi Kleinbaum successfully introduced some of the changes that Pinchas had hoped to institute, emphasizing music over English readings and singing more of the Hebrew liturgy, such as the full text of *L'chah dodi*. For some members, however, any change was too much. "For many people it was traumatic and they couldn't adjust to it. Maybe they just couldn't adjust to any rabbi, or Rabbi Kleinbaum was not their vision of CBST's rabbi," Jack Greenberg reflects. "For others, her being there was really positive, and many people came *because* of her. Eventually some of the other people left, and the changes were no longer so controversial. After two or three years, we really changed our style."

## Building a Culture of Respect

Like every living community, CBST naturally continued to evolve. At each stage of growth, some members could not accept the changes in the synagogue and left, others adapted personally as the community changed and continued to find fulfillment there.

The board culture also began to change. Catherine Sull became the second woman chair in 1993, the first of the new-generation of leaders to have come on the board under Mel Rosen's leadership. Before Yolanda Potasinski was elected president in 1996, the board had been restructured again, and it was time to take on some of the thornier issues of congregational culture.

Meanwhile Rabbi Kleinbaum tried to address the sometimes nasty tenor of contentious board meetings and factionalism within the synagogue. Periodically, the intense identification with the past and fear of change led to unfortunate and inappropriate expressions of anger. At times board meetings devolved into shouting matches, occasionally lasting into the late hours of the night. At one particularly rancorous meeting in the 1980s, an argument about installing an answering machine in the office got so out of hand that, in an effort to subdue an abusive board member, the board president threw a chair at him. In her "State of the Synagogue Address" at the 1997 annual congregational meeting, Rabbi Kleinbaum talked about the ways in which the community had endeavored to overcome this "culture of meanness" and the work still needed to heal internal rifts.

In one of the most difficult chapters at CBST, the board addressed the actions of one longtime member and lay leader who had demonstrated a long history of abusive behavior and had violently threatened another lay leader. After painful deliberations, and with a heavy heart, the board decided that this extreme behavior was beyond the acceptable bounds of conduct and voted to expel him. The culture of the synagogue since that time has changed dramatically. The board has evolved to a high level and the tenor of its meetings become so productive and courteous, that such episodes now seem unimaginable. The synagogue's prevailing vision of *menschlichkeit* and joy has enabled it to carry out its work and move into a new era.

# THE STATE OF THE SYNAGOGUE

> It became clear to me that a culture of meanness was preventing CBST from becoming the deep spiritual community I knew was possible. Some people objected when I used that phrase "There is no culture of meanness here. Don't be negative." Well, there was a culture of meanness here. The way people were interacting, on the board, on committees, in Friday night *onegs*, was often just plain mean. This wasn't true for everybody and in every setting, but I began to see that the meanness was not coming out of evil or malevolence. There were a lot of people in the synagogue who were hurt, felt ignored, or unappreciated, and reacted by attacking somebody else. It happened at board meetings; it happened at Friday night services, when some congregants would attack the people coming off the bimah because they didn't agree with the *drash* or objected to the service. It happened in any number of ways. It became clear that we as a community had to find a way to overcome that culture of meanness. I think, in large measure, that has happened. I have been very moved to watch how people from the synagogue have come together. While I don't think we're done with this process, I do think we've made tremendous strides.
>
> RABBI SHARON KLEINBAUM, MARCH 1997

## Pastoral Care

The pastoral care burden was immense when Rabbi Kleinbaum arrived at CBST, in large part because of AIDS. She officiated at so many funerals and memorial services—four in her first four weeks at CBST—that Dr. Ron Wolfson, who interviewed her for his 1993 book on Jewish mourning, dubbed her "Rabbi of Death." But as she told him, she felt blessed to be able to do what she believed was God's work. She saw her role as helping those with AIDS retain their humanity through their illnesses, offering the companionship of community in a context that strived to destigmatize AIDS.

Rabbi Kleinbaum provided pastoral support not only to people with AIDS but also to their loved ones. She frequently helped navigate the relationships between the family of origin and the partner or other family of choice. Sometimes painful conflicts arose if the family of origin, which usually had the legal decision making rights, wanted to make different choices. "My job is to reach out and comfort both groups." She tried to help the family of origin recognize the life partner as a spouse, who should be included in making funeral and shiva arrangements.

> When things get ugly, it is usually because the family of origin has not reconciled themselves to the fact that their child is gay. Often they will take their anger out on the life partner: "My child is not gay; this person was the evil influence." They will attempt to cut both the gay partner and the community out of the mourning process. Another way this denial works is when the family of origin does not want any mention of AIDS in the obituary or at the funeral. While the gay person may be "out," the family of origin is often still "in the closet," terrified of what their community would do to them if this got out. This fear denies them the support of their friends and families at the very time they need it most. This illness and death affects every member of the family. That the Jewish community does not allow homosexuality to be an open issue forces everyone into the closet.

**CONGREGATION BETH SIMCHAT TORAH**

**HIV/AIDS OUTREACH COMMITTEE**

We are trying to REACH OUT and MEET THE NEEDS of our members who are HIV+ and/or PWA's. We need to know:

WHAT DO YOU NEED FROM CBST?
WHAT DO YOU WANT FROM CBST?
WHAT CAN WE DO?

A PRIVATE, CONFIDENTIAL MEETING will be held by
RABBI KLEINBAUM and
DAVID STEINBERG,
our Cooperberg-Rittmaster Rabbinic Intern, at the home of Mark Janover on March 1, 1995, 7 p.m.

RSVP ASAP:
Mark Janover at (212) 633-8393 or
David Steinberg at the CBST office
(212) 929-9498 (leave a message)

PLEASE TRY TO ATTEND THIS IMPORTANT MEETING.
If you cannot, please contact David and give him your input.

Rabbi Kleinbaum initiated a number of AIDS outreach efforts.

At the funeral for CBST member Danny Jacobs, Riverside Memorial Chapel was filled with mourners in black: his Orthodox family of origin seated on one side of the aisle and his gay and leather community on the other. His partner, Gary Adler, recalls the estrangement between the two worlds. Gary clung to the side of one of Danny's Orthodox brothers at the cemetery, afraid that the family would leave him stranded at the cemetery as they had with the non-Jewish wife of Danny's late brother. Years later Gary reconnected with that brother and has visited him and his family during CBST trips to Israel.

With years of experience working on AIDS issues, both while she was a student at RRC and at the Religious Action Center, Rabbi Kleinbaum initiated many discussions examining the climate for PWAs at CBST. Always working to develop the role of the synagogue as a spiritual community, she worked with the Bikkur Cholim committee to expand its mandate of reaching out to CBST members with AIDS. Regina Linder recalls that before the Bikkur Cholim committee she and her partner Leah Trachten helped take care of their closest friends who had AIDS, like Sheldon Arden, who had accompanied Regina to her first service at CBST and died in 1988. Regina recalls, "Once Rabbi Kleinbaum came on board, Leah and I felt we could be helpful to people in the congregation who might not have been our best friends. There was a structure that allowed us to reach out to people, some of whom we knew, some whom we didn't even know." It was through the Bikkur Cholim committee that Regina and Leah became close to Carl Bennett and Walter Schwartz.

Carl, who as Regina remembers knew everything about the Jewish calendar, had a strong Jewish background and education. An early ritual leader of CBST, Carl was part of an intense circle of relationships, known as "The Carlettes." Together they explored the pleasures of the mind and body, engaged in serious Jewish learning, and were intellectual leaders of the synagogue. Regina recalls:

> Carl's key partner in that group was Walter Schwartz. Several died pretty early on, including, Michael Friedman, Roger Chung, and John Irving. Eventually Walter also got very sick and only Carl was there to take care of him. That was when Leah and I got involved. They were both at Cabrini Medical center, which was right near us. Partly we were shell-shocked. We had been through the process so many times that I'm not certain we were able to react very much. We knew there were ways we could expedite and make things a little easier and be there for them. Eventually, Walter died and Carl was alone and pretty quickly got sick. We were there for him the best way we could be. The very religious group, the Talmud class with Pinchas, was very much there for Carl, so he had a community. But it was all such a sad process, a chain of sickness and death. I was there with Rabbi Kleinbaum when she did the final confession for Carl.

Carl Bennett

## Cooperberg-Rittmaster Rabbinical Internship Program

In 1994 Bill Fern approached the rabbi wanting to make a significant gift to CBST to honor his close friends Irving Cooperberg and Lou Rittmaster. Initially he had in mind an annual award for outstanding work conducted within the Jewish LGBT world. After Rabbi Kleinbaum described the overwhelming need for pastoral support at CBST, she and Bill conceived of a rabbinical student internship program that would focus on pastoral care for congregants with HIV and AIDS. One Cooperberg-Rittmaster Rabbinical Intern (CRRI) was hired the first year, with the intention of the program expanding to three interns by the third year, but because of office space limitations the number stayed at two. Eventually the interns provided broad pastoral counseling, supported the various minyanim, assisted in the growing programs for families with children and adult education, prepared *drashot*, and led services. During the worst of the AIDS years, many Cooperberg-Rittmaster Rabbinical Interns spent much of their time visiting congregants with AIDS at home or in hospitals, most commonly at St. Vincent's Hospital, one of the epicenters of AIDS care in New York City, just blocks away from CBST.

The internship drew students from every non-Orthodox East Coast rabbinical seminary. Members of CBST, especially those who served on the intern search committees, felt protective and proud of the Cooperberg-Rittmaster Rabbinical Interns, eager to learn from them and to be a part of their educations. Bill Fern did not ask to be involved in selecting the interns or shaping the internship program, insisting only that the interns consistently use their full title, Cooperberg-Rittmaster Rabbinical Intern, so that the program would continue to be associated with Irving and Lou. This stipulation became even more important after Irving

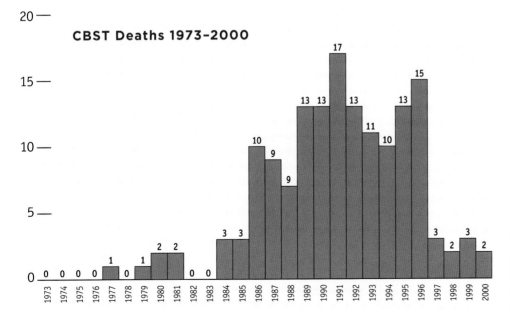

This graph reflects deaths of members from all causes. From 1981-1997 the vast majority of member deaths were HIV/AIDS-related.

died from AIDS and Lou moved to Florida, when many of the newer members and interns knew their names only through the internship program.

CBST embraced its new role as a rabbinic training ground, preparing a generation of rabbis to perform their work in a variety of rabbinic fields, applying their learned expertise in HIV and AIDS counseling, LGBT life, and queer liturgy.

## Growing Rabbinical Staff

As CBST continued to expand, the spiritual leadership also needed to grow to meet the increasing needs of the community. In 1999, CBST hired its first assistant rabbi, Roderick Young, who had served as a Cooperberg-Rittmaster Rabbinical Intern (CRRI) for two years and had been ordained at Hebrew Union College that year. In 2002, Rabbi Young moved back to his native London, and Rabbi Ayelet Cohen—who had just completed two years as a CRRI and was ordained at the Jewish Theological Seminary—was hired. She served at CBST for a total of ten years. When Rabbi Cohen left in 2010, Rachel Weiss, who had also served as a CRRI for two years while studying at the Reconstructionist Rabbinical College, was hired as assistant rabbi, working primarily with CBST's families with children.

While Rabbi Young served as assistant rabbi, tensions around the issue of gender balance on the bimah abated somewhat, but intensified again as the

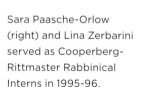

Sara Paasche-Orlow (right) and Lina Zerbarini served as Cooperberg-Rittmaster Rabbinical Interns in 1995-96.

### REFLECTIONS FROM MY YEAR AT CBST: CARING FOR ONE ANOTHER

One of the many times Marc Janover was hospitalized with AIDS, he asked me to hold his Tiffany earring from his beloved deceased partner, Clinton, while the technician inserted a Hep-Lock line. This was a particularly emotional process, as the Hep-Lock had signified a downturn for his partner. He asked me to sing a particular *niggun* and I stood behind his chair with my hands gently on his shoulder, singing, as the nurse did her work. After she finished, I needed to lie down. My pregnancy nausea had overwhelmed me and I could not stay upright. Marc happily proceeded to care for me as I regained my balance. Another time, at his apartment, Marc paused as he was about to offer me a joint and quipped, "Oh yes, you are on the job, and not good for the baby either."

The lesson that has stood by me is that we are in this world together. While I was clearly caring for him, he took pride in caring for me. It connected us both to a wellspring of *chesed* and God.

RABBI SARA PAASCHE-ORLOW,
COOPERBERG-RITTMASTER RABBINICAL INTERN, 1995–96

> **REFLECTIONS FROM MY FIRST YEAR AT CBST: FEAR OF COMING OUT**
>
> A few days before my internship began, I received a call from Tasha Calhoun, Rabbi Kleinbaum's assistant, asking me to go immediately to Cabrini Hospital, where a young man was dying from AIDS. An aspiring actor, he wasn't a CBST member, but had attended services and had many friends in the community. I grabbed a *Tanach* and dashed to the subway. By the time I arrived at the hospital, he had died. He was thirty-five years old. I sat with his parents in the family room next door. They learned only a few days earlier that their much beloved youngest son had life-threatening meningitis. Now he was dead. They had to digest his having AIDS, his death, and figure out what to say to their Jewish community at home. Years later the young man's mother recalled how compassionate and generous he was, noting that before coming out to her and her husband, he had attended a PFLAG meeting to learn how he could most sensitively tell his parents he was gay. She explained that he couldn't come to terms with his diagnosis, and neither sought treatment nor told his family until it was too late.
>
> This was in 2000, when AIDS education was everywhere. So many people talk about how easy it is for young people to come out now, decades after Stonewall, when the world has changed so much. But coming out is still scary and new for every person. When you're terrified of telling your parents you aren't who they wanted you to be, you're not thinking about how the world has evolved. You're just a kid who wants your parents to love you. I kept my notes from that first call from Tasha on my desk the whole time I was at CBST.
>
> RABBI AYELET S. COHEN,
> COOPERBERG-RITTMASTER RABBINICAL INTERN, 2000-01, 2001-02

rabbinical staff grew to include more women. When Rabbi Cohen was hired, CBST became one of the only synagogues in the country to have two female (and no male) rabbis. Rabbi Kleinbaum pointedly hired rabbis and interns (and later a cantor) who varied in age and came from every movement of Judaism—communicating the value of drawing from the variety and wealth of every Jewish tradition—and across the spectrum of gender identity and sexual orientation. The fact that the clergy represented a diversity of gender and sexual identity modeled a powerful statement about the nature of community, which CBST hoped would become a paradigm for Jewish communities throughout the world. Rabbi Kleinbaum repeatedly maintained that one service alone could not reflect the diversity of the community; each service would express an *aspect* of CBST, she insisted. It was the range of voices over time that truly conveyed the spirit of CBST.

# COOPERBERG-RITTMASTER RABBINICAL INTERNS

**Rabbi David Steinberg** (1994–95), Reconstructionist Rabbinical College, 1997

**Rabbi Lina Zerbarini** (1995–96), Reconstructionist Rabbinical College, 1997

**Rabbi Sara Paasche-Orlow** (1995–96), Jewish Theological Seminary, 1996

**Rabbi Joshua Lesser** (1996–97), Reconstructionist Rabbinical College, 1999

**Rabbi Roderick Young** (1996–97, 1998–99), Hebrew Union College–Jewish Institute of Religion, 1999

**Rabbi Daniel Judson** (1997–98), Hebrew Union College–Jewish Institute of Religion, 1998

**Rabbi Elisa Goldberg** (1997–98), Reconstructionist Rabbinical College, 1999

**Rabbi Edythe Held Mencher** (1998–99), Hebrew Union College–Jewish Institute of Religion, 1999

**Rabbi Mychal Copeland** (née Rosenbaum) (1999–00), Reconstructionist Rabbinical College, 2000

**Rabbi Rachel Gartner** (1999–00), Reconstructionist Rabbinical College, 2002

**Rabbi David Dunn Bauer** (2000–01), Reconstructionist Rabbinical College, 2003

**Rabbi Ayelet S. Cohen** (2000–01, 2001–02), Jewish Theological Seminary, 2002

**Rabbi Tracy Nathan** (2001–02), Jewish Theological Seminary, 2003

**Rabbi Ryan Dulkin** (2002–03), Jewish Theological Seminary, 2004

**Rabbi Darren Levine** (2002–03), Hebrew Union College–Jewish Institute of Religion, 2003

**Rabbi Lauren Grabelle Herrmann** (2003–04), Reconstructionist Rabbinical College, 2006

**Rabbi Michael Rothbaum** (2003–04), Academy of Jewish Religion, 2006

**Rabbi Ruth Gelfarb** (2004–05), Hebrew Union College–Jewish Institute of Religion, 2007

**Rabbi Darby Jared Leigh** (2004–05, 2005–06), Reconstructionist Rabbinical College, 2008

**Rabbi Reuben Zellman** (2005–06), Hebrew Union College–Jewish Institute of Religion, 2010

**Rabbi Rachel Kahn-Troster** (2006–07), Jewish Theological Seminary, 2008

**Rabbi Rachel Weiss** (2006–07, 2007–08), Reconstructionist Rabbinical College, 2009

**Ben Davis** (2007–08), attended Reconstructionist Rabbinical College 2005–2009

**Rabbi Cecelia Beyer** (2008–09), Jewish Theological Seminary, 2010

**Rabbi Melissa Simon** (2008–09, 2009–2010), Hebrew Union College–Jewish Institute of Religion, 2010

**Rabbi Yosef Goldman** (2010–11), Jewish Theological Seminary, 2013

**Ari Lev Fornari** (2010–11, 2011–12), Hebrew College

**Rabbi Guy Austrian** (2011–12), Jewish Theological Seminary, 2013

**Jason Bonder** (2012–2013) Reconstructionist Rabbinical College

**Margot Meitner** (2012–2013) Hebrew College

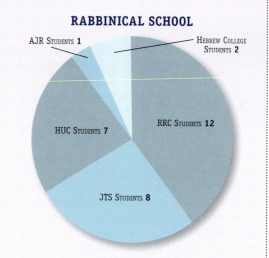

**RABBINICAL SCHOOL**
- AJR Students 1
- Hebrew College Students 2
- HUC Students 7
- RRC Students 12
- JTS Students 8

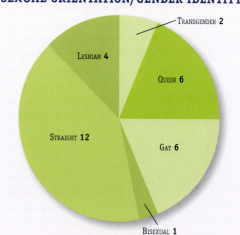

**SEXUAL ORIENTATION/GENDER IDENTITY**
- Transgender 2
- Queer 6
- Gay 6
- Bisexual 1
- Straight 12
- Lesbian 4

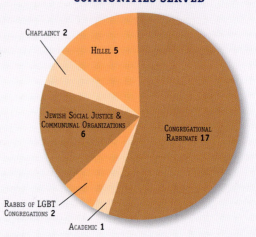

**COMMUNITIES SERVED**
- Chaplaincy 2
- Hillel 5
- Jewish Social Justice & Communal Organizations 6
- Congregational Rabbinate 17
- Rabbis of LGBT Congregations 2
- Academic 1

Rabbis Kleinbaum, Cohen, and Young at Rabbi Young's farewell party in 2002

## A Flourishing of Minyanim

Exposure to CBST's eclectic ritual mix became an important part of the interns' education. Rabbis Kleinbaum and Cohen deliberately assigned each intern to attend and support minyanim whose practices were different from the seminary in which they were training, frequently assigning interns from HUC and RRC to the Traditional Minyan and JTS students to the Liberal Minyan; RRC students found themselves leading *Musaf*, which is excised from the Reconstructionist Shabbat liturgy, and JTS students had to design creative, meditative services.

When Rabbi Kleinbaum came to CBST in 1992, the Mevarchim Minyan was the only regular monthly Shabbat morning service. At that time, the Mevarchim Minyan resisted celebrating lifecycle events for CBST members who weren't minyan regulars. Disappointed that more CBST members didn't attend regularly, some minyan members resented the idea that a person who never came to the minyan could be called up to the Torah and honored, never to return. Rabbi Kleinbaum established the Liberal Minyan in part to have a place for congregants to celebrate lifecycle events by being called up to the Torah.

LEFT TO RIGHT: Annette Miller, Sara Paasche-Orlow, Saul Zalkin, and David Flohr

## FROM INTERN TO RABBI

I moved to New York from London in 1988. Although I had been an out gay man for over ten years, I certainly had never been to a gay synagogue. I well remember my first visit to CBST, on a Shabbat morning about a year after my arrival in the city. There was only a small group of people davening. But the warmth was immediate, and I stayed for lunch. Who would have guessed that ten years later I would be CBST's first assistant rabbi?

In 1992 I graduated from JTS with a masters degree. The plan was to stay there and become a rabbi. But after I came out publicly to the chancellor that door was summarily closed to me, for in those bad old days the Conservative Movement refused to ordain LGBT people. HUC took me in instead and made my partner and me completely welcome. In my second year at HUC I had to choose a synagogue in which to work as an intern. Having now been to CBST several times, and having seen Rabbi Sharon Kleinbaum at work, I knew this was where I wanted to be and that she would be the rabbinical mentor and role model for me. But HUC was not happy. Not because CBST was an LGBT shul, but rather because it was not a member of the Reform Movement. After hitting wall after wall in the college, I went to Rabbi Kleinbaum and told her how unfair this policy was, given that an HUC colleague was at that moment working in a Conservative shul in Hoboken and another in a Conservative shul on the Upper West Side. "Really," she said. And she picked up the phone to HUC. By the end of that day, I was CBST's first Cooperberg-Rittmaster Rabbinical Intern from the Reform Movement.

I enjoyed the experience so much that two years later I came back to be an intern once again. When the synagogue asked me to stay on as their first assistant rabbi, how could I say no? That was the start of three marvelous years working full time at CBST, until I had to return to the UK in 2002 to look after my elderly mother.

RABBI RODERICK YOUNG, COOPERBERG-RITTMASTER RABBINICAL INTERN, 1996–97, 1998–99, CBST ASSISTANT RABBI, 1999–2002

FROM LEFT TO RIGHT: Gary Adler, Annette Miller, and Roderick Young, then a Cooperberg-Rittmaster Rabbinical Intern, at a Matthew Shepard vigil and protest, 1998

# AYELET COHEN AND THE CONSERVATIVE MOVEMENT

Although Ayelet Cohen had served as a Cooperberg-Rittmaster Rabbinical Intern for two years with the knowledge and support of JTS, the Rabbinical Assembly wouldn't allow her to apply for the position of full-time Assistant Rabbi after her ordination. They claimed it was because we weren't affiliated with the Conservative Movement, denying their decision was in any way related to the fact that we were an LGBT synagogue. At that time CBST was ineligible to affiliate with the Conservative Movement because our rabbis officiate at weddings for same-sex couples. Rabbi Cohen was required to get a waiver from the RA to apply for the job. Eleven years after its refusal to provide CBST with a rabbi made the cover of the Metro Section, the RA wanted the situation to disappear. Hoping to intimidate her and to keep the words "Conservative Movement" and "gay" out of the press, the head of the RA told her that taking the job with CBST would destroy her career. They falsely claimed that she had entered into an agreement with CBST before she received the waiver. Rabbi Cohen stared them down and began her work with CBST. While the Conservative Movement's policies had excluded and intimidated gay and lesbian rabbis for years, they were not prepared for a straight rabbi who was an outspoken and relentless advocate for LGBT equality.

Two years later the RA resumed the proceedings, threatening to expel Rabbi Cohen from the Assembly if she continued to work at CBST. They claimed it was about paperwork, but we knew it was about having a high profile Conservative rabbi serving in a highly visible New York LGBTQ synagogue. Rabbi Cohen refused to back down. She absolutely believed that the most important work she could do as a Conservative rabbi was to be a rabbi at CBST, which she continued to do in the face of tremendous pressure.

With the support of CBST and some colleagues and friends, Rabbi Cohen stood up to the RA and the Placement Commission, which ultimately voted to censure her but not expel her. The confrontation between Rabbi Cohen and the RA was reported in the *Jewish Week*, the *Forward*, and the *New York Times*. It forced the Conservative Movement's positions towards LGBTQ people back into the public eye, which helped motivate the movement to reevaluate its policies.

Rabbi Cohen has remained one of the most powerful voices for full equality for LGBTQ Jews in the Conservative Movement. Many at CBST were moved by her commitment as a straight ally, especially when she and her partner, Rabbi Marc Margolius, chose not to get legally married as long as legal marriage remained unavailable to same-sex couples.

RABBI SHARON KLEINBAUM

# EXCERPT FROM RABBI AYELET S. COHEN'S INSTALLATION *DRASH*

## SEPTEMBER 13, 2002/8 TISHREI 5763

On Pride Shabbat, CBST welcomes the new Cooperberg-Rittmaster Rabbinical Interns and ushers out the old ones. I remember one service, one of the first I ever attended at CBST, where I watched the Cooperberg-Rittmaster Rabbinical Interns being welcomed—among them Roderick Young—and I thought to myself, "I want to do that. I am going to do that." It was before I had even started rabbinical school, before I was even sure I wanted to become a rabbi. But I knew I had to do it. I had to come to CBST.

People ask me often why I want to be here. As a straight woman, as a Conservative rabbi, why a gay synagogue? Why CBST? Some people think they already know the answer. "She couldn't find another job." "She likes to make trouble in the Conservative Movement." That may be true, but it is hardly the foundation for a career. Some people are sure they have figured it out: "Her sister is a lesbian." Of course, that is only part of the story.

My first memory of being in shul is of *Kol Nidrei* in Jerusalem when I was three or four years old and my sister was six or seven. It was an Orthodox shul. The women were upstairs, the men were downstairs, and the kids were outside. This was before everything in Jerusalem was paved and developed, and the area around the shul was uncultivated, filled with thorny bushes and rocks. The Emas (the mothers) would make little *sakiot*, baggies of goodies, to get the kids through the long services.

Of course, our Ema made the best *sakiot* of anyone. One little boy wanted my sister's *sakit*. He chased her around the shul, through the brambles and over the stones, until she tripped over a root and fell and cut her knee. I remember seeing my big sister lying there on the ground, bleeding. I was terrified. I went into the shul, scared and tiny among all of the tall men in their white *tallitot,* to get the Abas (the fathers) to come outside and help.

For years, my sister Tamara had that scar on her knee. So I guess you could say it started then. By the time I got to college and was old enough to have some impact on my Jewish community, I knew that I had to create a community where my sister would never be chased until she fell and bled. And I realized something else: I don't ever want to be part of a community that chases anyone.

Part of the reason I wanted to become a rabbi in the first place, and a Conservative rabbi in particular, is that I want to help transform the Jewish world so that its values catch up with its rhetoric—so that moral leadership is really moral. And, to be honest, I don't want to let other straight people off the hook. Straight people, who happen not to have a lesbian sister or a gay uncle or a transgender child, too often think they can just sit back because "it isn't their issue." It's not about having a lesbian sister. It's about each of us doing the work we need to do to repair this world.

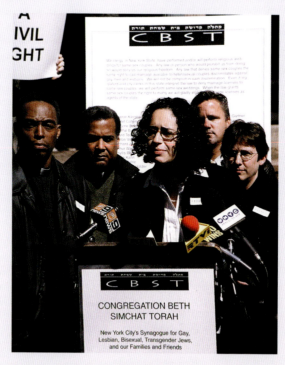

Rabbi Ayelet Cohen speaking at a marriage equality rally at One Police Plaza, 2004

But this too is only part of the story. Because what is the point of making a community inclusive if it is so spiritually empty and intellectually undemanding that no one cares if they are chased away?

CBST is a great synagogue. What we do here is a model for Jewish life in the twenty-first century. We are serious, we are engaged, we know how to have a good time. We love learning and davening and singing and asking questions. We are creating the answers to halachic and spiritual and liturgical questions that other communities have been afraid to even ask. This community, this shul, is so important to us that we rage and we hurt, deeply, when it is not giving us what we want. None of us has to be here. It isn't automatic; it isn't expected; it isn't easy. We have sought this place out and we demand that it meets our needs and we make it so.

Reb Nachman of Bratslav taught that each person in the world has at least a speck of goodness. Each person in a community, no matter how difficult he or she may be, has a speck, a dot, a *nekuda*, of goodness, some unique quality that belongs to no one else. I look around tonight and see each of you with your own *nekuda*, your unique gift. Reb Nachman

Officiating at the wedding of Joanne Jacobson (left) and Ellen Wertheim, June 2008

taught that a community is each of these *nekudot*, each of these literal dots, laid out on a scored piece of paper, so that each dot can be read as a musical note. Together they make up a piece of music, which becomes the *niggun*, the musical anthem of a community, composed of the *nekudot*, the unique gifts, of each member. I thank each of you here for inviting me to add my *nekuda* to the score of this community. I look forward to the music we will make together.

On the bimah at the Javits Center on Yom Kippur (from left to right) Cantor Berger, Rabbi Cohen, Larry Kay

## EXCERPT FROM RABBI RACHEL WEISS'S INSTALLATION *DRASH*

OCTOBER 15, 2010/8 CHESHVAN 5771

I'm not a New Yorker—I'm a Midwestern girl, raised Reconstructionist in Chicago, came out as a lesbian in Iowa. I had never been to Manhattan until the day I interviewed to be a Cooperberg-Rittmaster Rabbinical Intern in 2006. But I was already introduced to CBST in 1997. I attended a Jewish feminist college retreat at Yale University, where Rabbi Kleinbaum was our Shabbat luncheon speaker. I can tell you that I still remember what she talked about (although she may not), and sitting with a group of lesbian and bi college women, planning for rabbinical school, I didn't know at the time—which is usually how *bashert* works—what was to come.

So it was a huge joy and achievement to join CBST as Cooperberg-Rittmaster Rabbinical Intern in 2006 and to be granted a second year with you. The work I did at CBST was foundational. This is the most comprehensive, challenging, and innovative rabbinical and cantorial internship that exists anywhere. Period. While my classmates were visiting remote communities as monthly service leaders, I was engaging with congregants through intimate pastoral encounters, developing and leading lifecycle rituals, working with committees, and organizing public events.

Ten years ago, my partner Julia, my dad, and I were part of the Twin Cities to Chicago AIDS Ride. There was a sign at the exit of our pit stop, where we sent riders on their way with their Gatorade and Clif Bars, which read, *"Go confidently in the direction of your dreams. Live the life you've imagined."* These words by Henry David Thoreau couldn't be truer to my experiences these past years.

Rachel Weiss as a Cooperberg-Rittmaster Rabbinical Intern in 2007 with Shmelmo and Emmet Nathan Schatell-Prince at a Chanukah party

This is the place, the direction, and these are my dreams. I said, just the other night, I can't believe this is really my life.

In *Lech Lecha*, God tells Abraham not only to go to a physical land, but literally to go to himself. *Lech Lecha* . . . go to yourself. Go to the place where you will become yourself. Go to authenticity. Go to your own inner truth. Go inside yourself. Go to the place where you will walk confidently in the direction of your dreams. Go to the place where you will become your truest self, and you shall be a blessing.

As I envision our time together in the coming years, I envision working to create a place—even more so than we already have at CBST—where we will become our truest selves. A place where we will indeed be a blessing.

## Traditional Minyan

Once the Liberal Minyan was established, the Mevarchim Minyan became the Traditional Morning Minyan. It differed in mission from the Orthopractic Minyan, which initially had a more clearly articulated commitment to Orthodox and right-wing Conservative Judaism and was more ambivalent about women's participation, but there was a natural overlap in population. With time, those who were most virulently opposed to women's participation stopped attending CBST. The Traditional Evening Minyan also became a home for young graduates of yeshiva day schools seeking traditional davening in a positive LGBT setting.

All of these siddurim were used regularly by various minyanim at CBST (clockwise left to right) *De Sola Poole* (Orthodox Sephardic), *Siddur Sim Shalom* (Conservative), 1981 edition of *B'chol L'vav'cha* (CBST), *Book of Blessings* (feminist poet Marcia Falk), *Siddur B'chol L'vav'cha* (CBST), *Kol Haneshamah* (Reconstructionist)

The members of the Traditional Morning Minyan took great pride in its existence. David Feinberg, coordinator of the minyan for many years, proudly declared at every opportunity that it was "the only regularly scheduled traditional egalitarian LGBT Shabbat morning service."

The minyan was always predominantly male, although its ritual policies, like all of those at CBST, were egalitarian. In 2005, in part to combat the persistent perception that the minyan was not inclusive of women, Irene Korenfield became co-coordinator of the minyan and it was later renamed the Traditional Egalitarian Minyan.

Inherent in the Traditional Egalitarian Minyan's mission were some ongoing challenges. A number of potential and former members preferred to be closeted at Orthodox synagogues than pray in an egalitarian environment. CBST's location made it difficult for people who did not travel on Shabbat to attend the service. In time, some participants returned to stricter ritual observances, partly influenced by the minyan, and eventually stopped traveling on Shabbat. As more Conservative synagogues became welcoming to gay and lesbian members and some Orthodox synagogues became tacitly tolerant of gay men, many members of the Traditional Egalitarian Minyan found a home elsewhere. A few of its regulars didn't attend other services at CBST and weren't connected with the rest of the community. Several members of the Traditional Egalitarian Minyan felt that it was one of the last places at CBST where lay people still had reign over services; they welcomed CBST's clergy at the minyan, but were anxious that they not replace lay people on the bimah. Despite these issues, the minyan has a deeply devoted core and continues to meet monthly.

**Liberal Minyan**

In contrast, the Liberal Minyan, described by coordinator Liz Galst as "davening in a consciously modern context," welcomed support from the clergy on and off the bimah. The Liberal Minyan was very much a part of the changing face of CBST. Its membership was organically mixed in terms of gender and age, and the attendees were eager to embrace liturgical change and engage in the issues the larger community was facing. The Liberal Minyan encouraged all CBST members to come to be called to the Torah for their first *aliyah* after completing conversion to Judaism, or to take on a new Hebrew name as they underwent gender transition. Most of the adult b'nai mitzvah services were held at the Liberal Minyan. The Liberal Minyan thrived under the leadership of Rabbi Cohen, Neal Hoffman, Andrew Ingall, Liz Galst, and Shelli Aderman. It also became the locus of a significant emerging demographic at CBST: families with children.

Rabbi Kleinbaum, along with members Tova Klein and Ron Kohn, created a monthly Saturday morning Tot Shabbat "minyan," which later became Alef Bet Shabbat. As more and more core members of CBST began to raise children, they sought to maintain their connections with the larger community. While attending Friday night services regularly was not an option for most families with children, Shabbat morning was a more feasible alternative. Rather than lose its regular members who became parents, Rabbi Cohen helped transform the Liberal Minyan into a place where families with or without children could comfortably daven together. By 2005, the minyan had expanded to meet twice a month and was scheduled to coincide, rather than alternate, with services for families with children.

Tova Klein leads a Tot Shabbat program, 1994.

The Liberal Minyan, which also became an important gathering place for CBST's older members, took pride in its informal, multigenerational atmosphere. Yet that diversity brought its own challenges as well, as the minyan strived to create an environment that was welcoming and comfortable for those with young children and still prayerful and intellectually rigorous for adult members .

LEFT TO RIGHT: Aari Ludvigsen holding Simon Ludvigsen-Gaines, Liz Galst holding Naomi Springer-Galst, Nancy Mertzel holding Shari Potasinski-Mertzel, Mark Lerner (obscured) holding Derek Frank-Lerner, Steven Frank holding Malka Aderman-Alcorn, Shelli Aderman holding Owen Boone, Yael Bat-Chava holding Talia Green, Rabbi Jo Hirschmann (obscured) holding Shoshana Hirschmann

Andrew Ingall with Shirley Hoffman-Ingall at Alef Bet Shabbat, 2007

## Feminist Minyan

Yolanda Potasinski helped found the Feminist Minyan in 1991 while serving on the first board that included three women. As the original coordinators ascended to other board leadership positions, Sandy Warshaw took on the minyan's leadership. Feminist programming flourished at CBST during the 1990s. In addition to the Feminist Minyan, Sandy coordinated the annual feminist seder and other programs which attracted a wider audience. In 1997, Sandy created the Book of Blessings Minyan, a Shabbat morning minyan that met for several years using the newly published siddur, *Book of Blessings*, by feminist poet Marcia Falk.

The Feminist Minyan saw it as their responsibility to make sure there was a feminist space in the congregation. Some sought to remind Rabbi Kleinbaum not to be overly conciliatory to the antifeminist men in the congregation and to push her to articulate more feminist values. Many experienced her as an important mentor for women's religious leadership. "I learned from Rabbi Kleinbaum," Sandy recalls, "that it was OK if we rewrote our own prayers, that even from my 'revolving door' Jewish background I could absorb more Judaism and become a leader. We had begun to establish ourselves as a Jewish feminist place."

As women ceased to be marginal at CBST, the need for a women's prayer space felt less acute. Many of the women who once felt uncomfortable in the main Friday night service now stayed to attend it. Early minyan coordinators Catherine Sull and Yolanda Potasinksi both became board presidents. Eventually the Feminist Minyan became Lesbian Voices, a Friday evening study and discussion group. In 2005 the group's name was changed to Feminist Voices to be more inclusive of bisexual and transgender women and of men. It stopped meeting regularly in 2007. Jack Greenberg reflects on the two minyanim, "I think the Feminist Minyan overcame the need for a separate space. After many years, the minyan ceased

Sandy Warshaw on Simchat Torah

### HOW I GOT TO CBST

I was down in the Village one day and read that Rabbi Sharon Kleinbaum was going to be installed at CBST. I felt this was a great feminist happening and decided to go. I sat in the back of the room, near the hospitality corner displaying all kinds of flyers about what was happening in the synagogue. One of the flyers was about the Feminist Minyan, although it wasn't called that yet. I thought, "This would be an interesting reason to come back." And that was how I got to CBST.

I had a prayer I wanted to use for a buddy I lost, and at the Feminist Minyan they let me read it. I thought, "OK, this is a place where I can be. At that time the Feminist Minyan met once a month and afterward we would go out to dinner. A couple of members of the minyan used to stay for Friday night services. One evening I decided to stay. I sat next to Nancy Mertzel, who pointed out to me that moving into the *Ma'ariv* service the *Barchu* was like saying "Hey God, I'm here." So now, when we get to the *Barchu*, every now and then I'll say, "Hey God, I'm here."

I grew up as a Revolving Door Jew—in on Rosh Hashanah, out on Yom Kippur—so I wasn't used to Friday night services. Even now when we sing some of the prayers, especially in the *Kabbalat Shabbat* service, I say "Ooh, I remember learning this. This was the first one I learned." So I began through the Feminist Minyan and then continued through Friday night services to deepen my own Judaism.

It was a fine place for me to be, because I was in transition, the synagogue was in transition, and it was a nice place to transition. The Feminist Minyan became my base. I got to know Yolanda Potasinski, Tamara Cohen (the sister of Rabbi Ayelet Cohen), Rosanne Leipzig, Regina Linder, and Lisa Edwards, who is now a rabbi in Los Angeles. That's how I integrated into the synagogue.

SANDY WARSHAW, MEMBER SINCE 1992

### REFLECTIONS FROM MY YEAR AT CBST: *BOOK OF BLESSINGS*

During my time as a Cooperberg-Rittmaster Rabbinical Intern, there was a monthly Saturday morning minyan called Book of Blessings. The group, which had always been almost all women, prayed using the Marcia Falk *Book of Blessings* siddur. I believe I was the first male rabbinical intern to have been assigned to that minyan, and I was certainly the only man to show up every month that year.

We rarely made a minyan (there were often merely five or six of us present), and the prayer style was both consistent and informal: We sat in a circle, read aloud from the book (occasionally we chanted the prayers to some Linda Hirschhorn melodies), and talked. Yet, without fail, it was the spiritual highpoint of every month for me, my first experience of truly feminist worship style. We didn't attempt to "pray by the rules." We weren't led by a lay or professional figure of authority. We formed each service as much through the inspiration and conversational response to one another as through the printed words on the page. Each prayer moment became an opportunity for dialogue, exchange, teaching, and learning. There was almost no perceptible rhythm to the davening—we sat, we read, we chanted, and we talked—and I always left with an energized spirit and a gratitude to God and to the group which I have only infrequently found elsewhere.

RABBI DAVID DUNN BAUER,
COOPERBERG-RITTMASTER RABBINICAL INTERN, 2000-01

to have a need to exist. Women wanted to be part of everything." While Sandy and others still mourned the loss of a predominantly women's space, many of the perspectives of the Feminist Minyan were now a part of mainstream CBST. In contrast, the needs of some of the members of the Traditional Evening Minyan were ultimately incompatible with CBST's values. "They really needed their own space that was Orthodox, not orthopractic," Jack reflects. By 2001, the Traditional Evening Minyan barely had a minyan most Friday nights, and the following year they stopped meeting altogether.

The Shabbat morning minyanim became a meaningful way to satisfy the diverse congregation and provide intimate and specialized experiences of community and prayer. Saturday morning services rotated between the various minyanim, allowing CBST members to seek out the minyan that best met their spiritual needs. Some chose one minyan, others attended multiple minyanim, their attendance varying along with their own Jewish journeys.

CLOCKWISE FROM TOP LEFT:
Hanna Gafni affixes a mezuzah to the door of Holy Apostles.

Volunteers prepared the sanctuary for CBST's services. (from left to right) Mike Vine, Liz Dornfeld, Hanna Gafni, Liz Deutsch, Sandy Warshaw, Michael Levine, Leslie Deutsch, Rick Landman, Yolanda Potasinski, Dick Radvon, Glenn Mones

Hanna Gafni and Lisa Kartzman creating the bimah table for the Chelsea sanctuary.

## Moving Back to Chelsea

The ebb and flow of the minyanim was a natural part of synagogue life over the years, as the needs of the community evolved and changed. However, many congregants believed that the main Friday night service was sacrosanct. Rabbi Kleinbaum maintained that this was the one time when the whole community would come together to pray. Probably the greatest controversies after the hiring of a rabbi involved changing the location and time of the Friday night service. The Bethune Street sanctuary, originally intended to be only a temporary space for the congregation, was unable to accommodate the congregation. In the early 1990s, High Holiday services had moved elsewhere to contain the crowds. Special Friday night services, such as Chanukah and Pride Shabbat, were dangerously overcrowded. Many felt the sanctuary was uncomfortably crowded even on ordinary Friday nights, with attendance regularly surpassing one hundred. Meanwhile, a growing staff required more office space, which would further reduce room for the sanctuary overflow. For years, the synagogue had been searching for its own space with little success. Something had to be done.

In 1995, Rabbi Kleinbaum asked Bill Hibsher and Marcy Kahn to co-chair the Mishkan Committee, tasked with finding an alternate space for Friday night services. Bill Hibsher recalls, "A dynamic committee of real estate professionals and others scoured lower Manhattan for a facility that could seat 400, was proximate to public transportation and parking, and would commit to availability every Friday night. We considered more than fifty spaces and recommended renting the sanctuary of the Church of the Holy Apostles in Chelsea." Initially, no one on the committee realized that this was the same building where CBST had first convened in 1973. The 1999 Board decision to rent the space was highly controversial. For some, leaving the familiar Bethune Street sanctuary seemed like an exile from

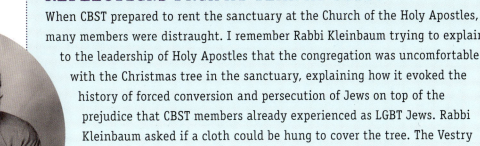

> **REFLECTIONS FROM MY YEAR AT CBST:**
> When CBST prepared to rent the sanctuary at the Church of the Holy Apostles, many members were distraught. I remember Rabbi Kleinbaum trying to explain to the leadership of Holy Apostles that the congregation was uncomfortable with the Christmas tree in the sanctuary, explaining how it evoked the history of forced conversion and persecution of Jews on top of the prejudice that CBST members already experienced as LGBT Jews. Rabbi Kleinbaum asked if a cloth could be hung to cover the tree. The Vestry voted that they didn't need a tree at all. They cared more about creating new memories of understanding, welcome, and empathy. They hoped CBST members would come to associate Holy Apostles with the friendship and respect offered by their neighbors, rather than the past mistreatment and harm that Jews have suffered. Rabbi Kleinbaum helped build bridges of understanding and the possibility of persistent hope and conversation in the face of distrust and hurt on all sides. I still can't tell this story without getting teary.
> RABBI EDYTHE HELD MENCHER,
> COOPERBERG-RITTMASTER RABBINICAL INTERN, 1998–99

home. The traditionalists were in an uproar, and the move became a lightning rod for members who had never accepted Rabbi Kleinbaum. They claimed their opposition stemmed from their discomfort davening in a church sanctuary. This was true for at least some of the dissenters, although one of the fiercest opponents to the move sang in a church choir. Some feared that the church sanctuary, which housed the city's largest soup kitchen, would be hazardous for people with HIV and AIDS, at risk for TB and other infections.

The board offered multiple forums to allow congregants to air their concerns. Rabbi Kleinbaum, Rabbi Young, and the Ritual Committee studied the halachic issues and determined that the sanctuary, with little Christian iconography, was an appropriate location for Jewish prayer. Many members from traditional and Orthodox backgrounds, like Daniel and Ian Chesir-Teran, felt satisfied with that determination. Indeed, in a city where real estate was at a premium, many New York synagogues shared space with churches. A number of members, like Bill Hibsher, who appreciated the poetry of returning to CBST's original locale, argued that CBST and Holy Apostles shared important values and that Holy Apostles' history of social activism, its early support of gay organizations, and its soup kitchen made it a profoundly holy place and a fitting home for CBST. Regarding the danger of infection, the board engaged experts to test the air quality in the

Holy Apostle's Rector William Greenlaw at the dedication ceremony

church sanctuary, and it was determined there was no health risk to people with compromised immune systems. In fact, the air circulation was actually better than in the windowless Westbeth space.

### Bethune Minyan

Unwilling to accept these arguments, a group of dissenters—led by past board chair Art Strickler—refused to move and continued to meet in Westbeth. The Bethune Minyan formed with the understanding that when the synagogue had its own space they would return to the main Friday night service.

The Bethune Minyan quickly reversed the changes they felt Rabbi Kleinbaum brought to the Friday night service. Some people were more comfortable in a smaller environment closer to the CBST of the 1980s, with more responsive English readings, abridged Hebrew liturgy, and where any layperson who wanted could lead from the bimah. Many members of the minyan eagerly greeted the rabbi, cantor, or intern who came once a month to lead services or to deliver the *drash*, although a few were less than enthusiastic.

After a few years, when the initial trauma of the split had faded, many of those who had originally opposed the move quietly returned to the main service at what became known as the Chelsea sanctuary. Others fell away from the synagogue altogether. By 2010, the group frequently struggled to get a minyan of ten.

### Service Time

The 8:30 PM start time of Friday night services originally echoed the late Friday night service of the Conservative Movement during the 1950s and '60s and was convenient for a population that went from shul to the bars. In the mid 1990s, the service time was changed to 8:00 PM, but by the early 2000s, with shifting community needs, many argued that even that was too late. In 2005, after a year's debate and experimentation with an earlier service time, the board voted to start weekly Friday night services at the Chelsea sanctuary at 7:00 PM. At a heated congregational meeting on the subject, objections ranged from personal convenience—when would people eat dinner?—to political undertones—were families with children trying to take over the synagogue? Some of the most impassioned objections focused on the parking rules near Holy Apostles. Some members preferred the later start, but ultimately attendance at Friday night services continued to grow.

The changes in time and location proved challenging for some of the Friday evening minyanim. The layout of Holy Apostles felt less hospitable for these events and services. The community Shabbat dinner, which started meeting in 1990, coordinated by volunteers including Larry Kay, Bill Rosenbloom, Sue Rosansky, and Ilene Block, had provided an intimate Shabbat table in a community where few people's apartments or family lives made it possible for them to host a Shabbat meal. After the Friday night service time changed, the community experimented with different start times for Shabbat dinner. Eventually, attendance declined and volunteer energy waned, and dinners were held only for special occasions.

## Evolution of the Ritual Process

Together, Rabbi Kleinbaum and Jack Greenberg redefined the role of the Religious Committee, now called the Ritual Committee, to adjust to the new reality of CBST with a rabbi. Rabbi Kleinbaum deeply appreciated Jack's immense Jewish knowledge, his staunch egalitarianism, and his openness to ritual innovation. She frequently remarked, "Any rabbi would be blessed to have a Jack Greenberg to turn to." For two decades, as Ritual Committee chair and *tefillah* coordinator, Jack worked closely with Rabbi Kleinbaum and later with Rabbi Cohen to design the ritual calendar and shape the ritual life of the synagogue.

As the congregation became more concerned with consistently raising the quality and musicality of services, it remained challenging to balance the presence of laypeople and clergy on the bimah. For many longtime members, nostalgic for the more homegrown services of the past, lay presence on the bimah remained important. Still, the congregation as a whole prided itself on the consistently beautiful and inspiring services that had become the norm. The rabbis had deep respect for the ritual lay leaders and took seriously their role of continuing to honor its lay-led past as a significant hallmark of CBST. Together with Jack Greenberg, the rabbis created a Service Leader's manual and offered classes and training for service leaders. Lay *darshanim* worked with a rabbi or a Cooperberg-Rittmaster Rabbinical Intern as they prepared their *drashot*. Reflecting on this mix of service leadership, Regina Linder said:

> I think the quality of services at CBST is unparalleled anywhere. Whenever I attend services at another congregation, I see the difference. The professional quality and the genuine Jewish sincerity of our services is just not equaled anywhere. Our spiritual leaders are all over the map in terms of age, education, in terms of religious training and backgrounds, and yet if you know each person individually you see they have a great deal in common, even going back to Reb Pinchas. They have a sincere traditional take on Judaism and a sincere desire to engage the congregation.

# 6. INSCRIBING THE TEXT

TRUE TO ITS "SHOPPING BAG" BEGINNINGS, CBST began holding Shabbat services before it had any of the trappings of a synagogue. Everything was borrowed or makeshift, from the kindergarten chairs in the Holy Apostles community room to the hand-lettered banners at the first Soviet Jewry rallies and Christopher Street Liberation Day Parades: the remarkable effort of a dedicated group of volunteers. While many members contributed to the ritual life of CBST from the bimah, others, like Dick Radvon, did their holy work setting up for services and keeping the synagogue's ritual objects in order. According to Pinchas ben Aharon, two older men named Al and Ben would buy the challah for those early services. He remembers that Ruth—an Italian American transgender woman who frequently attended CBST in its first two years—borrowed a few siddurim from an Orthodox synagogue. Before there were dues and a budget, someone would pass a basket on Friday nights, to gather donations to cover expenses, until, as Saul Mizrahi recalls, Carl Bennett objected that it was "too much like a church" and the practice was abandoned in the 1980s. But as the synagogue and its services expanded, CBST slowly began to gather the items it needed to function.

Candles, kiddush, and challah set up for a Friday night service, 1974

## The CBST Siddur

CBST's Friday night liturgy was always unique to its constituency, with its earliest leaders creating customized services from photocopied handouts. Yehuda Berger recalls that when Pinchas ben Aharon led services at CBST he would photocopy a new English reading every Shabbat to include in the service. The loose-leaf makeshift siddur was a constant work in progress. Soon Pinchas compiled his handouts into a makeshift Friday night siddur, which became affectionately known as the *Blue Shmatte* for the black and later blue cardboard report holder in which it was bound. The siddur was thirty-four pages and included a traditional, if abbreviated, Friday night service along with several additional songs and readings, most of which were copied from other siddurim. Most notably, this siddur contained Reb Pinchas's original translation of verses from the Prophet Isaiah,

CBST members marching with their hand-lettered banner at the Christopher Street Liberation Day Parade, 1976

transformed by his "midrashic" translation of the word *saris*, commonly translated as "eunuch," which Pinchas interpreted as "childless." This passage, as translated, has been included in every CBST siddur.

Let not the childless say,
"Behold I am a dry tree."

For thus says the Lord to the childless
Who observe my Sabbaths,
Who choose to walk in my ways,
And cling to my covenant.

I will give them a monument and a name
Better than sons and daughters.

I will give them an everlasting name
Which shall never be cut off.
If because of the Sabbath you will refrain
From doing your business on my holy day.

And will call the Sabbath a delight,
A holy and honored day of the Lord.

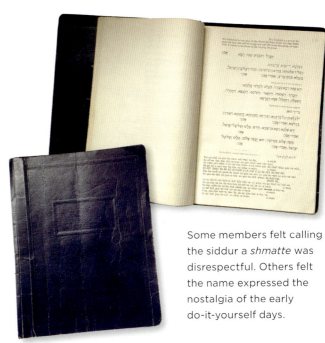

Some members felt calling the siddur a *shmatte* was disrespectful. Others felt the name expressed the nostalgia of the early do-it-yourself days.

## CLOSEUP: DICK RADVON

Richard Radvon came to CBST within six weeks of its founding and quietly made himself indispensable for more than thirty-five years. He grew up in the Bronx, the only child of secular parents. At age eleven, he asked his parents to send him to Hebrew School, but after two short-lived and traumatic attempts at nearby Orthodox and Conservative synagogues, he gave it up. "My Jewish life began with CBST," Dick later reflected. "When I came to CBST, I thought, my parents really should have forced the issue. They should have said, 'You're Jewish, you're going to be bar mitzvah.' But they didn't. It wasn't in them." Dick deeply regretted that he never had a bar mitzvah, not in the Bronx at thirteen, and not at CBST, where he joined the adult b'nai mitzvah program, but dropped out, overwhelmed at the prospect of learning to read Hebrew late in life. At CBST, he found his Jewish home. I thought, 'This is what I should have been doing all my life.'"

Out as a gay man in the 1950s at Bowling Green State University in Ohio, Dick joined a Jewish fraternity, one of two out of twelve on campus that admitted Jews. But he was mostly interested in exploring the one gay bar in town. After college, Dick joined the army and served in the Korean War. The end of a difficult sixteen-year relationship precipitated Dick's move to New York City where he made his home in a modest apartment in the Village.

At CBST, Dick made life-long friends with whom he bickered and laughed and enjoyed dinners out. Through CBST, Dick became close to women as well as men and to people of different ages. He embraced the presence of children at CBST and enjoyed being a bridge between the generations, passing down the lore from the synagogue's early days. "It's so important that we preserve the history of the synagogue," he reflected. But Dick struggled to tolerate younger people's embracing the word *queer*, with which he had been taunted during brutal schoolyard beatings.

"CBST is where my friends are. It's where I belong," Dick said. For decades, he and his close friend Michael Levine arrived early to set up for services together and went out for dinner afterward. Dick carefully put out the seat reservation signs and lovingly made sure the Torahs were properly dressed and displayed. His domain became the kiddush sponsorships, where CBST members would announce their milestones (sometimes in comical detail), carefully recording in his notebook each name, occasion,

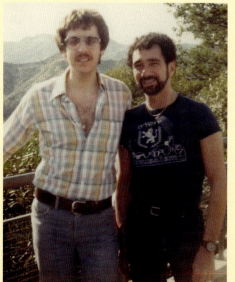

Michael Levine and Dick Radvon, 1978

and color of icing on the celebratory cakes.

Dick recalled that Arnold Mandelbaum, CBST's first board chair, invited him to a meeting at his midtown home. "Someone said, 'You're being groomed for the board.' I said, 'C'mon, that's outrageous. I don't know anything about Judaism, I never had a bar

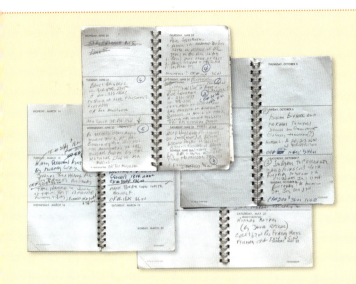

Dick's kiddush notebooks

Michael and Dick, 1990

mitzvah. I don't know what I'm doing." Dick went on to be CBST's longest standing board member, serving nineteen years, including terms on the Executive Committee and as vice president.

Dick often said that he got his Jewish education at CBST. He learned the services by rote, attending every week, and found the liturgy deeply resonant. He wept every year at the passage from the High Holiday liturgy "*al tashlicheini le'eit ziknah*, Do not forsake me in my old age."

Dick's last year of life was agonizing. After suffering a stroke on the eve of Passover in 2008, he moved between St. Vincent's Hospital and the Village Nursing Home, unable to speak or walk. Some close friends, including Michael Levine and his partner Ray Nacianceno, Robert Eppenstein, Ruth Gursky, and Judy Slomack, helped oversee his care. He died on the sixth day of Passover a year later, with Michael Levine and three members of CBST's clergy at his bedside. His illness helped bring to light the need to provide care for aging members without partners, children, or biological family. Robert Eppenstein reflects, "I think Dick would be happy that even at the very end he still had something to contribute."

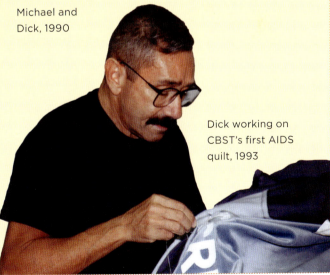

Dick working on CBST's first AIDS quilt, 1993

LEFT TO RIGHT:
Mark Bieber, David Krause, Yehuda Berger

These words were profoundly meaningful to a community of gay men, who in building the synagogue hoped they were becoming part of something that would serve as a beacon for other gay men and exist for generations to come. Most of them were childless—living at a time when being gay meant not having children or often being cut off from the children they had—but they dared believe they were creating something of profound value.

Always creating more handouts and wanting to deepen and develop the service, Pinchas had begun to work with Mark Bieber—for many years one of CBST's principal liturgists—on revising the siddur, but it was far from complete when Pinchas stepped away from CBST. In the late 1970s, the Religious Committee revived the siddur project. Yehuda Berger lobbied the committee to adopt *Siddur Likrat Shabbat*, which he liked and felt could be sufficiently customized for CBST by adding adhesive stickers with additional text, but the committee felt that no printed siddur would be adequate: CBST needed its own siddur. They appointed Mark Bieber, David Krause, and Yehuda Berger as editors. Yehuda recalls taking the PATH train to New Jersey on the weekends to work on the siddur in Mark's empty conference room at Best Foods, Mark painstakingly typing the edits on his Selectric typewriter and gluing the text on the pages with rubber cement.

### Siddur B'chol L'vav'cha

Completed in 1981, *Siddur B'chol L'vav'cha* was radical for its time. While it left the Hebrew text unchanged, the siddur eliminated exclusively male-gendered images of God from its English translations and included the names of the matriarchs, Sarah, Rebecca, Rachel, and Leah, alongside the patriarchs, Abraham, Isaac, and Jacob, in the translation. Those choices, determined by the three male editors, had an enormous impact on women joining CBST. Although in 1981 many members were still closeted outside the synagogue, while inside they could be openly and proudly gay. Giving new and profound meaning to the adapted texts, *Siddur B'chol L'vav'cha* consciously included the word *gay* (and, in later emendations, *lesbian*), which was not used in the *Blue Shmatte*. The English translations of the prayers and Psalms, mostly fashioned by Yehuda Berger, sensitively referred the truths of a gay and lesbian community. Echoing Reb Pinchas' teaching, from the paragraph of the *Sh'ma*, for example, "Teach them [i.e. God's commandments] diligently to your children" derived from the '*V'ahavta*,' while in the new siddur this was translated as "Teach them to the generations to come." In another example, verses from Song of Songs, allowed men to address male lovers using the words of the Bible. The translation of *L'chah dodi's* "God will rejoice in you as a groom over [his] bride" became "God will rejoice in you as lovers rejoice in each other." And in Psalm 118, where "*Kol rina vishua*" had been translated as "Hear the gay shouts of liberation . . ." became a song of victory against oppression and derision. Other prayers, like a prayer by Rabbi Chaim Stern that Yehuda Berger adapted for the siddur, expressed the longing for a time when it would be more possible to live fully and openly.

> קבלת שבת
>
> **kabbalat shabbat**
>
> **WELCOMING THE SABBATH**

A page from the 1981 edition of *Siddur B'chol L'vav'cha*

> O God of truth and justice, the evasions and deceits we practice upon others and upon ourselves are many.
>
> We long only to speak and to hear the truth, yet time and again, from fear of loss or hope of gain, from dull habit or from cruel deliberation, we speak half-truths, we twist facts, we are silent when others lie and we lie to ourselves.
>
> As gays, we often feel forced to pretend to be that which we are not, to present ourselves in ways which are not truthful, and sometimes with outright lies.
>
> But as we stand before You, our words and our thoughts speed to One who knows them before we utter them. We do not have to tell untruths to You as we are often forced to do in the straight world. We know we cannot lie in Your presence.
>
> May our worship help us to practice truth in speech and in thought before You, to ourselves, and before one another; and may we finally complete our liberation so that we no longer feel the need to practice evasions and deceits.
>
> Eternal God, purify our hearts to serve You in truth.

Prayers like this become words of inspiration and hope to LGBT people struggling for personal and political liberation. Some of the liturgical innovations of the siddur presaged the needs of the community. Long before it was fathomable that weddings would ever become a regular occurrence at CBST, the Prayer for Lovers, including an excerpt from the *Sheva Brachot* (seven wedding blessings), took its place in the siddur. The siddur also included a *Mi shebeirach*, the prayer for the sick, which by 1981 no other published siddur included in a Friday night service. As AIDS befell the community, this healing prayer would become an essential part of each Friday night service, and many new healing prayers would follow.

The siddur expressed a powerful vision of prayer and community that was compelling to members and non-members alike. On several occasions, visitors from other gay and lesbian synagogues took home copies of the siddur, changing the cover page and making photocopies for their own communities. One non-gay synagogue edited out the overtly gay and lesbian references to reproduce the siddur for their shul.

Nearly ten years after *Siddur B'chol L'vav'cha* was completed, the Religious Committee, then under the leadership of Saul Zalkin, initiated a plan to update the siddur, but the project never came to fruition, a casualty of the ongoing ideological conflict between ritual innovation and conservatism that flared at CBST during the early 1990s. (In fact, it would be more than fifteen years before a new siddur edition was ultimately completed.)

The 1981 siddur always regarded itself as a work in progress. Its editors intentionally skipped page numbers and bound the photocopied book in black cardboard thesis binders to facilitate the addition of new material. A few prayers were added to the binder, including Debbie Friedman's *Mi shebeirach*, other prayers for healing, and the Ladino Ein keloheinu, but more often the community resorted to the long-standing tradition of separate handouts for songs or special prayers.

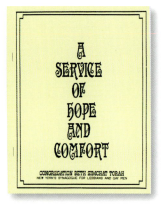

Yehuda Berger composed a service booklet with healing prayers during the AIDS crisis.

> At the rabbis' request, Reuben Zellman invited me to write something for the revised edition of *Siddur B'chol L'vav'cha*. To my total shock, it was included. I can't tell you how proud I am of that. Every time I open the siddur, I want to turn to that page. It's a very personal piece, in the voice of a young child. To me it's very tender, evocative, and also painful, but in a good way. That's what the piece is about. It's wonderful when it's read out loud during services. I love it every time.
> JILLIAN WEISS

### Siddur B'chol L'vav'cha, Revised Edition

One of the greatest examples of the way CBST evolved over its first three decades was the publication of the revised edition of the siddur, published in 2007. This was the first siddur to be professionally designed, edited, printed, and published, expressing a very different sensibility from that of the earlier offerings. Its pages reflect the significant resources and talents of CBST's members, and the awareness that a siddur created by CBST would be anticipated and read by the wider Jewish and LGBTQ world.

Editors Rabbi Sharon Kleinbaum, Rabbi Ayelet Cohen, Jack Greenberg, Yehuda Berger, and Marsha Melnick strove to create a new, inclusive, and relevant siddur. Under the direction of Rabbi Roderick Young, members of the Ritual Committee combed through existing siddurim and poetry books to suggest readings for the siddur. They also invited congregants to contribute original works. Rabbi Kleinbaum oversaw the ten-year process, contributing text and and commentary. Yehuda, still a creative and innovative liturgical force at CBST and the only editor of the original edition to collaborate on the new one, worked closely with Rabbi Cohen to create many of the translations in the siddur. Jack read and reread every draft, meticulously correcting every vowel in the Hebrew text. Rabbi Cohen wrote new liturgy, English translations, and shaped the structure of the siddur, while Tasha Calhoun, Rabbi Kleinbaum's assistant, secured permissions from sources that varied from the poet Marge Piercy to the estate of Reverend Martin Luther King Jr. With years of experience as an editor, member Marsha Melnick shepherded the unwieldy project to publication. Harriet Beckman, who worked in production, facilitated the printing and binding of both paperback and hardcover editions. Many CBST members and Cooperberg-Rittmaster Rabbinical Interns worked on the siddur, as well as Music Director Joyce Rosenzweig and Cantor David Berger, who contributed their expertise in Jewish liturgy, Hebrew, and song.

The siddur reflected the many changes within CBST and the landscape of Jewish liturgy since the 1981 *Siddur B'chol L'vav'cha*, its pages revealing the expansion of CBST's self-definition from "Gay" and later "Gay and Lesbian Synagogue," to include all sexual orientations and gender identities. The

One page from the 2007 revised edition of *Siddur B'chol L'vav'cha* illustrating Hebrew transliteration and commentary

קבלת שבת

התעוררי התעוררי      כי בא אורך קומי אורי
עורי עורי שיר דברי    כבוד יהוה עליך נגלה.

לכה דודי לקראת כלה פני שבת נקבלה.

לא תבושי ולא תכלמי   מה תשתוחחי ומה תהמי
בך יחסו עניי עמי       ונבנתה עיר על תלה.

לכה דודי לקראת כלה פני שבת נקבלה.

והיו למשסה שאסיך    ורחקו כל מבלעיך
ישיש עליך אלהיך       כמשוש לב באהבה.

לכה דודי לקראת כלה פני שבת נקבלה.

Hitor'ri hitor'ri, ki va orech kumi ori
Uri uri shir dabeiri, k'vod Adonai alayich niglah.
   L'chah dodi....
Lo teivoshi v'lo tikalmi, ma tishtochachi umah tehemi
Bach yechesu aniyei ami, v'nivn'tah ir al tilah.
   L'chah dodi....
V'hayu limhisah shosayich, v'rachaku kol m'valayich
Yasis alayich elohayich kimsos lev b'ahavah.
   L'chah dodi....

כמשוש לב באהבה/kimsos lev b'ahavah. The joy of the divine relationship with the people Israel is compared to the unique happiness of the heart or the soul rejoicing in love. While the traditional text reads כמשוש חתן על כלה/kimsos chatan al kalah, as a bridegroom rejoices with his bride, we expand the metaphor to embrace many configurations of love, knowing that our love for God—and God's love for us—encompasses the great diversity of love we may experience in our lives: romantic love regardless of sexual orientation, love between friends, between parents and children, love between other family members, and love within a community.

68

# REVIEWS OF *SIDDUR B'CHOL L'VAV'CHA*

"The introduction and history that Rabbi Kleinbaum provides not only explains and contextualizes this prayer book, it also constitutes a rich and inspirational contribution to Jewish prayer and human rights. The siddur itself is a brilliant combination of the old and new. It roots itself firmly in the soil of Jewish liturgical tradition and draws creatively upon a whole variety of Jewish sources, while providing a host of innovative and imaginative poems and prayers. *B'chol L'vav'cha* publicly affirms the pride GLBT Jews possess today, and provides a message of tolerance, inclusion, and inspiration that will facilitate meaningful moments of communal and personal devotion and joy for all Jews."

**RABBI DAVID ELLENSON**
**PRESIDENT OF HEBREW UNION COLLEGE-JEWISH INSTITUTE OF RELIGION**

"*Siddur B'chol L'vav'cha* represents a magnificent achievement and a cause for celebration—a prayerbook that is traditional in content, open and embracing of the range of human beings and their loves, stunningly beautiful in layout and look, and suffused with grace. Each page invites contemplation and prayer. Each *tefillah* glows with a love of our rich heritage and a yearning for the divine. And each new poem or prayer artfully blends contemporary voices with the depth and vision of Jewish sacred sources. This is a *siddur* that opens hearts even as its beauty and wisdom open the heavens."

**RABBI BRADLEY SHAVIT ARTSON**
**DEAN OF THE CONSERVATIVE MOVEMENT'S WEST COAST ZIEGLER SCHOOL OF RABBINIC STUDIES**

"I am in awe of the way you managed to create a liturgical work that is so deeply traditional and at the same time so revolutionary. The wonder is that it does not feel didactic or preachy—it actually feels like prayer. I always wondered exactly how Abraham J. Heschel thought prayer could be subversive and, at the same time, a humble response to the surprise of being alive. I think you have pulled it off."

**RABBI NANCY FUCHS-KREIMER**
**DIRECTOR, RELIGIOUS STUDIES PROGRAM AND ASSOCIATE PROFESSOR OF RELIGIOUS STUDIES, RECONSTRUCTIONIST RABBINICAL COLLEGE**

Siddur committee (counter clockwise) Yehuda Berger, Tasha Calhoun, Rabbi Ayelet Cohen, Jack Greenberg, Rabbi Sharon Kleinbaum, Marsha Melnick

new edition includes contributions by Jewish and LGBT writers who identify across the spectrum as lesbian, gay, bisexual, queer, and straight, as women, men, transgender, and intersex. Not only the English translation but also the Hebrew liturgy expresses a queer and feminist sensibility. The siddur features a vastly expanded section for lifecycle transitions and for holidays and special days throughout the year. Extensive and nuanced sections for World AIDS Day, Yom Hazikaron (Israel's Remembrance Day) and Yom Ha'atzmaut (Israel's Independence Day), and LGBT Pride express the community's struggles, maturation, and celebrations through the decades.

To involve the entire community in the project, and to ease the transition to the new edition, a paperback pilot edition of the siddur was used for a full year. The rabbis and Jack solicited congregational feedback on everything from the size of the page numbers to the language of the instructions on the page to the liturgical innovations. Many of those suggestions were incorporated into the completed hardcover edition. For the first year of its publication, one Friday night *drash* a month was devoted to exploring an aspect of the siddur. CBST members and authorities on Jewish liturgy greeted the siddur with great interest and enthusiasm. Many reviewers regarded the siddur as a major contribution to progressive Judaism.

### *Klei Kodesh*

Bill Fern recalls searching for a Torah to borrow for the 1974 High Holiday services. CBST approached a number of synagogues before finding Temple Sha'arey Tefillah on 79th Street and Second Avenue, which agreed to lend them a Torah. "I was one of the few people who had a car, so I wrapped up the Torah, stuck it in the trunk, and drove it down to CBST," Bill remembers. Volunteers fashioned an ark out of an orange crate with a curtain draped over it.

"Between Rosh Hashanah and Yom Kippur," Bill continues, "I stored the Torah in my clothes closet. After Yom Kippur, Irv said to me, 'Just leave it there until we get a chance to bring it back to the synagogue.' A year went by, and the Torah was still sitting on the second shelf of my clothes closet. I said, 'Irv, we've got this Torah.' He had never told the synagogue that we still had their Torah. I said, 'Irv, I cannot deal with this.' 'Don't worry,' Irv reassured me, 'I'll take care of it.' I drove him and the Torah to the synagogue. He went inside to explain, saying, 'We borrowed your Torah last year, and I apologize, but we never brought it back.' They said, 'We wondered where that went.' Irv asked if we could use it again for that year's High Holidays. And they told him, 'OK, you can take it!'" In the spring of 1976, CBST received a Torah of its own as a permanent loan from the Reform Tremont Temple Gates of Mercy in the Bronx, Bruce Friedman's childhood synagogue. By then the Jewish population of the South Bronx had declined to the point where it could no longer sustain the many synagogues that once

Irving Cooperberg (top) and Bill Fern

flourished there. The synagogue sold its building to the First Union Baptist Church, bestowing upon CBST both a Torah and the metal gates of its ark, which later became the centerpiece of CBST's memorial board. On June 4, the second night of Shavuot, CBST dedicated the Torah. Lou Rittmaster remembers driving to shul one Friday night, when Irving spotted a discarded chest of drawers on the curb. "Irv told me to pull over and put the chest in the car. 'Don't bother with the drawers,' he said. We tied the dresser onto the top of my VW Bug. That became our ark."

Unfortunately, the Hebrew script of the Tremont Torah was difficult to read, and the poor condition of its parchment made it almost impossible to keep it ritually kosher without constant repairs. The October 1978 newsletter announced the purchase of a second Torah, mantles, and silver, after six months of fund-raising for that purpose. As CBST held more morning services and the

BELOW: The ark constructed from the salvaged dresser, 1975

RIGHT: Lou Rittmaster in the sanctuary at 155 Bank Street before High Holiday services, 1975

CBST Newsletter, July 1976, announcing the arrival of the Tremont Torah

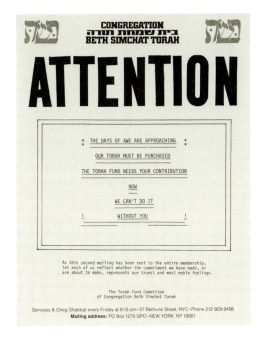

FAR LEFT: CBST appealed to its entire membership to donate to the Torah Fund, saying, "let each of us reflect whether the commitment we have made, or are about to make, represents our truest and most noble feelings."

LEFT: CBST's three Torahs with their silver adornments

Torahs were read more frequently, the Religious Committee recommended the purchase of a third Torah, a decision the board fully supported. Members of the Religious Committee, including Saul Zalkin and Jack Greenberg, took great pleasure in going to the Lower East Side to select a Torah, which was dedicated on Shavuot in 1982. The board easily approved the cost of the Torah, raised through the Torah Fund in a few short months. But when Mark Bieber and Saul approached the board, requesting funds to buy a silver crown for the new Torah, the discussion became contentious. Saul recalls, "CBST had bought silver for the Torahs it already had. Mark and I went to the board, saying, 'This Torah needs to be equally honored.'" Saul remembers the outrage at the board table over the idea of spending money on what some felt was unnecessary adornment for the Torah. "Irving made a speech about how focusing on the silver is like worshipping the golden calf. The board simply wouldn't allow it. At the next Rosh Hashanah services, when Irving saw the two Torahs that were dressed, next to the new one that wasn't, he went out and paid out of his own pocket for a *keter* for the new Torah." That story, which aptly describes Irving's extremely generous, if often unilateral, leadership style, also points to a conflict that continually reemerged: who had the right to make aesthetic choices about ritual objects. "It was really wonderful that Irving contributed the *keter*," Saul reflects, "but we didn't think it matched what the synagogue already had."

*Congregation Beth Simchat Torah expresses profound gratitude for your generous donation to the Torah Fund*

BELOW, CLOCKWISE: Jack Malick accompanies the Torah on the flight back from London.

Bill Wahler (right) carries the Holocaust Torah under a chuppah through the streets of the Village; Jared Matesky (left), Sam Levine (center).

Yehuda Berger with a klezmer band at the entrance to CBST

Hanna Gafni crafts the cabinet for the Holocaust Torah.

## The Holocaust Torah

When Bill Wahler learned that Congregation Mishpachat Am of Phoenix had obtained a Holocaust Torah from the Westminster Synagogue Trust in England, he was determined that CBST should have one as well. Acquiring a Holocaust Torah would further connect CBST to the global Jewish community, and it felt particularly meaningful because many children of survivors were members of CBST. Jack Malick flew to London to receive a Holocaust Torah rescued from the Kladno Jewish community. The November 1990 dedication of this was a momentous community event. The community's leaders carried it through the West Village in a procession from the Lesbian, Gay, Bisexual and Transgender Community Center to CBST. The Torah was displayed in a special cabinet built by member Hanna Gafni, whose own parents were survivors of the Holocaust.

## THE LITTLE TORAH

CBST member Richard Landman is the child of a Dachau survivor and a family of German Jewish refugees. His grandfather returned to Germany after the war and brought back three rescued Torahs, giving one to his synagogue and one to each of his grandsons.

Rick wrote, "I always felt a special duty to watch over this little 200 year-old Torah that survived the Holocaust. I was its guardian. Instead of having the Torah displayed in a Holocaust Museum, I wanted it to be used by people whose love of life and Judaism would be worthy of this old Torah. I also wanted to make sure this Torah would help continue to direct the history of the Jewish people for the next hundreds of years.

"My earliest memories of the Torah were when I discovered it lying on top of my bedroom closet while I was attending Hebrew School. At first I thought every home had its own Torah, sort of like a *mezuzah* on a door. But as I grew older, I felt uncomfortable seeing it every morning, so I made a curtain and turned the top of my closet into a small ark."

Initially Rick lent the Torah to his family's synagogue in Queens, later moving it to CBST, where it was used for almost a decade. In 2004, inspired by the reemergence of Progressive Judaism in Germany, Rick donated the Torah to the World Union for Progressive Judaism, to be used at Congregation Beth Shalom in Munich, where Rick's father's family lived before the war. Rick stipulated that the Torah always be used by a progressive synagogue. "I pray that the Torah will bring years of study and joy to the members of Congregation Beth Shalom and will encourage the regrowth of modern Reform Jewry in Germany, a theology based on progressive interpretations of the Torah, rather than those that promoted discrimination and the hatreds of the past. I believe it is *bashert* that I am in the position to give a Torah to the Progressive Movement. I want the new German Jewish community to continue studying the Torah and find the love, respect, and intelligence therein to help us all live in peace and grow as human beings. I think my grandfather would be proud: at first, a fledgling congregation in Queens, New York City had the honor of learning from this Torah, and then New York City's lesbian and gay congregation made a home for the Torah. My grandfather would be really happy that it was able to return to a Germany where Jews were once again full citizens and where tolerance of Jews is now the norm."

Rick Landman carries the Holocaust Torah under a chuppah through the streets of Munich, accompanied by the leadership of Congregation Beth Shalom.

### With Our Own Hands: The CBST Torah Project

On the first night of Shavuot 2010, almost thirty-four years to the day of the Shavuot dedication of the Tremont Torah, CBST dedicated a brand-new Torah scroll. Always seeking ways to encourage more members in every aspect of services, the regulars of the Shabbat morning minyanim had long wished for a Torah that was easy to read and light enough to lift and carry. Felix Wolf had been one of the members most frequently designated for *hagbah* in both minyanim for nearly a decade, skillfully unrolling the Torah to show much more than the required three columns, and lifting it high in the air, often while wearing one of his three children in a baby carrier on his chest. He was eager to share the role with others who were afraid to lift the heavy scrolls.

Shortly before she died, CBST member Myrna Reich met several times with Executive Director Ilene Sameth to discuss a bequest to CBST. While she didn't attend CBST frequently, Myrna felt deeply connected to its mission. "Myrna often told me that one of the greatest gifts she ever received was having an *aliyah* at CBST on Yom Kippur," her friend Danielle Korn recalled, explaining the reason Myrna left funds dedicated for a new Torah.

CBST decided to commission a new Torah of its own, transforming Myrna's bequest into a yearlong community experience of learning and exploration. Rabbi Cohen and Ilene Sameth interviewed numerous *sof'rim* who had worked with other progressive synagogues in order to find someone who would openly and enthusiastically embrace the experience of creating a Torah for an LGBT synagogue. Jack Greenberg and the rabbis examined dozens of handwriting samples to choose the *sofer* who would write the bulk of CBST's Torah and sought out a woodworker in Vermont to fashion the *atzei chayim* out of Forest Stewardship Council certified sustainable wood. The project committee, chaired by board member Sherri Dratfield and Jack Greenberg, included members Nicole Fix, Sandy Warshaw, Aari Ludvigsen, Laurie Siegel, Jack Nieman, and Judy Hollander, with Peter Klein and Liz Galst contributing their professional expertise. Ellen Wertheim designed a new mantle for the Torah, matching those she had been commissioned to make earlier for CBST's Torahs on the shul's twenty-fifth anniversary. Rabbi Cohen and the committee created a full year of programs, including learning opportunities with *soferet* Jen Taylor Friedman, *soferet* Rabbi Linda Motzkin, and *sofer* Rabbi Gedalia Druin. All CBST members were invited to write a letter in the Torah scroll under the guidance of Jen Taylor Friedman or Rabbi Druin, to embroider a few stitches in the *gartel* created by Ellen Wertheim

Danielle Korn (center), whose dear friend Myrna Reich left a bequest for the dedication of a new Torah

or mold a keepsake letter out of clay under the direction of Irene Riegner.

The Torah project was particularly meaningful to CBST members, many of whom had struggled to integrate Judaism with their LGBT identity. The two Leviticus verses interpreted as proscriptions of homosexuality are frequently used to justify cutting LGBT people out of religious life. Now CBST members could literally *inscribe the Torah* with the fullness of their Jewish lives and sexual identities and could take pleasure in knowing their Torah would be passed down to future generations of CBST members. Member and frequent Torah reader Leslie Bernstein reflected on sharing this experience with her daughter Emily, "Writing the letter in the Torah was a thrill—I don't think the effect of *l'dor v'dor* hit me until much later, and then I was totally awed. I kept humming "Oyfn Pripetchik" (the Yiddish folksong about teaching a child the *alef bet*). The Torah experience deepened my understanding of those *oysyus*. It was truly an experience of a lifetime that will stay with us all."

DECEMBER 9, 2009
RE: TORAH PROJECT OPENING CEREMONY

Dear All,
Last night was a wonderful moment in the life of our Congregation. The evening was a tremendous success--from Rabbi Cohen's moving introduction, to Ilene's touching words about Myrna Reich, to Rabbi Motzkin's fascinating presentation--and the effort and attention to detail that were involved in planning it were obvious. I was, frankly, blown away by the turnout (as I know others were), and the energy and excitement in the room were palpable. The creation of this Torah is a historic event for CBST, and you each deserve tremendous credit and thanks for your hard work and commitment to this important project, and for putting together yesterday's enormously successful kickoff. I am inspired by all you do for CBST.
With thanks and deep appreciation.

STEVE FRANK

# WRITING THE SACRED LETTERS

CBST members with *soferet* Jen Taylor Friedman and *sofer* Rabbi Gedalia Druin:
TOP ROW: (left) Sherri and Simon Dratfield, (right) Tasha Calhoun. SECOND ROW: (left) Gerry Faier, (middle) Laurie Siegel, (right) Harry Lutrin. THIRD ROW: (left) Josephine Kleinbaum, (middle) Nancy Meyer, (right) Stan Moldovan. BOTTOM: Maryann King

"It was both a privilege and an honor to be a part of this historic Torah project at CBST and to record in photographs these very personal moments during the act of writing the sacred scroll. This experience truly connected us all as a community to the receiving of the Torah at Mount Sinai." JACK NIEMAN

TOP ROW: (left) Matthew Gore, (right) Derek Frank-Lerner. MIDDLE ROW: (left) Jack Greenberg, (right) Barbara Dolgin and Hanna Gafni. BOTTOM ROW: George Perlov embroidering the *gartel* designed by Ellen Wertheim, (right) Laural Boone helping Owen Boone mold a letter out of clay. RIGHT: Shelli Aderman and Malka Alcorn-Aderman

# DEDICATION OF THE TORAH

TOP ROW: (left) Felix Wolf, (middle) Leah Trachten and Regina Linder, (right) Ron Weiss and Jack Greenberg. SECOND ROW: (left) Tom Mendel and Alex Weissman, (middle) Gary Adler and Andrew Berger, (right) Sandy Warshaw, Janet Zaleon, and Lea Rizack. THIRD ROW: (left) Charles Achuff and Adam Bender, (right) Sheila Pack and Ruth Gursky. BOTTOM ROW: Janet Pavloff. INSET: Jonathan Sheffer

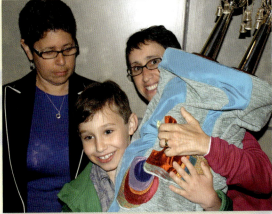

TOP ROW: (left) Tibarek Vexler, (right) Laurie Hanin, Jonathan Green, Lisa Green. SECOND ROW: (left) Shep Wahnon, (middle) Andrew Berger and Susan Ingerman, (right) Saul Zalkin and Michele Zalkin. THIRD ROW: Rafaela Anshel, (middle) Spencer Shear, (right) Shari Klugman and Debbi Berman. BOTTOM ROW: (left) Andy Austin and Joseph Cunin, (right) Stacey Harris

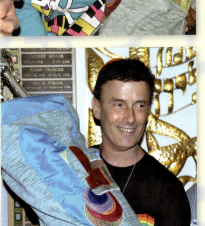

# 7. DAYS OF CELEBRATION AND AWE

From the outset, CBST celebrated every traditional Jewish holiday and, over the years, added some new ones, such as LGBT Pride, World AIDS Day, and Transgender Day of Remembrance, bringing a Jewish sensibility to days that became significant on its yearly calendar. Members also brought their own traditions to the shul, creating an eclectic ritual mix that became characteristic of CBST's celebrations and observances.

Since CBST functioned as a Jewish family for so many members, the shul made sure to offer home-style celebrations of several holidays, hosting festive meals, Passover *sedarim*, and break-fasts. Whether grand and awe-inspiring like the High Holidays or *heimish* and informal smaller gatherings in the sanctuary, each holiday was uniquely CBST. Encountering certain holidays for the first time at CBST, some members could not imagine them being observed any other way.

## The Festivals

Reb Pinchas recalled that, after the first lightly attended High Holiday services in 1973, Sukkot services, by contrast, were packed with people who sought out a Jewish community during the early days of the Yom Kippur War. Many of

For decades, member Earl Anthony Giaquinto adorned the sanctuary with his distinctive decorations for holiday services and celebrations.

those who attended that fall became longtime members. In later years, the Ritual Committee, the volunteer lay leaders from the Shabbat morning minyanim, and the rabbis coordinated evening and morning services for the three major festivals—Sukkot, Pesach, and Shavuot. For Sukkot the congregation built a sukkah (for many years both at its Bethune Street and Chelsea locations) in which members gathered for kiddush and meals during the holiday.

Simchat Torah, the synagogue's namesake holiday, was always a joyful celebration with spirited dancing. Rabbi Kleinbaum introduced the tradition of unrolling the entire Torah scroll, leading the assembled congregation through a Torah Travelogue as she and the other rabbis and interns point out the highlights of the five books and Joyce Rosenzweig and Larry Kay sing songs from each *parashah*.

TOP LEFT AND BELOW LEFT: The CBST sukkah built in the Westbeth courtyard in 1997 was a group effort.

TOP RIGHT: The sukkah was constructed and painted in part by Ruth Berman (standing) and Lisa Kartzman.

ABOVE RIGHT: Ellen Wertheim, Dean Dressler, and Cindy Levitz review what needs to be accomplished for its design.

# SIMCHAT TORAH

Before CBST, I went to a Reform synagogue for Simchat Torah. The rabbi announced that fathers and sons could get up and dance with the Torah. I asked him, "My son's father is gone, and my son wants to dance with the Torah. Can I do it with him?" He said, "No, only fathers and sons can dance with the Torah."

When I came to CBST, one of the happiest moments of my life was dancing around and holding the Torah on Simchat Torah. It's very spiritual for me. Every year I do it. One year I wasn't well and couldn't get up to dance. The rabbi put me in a chair in the middle of the circle and I held a Torah in my lap.

ANNETTE MILLER, MEMBER SINCE 1977

LEFT: Ruth Friedkin (left) with Annette Miller

BELOW: Sydney Rosenberg dancing with the Torah at a celebration in the 70s

ABOVE: Daniel Chesir-Teran (left) dancing on Simchat Torah in the Westbeth courtyard, 1998

LEFT: Simchat Torah in the Westbeth courtyard, 1992

TOP LEFT: In the Torah Travelogue the entire Torah is unrolled and summarized.

TOP RIGHT: Molly (left) and Liba Wenig Rubenstein at Simchat Torah services in the early 90s

MIDDLE RIGHT: Jerry Ganz dancing with the Torah, 1992

RIGHT: Dancing in the courtyard: Sariel Beckenstein (left), Jack Greenberg (far right) with the Torah

CLOCKWISE: Gloria Weiner and Dick Radvon on Passover

A table set for the seder on Bethune Street.

Bill Fern sits at the head of the seder table, 1975

BELOW: Rabbi Kleinbaum raising the matzah during the seder, 2007

Since 1975 CBST has held a community seder on the second night of Pesach, first at the McAlpin Hotel on 34th Street and Broadway and for decades later at its Bethune Street home. Saul Mizrahi helped match members seeking a first seder with willing hosts. With the creation of the feminist seder later on, the holiday observance was further expanded. In time the celebration of the second-night seder at the synagogue developed a more feminist sensibility and the Haggadah it used, the Reconstructionist Movement's *A Night of Questions*, included many readings by feminist and LGBT rabbis and scholars.

LEFT: Danny Pollock leading Israeli dancing at the Shavuot Tikkun, 1998

BELOW: Purim flyer, 1972

BOTTOM RIGHT: A Purim *shpiel*, 1981

BOTTOM LEFT: Elenore Lester, Yehuda Berger, Lou Rittmaster, and David Carrey on Purim in the Holy Apostles Community House, 1974

In her first year, Rabbi Kleinbaum instituted a Tikkun Leil Shavuot evening of study, which soon extended to last all night, as is customary on Shavuot, followed by a sunrise *Shacharit* service at the Hudson River. In true CBST fashion, the night of Torah study, taught by CBST's rabbis, interns, and members with occasional special guests, was punctuated by Israeli dancing at 2:00 AM, a tradition led for years by member and master Israeli dance instructor Danny Pollock, who connected the dances to the study theme of the night.

## Other Holidays, Traditional and Innovative

Early Purim celebrations at CBST featured elaborate Purim *shpiels*. Reb Pinchas affectionately recalled an Orthodox woman who came to one of the first Purim celebrations, held in the basement of an Episcopal Church. She had seen the *Village Voice* ad, "Gay synagogue Purim party." Fearing she was in the wrong place, Pinchas, who was dressed for Purim in a *streimel* and full Chasidic costume, asked

what brought her there. "She said, 'I heard about a gay synagogue. That's what I want, happiness.' I said,'You realize that gay means homosexual?' to which she replied, 'Oh no, there's no such thing as a homosexual Jew.'"

For many years, Purim was an opportunity for Orthodox gay people to visit CBST for the first time in the safety of the holiday's revelry, since traveling is permitted. Decades before there were any other gay Orthodox megillah readings, people flocked from afar to attend CBST's all-Hebrew reading. Inspired by the Talmudic authorization to chant megillah in any vernacular, CBST's main reading evolved into a multilingual extravaganza, with the rabbis costumed for many years by Rick Landman. Later Rabbi Cohen introduced a yearly costume theme for the entire congregation. The year *Brokeback Mountain* was nominated for an Academy Award, for example, the entire sanctuary was filled with cowboys.

## CLOSEUP: SAUL MIZRAHI

It used to be that you were either a religious Jew or you were gay. Not both. You do your job all day, you see your family, you keep your mouth shut. Then you run to CBST and you can be who you really are in all the fullness of your dimension. At CBST you can hold on to three thousand years of religious beliefs, which you have to do if you're gay because we are so persecuted. At the same time, we are also able to dress up as Queen Esther.

In the old days, I always played Queen Esther in the Purim plays. Everyone was in costume, and the songs were in Yiddish. Phil Katz, an active member back then, wrote 99 percent of them. They were fantastic.

Recently on Purim I was dressed up in my beautiful costume, and a little kid said, "Wow!" I replied, "Who are you? You look like a wizard." He said, "I'm Dumbledore," and I thought, maybe that's what it's all about. He loved my costume, and I loved his. He's a little doll, a little munchkin. I recognized that and I said, "it's a blessing." At first, at CBST, we had only ten men and one woman. And from there we have all these beautiful kids. That's CBST's evolution.

SAUL MIZRAHI, MEMBER SINCE 1973

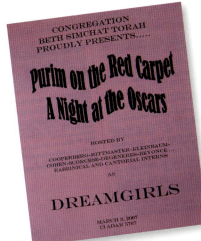

TOP ROW, LEFT TO RIGHT: Poster announces the theme of Oscar Night for Purim, 2007; Rabbi Roderick Young poses as the Queen Mother; Rick Landman dresses as Mae West.

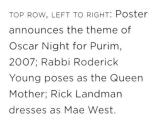

MIDDLE ROW, LEFT TO RIGHT: Earl Anthony Giaquinto as Queen Esther; Simon Ludvigsen-Gaines as an Oscar statuette, 2007; Rabbi Kleinbaum, Rabbi Cohen, and Cooperberg-Rittmaster intern Darby Leigh are cowhands from the film *Brokeback Mountain*, 2006.

BOTTOM ROW, LEFT TO RIGHT: Steve Fruh and Paul Marsolini come in from the rain for Purim; Ivan Zimmerman reading from the megillah; Mike Finesilver dressed for a masquerade; Jacqueline Jonée performs at the piano.

As most Jewish festivals include an exhortation to give *tzedakah* as part of the holiday observance, CBST chose an organization or issue in concert with the spirit of each holiday. On Purim, *tzedakah* is raised for Project Ezra, an organization that provides food for Jewish elderly on the Lower East Side; on Pesach, *tzedakah* is raised for Mazon, a Jewish Response to Hunger, or Rabbis for Human Rights' (now called T'ruah: The Rabbinic Call for Human Rights) anti-slavery campaign. By offering classes in preparation for the holidays, each became a significant point of connection with Jewish tradition as well as an opportunity for congregants to make the holidays relevant to their lives and to the contemporary world.

Yehuda Berger always encouraged CBST to challenge itself ritually and liturgically. He created a Birkat Hachamah celebration in 1981, the blessing of the sun observed only once every twenty-eight years, at the point when the rabbis believed the sun was in the same position in the sky as it had been at creation. Cooperberg-Rittmaster Rabbinical Intern Cecelia Beyer consulted with him to create the next sunrise ceremony in 2009.

Yehuda also introduced CBST to the idea of holding a Tu Bish'vat seder when the practice of celebrating the New Year for the trees was revived by progressive Jewish communities in the 1980s. The Feminist Minyan assumed leadership of the Tu Bish'vat seder as one among newer rituals members were exploring. Eventually that celebration expanded to include the entire community, featuring a Tu Bish'vat seder

Cooperberg-Rittmaster Intern Cecelia Beyer leading Birkat Hachamah , 2009

Tu Bish'vat Seder, 1996

integrated into the Friday night service or a guest speaker invited to talk about environmental issues in a Jewish context.

The shul's annual Yom Hashoah commemoration often features speakers who were survivors of the Shoah, including Lee Potasinski (board president Yolanda's father), George Vine (board president Mike Vine's father), and member Lea Rizack. On many occasions, CBST joined with other downtown synagogues for a community Yom Hashoah observance. When CBST first hosted the commemoration in 1991, two hundred people from ten downtown synagogues attended. In later years, the service has been coordinated through the Downtown Kehillah, a consortium of downtown Manhattan synagogues and organizations, with Joyce Rosenzweig frequently conducting a chorus created for the occasion, and composed of members or the cantors and cantorial soloists from the local synagogues. Thanks to the energies of member Rick Landman, CBST was one of the few synagogues to continue holding an annual Kristallnacht remembrance well past the seventieth anniversary of the event. That program has evolved into a special Friday night service, with organ and choir, devoted to the music of the German synagogues vandalized and destroyed on Kristallnacht.

Like most American non-Orthodox synagogues, CBST marks secular American holidays, such as Thanksgiving and Martin Luther King Day, with a reading or song in the service. The synagogue also observes significant days for the LGBT community, including World AIDS Day and Transgender Day of Remembrance, community milestones, such as the anniversary of its founding

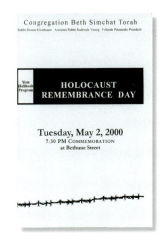

Yom Hashoah program

## YOM HASHOAH

As a Salvadorean who watched many of my people being murdered just because of who they were, by people who wanted power and believed they were superior, I have always felt connected to the Holocaust. My own survival, and the survival of the Salvadorean people and the Jews, gives me hope. As the years pass, generations keep healing and new ones are born beyond the evil. Many Holocaust survivors can still tell their stories, which carry the power of miracle and survival. Through the survival stories of Jews and Salvadoreans in exile, I hope to teach our future generations. They should be proud that, although we have a painful past, we also have a present and a future that reflects the bravery of our people.

PATRICIA MARTINEZ, MEMBER SINCE 2009

Patricia Martinez (right) and Zachary Metz at a CBST rally

BELOW: Molly Wenig Rubenstein inspects the Menorah.

BOTTOM: Rabbi Kleinbaum, Cantorial Intern Dan Singer, and Judy Ribnick leading Shabbat Chanukah services with chorus and sign language interpreter Jessica Ames, 2004.

and other significant anniversaries, as well as the installation of its clergy and the installation each year of its new Board of Directors. The 2007 edition of the siddur includes an extensive selection of readings for these occasions written by LGBT and Jewish poets and a few of CBST's own liturgists, Ron Weiss, Richard Howe, and Cantor David Berger.

The editors of the 1981 CBST siddur chose selections from Hallel—the psalms of celebration traditionally recited in the mornings on festivals, Rosh Chodesh, Chanukah, and Purim—to be recited on the Friday nights coinciding with those holidays as well as during the congregation's anniversary Shabbat and on LGBT Pride Shabbat. In 1981 this was a radical and meaningful innovation for a traditionally oriented synagogue, which regarded these occasions as religious celebrations of significance, beyond the immediate CBST community. Following CBST's example, LGBT Pride is celebrated at other LGBT and a few LGBT-affirming synagogues.

The Family and Friends Shabbat service is held the week before Pride. In the earliest years, when many CBST members were closeted in their lives

ABOVE: Rabbi Kleinbaum with Florent Morellet

LEFT: The Chelsea location is filled to capacity at Pride Services led by Cantor David Berger, Rabbi Cohen, Rabbi Kleinbaum, with Judy Ribnick and the chorus.

BOTTOM: Mayor Michael Bloomberg speaking at Family and Friends Shabbat, 2009

outside the synagogue, some felt this Shabbat service was a safe week to invite straight family and friends, because having so many guests made it harder to tell who was a CBST member and who was a straight visitor. It soon became a celebratory kickoff to the week of Pride celebrations, frequently accompanied by a festive dinner, and often an opportunity to hear from a straight or non-Jewish ally of the Jewish LGBT community. CBST's Pride Shabbat service has become a destination for Jews from all over New York and for anyone coming to New York for Pride. Both services have attracted notable guest speakers active in the movement for LGBT equality.

# NOTABLE GUEST SPEAKERS

CBST has built relationships with many communities and entities—LGBT, Jewish, New York City, New York State, the United States, and the State of Israel—and has attracted distinguished visitors from each of them, many of these political, literary, and religious leaders. Distinguished guests who have addressed the congregation include:

Frank Rich with Ruth Messinger and Rabbi Kleinbaum, 2001

Bill Hibsher, Dr. Mathilde Krim, Rabbi Kleinbaum, and Yolanda Potasinski, Family and Friends Shabbat, 1998

Tony Kushner and Rabbi Kleinbaum, Pride Shabbat, 1998

**1978** Manhattan Borough President Andrew Stein; U.S. Congressman Theodore Weiss; Rabbi Hershel Matt, early Conservative movement advocate for gay and lesbian inclusion

**1979** Rabbi Allen Bennett, Congregation Sha'ar Zahav

**1980** New York City Comptroller Harrison J. Goldin

**1981** New York City Council Member Miriam Friedlander; Rabbi Balfour Brickner, Stephen Wise Free Synagogue; Bishop Paul Moore Jr., Episcopal Bishop of New York City

**1982** New York City Council President Carol Bellamy; Manhattan Borough President Andrew Stein

**1985** New York City Council President Carol Bellamy; Mayor Ed Koch

**1986** Dr. David Axelrod, New York State health commissioner

**1987** Manhattan Borough President David Dinkins; Member of Knesset Shulamit Aloni

**1989** Rabbi Marshall Meyer, Congregation B'nai Jeshurun

**1990** Mayor David Dinkins; Thomas B. Stoddard, executive director of Lambda Legal

**1991** U.S. Congressman Bill Green; New York State Assembly Member Deborah Glick

**1992** Tim Sweeney, executive director, GMHC; Rabbi Alexander Schindler, president, UAHC

**1993** Georgetown University Law Center professor Chai Feldblum, principal author and negotiator for the Americans with Disabilities Act (ADA)

**1994** Composer and lyricist William Finn; member of Knesset Yael Dayan

**1995** Roberta Achtenberg, former HUD assistant secretary; Michael Lerner, editor, *Tikkun*

**1996** Evan Wolfson, Lambda Legal; Robin Shahar, plaintiff, *Shahar v. Bowers* landmark LGBT workplace discrimination case

**1997** Gad Beck, Gay Holocaust survivor and resistance fighter; Bishop Zachary Jones, Unity Fellowship Church

**1998** Dr. Mathilde Krim, founder of AmFAR; Tony Kushner, playwright

1999 Alan Hevesi, New York City comptroller

2000 Activist Reform Rabbi Balfour Brickner; Michal Eden, Tel Aviv City Council member

2001 Israeli consul general Alon Pinkas; Rabbi Robert Levine, Congregation Rodeph Shalom

2001 Ruth Messinger, former Manhattan Borough President and president of the American Jewish World Service

2003 New York City Council Speaker Gifford Miller; Richard Burns, executive director, LGBT Center

2004 Dr. Barbara E. Warren, LGBT Center; Alan van Capelle, executive director, Empire State Pride Agenda

2005 The Right Reverend Gene Robinson; U.S. Representative Jerrold Nadler; Rabbi Lynne Landsberg, Religious Action Center

2006 Scott Stringer, Manhattan borough president; New York City Council Speaker Christine Quinn

2007 Frank Rich, New York Times columnist; Randi Weingarten, UFT president ; Rachel Tiven, executive director of Immigration Equality; Rabbi Lawrence Troster, Coalition on the Environment and Jewish Life; Noa Sattath, executive director, Jerusalem Open House

2008 New York City Comptroller William Thompson; Dr. Marjorie Hill, executive director, GMHC; New York State Assembly Member Deborah Glick; Tom Weber, SAGE; Kevin Cathcart, executive director of Lambda Legal

2009 Mayor Michael Bloomberg; Evan Wolfson, Freedom to Marry; Hagai El-Ad, executive director of the Association for Civil Rights in Israel; Professor Susannah Heschel

2010 U.S. Senator Kirsten Gillibrand; Rickke Mananzala, executive director of FIERCE

2011 Gilbert Baker, creator of the rainbow flag; Cynthia Nixon, actor and activist

2012 Newark Mayor Cory Booker; Kate Bornstein, transgender activist and performance artist

2013 U.S. Senator Charles E. Schumer; Roberta Kaplan and Edie Windsor, lawyer and plaintiff, *Windsor v. United States*

Assembly Member Deborah Glick with the CBST community chorus and leadership, Pride Shabbat, 2000

Member of Knesset Yael Dayan and Rabbi Kleinbaum, Yom Kippur, 1994

U.S. Senator Charles E. Schumer, at Family and Friends Shabbat, 2013

### Days of Awe

CBST's Rosh Hashanah and Yom Kippur services have come to be iconic for the synagogue. The first High Holiday services in 1973 were very small, held in the failing Presbyterian Spencer Memorial Church in Brooklyn Heights. The following year, much larger services were held at the Church of the Beloved Disciple, the gay-friendly Catholic Church on West 14th Street. Bill Fern recalls:

> We had no money, so the only cantor we could afford couldn't really sing. He would change key in the middle of the same prayer and everybody would scramble to change key with him. The service was very abbreviated. I said to Irving, "I don't know if I can spend the rest of my life going to High Holiday services like this." He assured me, and I half believed him because I wanted to, "It'll get better," never dreaming at the time that it would become as glorious as it is today.

Rosh Hashanah services were first held at Westbeth in 1975 and could be accommodated at Bethune Street for more than twenty years. The Ritual Committee chose High Holiday service leaders and *darshanim* from among the most skilled lay leaders, wanting to provide beautiful and spiritually uplifting services for both CBST's members and the many guests who joined the community for the Days of Awe. Murray Lichtenstein, Jay Azneer, Shami Chaiken, and David Asch were among the most frequent High Holiday *ba'alei tefillah*, later expanding to include Rosanne Leipzig, Sariel Beckenstein, and Larry Kay. They shared the bimah with service leaders Saul Zalkin (who served in both roles), Mark Bieber, Jack Greenberg, and many others. For some members, the festive Rosh Hashanah

TOP: The first High Holiday service in 1973

ABOVE: CBST is proud to never have charged for High Holiday tickets.

## THE OPEN DOOR

In August 1975, as CBST prepared for the first High Holiday services in its new home in Westbeth, the newsletter proudly announced the decision to make admission free. Irving Cooperberg coined the phrase *Open Door* to describe CBST's philosophy of welcoming everyone, at no charge, to High Holiday services. As Dick Radvon expressed it: "We don't charge to pray, we don't ask if you're gay or lesbian. We just say: 'Welcome!' That's how it should be. That was Irving Cooperberg; he insisted on the Open Door policy. Some said, 'We can't afford this. Once Irving is gone, we'll have to make some changes.' Fortunately, no changes were ever made. Irving is gone—but it's an Open Door, and that's the way it is."

While orchestrating High Holiday services grew increasingly costly, the congregation remained committed, with the leadership repeatedly reaffirming the value of providing a free place for all who needed to daven.

meals, the work of such dedicated volunteers as Lee Levin, Irving Cooperberg, Lisa Kartzman, and Ilene Block were as essential to the celebration of the holiday as were the services.

By 1990, attendance at Rosh Hashanah had swelled to the point that chairs had to be set up throughout the entire synagogue, extending past the sanctuary into the kiddush area, out of view of the bimah. Closed-circuit televisions were arranged so that those not seated in the sanctuary could watch the service. In 1992, in anticipation of the first Rosh Hashanah with Rabbi Kleinbaum, CBST decided to hold two consecutive first-night services, one at 6:15 PM and one at 8:30 PM, with the rabbi and president repeating their remarks at both services. Despite exhortations that the two services would be identical, several members, knowing that Rabbi Kleinbaum didn't speak from a written manuscript, attended both services to hear if the *drash* changed significantly from one to the next. Two years later, the synagogue held a second, "liberal" first-day Rosh Hashanah morning service, which helped diffuse the numbers.

No matter how CBST tried to accommodate the increase, by 1997 the Bethune Street space was simply too small for the Rosh Hashanah services. The congregation convened at the Metropolitan Pavilion, a move Irving Cooperberg orchestrated shortly before his death, made possible only because of the extensive process a few years earlier that ultimately led to conducting Yom Kippur services at the Jacob Javits Center. As the

ABOVE AND LEFT: Observances of *Tashlich* at the Hudson River, 1975

services continued to expand, and the High Holiday service venue needed to accommodate space for children's services, CBST experimented with different locations for Rosh Hashanah, including the Hammerstein Ballroom and, for a number of years, Town Hall.

## The Crowds Assemble

As early as the mid 1980s, Yom Kippur services at Westbeth were full to overflowing. The board first debated moving elsewhere for the holiday after the 1986 services, and conducted a congregational survey and a special board meeting to reach a decision in time for Yom Kippur the following year. Some members passionately argued against being "exiled" from CBST's home on the holiest day of the year, launching a debate that foreshadowed the discussions about moving Friday night services to Chelsea ten years later. As a compromise, the board determined to stay at Bethune Street for the service, trying various solutions for managing the crowds. In 1987, a parallel *Kol Nidrei* service primarily for nonmembers was held in the Westbeth Theatre off the Bank Street courtyard. The two services were originally intended to be identical, but by the following year the overflow service was billed as an "alternative" service. The main traditional service continued to be reserved only for CBST members and their guests, whereas the alternative service was open to nonmembers as well. Some members grew to prefer the alternative service because it included more English and contemporary readings, but others regarded it as second-class and were disappointed if they arrived too late for a seat in the main sanctuary. Mel Rosen

BELOW, CLOCKWISE: A holiday meal in the mid 70s; chairs at Bethune crowded on all sides for Rosh Hashanah, 1991; Lisa Kartzman preparing a holiday meal, 1998

described the scene this way: "Over an hour before services, people line up for the doors to open, then race up the ramp to grab the seats in the front that aren't already reserved. People should be enjoying a festive holiday meal before Yom Kippur, not doing a hundred-yard dash."

With numbers growing each year, in 1991 CBST experimented with reserving preferred seats for members at the more heavily attended services and limiting the number of guest tickets. Even using this system, both services were filled beyond capacity. The rooms were sweltering and overcrowded. More members watched the service on the closed-circuit TV screens than could actually see the bimah. "Sitting and facing a TV screen is really not my idea of an appropriate atmosphere for davening," Irving Cooperberg remarked, while acknowledging that it was preferable to the alternative of turning people away for lack of space, which had created a great deal of ill will.

At the height of the AIDS epidemic, when so many people attended the Yizkor service, even the Yom Kippur day services had become dangerously overcrowded, with a thousand people attending, three hundred standing inside lining the walls and blocking the fire exits. Yom Kippur in 1991 was unseasonably warm. There was no air conditioning in the Westbeth Theatre, and the weak system in the main sanctuary meant that both services were unbearably hot. Despite the ongoing objections to leaving Westbeth, the leadership had genuine concerns about safety.

In his signature style, skillfully walking the congregation through a controversial change, board chair Mel Rosen wrote an article in the November newsletter describing the three records that had been broken on Yom Kippur: the heat, the numbers attending services, and the pledges handed in on *Kol Nidrei*. "People just wilted," Mel wrote. "The second service in the Westbeth Theatre was like an oven… All five hundred chairs were occupied, and people were lined out the door. It was like a furnace… If any of you were angry at the heat or standing room only, let me take this opportunity to apologize. The day after Yom Kippur, I appointed a committee headed by past chair Mark Bieber to review (as we did only a few years ago) all our options for next Yom Kippur."

The committee considered renting a single space in another location or—as a stopgap measure—holding a second Yizkor service in the afternoon. Mel wrote, "I was one of the congregants a few years ago who wanted to stay in the current space mostly for reasons of emotional attachment and familiarity, but we now need to analyze this from many points of view: our mission, comfort, costs, and safety."

The 1991 newsletter announced the recommendation that Yom Kippur service be held in a larger venue.

# THE WANDERING JEWS OF NEW YORK

### FRIDAY NIGHT/SHABBAT MORNING SERVICES:

| | |
|---|---|
| 1973–75 | Holy Apostles Community Room (300 9th Avenue) |
| 1975–76 | 151 Bank Street, Westbeth |
| 1976–2013 | 57 Bethune Street, Westbeth |
| 1999-2013 | CBST's Chelsea location (Holy Apostles Sanctuary, 296 9th Avenue) |

### HIGH HOLIDAYS

| | |
|---|---|
| 1973 | Spencer Memorial Church (Pierrepont Street/Monroe Place, Brooklyn Heights) |
| 1974 | Church of the Beloved Disciple (348 West 14th Street) |
| 1975 | 151 Bank Street, Westbeth |
| 1976–1996 | 57 Bethune Street and other locations within Westbeth |
| 1992-2013 | Jacob Javits Center (655 West 34th Street) (Yom Kippur) |
| 1997 | Metropolitan Pavilion (125 West 18th Street) (Rosh Hashanah) |
| 1998 | St. Bart's Church (325 Park Avenue) (Rosh Hashanah) |
| 1999–2002 | Metropolitan Pavilion (125 West 18th Street) (Rosh Hashanah) |
| 2003–2005 | Hammerstein Ballroom (Manhattan Center, 311 West 34th Street) (Rosh Hashanah) |
| 2006-2012 | Town Hall (123 West 43rd Street) (Rosh Hashanah) |

### PRIDE SHABBAT SERVICES

| | |
|---|---|
| 1975-1996 | 57 Bethune Street, Westbeth |
| 1997 | NYU's Loeb Student Center (566 LaGuardia Place Washington Square South) |
| 1998 | Congregation Ansche Chesed (100th Street and West End Avenue) |
| 1999, 2000, 2005 | Ethical Culture Society (2 West 64th Street) |
| 2001 | Stephen Wise Free Synagogue (30 West 68th Street) |
| 2002-2013 | CBST's Chelsea Location (296 9th Avenue) |

## The Javits Center

Irving Cooperberg understood that there was more at issue than overcrowding. He saw the need to find a new venue for services as an opportunity to realize a vision for CBST, to do what no one else in the Jewish world was doing at that time: to offer anyone who wanted, at no cost, a place to daven on Yom Kippur. Irving wanted to hold services at the new Jacob Javits Convention Center, a space that could comfortably accommodate two thousand people in one room. He offered to personally launch a new fund-raising effort that would cover the cost of the space.

Finally, in December 1991, the past chairs issued their recommendation to rent the Javits Center for Yom Kippur. A congregational meeting held that month allowed the whole community to voice their opinions about the move. Member David Ehrich recalls some of their fears: "It was unthinkable at the time: Would Javits even rent to a gay group? Would we be able to fill the space? Irving was a visionary. He was the person who was ten feet ahead of everyone else, opening the gate, leading everyone through it." After evaluating the community response, the Board of Trustees voted unanimously to move Yom Kippur services to the Javits Center in 1992. Irving raised the money single-handedly, following the board's mandate to solicit only people who were not already donors to CBST in order to avoid competition with the existing High Holiday Appeal.

When he stood to make the annual High Holiday Appeal during the first *Kol Nidrei* service at the Javits Center (Rabbi Kleinbaum's first at CBST), Irving articulated the significance of the moment. "Wherever we come together as a community, that is CBST. And on this night, this Javits Center room becomes our sanctuary. It becomes a home for the largest gathering of gay and lesbian Jews probably in history. I doubt if there have ever been over two thousand gays and lesbians congregating to daven—not to dance, not to rally, but to daven, and be part of a *kehillah*." CBST's Yom Kippur Open Door services at the Javits Center would become legendary in New York's Jewish life. Irving's vision represented the gift of the LGBT Jewish community to all New York Jews seeking a home on Yom Kippur not, as he said, "in the third catacomb of an immense stone building," but gathered in one room, together, with access to the "first string" rabbis and cantors.

> Dear Irving,
> I could not sleep last night after the High Holiday service. Being part of CBST at Kol Nidrei was so meaningful and exciting. After not having been part of a synagogue for nearly twenty years, I found I could be my Jewish and Gay self at the same time.

Gay legal activist Mark Turkel, in a letter to Irving Cooperberg, 1981

# KOL NIDREI APPEAL, 1992

Tonight's service was underwritten by about twelve or fifteen individuals. I asked people in the community (not too many members of the synagogue, because I didn't want to interfere with our High Holiday appeal, which I'm getting into now). I asked people who are known Jews in our community who had never been part of our community to help us. The first person I called said, "You know Irving, I'm not a religious Jew; I haven't been to synagogue in maybe twenty or thirty years." I said, "That's not what we're talking about. We're talking about our obligation to make sure that anybody who wants to go to a synagogue will have a place to go." That's what this is all about. It doesn't matter if you daven or not, whether you want to give out yarmulkes in the hallway, whether you want to be the parking lot attendant. The important thing about Jewish life is that we work toward our vision. He understood the vision right away. He said "Irving, would $5,000 be OK?" I said yes. I hung up the phone and bawled for ten minutes, because I was so thrilled. Right after that we got another $5,000 and a couple of thousands here and there. I'll tell you, I didn't get one refusal out of the fifteen people I asked. I am saying this because I want you to know that we're not alone. There are people who care about us.

We need to raise $200,000 this evening. We will not have comedians on the stage, we will not entertain you with Broadway personalities, but it is extremely important that we do this. We need at least a hundred people in the thousand to five thousand dollar category. There are, out of these two thousand people, a hundred people who will know what the stakes are, and what we should be doing, and be able to give that amount. We need another hundred people in the $500–$1,000 category, which is about $10 a week to $12 a week, so if you're in that category declare yourself tonight. And if you are in the $360–$500 category, declare yourself in that. And if you're unemployed, and you don't have anything, put a dollar in the envelope. The envelope you have tonight is a vote of confidence in what we are doing by having these doors open at all times, to make sure that there is a *kehillah* here, that we can take care of the needs of the community. We're not trying to convert anybody, were not trying to change anybody, we're just telling you that it's available and that we all have a responsibility. We're making an investment today for ourselves.

IRVING COOPERBERG

## The Preparations

Like everything else undertaken at CBST, the annual move to Javits was orchestrated by volunteers for many years. Yolanda Potasinski recalls the tremendous effort: "all of us shlepping prayer books, the bimah, *tallitot*, the *kippot*, the Torahs, and everything else we needed. The group generally included Dick Radvon, Michael Levine, Lisa Kartzman, Sandy Faddis, and Robert Eppenstein, a small number who worked really hard." As the service and the synagogue staff expanded, the team has grown to include several staff members and a professional stage manager to prepare for the four thousand people who regularly attend the *Kol Nidrei* service. (In 2001, just days after the September 11 terrorist attacks, six thousand people came to daven with CBST for *Kol Nidrei*. The service was held in the basement, while New York State Troopers were stationed in the windowed space upstairs.)

Even before services begin, the atmosphere at Javits is electric. Year after year, CBST member volunteers, clergy, and staff who arrive early to prepare for the service remark that it is thrilling to be in the stillness of the immense room, overlooking the endless rows of empty chairs waiting to be filled. The hum of activity slowly increases, as people dart through the room, making sure everything is ready. When the doors finally open, lines of people are waiting to file in, to assemble in one room, experiencing the darkening sky through the vast windows, the late afternoon light reflecting on the Hudson River.

CLOCKWISE FROM LEFT TO RIGHT: The sign welcoming all who arrive at the Javits Center; prayer books are readied for the thousands who enter; the massive number of chairs will soon be filled; volunteers—Linda Vogel, Danielle Korn, Judy Hollander, and Josephine Kleinbaum—are set up to register attendees who are waiting for the doors to open.

## CLOSEUP: IRVING COOPERBERG

Irving Cooperberg had three great loves: Lou Rittmaster, CBST, and the LGBT Center. He often said that his best contributions were the hiring of Richard Burns as executive director of the Center and Rabbi Kleinbaum at CBST. He acted as a father to both.

Born in Bushwick, Brooklyn, Irving's family lived behind the store where his mother, a smart, strong-willed business woman, worked twenty hours a day. Irving attended pharmaceutical college before enlisting in the U.S. Army and serving in Korea, administering blood banks for mobile army surgical units. He worked for Pfizer upon his return, establishing and operating storefront blood banks. In 1963, Irving opened his first coin-operated laundry on 34th Street. That year, he also bought a home in the fledgling gay community on Fire Island Pines. His laundries and real estate investments made him a wealthy man. His parents' values of tolerance, commitment to community, and *hachnasat orchim* (welcoming guests) informed the generosity and community building that became Irving's hallmark. As Bill Hibsher recalls, "Irving helped teach a tradition of giving." Irving remained deeply connected to his Orthodox family of origin, a connection that Lou Rittmaster maintained long after Irving's death, traveling long distances to attend family *simchahs*.

When Irving came to CBST in its first year, just after the Yom Kippur War broke out, he immediately made the shul his home. Lou remembers that their first date was at the synagogue. "We went to meetings, we went to shul; we talked synagogue. We dated every day for two weeks and then I moved in. Irving forgot to tell me that the day I was moving in he had invited about twenty people to the apartment for a synagogue consciousness-raising and fund-raising drive. I traipsed back and forth right through the meeting in the living room, carrying shopping bags that contained all my worldly possessions." Their home on 35th Street became a gathering place after services and for Rosh Hashanah dinners, seders, and synagogue meetings. Irving often said his home with Lou gave him the support to do the work about which he felt so passionate.

Irving collected people. Bill Fern recalls that Irving was skilled at spotting young people who seemed to have great potential. He and Lou served as surrogate fathers, mentors, and protectors for many of them, giving them jobs in the laundry while they finished their dissertations or struggled to put themselves through school. For member Asher Quell, Irving's "outstretched hand of friendship, patient counsel, and parental prodding were very important elements in my life.... He was incisive, wise, and helpful, constantly reminding me to participate in family and community and not to cut myself off. He always backed up his lessons by personal example." Lou once said to Irving, "If you were straight, you could have stayed *frum*, raised a bunch of kids, and lived an ordinary life." Irving's response: "It wasn't meant to be. My family is the community. I can do better than raise four or five kids. I can raise hundreds." Indeed, Irving left behind dozens of adopted children and protégés, and countless people whose lives were transformed by the work of CBST and the Center.

Irving lived openly and courageously with AIDS for twelve years, an astounding survival in the early days

Irving and Lou at a Soviet Jewry rally in the 1970s

of AZT. He told everyone of his illness, insisting it was possible to live with AIDS, and encouraged gay men to get tested so that they could live with knowledge rather than fear the possibilities. When Irving was first diagnosed Lou asked, "What should we do? Should we go on a trip around the world?" "No," Irving replied, "I'm doing exactly what I want to be doing now." He and Lou had a "good-bye" party for their thirteenth anniversary, thinking they had little time left—and then another celebration for their twentieth anniversary.

Irving was idiosyncratic and could be difficult to work with—he wasn't always patient and sometimes lost his cool, bulldozing those who disagreed with him. His confidence in his rightness was maddening to his opponents, especially when he turned out to be right. But that didn't stop Irving. He was determined to act on his vision, even if it meant people didn't like him.

Irving served as board chair twice, first in the 1980s and then again to preside over Rabbi Kleinbaum's arrival when Mel Rosen was dying of AIDS. For Rabbi Kleinbaum, Irving was one of the most profound teachers of her life, and his imprint is still evident in her leadership of CBST.

Stepping down as chair of the board in 1994, Irving wrote in his farewell speech, "I've always been proud of whatever role I have taken with CBST these last twenty years. My energies are now limited, allowing me time to work only on specific projects, such as long-range planning to

ensure that CBST is prepared for the twenty-first century as a major force for justice and rights for lesbians and gays throughout the world, the Jewish community, and people everywhere. Thank you for giving me the opportunity to help these past twenty years."

As a founder and first president of what is now called the Lesbian, Gay, Bisexual & Transgender Community Center, Irving orchestrated the purchase of a vacant building from the city, almost single-handedly raising the money before the city deadline, largely with contributions from CBST members.

Irving keenly understood the importance of the daily work of CBST, but also its larger significance. "The basic thing is to have courage," Irving said. "On good days, we do everything we can. Bad days take care of themselves."

Booklet created for Irving's funeral

The *Kol Nidrei* service begins (top): Adria Benjamin (above) plays the viola for one of the recitations of *Kol Nidrei*.

### The Music

When Joyce Rosenzweig became CBST's part-time music director in 1994, she coached the *ba'alei tefillah* and rehearsed the newly created CBST Community Chorus, which sang a few pieces during High Holiday services. Joyce recalls writing an arrangement of *Kol Nidrei* for *ba'alat tefillah* Karen Krop to sing and for Adria Benjamin to play the viola. Adria's viola has become a moving element of *Kol Nidrei* every year. Soon Joyce joined CBST for High Holiday services, first conducting the a cappella chorus and later playing piano to accompany the chorus and cantorial voices. Under her direction, the music grew increasingly elaborate and the task of the High Holiday *ba'alei tefillah* became more complex. Joyce introduced musical settings from throughout the Jewish world, rehearsing the chorus for months to prepare for the High Holidays. In 1999, after an extensive congregational search process, CBST hired members and frequent Friday night *ba'alei tefillah* Larry Kay and Judy Ribnick— both of whom had professional cantorial experience at High Holiday services held at other synagogues—as the main High Holiday *ba'alei tefillah*. The two led High Holiday services for six years. Since 2005, Larry Kay has led the major services with cantorial intern (later Cantor) David Berger and with cantorial interns and soloists Jason Kaufman, Magda Fishman, and Re'ut Ben Ze'ev.

## The Liturgy

In keeping with CBST's ritual practices, the High Holiday services have been an eclectic mix of progressive and traditional Judaism. In 1999, the congregation began using the Reconstructionist movement's *Kol Haneshamah machzor*, replacing the Conservative Harlow *machzor* and the photocopied *machzorim* the Religious Committee had created for use at nearly every service. Pinchas ben Aharon remembers a conflict over doing *koreen* (full prostration) during the Yom Kippur service: "The first Yom Kippur at Westbeth I said we should do *koreen*. Irving Cooperberg was totally opposed to it, saying, 'This place looks like a mosque.'" Personally Pinchas recognized this as a moment when his increasing traditionalism might be incompatible with CBST's customs. Years later, when Rabbi Cohen led the Yom Kippur *Musaf* service, emphasizing its drama and theatricality, she encouraged the congregation to try out *koreen*, and, as the years moved on, more and more people have adopted the practice.

Some of the High Holiday prayer books and supplements created by CBST through the years, and the *Kol Haneshamah machzor* CBST eventually adopted.

## Experiencing the Awe

Although the sheer size of CBST's High Holiday services is remarkable, the spirit of offering an open door provides a far deeper significance. Standing on the bimah for the first *Kol Nidrei* service at Javits, Jack Greenberg was overcome by the sea of two thousand people before him. Saul Zalkin recalls leading a *Shacharit* service with Larry Kay at the Metropolitan Pavilion. "I was moved not because I was saying anything remarkable or brilliant but because we together—Larry and I and the congregation—were creating something wonderful. We sang together, we read together, and, as the service went on, the crowd got larger and larger. Unless you're on the bimah, looking out at the community, you have no idea of the magnitude of the congregation. *Ba'alat tefillah* Judy Ribnick recalls, "It was both thrilling and an awesome sense of responsibility reaching out to have my

### SOCIAL JUSTICE ON THE HIGH HOLIDAYS

Without question, Rabbi Kleinbaum's *drashot* access the spiritual through the political. How can one consider oneself spiritual without also being righteous, speaking out against injustice? Remove the moral impetus and what's left is a hollow spiritualism. I was deeply moved by the connection she made.

NICOLE FIX, 2010

## A SPIRITUAL MOMENT TOGETHER

It was Rosh Hashanah of 2004, and we were standing at the bimah on stage at the Hammerstein Ballroom in front of over fifteen hundred people.

We were about to sing a meditation before the *Sh'ma* by Jeff Klepper called "Open Up Our Eyes." I looked to my left at Rabbi Kleinbaum to see what she would say to introduce the piece. As a profoundly Deaf individual, I find the spoken word is much more challenging to understand than Sign Language. I depend heavily on lipreading to understand hearing people, so I had to turn to her to see what she would say.

As we made eye contact, she said, "Why don't you teach us to sign this." I must have mislipread her. My expression belied my confusion, and so she repeated herself, slowly, speaking directly to me. "Teach us to sign it." I glanced down at the words of the song.

She was serious. I took a deep breath and leaned toward the microphone. "We're going to try something a little different. We're going to sing this next song in English and in American Sign Language." I demonstrated the ASL translation for each phrase and within a matter of minutes I was conducting the largest ASL choir I had ever seen in my life. The focus and care that every individual brought to each sign was powerful, as the hands and voices and souls of fifteen hundred people joined together.

Rabbi Kleinbaum and this experience taught me that it is indeed possible to work together to create a spiritually powerful moment for a community, no matter how small or large. On a personal level, it (and she) reinforced for me that as a Deaf person/rabbi, I too could bring something meaningful to that process.

RABBI DARBY JARED LEIGH, COOPERBERG-RITTMASTER RABBINICAL INTERN, 2004-05, 2005-06

Cooperberg-Rittmaster Rabbinical Intern Darby Leigh preparing to help lead a service

spirit extend to all the corners of the room. Although I am more comfortable in a more intimate *shtiebel* environment, I experienced amazing moments of intimacy, of connection, that were really profound. To daven with a *shtiebel* is one thing, to daven with three or four thousand people is astounding. To hear so many people stamping and chanting with a Chasidic *niggun*. . . . It's a sacred and challenging endeavor." Irving Cooperberg described the first *N'ilah* service with Rabbi Kleinbaum at the Javits Center. "All major artificial lights were turned off. The slowly setting sun was visible through the glass walls. Our rabbi, as service leader, and Larry Kay, as *chazzan*, were flanked by the former past chairs of the synagogue (a custom that grew to include the entire board) as the assembled

As the sun begins to set, congregants listen expectantly for *Kol Nidrei* to begin.

congregants prayed through the hour-long service, creating an awe of divinity."

Members look forward to the different voices that have come from the bimah on the High Holidays: Rabbi Kleinbaum's mix of humor and depth as she welcomes the community to services, the moving membership and Yizkor speeches given by members, Rabbi Cohen's scholarly and poetic Rosh Hashanah *drashot*, Rabbi Kleinbaum's fiery and funny *Kol Nidrei drashot*, Rabbi Weiss's joyful children's services, even the board president's lovingly crafted *Kol Nidrei* appeal. Past board president Lisa Kartzman describes how she came to feel when Rabbi Cohen led the Yom Kippur *Musaf* service. "I used to have every excuse in the world not to sit through *Musaf*. 'Just get me out of there!' But it's changed me to be able to sit through it and listen to the stories and learn." Saul Zalkin recalls a particularly moving moment one Yom Kippur when Cantor David Berger was leading the service. "It was during the *Unetaneh tokef* prayer on Yom Kippur, when we talk about who will live and who will die. Here I'm standing, before the ark at the Javits Center—I still get chills. It's the closest we have to being in the holy of holies."

# 8. SINGING A NEW SONG

Music has always played a key role in elevating the spiritual experience of Friday night services at CBST. Pinchas ben Aharon played recorded music during services, his partner Jerry operating the tape recorder or record player as daveners leapt to their feet after *L'chah dodi* and danced. Members Murray Lichtenstein and Jay Azneer brought the flavor of classical *chazzanut* to the services they led. The joyful davening of the *ba'alei tefillah* conveyed their love of music and liturgy, and gratitude for the freedom to lead prayer openly and honestly as LGBT Jews. Congregants agreed that the informal atmosphere and spirited singing set CBST apart from the stultifying, passive synagogue experiences of their childhoods. From the outset, the entire congregation actively participated in the services.

## Music in the 1970s and 1980s

While some *ba'alei tefillah*, like David Asch and Saul Zalkin, were trained musicians, they didn't necessarily carry their secular musical influences into their service leadership. Typically, the *ba'alei tefillah* in the early years drew from a fairly

Ya'akov Gladstone conducts an early volunteer chorus on Chanukah, 1979.

The Flirtations perform at CBST in the 1980s (Elliot Pilshaw is second from the right).

BELOW: Elliot Pilshaw and Lorin Sklamberg performed at an *oneg* in June 1984.

**GAY MUSIC MAKING**

The evening of Saturday, June 25, is sure to enter the annals of gay music-making in New York City, when two major West Coast talents appear here for the first time. The Peoples' Voice Cafe, at 388 West Broadway, in Soho, will present a double bill of Elliot Pilshaw & Lorin Sklamberg and The Choral Majority. The program starts at 8 PM. Admission is $4 or TDF voucher.

ELLIOT PILSHAW & LORIN SKLAMBERG

Elliot and Lorin, who will be appearing the previous evening at CBST's Oneg Shabbat program, have a repertoire of songs that are challenging and questioning, angry and uplifting, hopeful and soothing. They draw from many musical sources, including beautiful Hebrew melodies and contemporary women's movement songs.

The Choral Majority is a bold, blaspheming quartet crusading and caroling against the New Right, Reaganomics and all things homophobic and politically incorrect.

So, before you head down to our Gay & Lesbian Pride Dance on the 25th, pay a visit to Peoples' Voice Cafe to hear some fine music for this special weekend.

standard Conservative and Orthodox Ashkenazi canon, although there were some forays into newer settings, such as those written by Debbie Friedman and other contemporary composers. Member Shami Chaiken's composition for *V'shamru* was a regular feature at services for many years and, decades later, would be sung on CBST's anniversary Shabbat service to evoke the spirit of that era.

While the music for services was familiar, if fairly predictable for a musically sophisticated congregation, the experience of the service varied greatly depending on the volunteer *ba'al tefillah*. Ruth Plave recalls, "You never knew what you were going to get in a service." Some *ba'alei tefillah* were quite musically accomplished, like Elliot Pilshaw, a founding member of the gay activist a capella group, The Flirtations. Judy Ribnick arrived in 1985 with years of experience leading services at her home Conservative synagogue in Minneapolis and comfortably assumed a role on the bimah. She taught a CBST music workshop in 1987 in which several frequent *ba'alei tefillah*, including Rafaela Anshel, Janet Sonnenstein (now Shayna Caul), and Shami Chaiken participated. In the late 1980s, Judy assembled a modest volunteer chorus that sang occasionally at special services or events, one of a few such efforts over the years. Before moving to New York in 1989, Larry Kay had served as part-time cantor at a Connecticut Conservative synagogue. He too became a regular Friday night and High Holiday *ba'al tefillah*.

## Joyce Rosenzweig Comes to CBST

In her 1992 installation address, Rabbi Kleinbaum invited members to "imagine a CBST that is a center for Jewish arts. Our members are among the most talented artists in this city. Let us create a Jewish community where music, theater, literature all flourish and our souls are enriched." With her deep appreciation of music, Rabbi Kleinbaum maintained that a community with so many skilled musicians and avid music lovers offered great potential to expand musically. She invited ApiChorus, an a capella singing group from RRC, to sing at her installation, in part to model how a wider repertoire of music might transform services at CBST.

In early 1994, knowing of Rabbi Kleinbaum's interest in building a great music program at CBST, Rabbi Margaret Moers Wenig, her partner at that time and a colleague of the highly respected musician Joyce Rosenzweig, suggested that Joyce be hired to direct that program. Without ever having met Joyce before, Rabbi Kleinbaum went to HUC trying to convince Joyce to come to CBST. According to Rabbi Kleinbaum, she dropped to the floor, begging Joyce to come to CBST. Joyce remembers the invitation as somewhat less dramatic but still surprising. After all, she and Rabbi Kleinbaum had never met, although Joyce, a friend of one of the founders of ApiChorus, had attended Rabbi Kleinbaum's installation. According to Joyce, "Rabbi Kleinbaum came to my office and proclaimed, 'We want you to come to CBST to enhance the music of services, but we're not sure what we want you to do.' I said, 'I'm a pianist, I can come and

Newsletter announcing the recruitment of Joyce Rosenzweig to direct an experimental chorus to celebrate CBST's twenty-first anniversary, March 1994

### Ad Hoc CBST Community Chorus Adds to Anniversary Shabbat

By Michael L. Lehrman

A festive Shabbat service on February 4/23 Shevat heralded the observance of CBST's 21st anniversary. The shul ushered in this landmark occasion with flair and pizzazz, as a newly formulated in-house chorus for Congregation Beth Simchat Torah was introduced. During scheduled celebrations featuring Rabbi Kleinbaum and Larry Kay leading Friday night services, the community chorus and general membership of the congregation joined forces participating in several t'filot. The chorus was comprised of ba'aley t'filah (singers) from each of our minyanim: the 8:30 service, feminist, traditional, Shabbat morning, and Tot Shabbat.

Rabbi Kleinbaum recruited Joyce Rozensweig to direct an experimental chorus for the occasion. Joyce is an accomplished musician and one of the leading experts on monies written by Joyce for the occasion. A chant introducing the Amidah (Silent Devotion) provided a beautiful transition between sections of the service, effectively executed a capella: humming a lovely lyric phrase, then alternating the line in Hebrew and English. Following the Silent Devotion, CBST member Sariel Beckenstein was spotlighted in a moving solo, Gershon Kingsley's "Yih'yu L'Ratzon" (May the Words) originally commissioned by Park Avenue Synagogue, ably and beautifully backed by the chorus. The practice periods were demanding but fun and the results at Shabbat services were well worth the extraordinary effort, contributing to an uplifting, inspiring and memorable religious ceremony.

Most appreciative thanks to Rabbi Kleinbaum, Joyce Rozensweig and all participants (see list). (Maybe we can do this again for Pride Shabbat and the High Holy Days as well?)

**Members of the Ad-Hoc Community Chorus**
Joseph Alberts
Sariel Beckenstein
Zev Ben-Yehuda
Mark Bieber
Ron Citro
Janet Englund
Geoffrey Goldberg
Rachel Kaufman
Larry Kay
Ellie K.
Ron Kohn
Michael Lehrman
Rosanne Leipzig
David Spegal
Diane Temkin
Janet Zaleon

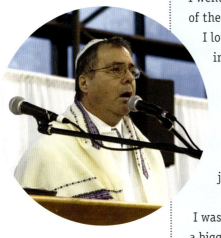

Larry Kay as *ba'al tefillah* at Javits

> ### HOW I GOT TO CBST
>
> I went to CBST a few times in 1984. I lived in Connecticut at the time and was part of the Jewish gay group there. I remember being thrilled with the CBST siddur. I loved the translations. I loved the GLBT additions, the degenderization, the inclusion of the matriarchs. It was a real revelation to me.
>
> By 1986 my partner Bob Christensen was living in our Varick Street apartment full-time on weekends, and I was part-time cantor in Hamden, Connecticut. I came in from Connecticut on a Thursday evening to attend the CBST Talmud class. I realized two things. First, coming in from Connecticut on a weekday evening was impossible. Second, the Talmud class just wasn't my thing. I wanted to be there on Shabbat.
>
> I was too scattered. I lived a double life. I worked in Fairfield county; I was closeted in Connecticut. I had my life with Bob in New York. It had to be a bigger commitment than that. So in 1989 I moved to New York, for Bob and for CBST. I was painfully shy. I went to someone and asked him about being *ba'al tefillah*. He said, "OK, the first time you only lead one thing." I led a *Tov lehodot*. That was my entrée into getting to know people at CBST, something that otherwise would have been very difficult.
>
> I loved the siddur and the democratic spirit of services. You had much more latitude than in many other synagogues. But it was a little same old, same old. Hiring Joyce was such a critical thing. Over the years, services gradually changed from being totally democratic, but often uninteresting, to a service that was always interesting and about music and piano and singing. The rabbis set up the songs beautifully and make them mean something very profound. All these changes happened very slowly, so that one day I turned around and it was different. I was sad to lose the *chavurah* feeling, but I love that our Friday night services are so much grander and more exciting.
>
> My life is open and deeper, and I have had the opportunity to develop as a *ba'al tefillah* in ways that would have been unimaginable in New Haven.
>
> LARRY KAY, MEMBER SINCE 1989

play.' She replied, 'We don't use piano in our services. Come conduct a choir.'" Joyce had never conducted before. Rabbi Kleinbaum insisted, "You can do it." She assured Joyce that she would recruit enough congregants to sing for CBST's upcoming twenty-first anniversary Shabbat service. "Come to some rehearsals. It will be fine." Joyce is still surprised she agreed. After that meeting, Rabbi Kleinbaum wrote to the frequent *ba'alei tefillah*, inviting them to participate and declaring her commitment to deepening the spirituality of services. "Music

When the chorus first sang at High Holiday services in 1995, they sang a capella. They rehearsed with Joyce, but she did not conduct them because she had a High Holiday position as an accompanist elsewhere.

and song will help us to reach new heights in prayer." At the rehearsals, Joyce introduced new harmonies to familiar settings and some from Sephardic and North African settings—a taste of what she would bring to CBST in years to come. Joseph Alberts (now Rafaela Anshel), Sariel Beckenstein, Bill Rosenbloom, Mark Bieber, Ron Citro, Janet Englund, Geoffrey Goldberg, Ellie K., Rachel Kaufman, Larry Kay, Ron Kohn, Michael Lehrman, Rosanne Leipzig, David Spegal, Diane Temkin, and Janet Zaleon constituted that first chorus. Some of these original members are still singing in the CBST Community Chorus nearly twenty years later. While a few members carried negative associations with choirs from their former synagogues, most were excited by the energy and musicality of incorporating a chorus into services. In the spring of 1994, Rabbi Kleinbaum and board chair Catherine Sull hired Joyce as CBST's part-time music director. She conducted the chorus, coached *ba'alei tefillah*, taught master classes, and introduced new music to Friday night services.

It took several years before Joyce began to play piano at services. CBST Friday night services did not customarily include instrumental music and Rabbi Kleinbaum hesitated to introduce the change too quickly. They initiated the piano in services tentatively, first with one accompanied selection per service, then having Joyce play during an entire service once a month. Some members from more traditional Jewish backgrounds avoided that service, feeling that instruments were incompatible with their experience of Shabbat prayer. But Joyce, frequently described by Rabbi Kleinbaum as "davening through her fingers," believes that musical instruments significantly enhance the depth, rhythm, variety and flow of the service, connecting the prayers and the diverse musical styles. In time the services that included Joyce became the most popular of the month. Her role expanded to playing piano on most Friday nights, High Holidays and special services, and conducting the chorus' more frequent participation. The rabbis and Joyce worked closely together, with profound respect, affection, and enjoyment, to craft services that were emotional, challenging, eclectic, and deeply sacred.

## A LABORATORY FOR MUSIC

The music program at CBST is one of the things that has given me the most pleasure in my life. In so many shuls, people think if there is a choir that means they can't sing. But I always try to make the chorus a force for encouraging even more participation. They might sing a special new piece, but it always leads into something for the congregation to sing. People sing with so much enthusiasm, it's contagious. The choir adds energy and excitement to services. CBST has been the greatest laboratory for bringing all the music that I know and developing it into something wonderful. The music of CBST has become a model for synagogues throughout the United States.

The music program has been able to develop as it has because of Rabbi Kleinbaum and Rabbi Cohen. I always tell my students at HUC and JTS that music can't be separated from everything else that goes on in the shul. It has to be integrated. There's got to be buy-in, respect, and complete collaboration. When Rabbi Kleinbaum or Rabbi Cohen give a charge to the choir before a service or a concert, it helps members understand the sacred work that they are a part of. Rabbi Kleinbaum talks about music and how important it is all the time. When a congregation knows that their rabbis value music, they understand that the music is something to take seriously.

JOYCE ROSENZWEIG

Joyce conducting the chorus, Shabbat Shirah, 2008

# THE GIFT OF JOYCE

Joyce is my partner in creating a religious life at CBST that is soulful and Jewishly rich. She adds immeasurably to the spiritual life of our congregation. Her depth as a person, as a Jew, as a musician enables her to use music as a way for our community to reach new heights.

Joyce has taught, coached, nurtured, inspired, and deepened the lives of hundreds of cantors and synagogue musicians. She brings expertise in a range of Jewish music: traditional *nusach*; Jewish art song; Yiddish, Sephardic and Mizrachi music; as well as contemporary creative liturgy. Many are expert in one or two of these areas; Joyce is fluent in all of them.

Under Joyce's direction, we have had *shabbatot* dedicated to German Jewish synagogue music, Moroccan Jewish music, Ladino music, Yiddish music, Shlomo Carlebach, and music from Israel. Joyce is brilliant at working with our community chorus. She has taken our members and crafted a fine and exquisite choral group to lead our congregation in prayer and celebration, mourning and grief.

We are grateful to the Holy One for the gifts of the spirit, the gifts of music that Joyce Rosenzweig has brought to us.

RABBI SHARON KLEINBAUM

RIGHT: Joyce rehearsing the chorus

BELOW: Rabbi Kleinbaum speaks to the chorus before Pride Shabbat services, 2008.

## CBST Community Chorus

By Pride Shabbat 1994, the chorus was open to all CBST members. While auditions were required, Joyce saw the love of Jewish music in everyone and hated to say no. A brilliant conductor, she led the chorus with sensitivity and generosity. While some chorus members were experienced singers or musicians, many had never sung in public before. Some didn't read music. Some didn't read Hebrew. Yet all wanted to sing and daven beautiful music, which Joyce's direction made possible. Joyce's efforts have made services accessible to many chorus members and deepened their understanding of the liturgy. Scores of CBST members have sung in the chorus over time and, whether singing from the bimah or among the congregation, their voices immeasurably deepen the CBST prayer experience.

The chorus now sings at High Holiday services and at the five major Friday night services each year: for Chanukah, CBST's anniversary Shabbat,

### HOW I GOT TO CBST

It was 1998 and I had just recently transitioned. My cousin Marsha told me there was a gay synagogue in New York City. I had grown up very religious; I wasn't religious at that point but thought it would be a good idea to check out CBST. I went for a Friday night service and was totally blown away. I was in tears by the end of the service. I felt like I had come home.

I had played piano seriously as a youngster, and music was very important to me. I wanted to be in the chorus, but I didn't know where my voice would fit. I went to Joyce. She was very open and said, "Let's try it." I auditioned and she said, "You're in."

It was a little difficult at first. I had just gone through the transition and I was a little unsure about how to be. At that point my transition was very obvious, at least to me. Some people said some hurtful things, even though it was a gay synagogue. It was a very awkward phase. But by and large people were very friendly.

I remember going to an early chorus rehearsal. Marc Janover was passing around some candy. I thought it was being passed to someone else; I didn't realize it was for everyone to share, so I just passed it along. Marc said, "Take one." He told me later that seeing me pass along the candy without taking any broke his heart. Before CBST, I really hadn't been a part of queer community at all and didn't know what to expect. I didn't know how accepting people would be to someone who was transgender. But after I got over my own initial shyness, I felt really comfortable. I didn't have any other place where I could be completely myself with the whole part, Jewish and queer.

JILLIAN WEISS, MEMBER SINCE 1999

RIGHT: The chorus preparing for Chanukah services in 2004

BELOW: Under the direction of Joyce Rosenzweig the chorus recorded two CDs: live at the North American Jewish Choral Festival (2002) and in celebration of Shabbat services at CBST, 2007.

Yom Ha'atsmaut, Family and Friends, and Pride, as well as special *shabbatot* and community programs honoring Martin Luther King Day, Yom Hashoah, and Kristallnacht. At each event, the chorus explores Jewish music from around the world. Thanks to Joyce, the chorus has transformed from a rag-tag group of enthusiastic volunteers to a remarkable ensemble that has performed on several occasions at the North American Jewish Choral Festival, the celebrated annual national Jewish music event in the Catskills.

## MAKING MEANINGFUL MUSIC

When Joyce first talked to me about joining the chorus, I was flattered but petrified. I had never sung in a chorus before, and I didn't think I could keep up. As it turned out, singing in the chorus was transformative for me. Joyce has taught me so much about music and singing in general, and Jewish music in particular. This has given me the confidence to expand and deepen my participation as a leader in Shabbat services.

For me, music is the most direct path to the transcendent. There are times when I feel as well as hear the harmonies and the blending of voices into one sound as a truly religious experience. I am so grateful to Joyce and my fellow chorus members for the opportunity to make joyous, meaningful music together.

ILENE BLOCK, MEMBER SINCE 1999

## Shabbat Shirah

It had long been a dream of Rabbi Kleinbaum's for CBST to become an LGBT 92nd Street Y, offering its cultural gifts to the broader New York community. At a summer barbecue in 1995, she told member and musician Adria Benjamin that she hoped CBST could hold a major arts festival every year. "I explained that Shabbat Shirah (Shabbat of Song) is the Shabbat on which synagogues throughout the world sing *Shirat Hayam* (the Song of the Sea) celebrating our survival through song and dance. I wanted to mount a week-long arts festival around the time of Shabbat Shirah. I wanted an eighty-person orchestra, choruses, and performances of all kinds." Adria suggested they start with a chamber music concert. That year, Adria worked closely with member Jill Vexler, a curator, and Joyce Rosenzweig to plan a gala chamber music Shabbat Shirah concert. CBST's first concert in February 1996 was held at the crumbling historic Orensanz Synagogue on the Lower East Side. The beautiful old building was yet to be restored and had no working heat. "It was freezing," Joyce recalls. "Everyone sat there shivering in their coats. The musicians wore gloves with the tips cut off." But the cold couldn't dampen the excitement. From then onward, the concert has become an annual tradition, each year featuring a different style of music, held in a venerable New York synagogue or performance space. Shabbat Shirah concerts have presented instrumental, choral, and solo music featuring guest musicians such as Danny Maseng and Debbie Friedman, exploring baroque to Bernstein, Aaron Copland, William Finn, and Giuseppe Verdi, with the CBST community chorus participating under Joyce's direction.

ABOVE: Dean Feldman and Jill Vexler, the event coordinators

LEFT: The first Shabbat Shirah concert, celebrating CBST's twenty-third anniversary, 1996

RIGHT: Joyce and the chorus at the 2001 Shabbat Shirah concert held at Ansche Chesed.

MIDDLE: The 2008 Shabbat Shirah concert, a musical celebration of Israel at 60, featured Debbie Friedman.

BELOW: Bill Finn and his music were the centerpiece of the Shabbat Shirah concert at Merkin Hall, 2009.

An array of Shabbat Shirah programs

LEFT: Pierre Vallet, honoree of the 2012 Shabbat Shirah concert, performs with cantorial soloist Re'ut Ben-Ze'ev at the Merkin Concert Hall.

BELOW: The 2013 concert at Stephen Wise Free Synagogue honored composer/conductor Jonathan Sheffer (third from right), and featured Christine Ebersole, and cantorial soloist Re'ut Ben-Ze'ev, among others.

## Musical Transformation

As music continued to flourish at CBST, members such as Assaf Astrinsky, Karen Krop, and Graham Parker joined the ranks of frequent *ba'alei tefillah*, with Joyce coaching and introducing them to the vast array of liturgical music in which she was fluent. Strong singers developed more fully under her direction, and those with knowledge of Jewish music collaborated with her to further enhance their repertoire at CBST's services. Judy Ribnick recalls having discovered a melody in a collection of Chasidic *niggunim* and sharing it with Joyce, who set *Hashkiveinu* to the classic melody. "It was like a light bulb going off," Judy recalls. "It was a great collaboration."

Member musicians also enhance services with their talents: Adria Benjamin plays viola each year for *Kol Nidrei*, and percussionist Barbara Freedman regularly joins Joyce accompanying Friday night services. Judy Ribnick frequently plays clarinet when serving as *ba'alat tefillah*. Simon Dratfield plays the flute. It is a testament to CBST's musical success that renowned professional musicians, such as Jonathan Sheffer and Metropolitan Opera vocal coach and conductor Pierre Vallet, are proudly associated with

Graham Parker rehearsing before Yom Kippur, 2007

LEFT TOP: Karen Krop
LEFT BOTTOM: Barbara Freedman
BOTTOM MIDDLE: Judy Ribnick
BELOW: Simon Dratfield

## HOW I GOT TO CBST

I went to a twenty-something group at the Center, where I met Robert Eppenstein, who told me about CBST. The first time I went to a service, the room was packed. It was like nothing I had ever been to before—I didn't grow up religious. But I liked all the singing. That's what made me feel at home.

We used to sit in the back row—they called us the boys in the back: Robert, Daniel [Chesir], and Ian [Teran]. Pretty quickly that was what I was doing every Friday night. There were other people like me, and other young people. It was a community. A way of feeling Jewish, and accepted, and welcomed.

Daniel and Ian asked me to sing one of the *Sheva Brachot* at their wedding. After the wedding, Rabbi Kleinbaum said, "You should join the chorus." I wasn't interested. The chorus was just getting started and they were mostly singing in unison. Rabbi Kleinbaum hounded me week after week until I finally spoke to Joyce. I joined the chorus. It was an amazing experience. I said to myself, "What was I thinking that I didn't want to do this?"

They held classes for people who wanted to become lay service leaders. At first it didn't even occur to me that I could do that. I was very scared of public speaking and being on stage. So the chorus helped me a lot in terms of gaining confidence. To be up there and lead congregants in prayer . . . I felt people were with me. It is a real *kavod*. All my great friends who played such a central role in my life came from CBST.

ASSAF ASTRINSKY, MEMBER SINCE 1994

CBST's music program and excited by its increasing range and sophistication.

Joyce began inviting her cantorial students from Hebrew Union College to serve as occasional guest cantors. While the response was enthusiastic, when Joyce expressed her hope of CBST hiring a cantor or cantorial intern at a congregational strategic planning session in 1998, many congregants expressed misgivings. The congregation was loathe to lose the *heimish* feeling of services and lay *ba'alei tefillah* were not ready to cede their place on the bimah.

Joyce continued working closely with *ba'alei tefillah*, coaching them on *nusach* and introducing them to a diverse repertoire, increasing the quality of singing on the bimah. When some of the strongest *ba'alei tefillah* were offered paid positions at other synagogues or left the New York area, CBST revisited the concept of a cantorial internship. In 2003 the time had come. The first cantorial internship, modeled after the Cooperberg-Rittmaster Rabbinical Internship, was launched.

## Cantorial Program

The search committee, which included Sari Kessler, Steve Fruh, Jack Greenberg, Rabbi Kleinbaum, and Rabbi Cohen, chose Daniel Singer, a cantorial student at the HUC–JIR School of Sacred Music, as CBST's first cantorial intern in 2004. The cantorial interns have worked closely with Joyce, who relishes the opportunity to lead students devoted to liturgy, *nusach*, and a diverse repertoire of Jewish song. They became part of CBST's clergy team, working with the rabbis and the Cooperberg-Rittmaster Rabbinical Interns to be a pastoral and educational presence at CBST.

After two years as CBST's second cantorial student intern, Cantor David Berger was hired in 2007 as CBST's first full-time cantor upon graduating from HUC–JIR. With a deep respect for Hebrew and an enthusiasm for davening from different traditions, David worked with Rabbi Cohen to develop the Shabbat morning minyanim. He shared Joyce's love of Jewish music from around the world, and they collaborated on many projects, including a professionally recorded CD of the music of Friday night services, a project begun when Daniel Singer was cantorial intern. After Cantor Berger moved to Los Angeles, CBST resumed hiring cantorial interns and soloists, including Jason Kaufman, Magda Fishman, and Re'ut Ben-Ze'ev, each bringing his or her own talents and unique musical style.

CBST services have evolved to integrate myriad and diverse musical voices through generations and from across the Jewish experience, including Uganda, Morocco, Germany, Israel, and Paris. Joyce's particular interests in art song, as well as Yiddish and Sephardic music, have introduced the congregation to a broad variety of texts, textures, and new sounds. Reinforcing the principle that Jews from Sephardic and North African backgrounds are equally welcome at CBST, Joyce includes such liturgical music as the Sephardic *piyyut Achot k'tanah* to begin Rosh Hashanah services each year.

BELOW LEFT: Cantorial intern Dan Singer on the bimah

BELOW RIGHT: Outgoing cantorial intern Dan Singer, Joyce Rosenzweig, and incoming cantorial intern David Berger, 2009

LEFT: Cantor Berger, Joyce Rosenzweig, and Adria Benjamin preparing for a service in 2007

BELOW: Cantor David Berger leading Family and Friends Shabbat Services in 2009 with Rabbi Kleinbaum, Larry Kay, and Judy Ribnick

Reflecting on the musical evolution at CBST, Joyce observes that "the growth in musical sophistication parallels the intellectual seriousness that comes from the bimah and the shul's involvement in social justice. The rabbis speak with such intelligence and awareness of the world that it wouldn't make sense to have a service composed entirely of 'ditties.' There is a beautiful marriage now between the intellectual and cultural aspects of Judaism and a shul that reverberates with soulful, ecstatic, and joyous davening."

## REFLECTIONS FROM MY YEAR AT CBST: BEYOND THE MUSIC

As soon as I became aware of CBST, I dreamed of being a part of its leadership. I was in awe of the musical excellence of the synagogue as well as its commitment to social justice and human rights. My dream came true in 2008 when I was selected to serve as the cantorial intern. I was so overjoyed and humbled that I spent the entire summer before my internship endlessly preparing for High Holiday services. What complicated matters was that at the same time I was serving as a summer cantorial intern for a community in Melbourne, Australia. I traveled through Australia with my CBST High Holiday music binder in one hand and my iPod full of recordings from the previous CBST High Holiday services in the other. My cantorial professors in New York even coached me on Skype, sometimes into the late hours of the morning.

As I began my time with CBST, I was so focused on getting the music right and trying to sing everything perfectly, that it took a congregant to remind me of my true purpose as cantorial intern at CBST. After service, one Friday evening, early in my internship, a man in his late seventies approached me. He was in awe that I, a young man in my twenties, was leading a congregation as an openly gay cantorial intern. He told me that he was jealous of the fact that someone my age could be openly gay, without fear of shame or rejection, in a way that he was not able to when he was my age. At that moment, I was reminded of the sacrifices and struggles that others experienced so I could have the opportunities that I now enjoy.

I hold this story close to my heart. It serves as a constant inspiration for me, for the ways in which I need to work to transform my world, so that the next generation may have opportunities that I once considered unimaginable.

JASON KAUFMAN, CANTORIAL INTERN 2009–2010

Magda Fishman performing at the Shabbat Shirah concert in Merkin Hall, 2011

## CANTORS, INTERNS, AND SOLOISTS

**Cantor Daniel Singer**, cantorial intern, Hebrew Union College–Jewish Institute of Religion (2004–05)

**Cantor David Berger,** cantorial intern, Hebrew Union College–Jewish Institute of Religion (2005–07), cantor (2007–09)

**Cantor Jason Kaufman**, cantorial intern, Hebrew Union College–Jewish Institute of Religion (2009–10),

**Cantor Magda Fishman**, cantorial intern, Jewish Theological Seminary (2010–11)

**Re'ut Ben-Ze'ev**, cantorial soloist (2011– )

## SINGING JOYFULLY

I remember a few years ago my family was at a family bat mitzvah and somebody started singing a song and I joined in. My sister had never heard it, and she asked me how I knew it. I said, "Because I go to CBST. We sing everything." I'm very proud of that. Joyce has introduced all kinds of new music that perhaps we wouldn't have been introduced to in another setting. It's not just the different kinds of music, it's a joyful and participatory kind of music. This is not a congregation where just the cantor sings. I've been exposed to so much that I really see a joyful take on Judaism that I didn't have when I was growing up.

LAURIE SIEGEL, MEMBER SINCE 1991

BELOW LEFT AND BOTTOM: The community chorus sings out with great spirit.

BELOW: Cantorial soloist Re'ut Ben-Ze'ev leads services with the chorus.

# 9. A SACRED COMMUNITY

CBST IS NOT ONLY A PLACE TO PRAY, but also to gather and share ancient and emerging Jewish rituals. As members choose to make CBST their spiritual home for Shabbat and holiday davening, they naturally want to observe the significant moments in their lives there as well, openly, in the fullness of their identities.

## The First Weddings

According to Reb Pinchas, there wasn't much demand for ceremonies of commitment during the 1970s. Few men were in long-term relationships, and the few women members who were in couples were uninterested in having ceremonies. Yet long before weddings became popular among same-sex couples, Reb Pinchas officiated at a few ceremonies. After he returned to Orthodoxy, Pinchas no longer sanctioned commitment ceremonies. Even in the 1970s he was careful not to call these ceremonies weddings, which would be prohibited according to his Orthodox interpretation of halachah.

> We do not seek to duplicate, approximate, or imitate the marriage ceremony as performed at the wedding of a man and a woman. The traditional Jewish understanding of marriage as a social and legal institution is based on considerations quite different from what applied to the needs and wishes of Gay people. To mindlessly force the words and acts created for specific purposes into the very different context of this occasion allows us to lose sight of our uniqueness, and the potential value that uniqueness can have in the life of our tradition.

Still, his ceremonies incorporated many elements from the Jewish wedding. "Precisely because we do cherish our tradition, and see ourselves as part of it, the celebration we now share draws freely upon the traditional formulations, but does so with appropriate innovation and change." And, as the December 1976 newsletter attests, the congregation, albeit with a sense of humor, experienced it as such.

> A posh West End Avenue apartment was the recent setting for a ceremony of unity between two members of our congregation—Frank and Leslie. Under the velvet canopy the *rebbe* presided, as the two *chasonim*, both dressed in light tan suits, with matching brown ties, exchanged vows of love in the presence of their closest friends. The several male attendants wore light blue turtleneck sweaters and hand knitted blue and white

A
CELEBRATION
OF
LOVING DEDICATION

Charlie and Steve

October 8, 1977

Service booklet for early commitment ceremony

yarmulkes. The ceremony was concluded with the mutual breaking of wine glasses as those who had gathered together burst into song—*Siman Tov* and *Mazel Tov*. Dancing and salads were enjoyed by all. The couple will continue to reside in their Brooklyn apartment.

As time went on, more CBST couples in long-term relationships celebrated anniversaries with parties and kiddush sponsorships, but weddings would not become a regular part of CBST culture for almost two decades.

Most members associate the first CBST wedding with the controversy that arose in 1988, when Dr. Rosanne Leipzig and Ora Chaikin (then known as Judy Mable), announced their intention to celebrate their *brit ahavah* (literally "covenant of love"). At a time when gay life was still criminalized and marginalized, most gay men and lesbians believed that being out of the closet meant that neither legal nor religious marriage was a right that was available to them. Some considered gay wedding ceremonies as simply aping heterosexual customs and abandoning gay culture. Others believed that same-sex marriage could not be sanctioned by Jewish law and feared the practice at CBST would further damage its credibility among Orthodox Jews, alienating the wider Jewish world. While the Religious Committee had no formal policy relating to commitment ceremonies, many people responded as if there were an unwritten rule against it. Rosanne and Ora had to lobby the board and the Religious Committee to sanction their ceremony.

## Brit Ahavah

After some debate, the synagogue ultimately agreed to hold a *brit ahavah* for Ora and Rosanne at Bethune Street in 1988. There was no precedent for the wedding, which meant that they crafted their own ceremony. They started with a copy of a ceremony created by Reform Rabbi Stacy Offner, a former CBST member, and Anita Diamant's useful book, *The New Jewish Wedding*.

Rosanne and Ora at their *brit ahavah*

Rosanne recalls the significance of the ritual, "Putting all parts of my life together was one of the most meaningful experiences I'll ever have. I wrote a letter to my relatives, saying, 'Something wonderful has happened to me. I've fallen in love. And we want to have a commitment ceremony.' (People did not use the word wedding in those days.) I assumed they knew this about me, but I wanted to be clear when I wrote 'I'm a lesbian, I love women, and I've found the love of my life.' We sent the letter out with a Save the Date card to everyone who had attended my brothers' weddings, assuming that maybe two or four would come, out of a family of around sixty. The response was amazing. We received heartfelt, beautiful letters back. It melted my heart.

Rabbi Helene Ferris under the chuppah designed and embroidered by Sheldon Post (in wheelchair) with his partner Jay Lesiger

"For us it was very profound to create our own rituals for the ceremony. We asked people to send us a meaningful piece of fabric, from which we made the chuppah. Our friend Shelly Post embroidered the center of the chuppah while he was very sick with AIDS at St. Vincent's Hospital. He took the image from our invitation—two women dancing in a circle surrounded by other people dancing—and embroidered our names in Hebrew, 'with love from Shelly and Jay,' his lover. Then he joined all the fabrics around this centerpiece. The day after he completed the embroidery, he lost the use of his right hand. He managed to regain some use for a short time and was able to sign our ketubah. He died a few months later.

"People told us it was the most joyful experience of their lives. Many said it was the most Jewish wedding they'd ever been to. The gay men and lesbians who were there commented that they never thought they would ever see anything like this. I have pictures of my eighty-five year-old relatives dancing with Saul Mizrahi."

Rabbi Helene Ferris of Stephen Wise Free Synagogue and CBST *ba'alat tefillah* Judy Ribnick officiated at the groundbreaking ceremony. The published accounts of their *brit ahavah*, which appeared in the book *Ceremonies of the Heart* and *Lilith* magazine, were among the first within the Jewish and lesbian and gay world.

### Commitment Ceremonies, Civil Unions, and Weddings

Before CBST had a rabbi, members and nonmembers alike regularly approached the synagogue for help with lifecycle rituals. As Religious Committee chair in the late 1980s, Saul Zalkin reached out to local rabbis to inquire about their policies and practices concerning commitment ceremonies so that he could refer interested members to rabbis who would agree to officiate. Later, when the need arose, Jack Greenberg developed a *get*, using the traditional divorce document as a template and making it gender sensitive.

In time, marriage increasingly became part of the cultural vocabulary for same-sex couples. Younger gay couples felt that a wedding was a rite of passage available to them too. By the spring of 1993, with a rabbi in place, the demand for commitment ceremonies was so great that Rabbi Kleinbaum held a group information session: "Everything you wanted to know about planning a commitment ceremony, from ketubah to chuppah to canapés."

For some couples, getting married was a way of proclaiming the legitimacy of their relationship and reminding friends and family that it was cause for celebration and recognition as automatic as that enjoyed by their heterosexual siblings. For many, this demanded a more radical coming out—to their extended family, family friends, and colleagues from work. The process could be complicated and even painful. Some parents who may have been willing to tolerate their gay children could not bring themselves to dance at their weddings; other parents refused to invite their friends or their own parents. For some families, the process leading up to a wedding offered an opportunity for repair. For others, it was a moment of deep hurt and disappointment, such as in the case of Yolanda Potasinski and Nancy Mertzel.

"Nancy and I were married by Rabbi Kleinbaum on September 7, 1997," Yolanda remembers. "For me the ceremony was more than just a ritual and a

## AN INTERVIEW WITH ROSANNE AND ORA

**Rosanne:** In planning our *brit ahavah* we dealt with people who had never thought of gays and lesbians as human beings with the same needs and wants as others. After meeting with us, most came to relate to us as a couple in love, as lesbians in love. There's a term in Hebrew, *tikkun olam*, which means trying to mend or repair the world. We began to feel that by doing all this we were starting to participate in the process of *tikkun olam*.

**Ora:** We told the woman who designed our rings that we wanted to have them engraved in Hebrew. She said the engraving would have to be done by the Chasidic men in the jewelry district. We were a little concerned about how these Orthodox men would deal with all this, but we went ahead and sent her this inscription: *ahuvot chaim* [beloveds for life] 3/20/88. Soon the designer called with a big problem, the engraver told her, "Whoever wrote this inscription does not know Hebrew." All Hebrew nouns are gendered, and to the engraver it was impossible that we would want both rings inscribed with the female form of "beloveds for life." I told her to have it engraved in exactly the way it was written. I don't think it ever occurred to him that the rings were really for two women. I bet he's still convinced someone made a mistake.

**ADAPTED FROM *LILITH* MAGAZINE, 1992**

Yolanda and Nancy dancing at their wedding, September 7, 1997

celebration. Religious marriage was serious for me. It was about fulfilling the values of my Jewish upbringing, although it was totally counter to my parents' own Jewish beliefs. I was in terrible conflict about this. My parents just couldn't reconcile it. Nancy and I tried everything to convince them, but they never acknowledged our wedding. I knew I just had to move on. I remember putting on my dress before the ceremony and falling to the floor, weeping, and feeling so alone, and trying to find the strength to go on. It was another moment, another passage in my life when I felt I had to grow up on my own. And that's exactly what I did."

Yolanda continues, "We had 400 people at our wedding, which ironically is the same number of people as my parents had at their wedding in Caracas. I remember the joy of walking down the aisle with Nancy and standing under the chuppah, such a spiritual, powerful moment that was filled with the love and caring that came from CBST members and the family members who did come. It turned out to be one of the most beautiful days of my life."

Daniel and Ian Chesir-Teran were the first in their age cohort to marry. They each grew up in traditional Jewish communities where marrying young was expected. They worked closely with Rabbi Kleinbaum to craft a traditional ceremony. "We made our chuppah, we went to the mikvah, we had *tisches*, we had members of CBST and friends of ours participating in all parts of the ceremony." Ian recalls his parents' discomfort

Invitation to Daniel and Ian Chesir-Teran's wedding, September 14, 1997

with the one aspect of their 1997 wedding: "For us getting married was a political act, and we put postcards on all the tables for people to send in to their representatives against the Defense of Marriage Act (DOMA). My parents felt very uncomfortable. The wedding had to be consistent with their Long

Island sensibilities." Daniel chose his friend Susie Silverstein to represent his family, who didn't attend the ceremony but came for the reception. Daniel and Ian are proud to have planned a "very CBST wedding," which served as a model for other young lesbian or gay couples preparing for a Jewish wedding.

On the other side of the family spectrum, in 1993 Jay Fischer and Michael Lehrman, held their commitment ceremony jointly with Jay's parents, Rita and Alex Fischer, who were celebrating their 50th wedding anniversary. Michael recalls being inspired by Rosanne and Ora's *brit ahavah*, "It made Jay and me think maybe we wanted one too." Nine years into their relationship, they had exchanged rings and vows privately on a trip to Israel but wanted to do something more public. They asked Rabbi Kleinbaum to officiate and invited Rita and Alex to share in their celebration. Rita describes it as a highlight of her life, "When Alex and I walked Jay down that aisle, I thought, 'This was it.' Who would ever dream that a mother of a gay child would walk that child down an aisle?"

As civil unions and then same-sex marriage became legalized in more and more states, CBST couples planned

ABOVE: (left to right) Michael Lehrman, Jay Fischer, Rita and Alex Fischer at their combined *brit ahavah* and 50th anniversary celebration, August 1993

RIGHT: Longtime CBST couple Erika Karp (center) and Sari Kessler (left) were among the first in line to receive their marriage license. Rabbi Kleinbaum officiated at their wedding, surrounded by their three daughters (Ruby, Hanna, Molly) and Sari's brother.

LEFT: Mitchell Davis and Nathan Goldstein rejoicing at their wedding in May, 2012

BELOW: Marsha Melnick and Susan Meyer, married at the City Clerk's office, September, 2011, stand before a painting of City Hall with signs made by Richard Orient.

weddings. When same-sex marriage was legalized in New York State in the summer of 2011, many couples who had been together for decades without a ceremony, or who had celebrated in religious ceremonies years before, could now participate in legal ceremonies as well. On the first day, CBST set up a rainbow chuppah outside the city clerk's office, where the rabbis officiated as couples emerged with their marriage licenses.

## A Place for New Rituals

Over time, CBST created lifecycle rituals that suited not only its congregants, but also evolved into a central source for non-members as well. Jack recalls researching ritual issues to help those who reached out to CBST. "I'd say, 'why not become a CBST member, get involved, and create the process for the next person who calls?'" Once Rabbi Kleinbaum was hired, requests skyrocketed. Art Leonard cautioned, "while it might seem ideal to regard Rabbi Kleinbaum as rabbi for the entire Lesbian and Gay community of the metropolitan area, such a task would be too great for anyone to assume, and we can't expect her to assume it all." Still, CBST became a magnet for LGBTQ people from all over the country and, with the advent of the internet, from all over the world, seeking spiritual connection and Jewish guidance.

When the rabbinical presence expanded to include the Cooperberg-Rittmaster Rabbinical interns and Rabbi Young, Rabbi Cohen, and Rabbi Weiss, CBST was able to handle more of these inquiries. These questions ranged from counseling gay Chasidic men who called anonymously from phone booths in Brooklyn to young queer people writing from the rural south who feared there was no one else like them in the world. Rabbi Cohen studied Jewish legal sources and resources from the various Jewish movements to develop responses to new halachic questions that arose with LGBT parenting and gender transition, among other issues.

CBST has consciously embraced rituals celebrating all aspects of Jewish life, for members who are single as well as partnered, with and without children. The congregation has marked such occasions as retirement, significant birthdays, and moments within the community like board installations and the synagogue's anniversary. CBST's rabbis and interns work with congregants in order to develop new rituals and liturgy—some privately, others celebrated with the community—around coming out, name changes, and gender transition. The 2007 edition of the siddur, *B'chol L'vav'cha*, includes liturgy for many of these events. CBST's clergy has continued to share these resources with rabbis throughout the country who have reached out for help with LGBT pastoral questions. The rabbis have also taught seminars at JTS, HUC, and RRC on pastoral issues facing LGBT congregants, filling significant gaps in rabbinical school education.

---

ON COMING OUT

As God blessed our ancestors as they came out from Egypt, may you be blessed as you come out as lesbian/gay/bisexual/transgender/queer. Let the wisdom of your ancestors guide you as you begin this new journey through life. May you learn from Moses to enjoy every day of the journey, because there is no guarantee of reaching the Promised Land. May you learn from Lot's wife to keep your gaze on the horizon, because living in the past freezes you in your tracks. May you learn from Joseph that there is a place in the world for a dreamer. May you learn from Ruth and Naomi that love, friendship, and loyalty are not the entitlements of family, but its main ingredients. And may you learn from Caleb and Joshua to have the courage of your convictions and to find sweetness and hope in all that you set your eyes upon.

בְּרוּכִים אַתֶּם בְּבֹאֲכֶם וּבְרוּכִים אַתֶּם בְּצֵאתְכֶם.

May you be blessed in your coming home and in your coming out.

ON RETIREMENT

As God blessed our ancestors on their journeys, so may you be blessed as you embark on the journey of your retirement.
May you find rest and challenge, quiet and adventure.
May you be sustained by the achievements of your work life and inspired by the possibilities of what lies ahead.
May you allow yourself to experience silence and rest, and may you open yourself to the new music that may emerge from that silence.

RENAMING BLESSING FOR THOSE WHO ARE TRANSITIONING

מִי שֶׁבֵּרַךְ אֲבוֹתֵינוּ אַבְרָהָם יִצְחָק וְיַעֲקֹב,
וְאִמּוֹתֵינוּ שָׂרָה רִבְקָה לֵאָה רָחֵל, בִּלְהָה וְזִלְפָּה,
הוּא יְבָרֵךְ אֶת אָחִינוּ הָעוֹבֵר אֶת מַעֲבָרוֹ לְיַחֵד גּוּפוֹ וְנַפְשׁוֹ/
הוּא יְבָרֵךְ אֶת אֲחוֹתֵנוּ הָעוֹבֶרֶת אֶת מַעֲבָרָהּ לְיַחֵד גּוּפָהּ וְנַפְשָׁהּ
וְיִקָּרֵא שְׁמוֹ/ שְׁמָהּ בְּיִשְׂרָאֵל _____.
יְהִי רָצוֹן שֶׁיַּצְלִיחַ בְּדַרְכּוֹ וְיִרְאֶה בְרָכָה בְּכָל–מַעֲשֵׂה יָדָיו/
יְהִי רָצוֹן שֶׁתַּצְלִיחַ בְּדַרְכָּהּ וְתִרְאֶה בְרָכָה בְּכָל–מַעֲשֵׂה יָדֶיהָ,
וְנֹאמַר אָמֵן.

May the One who blessed our ancestors Abraham, Isaac, and Jacob, Sarah, Rebecca, Leah, Rachel, Bilhah, and Zilpah,
Bless our brother/sister, who is undergoing his/her transition to unite body and soul.
May he/she be known among the people Israel as_____.
May it be God's will that he/she succeed in his/her way and see blessing in all the works of his/her hands, and let us say, Amen.

From the 2007 edition of the CBST siddur

## Choosing Judaism

Some of the synagogue's most active members are Jews by choice. Seeking a place that would affirm their unique spiritual path and celebrate their gender identity and sexual orientation, they chose to study for their conversion to Judaism at CBST. Some—such as Maryann King, Aari Ludvigsen, Paul Marsolini, Jack Nieman, and Lisa Springer—had been partnered with Jews for a decade or more and living a Jewish life to a greater or lesser degree for some time. Jack Nieman took his son to Hebrew school to make sure he was prepared for his bar mitzvah. Aari was responsible for her family seder every Passover. When Paul's partner, Steve Fruh, lost his father, Paul brought Steve to CBST to say Kaddish, and they began attending every Friday night. CBST's intensive conversion program challenges its students to claim a Jewish identity that is authentically their own, becoming lifelong Jewish students and engaging fully in all aspects of Jewish life.

CLOCKWISE RIGHT: Paul Marsolini (center), who completed his conversion to Judaism in 2011, sings with the CBST Chorus at a Shabbat Shirah Concert; Lisa Springer (behind) completed her conversion to Judaism in 2003, pictured here with her partner Liz Galst and their children Aviv and Naomi; Beth Rosen (left) and her partner Maryann King, who completed her conversion to Judaism in 2003.

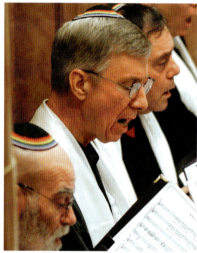

# EL AL SECURITY CHECK, JFK AIRPORT, DECEMBER 20, 2003

Rick and I dutifully arrived at JFK airport four hours before our departure to Tel Aviv. Rabbi Kleinbaum called the Jews by choice over in a huddle to brief us on what was going to happen when we were questioned by Israeli security. Apparently, Jews by choice fell into a different category of security risk. Although Rabbi Kleinbaum's guidance was comforting and helpful, nothing could have prepared me for what was about to happen.

After producing my passport and ticket, I was asked if I attended synagogue. Of course I had attended shul—every week for so many years I could not remember. I was in the b'nai mitzvah program after all. I had been through *hatafat dam brit* with an Orthodox mohel and had recently taken the plunge in an Upper West Side mikvah with Rabbi Kleinbaum, Rabbi Cohen, and Rabbi Young on my *beit din*. I had the all-star rabbinical dream team on my side! But, how Jewish was I? I would soon be put to the test.

"Which synagogue do you attend?" asked a tall blond-haired woman in her early twenties. Naomi was her name.

"Congregation Beth Simchat Torah," I responded in my best Hebrew pronunciation.

"Where is it? How long have you been a member?"

"I am a Jew by choice," I told her.

"Oh," she said, "Why did you do that?"

I told her it was a long story—I had married and divorced a Jewish woman and raised my son as a Jew. I left my soon-to-be-husband Rick out of the story; we planned to be married in Jerusalem, at the King David Hotel, no less, by Rabbis Kleinbaum and Cohen. But why complicate things even more? She asked me if I was going to have a bar mitzvah; I told her I was studying right now and would become a bar mitzvah in 2005. From there I was interrogated about the origin of my last name ("German"), my favorite holiday ("Purim") and why ("dressing up and reading the megillah of Esther"), how we spent the previous evening ("lighting Chanukah candles"), and the day before that? ("Sukkot and Simchat Torah") and what other holidays ("Rosh Hashanah and Yom Kippur") and could I read Hebrew ("Yes, thanks to Jack Greenberg").

Baggage check went smoothly, with no questions except for "What's this?"

"Oh, Venezuelan chocolate." How could anyone leave home without their Venezuelan chocolate?

"Did you buy it?"

"Yes, at Fairway." Uh oh, too much information?

I could not wait to go and sit and relax in my seat 50A. Shalom at last.

JACK NIEMAN

Jack Nieman (left) and Rick Reder in Jerusalem

### HOW I GOT TO CBST

I grew up in an Evangelical church. I started my conversion to Judaism when I was in graduate school in Michigan, but was only about halfway done when I graduated and moved to New York. My rabbi gave me the names of two synagogues, one near where I would be living and CBST. He went to school with Rabbi Cohen and suggested that I seek her out. I really didn't want to go to an LGBT synagogue. I was an activist all my life and I wanted to go to a "normal" synagogue. I tried the other synagogue first, and it was horrible, so I went to CBST. I remember that first Friday night service, feeling completely at home, even though I didn't really know what was going on. Rabbi Kleinbaum often says that everyone who comes to CBST is there because he or she wants to be there, not because they are compelled to go or to impress somebody. People go because they want to participate in Judaism; they want that spiritual community.

I went to a Conversion Open House with Rabbi Cohen, who explained that "over the course of your conversion process, you're going to discover which aspects of Judaism you relate to—which you connect with. It may be the religion, it may be the humor, it may be the intellectual, it may be the history, or it may be the food. Whatever it is, it's ok." I thought that was a beautiful way of putting it. The journey has been incredible: Ten years ago, I could not have imagined I would ever become a Jew. I could not have imagined the sense of fulfillment I would receive from religion. I hesitate to merely call it a religion. It's so much more than that: It's who I am. To have something that validates every fiber of my being on a regular basis is amazing. I feel so lucky to have already come to that place at the age of twenty-nine. The services never cease to touch me, which is probably why I cry every time we say the *Sh'ma*.

KATE GEITNER, MEMBER SINCE 2009

### B'nai Mitzvah

There were very few b'nai mitzvah at CBST in the early days. A few children, mostly of straight couples conveniently living in Westbeth but not involved with the synagogue, were tutored by CBST members for a bat or bar mitzvah at the shul. The first adult bar mitzvah was held in 1976, one of a small number of adults who studied with CBST members toward celebrating this milestone during the synagogue's first two decades.

Once CBST had a rabbi, more members sought to celebrate lifecycle events— more adults approached Rabbi Kleinbaum to express their interest in studying for b'nai mitzvah. In late 1993 and early 1994, members Jonathan Sheffer and Janet Englund

## I DIDN'T GO THROUGH IT ALONE

In 2005, I was diagnosed with breast cancer. I let the rabbis know and my friends rallied around me. I found that people were there for me. It was an experience I will never forget. It will always remain in my heart. I don't even know how to thank people like that. My CBST friends really made sure I was taken care of and that I didn't go through it by myself.

LAURIE SIEGEL

Ken Binder, Judy Hollander (behind), Sandy Warshaw, and Laurie Siegel at their b'nai mitzvah on February 26, 2005

celebrated their b'nai mitzvah. Inspired, several others wanted to follow suit. Rabbi Kleinbaum created an adult b'nai mitzvah program in 1994 that became a focal point of communal and educational life.

Throughout the years the adult b'nai mitzvah program has become a profound experience of education and of community. Its students often form the core of CBST's adult education program. The cohort that began studying with Rabbi Cohen in the fall of 2002 was the largest CBST had ever seen, a number that included members from seven countries, ranging in age from young thirties to seventies, who identified as lesbian, gay, bisexual, straight, transgender, and queer. For many of the participants, completing the program felt as if it validated their legitimacy as Jewish learners. Upon his bar mitzvah in 2005, Ken Binder said in amazement, "Whoever would have thought a scared little kid from South Dakota would grow up to be a nice Jewish gay boy from New York City—and be able to read Hebrew and have a bar mitzvah? Impossible dreams do come true."

The b'nai mitzvah group often becomes a close-knit community within the larger community, coming together to support one another in difficult times. Laurie Siegel and Ken Binder both fought cancer during the program; Barbara Dolgin had to delay her bat mitzvah while she was caring for her ailing parents. Their classmates were especially present for them during their struggles, and their hard-earned b'nai mitzvah celebrations were particularly joyful.

## Families with Children

Unlike many primarily heterosexual congregations—which tend to organize around the needs of families with young children—CBST developed rituals and services for virtually every other stage of life long before it became common to welcome babies into the community. Jack Greenberg recalls naming a few babies at CBST, including some of Annette Miller's grandchildren. There were always a few congregants with children and grandchildren from previous straight relationships, and some occasionally brought children as early as the 1970s. Marilyn Mishaan

loved bringing her son Shemmy each year on Simchat Torah. "He was young enough to be picked up and carried by one of the guys as we danced with the Torah. It was warm and welcoming and so much fun. At the age of forty-two, he still comes to CBST with his partner and friends…and still feels at home." Wayne Steinman and Sal Iacullo were among the founders of Center Kids, a program of the Gay and Lesbian Community Services Center that provided support and community for LGBT people who were considering parenting and raising children. They were virtually the only gay couple to bring a young child, their daughter Hope, to services regularly in the 1980s. Jack Greenberg recalls Irving Cooperberg frequently invoking "precious Hope" in his *drashot*, "pointing out how far we had come as a community." But until the late 1980s few members brought children to shul with any regularity. Many members recall the firestorm that erupted after member Rabbi Joan Friedman delivered a controversial *drash* in the late 1980s. "We have a right to have children and we should be doing it, not giving up that right to people who don't want to let us do so," Jack Greenberg recalls her saying.

TOP: Marilyn Mishaan and her son Shemmy, with *sofer* Gedalia Druin, 2010

ABOVE: Ron Kohn with his daughter Hannah, 1992

The subject of children was painful for many at CBST. After coming out, some members lost contact with their children in brutal custody battles or were estranged from children who rejected them when learning their parent was gay. Many had come out at a time when having children simply wasn't an option for gay people. Some were happy to live without the complications of children, while others, who chose to live openly as gay men or lesbians, felt the excruciating loss of the possibility they would ever raise children.

In the 1990s, CBST began to witness a transition to intentional LGBT families: Ron Kohn and Richard Connolly, and Judy Ribnick and her partner Diane, were among the earliest of CBST couples to choose to have children. Technology and law, as well as a sense of greater possibilities for gay people, were catching up to the times. While Rabbi Kleinbaum officiated at numerous funerals and memorial services during her first month at CBST, she also attended to what was then a rare lifecycle celebration: a baby-naming, made even more notable because the ceremony was for twins.

A decade later, baby-namings far outpaced AIDS funerals, as more members began raising children of their own. Some congregants watched these rituals wistfully, witnessing something they had considered impossible in their own lives; others were inspired by models of a family they too could create. Longtime member Sydney Rosenberg reflects, "I know that if I were thirty years younger and my late partner Bill Zenzel were still with me, we would have adopted a child. But in 1960 it was unheard of. I remember the first person who adopted a child at CBST. It's a wonderful thing to see children here."

Partners Liz Dornfeld (left) and Liz Deutsch gave birth to their two children within a few weeks of each other, 2001.

Twins Samantha and Allen Paltrow-Krulwich were the first children named at CBST who also celebrated their b'nai mitzvah there, marking a new era in the history of the synagogue: an education program to carry children from infancy through adulthood. Before that, most CBST families with children joined a second synagogue to find a peer group with whom their children could study. The few b'nai mitzvah held at CBST were transformative and moving occasions: the children, most of whom did not identify as LGBTQ, brought their friends and extended families into the shul, offering them a glimpse of CBST's vision of Jewish family and Jewish life.

### NAMING OUR TWINS

Although we had been members of CBST for years, it wasn't until the birth of our twins, Allen and Samantha, when we actually needed more than a seat during the High Holy Days. Now we needed help planning a naming ceremony, and ended up calling Rabbi Kleinbaum.

A friend summed up the ceremony this way: "On the surface it seemed like a familiar Jewish event with a traditional-sounding rabbi. It was only in stepping back that I realized how radical it was for so many people to celebrate a lesbian couple and their new family."

LYNN PALTROW AND SARA KRULWICH, NEWSLETTER, NOVEMBER 1993

Lynn and Sara with Allen and Samantha at their naming in 1993

BELOW: Sara with Allen wearing the tallit he designed for his bar mitzvah

BOTTOM: Samantha breathing a sigh of relief with Lynn after the service

### Obligations of a Jewish Community

CBST has become a family of choice for many. Members share a strong sense of community responsibility, stepping forward for one another in times of need. For years, member Marc Janover assumed the administration of the Bikkur Cholim Committee, making many of the visits himself. Longtime shiva minyan coordinators included Lisa Kartzman and Mike Finesilver. Member Gary Adler is still in awe at the *"neshamah* of CBST," at the emotional generosity of CBST members when he first came to services to mourn his lover Danny Jacobs. "I would weep in front of strangers every week, and they would talk to me and try to comfort me, and still come back and talk to me the following week. And I would do the same with other people. Every time I stood for Kaddish on Friday night, there was a hand on my shoulder when I sat back down."

The Bikkur Cholim committee was also responsive to members who were ailing. In 1994 Susan Meyer was undergoing a stem-cell transplant, the most aggressive treatment for lymphoma used at that time. Since few hospitals in New York City were chartered to perform the treatment, she was sent to the children's division of Long Island Jewish Hospital, where she was confined in a sterilized room for three

## TO BELONG TO A COMMUNITY

On the thirtieth day after we buried my mother, Rabbi Cohen and the shiva committee helped me to arrange a minyan. My partner Shelli and I were just back from California. We had buried my mother, cleared out her apartment…I was still a mess and so exhausted. The morning of the minyan I remember being afraid—not about having the minyan—but afraid that no one would come. As a black Jew by choice, I often grapple with feeling as if I am "the other." I grapple with embracing a covenant that includes a people who have sometimes shunned me because I look different, because they don't consider me a real Jew. In worrying about who would come for the minyan, I was so wrong. In our small, uptown apartment, so many people came that we ran out of places to sit. So many members of CBST came whom I only knew by sight, not even by name. And as we prayed, as I said Kaddish, as I shared a little about my mother, I was not alone. To belong to a community that embraced me so wholly, that understood I needed to mourn with them as a Jew, this meant the world to me. I am forever grateful.

NARDA ALCORN

Narda Alcorn (right) and her partner Shelli Aderman

weeks. Susan's partner, Marsha Melnick, stayed at her mother's apartment nearby. Every evening she scrubbed up at the hospital so she could enter the room to visit Susan. One morning, as Marsha was commuting to the city, she ran into Yolanda Potasinski on the train to New York. When Yolanda learned why Marsha was there, she asked if Susan would appreciate phone calls from the Bikkur Cholim committee. "Susan was not very active at CBST," Marsha remembers, "and she was feeling weak and depressed, which is why I was surprised she agreed to take the calls." As it turned out, Susan received comforting calls from nine people. "I didn't know any of them then," she says, "and I'm still not sure who all the callers were. It was such a powerful experience of support from the community that after I recovered, I became involved in CBST and signed up for the first bat/bar mitzvah class."

Before AIDS, funerals were rare in the congregation. CBST members would step in when there was no family rabbi to officiate. Reb Pinchas officiated at the

---

APRIL 14, 2009

DEAR RABBI COHEN,

Sitting with Dick's body last night was quite an experience. Four years ago on April 13, my mother died, and on the 14th my mother's body was transported to the funeral home where others performed the service of *shmirah* for her. Serving as *shomer* for Dick was a direct way of giving back to those who did this for my mother, and for me to remember her.

When I arrived, I was taken to a lovely and comfortable sitting room. Dick's body was on a copper table, overlaid with a blanket. I brought two books with me--the JPS *Tanakh*, and Paul Monette's *Last Watch of the Night*. I read from both, sometimes aloud and sometimes silently. I found psalms I had never read before, some of which felt deeply relevant and others that didn't. I'm not so comfortable with the ones calling for the destruction of my enemies, but I know that Dick, like me and all gay people, have enemies that are both external and inside us, and we need help with all of them.

At some point, my cell phone rang. I thought I had turned off the ringer, but I hadn't. It was Rick Reder and Jack Nieman. They asked me if they could come and sit with Dick. They had no idea I was already there, and I was glad to have them relieve me, so I didn't have to leave Dick alone with a stranger.

This business of community is quite a miracle. There were several times I found myself imagining how to explain to others why I would spend an evening alone with a dead body, reading to it. In a city like New York, this seems so odd and anachronistic. Of course, we don't only do it for the dead, even though our tradition tells us otherwise. We do it for ourselves, to remind us of the people who are important to us, to create continuity, a constant chain of support that will eventually come around to me again, the next time someone I love dies, and ultimately for those who love me.

I'm glad you arranged for us to have this opportunity.

Eric Rosenbaum

In 1991, Harry Lutrin helped assemble a booklet for memorial services.

first CBST funeral, for member Eugene Berman, an older man who died of cancer. Although the family attending didn't fully understand what CBST was, they appreciated the devotion shown to Eugene. On several occasions, CBST members, often coordinated by Art Strickler, raised funds for members who could not afford proper burial. The rabbis have continued that tradition. The community ensures that mourners can travel to the cemetery and will organize shiva at the synagogue if a member leaves behind no partner or family.

In 2002, CBST dedicated its own cemetery, fulfilling a goal first articulated more than two decades earlier and fulfilling the tradition that a community establish a cemetery even before it constructs a synagogue building. Yolanda Potasinski, board president from 1996–2001, and Cemetery Committee co-chair Ron Kohn, worked closely with board member Louis Urban, a funeral director who helped secure plots at Cedar Park Cemetery in New Jersey, and raised funds to establish the cemetery. CBST can now bury its members with the dignity and honesty many struggled to achieve throughout their lives.

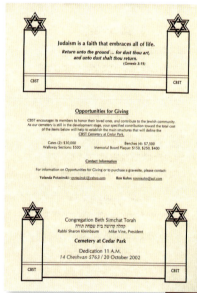

ABOVE: Invitation to the dedication of CBST's cemetery at Cedar Park, New Jersey

ABOVE RIGHT: The cemetery stone marker seen from the English and Hebrew sides

RIGHT: October 20, 2002: the cemetery dedication

## The Community Diversifies

As CBST continued to grow, various affinity groups developed to support and encourage the emerging populations of different demographics. Soon after its founding CBST tried various initiatives to attract more women members, with varying degrees of success. The creation of the Feminist Minyan laid the foundation for the sea change that ensued with Rabbi Kleinbaum's arrival, when the shul finally achieved a gender balance.

Over the years, CBST was home to a Zionist *chug*, a leather group, a Sephardic and Mizrachi group (initiated by member Shep Wahnon), and a Russian group (created by member Yelena Goltsman), among other affinity groups. CBST members formed the core of Lesbian Daughters of Holocaust Survivors and provided a support base and jumping-off point for many other LGBT Jewish groups, such as Orthodykes.

CBST also began focusing on members who didn't define themselves as gay or lesbian. Regina Linder recalls, "There were always transgender people in our community, but we didn't have language for them. Early on, we had a group, then probably called transvestites, who attended CBST's High Holiday services. Our intention was to be welcoming from the get-go. Our commitment to the transgender individuals among us is critically important, especially because the community is still so marginalized in society." In early 2000 CBST's mission statement was amended to include bisexual and transgender Jews. Although the synagogue quickly adopted the language GLBT or LGBT to describe itself, CBST didn't really address transgender inclusion until a few years later.

Jill Weiss remembers meeting one other transgender person when she first came to CBST in 1998. "The organization had started to move. There was interest, but people weren't really aware. When I told some people that I was transgender, they seemed confused, uncomfortable, and some were even hurtful. Mostly they evolved and, later on, apologized." Mike Waldman recalls wondering if he would be welcome to the adult b'nai mitzvah program as a trans person. "It was really scary. I called the office several times to make sure it was OK for me to take the class, if my gender and pronouns would be respected. I had to find where CBST stood in this respect. I read all the synagogue's literature and I looked at the website, but still felt it wasn't clear I would be welcome. That segment of the membership was just not as visible as it is now." In the class Mike was relieved to find playwright and actor David Harrison, whom he had read about in one of his books on trans people.

Activities sponsored by a variety of groups over the years.

The synagogue began to make transgender inclusion a priority in the early 2000s. Before moving to Boston in 2001 to begin graduate school, Jill Weiss met with Rabbi Kleinbaum and encouraged her to do outreach to transgender people. "I said, 'We're out there, and we don't know whether CBST is here'." When she returned in 2005, Jill discovered the climate to be quite different. Rabbi Kleinbaum had initiated a number of community conversations and educational initiatives. A *drash* by Rabbi Cohen on transgender inclusion had been published online, and later appeared in the book *Torah Queeries*, edited by former rabbinic intern Joshua Lesser. Jacob Lieberman gave the Rosh Hashanah membership appeal, talking openly about his experience as a transgender man. Reuben Zellman, the first openly transgender person to be admitted to rabbinical school, served first as children's educator and then as Cooperberg-Rittmaster Rabbinical Intern and, with Mike Waldman, helped create the Trans Working Group, now called the Trans Empowerment Committee (chaired by Jase Schwartz) as a welcoming and visible transgender presence.

CBST also became more thoughtful about the role of straight members. Nancy Meyer and her husband Marc Weiss preferred having their children, Amy and Isaac's b'nai mitzvah at CBST because of its progressive values. Ivan Zimmerman became the first straight member to serve as board vice-president. Avi Ofrane, a straight Moroccan Jewish father of twin sons—one straight, one gay—said he found in CBST the community he had been looking for his whole life: "This was equality, this was respect for the individual; this was truly a *kehillah kedoshah,* a holy congregation. This is

## ORTHODOX AND QUEER

Between 1992 and 1998 I was involved with several activist, religious and social groups that cropped up in New York City for twenty- and thirty-somethings. The first was the Alliance for Judaism and Social Justice. This group gave birth to JAGL (Jewish Activist Gays and Lesbians), which spawned GLYDSA (Gay and Lesbian Yeshiva Day School Alum Association) and later, the Orthodykes. During this time of movement building, CBST was the backdrop and home base for Orthodox GLBT Jews. CBST tried to satisfy some of our needs by hosting a "Friday Night Minyan with a twist." The twist was that it was traditional, but consisted of people with a GLBTQ identity. We wanted to re-create what we had grown up with, the same liturgy and davening experience. There was no place we could go to find both a queer and traditionally Jewish space; but we could make it happen at CBST.

CBST was a natural place for us to feel comfortable because we had heard about some of the men who started CBST, who were now either Orthodox or Chasidic. Also, it felt like a bit of a smaller world in the 90s. Things were newer for CBST then and the GLBT Orthodox scene was just beginning. We needed each other.

As an alum of Frisch, the Yeshiva high school, I know that Rabbi Kleinbaum understands the challenges of being Orthodox and gay and that she, in fact, comes from a very similar place. The love of the tradition that will not fully embrace you exists side by side with the sense of alienation that comes from being unwelcome in those traditional spaces.

MIRYAM KABAKOV

## THE TRANS EMPOWERMENT COMMITTEE

When I got to CBST, I had a lot of conversations with friends who hadn't met many trans people. I was definitely one of the first trans people they ever met. Part of me was accustomed to that situation—a lot of places added the *T* but didn't do anything about it, which was disappointing. There were moments when I found it challenging, especially earlier in my transition when I wasn't passing. People saw me ushering on High Holidays in my suit and just assumed I was a dyke.

Even so, it was exciting to be there from the beginning and witness the changes over time. I have been one of the more "out" trans people at CBST, and I think I've educated a lot of people along the way and have felt really supported. Rabbi Cohen was important in helping me feel welcome, and Rabbi Kleinbaum frequently talks about trans issues. There are many more visible trans people at CBST now. Even the fact that there is a transgender category on the website and that there is a gender-neutral bathroom.... Wherever I see those things I feel comfortable and I can tell the organization is thoughtful. We have also incorporated transgender ritually—sometimes at services, or at a name change ritual, just like a baby naming. This is part of community life.

The Trans Working Group was launched when Reuben Zellman came as a rabbinic intern. It was very meaningful to have a transgender person in the clergy. Even when the group has fluctuated in size, we kept it going, because it was important it stay alive. When Melissa Simon came as an intern we got a second wind and changed the name to the Trans Empowerment Committee, and others joined. Now there are more trans people who come regularly and are more engaged in community. We're a more visible presence, and congregants are more aware of trans people in the community.

Some of the younger members of the committee think we don't do enough, but they don't have the perspective to see how much we've done and how much has changed at CBST and in the world. They get frustrated that we have to keep educating. I was more impatient when I was young too. It's good to be frustrated. There is still work to do.

It's amazing that we can have such a diverse community, with so many opinions and viewpoints, where people worship so differently and believe such different things, and at the same time still care about one another.

MIKE WALDMAN, MEMBER SINCE 2002

---

truly a house of God where no one is made to feel inferior, where righteousness does not depend on the color of your skin or your sexual orientation, where one's beauty is not seen through the filters of bigotry." Some members resisted the "alphabet soup" that came from increasing efforts at expansiveness within the LGBTQ community, as the acronyms grew to include queer, questioning, intersex, and straight. Others have come to prefer the less restrictive *queer*, although many older members struggled to overcome their pejorative associations with the word. Some even came to believe the time has come for CBST to stop defining itself in terms of sexual orientation and gender identity.

### Crossing the Generations

For many CBST offered an opportunity to socialize with people from different generations, a phenomenon experienced both as a blessing and a challenge. Daniel Chesir-Teran (then Daniel Chesir), who first came to CBST shortly after graduating from Yeshiva University, remembers feeling conspicuous even at gatherings of the younger men, who were mostly in their thirties and forties. As more people in their

## WHY NOT CBST?

We are sometimes asked the question, "Why CBST?" The subtext to this question is, of course, why would a straight family join a primarily GLBT congregation? I hope that someday the question will be "Why not?"! But in the meantime, some history.

When I first met Rabbi Sharon Kleinbaum, she told me about CBST's High Holiday services that are free and open to everyone, regardless of Jewish background, sexual orientation, or membership status, regardless of anything that has historically stood in the way of full participation in Jewish life. I was intrigued. Hearing that *Kol Nidrei* services might draw 4,000 people, I privately thought that I would try it just once and in fall of 2000, I went for the first time. Through all of my adult years, trying many and various High Holiday services, I had never felt more at home. I had not ever attended a service that felt more intimate, more inclusive, more accessible, and more meaningful, in spite of the huge number in attendance.

I grew up in a reform congregation in the Midwest and have spent my adult life primarily on the East Coast. I know I am not alone in having attended services where, as a Jew, I could often identify more with non-Jewish visitors than with the members of the congregation, as far as understanding what was going on, and feeling as if whether or not I understood was completely unimportant to anyone there.

At CBST we have found a congregation that is welcoming in ALL respects. As Rabbi Cohen said recently, "Here, people come as they are." At CBST, our family has found a place of learning, a place dedicated to social justice and social change, a place where there is as much room for the devout as for the alienated, for our different ages, and for the full range of our different desires for participation. And yes, there is very much room for us as a straight family. I am continually moved by the fact that of all the many, many Jewish communities in New York, it is precisely the community of GLBT Jews that works so hard to raise enough funds each year to rent a place as large as the Javits Center, so that everyone is welcome. I am continually moved by the fact that it is precisely a GLBT community where there truly is room for all.

Here my children, Isaac and Amy, have been able to study, learn to read and chant Torah and Haftarah, learn about the history of Eastern European Jewry, join in the tradition of becoming a bat and bar mitzvah, and they can now define their own places within the traditions of their family and ancestors, whatever that place may be—all in a congregation where there is liturgical and ritual tradition, beautiful music always, and where there is room for the full and varied range of belief and practice within their own small family, extended family, and beyond. So in the end: Why not CBST?

NANCY MEYER, MEMBER SINCE 2000

early twenties started coming to the synagogue, they formed their own group, working with Rabbi Kleinbaum to create a safe space. The new group, which happily included women, debated an age cutoff. "We were very organized," Daniel recalls. "Each week we had someone greet young people at the door, so they would feel safe knowing they were not going to be preyed upon. We organized great activities, and there were always twenty or thirty of us who went out to dinner after shul. After I met my husband Ian, we moved to New Jersey. When we came back for Pride with our kids, we realized we weren't the 'young people' anymore." As one demographic aged into the next, the twenties and thirties group was reconstituted, and new groups formed as the synagogue adapted to meet the needs of its members.

David Levin was seventy-three in 2006 when he was taken to Mount Sinai hospital for a quintuple bypass. He recalls, "Quite a few friends from CBST visited me at the hospital and later at the rehab facility and then at home. They came to take me out for a walk when I couldn't do it on my own. Based on this experience, my friend Marilyn Tessler and I identified the strong unmet need in the congregation for the social and health situations of seniors, many of whom become isolated as they age and develop infirmities. We talked to the rabbis and the executive director, and explained that we would like to lead this initiative. We got their support."

In 2006 Marilyn and David launched the Mishpachah, a group they described as serving members who are "chronologically mature," creating varied social and cultural programming throughout the year. Stan Moldovan initiated a weekly lunch group at the Dish, a restaurant in Chelsea, where members could meet for an informal lunch and conversation. Both groups have fostered a warm sense of community among their regulars, retirees as well as those with flexibility during the day.

TOP LEFT: The 20s and 30s contingent at the 2004 retreat. (back row) Steve Frank, Adam Berger, Miya Rotstein, Mickie Trester, Ann Macklin, Melissa Comerchero. (front row) CRRI Darby Jared Leigh, Joseph Cunin, Marisa James, Ruby Thomasson, Rabbi Cohen

TOP RIGHT: (left to right) Ann Macklin, Mickie (Michelle) Trester, and Noa Sattath. Mickie revitalized the 20s and 30s committee in the early 2000s and served as its chair for several years.

ABOVE: David Levin at a luncheon with Aviad Doron from the Jerusalem Open House

These initiatives have focused attention on the needs of CBST's senior members. As the shul's aging population has grown, the community has developed resources to care for members without biological family or partners, and to support those who have become caregivers for partners and friends. For example, CBST and SAGE (Services and Advocacy for GLBT Elders) secured funding from UJA-Federation to develop programs and support for Jewish LGBT seniors.

Soon after the Mishpachah was established, a forties and fifties group—for couples and singles—was organized as well. The group organizes events out on the town, from guided tours of historic Jewish neighborhoods, to ice skating, and brunch out. Committee chairs included Joseph Cunin and Evelyn Shaw.

Each of these age-related groups supports social interactions and cultural activities. Far from feeling segregated, the members of each remain attached to the synagogue because CBST welcomes all aspects of the community.

### HOW I GOT TO CBST

Visiting New York for a weekend, I decided to go to Shabbes services at CBST. Afterward, Irving Cooperberg came up to me and said, "I see you know how to daven." I said, "I do." He asked if I lived in New York, and I told him I was thinking about it. He said, "Oh, you'll move here." I didn't know who he was at the time; I just thought he was some crazy *meshugeneh alte kaker* and was also really funny, so I said, "Ok, I'll do that." I chatted with a number of people that night and thought, "this isn't a bad place." In fact, CBST played into my decision to move to the city about six months later.

I came to services a few more times, looking around for others my age. Irving found me again and asked, "Did you move?" I was surprised he remembered me. When I told him I had, he asked, "Did you join yet?" I hadn't. He said, "You'll join." And I did. Then he said, "You'll get involved. You'll join a committee. You'll even chair a committee." I said to myself, "I don't have time for this," but I found myself joining committees, chairing a few, and, at Irving's prodding, running for the board.

My parents raised me to be a doer and a shlepper. You need boxes moved, I'll do it. Soon I became a fixture on Friday nights. I made friends with people my age and older, men and women. My ex-partner and I had a housewarming party; some of the older lesbians were the first to come. One couple, Ruth and Connie, arrived with practical gifts—cooking utensils, spatulas, cookbooks—the kind of things you don't think about buying but always need. They are good friends to this day.

ROBERT EPPENSTEIN, MEMBER SINCE 1994

## A SECOND CHANCE

At the end of her life, in August 2006, Marilyn Tessler self-published a book of poetry with the help of Tasha Calhoun and Rabbi Kleinbaum. A psychotherapist, she came to poetry late in her life.

A wily thief
Crept into my room
Last night
As I traveled along
A rocky shore

Inspecting the furthest corner
With great agility
Wrapped in his great coat
He kicked some rocks into the sea
Letting me
Boogie away

But his calling card
Wafted over to me
Warning me
To find my way
Or he would be waiting for me
Deciding to stay
That day
The angel of death

Marilyn Tessler reading her poem "A Second Chance," 1992

Gerry Faier, who had just turned 100, with three-month old Galia Cohen-Margolius, at *Kol Nidrei*, 2008.

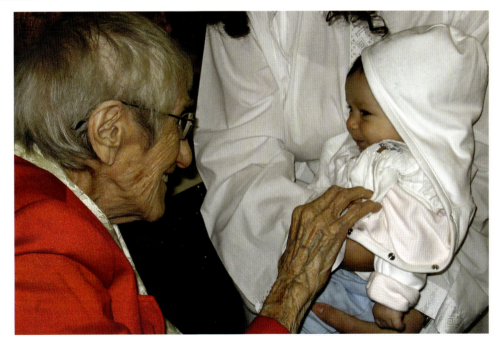

# 10. COME OUT AND LEARN

From its earliest days, CBST members have expanded their Jewish knowledge in a context that felt safe for questioning and exploring. Because so many CBST members were at home in a Jewish setting for the first time, they found a community where they could integrate every aspect of their identity—a place where they could challenge their minds, develop their skills, and examine the intersection of Judaism and sexual orientation and gender identity, while studying with others who would often become lifelong friends.

Before being introduced to CBST, Susan Meyer—the daughter of intellectual bohemian atheists—had no exposure to religious Judaism. Although her mother's first language was Yiddish, the religious aspect of Judaism seemed "remote and irrelevant." For others, CBST offered an opportunity to reconnect with Judaism, liberated from the traumatic associations of a Hebrew school, yeshiva, or Jewish community where they had been bullied or forced to hide their sexual identities. Ian Chesir-Teran, who graduated from Hebrew Academy of Nassau County, a yeshiva high school, recalls the letter his rabbi wrote to all college-bound seniors: "I imagine that there are going to be some of you reading this letter who are gay. The Torah makes very strict demands on you that you must lead a celibate life." Somehow, I knew this applied to me. His writing seemed compassionate, but expressed a very harsh vision of life for someone like me. I thought, if I need to come out, I can't make Judaism part of my life. I went to college carrying this sense of irreconcilable identities."

Ultimately, education at CBST is an experience of community.

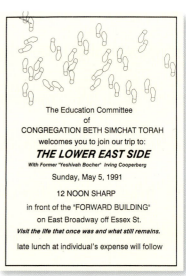

A typical Education Committee flyer from the early '90s

## A House of Learning

The first educational offerings were the Friday night *oneg* programs organized by Elenore Lester and Ros Regelson. The topics were as eclectic as CBST's members, spanning the political and cultural spectrum, for example, "Vladimir Jabotinsky, Rediscovered" or "A Bicentennial Celebration," with such guest speakers as the Reverend John McNeil, author of *The Church and the Homosexual*, and Rabbi Herschel Matt, Hillel Director of Princeton University, who wrote *A Jewish Approach to Homosexuality*.

While some *oneg*s were more intellectual, others, such as the "Bintel Brief," a theatrical presentation of letters addressed to CBST, which was a nod to the classic advice column in the Yiddish *Forward*, were purely entertaining. Some programs offered support for those struggling with coming out. Bruce Friedman recalls a panel composed of three mothers of CBST members: Barbara Brick (Barrett Brick's mother), Ethel Bieber (Mark Bieber's mother), and Selma Friedman (Bruce's mother). "Somebody from the audience asked, 'Are you happy your son is gay?' My mother was feisty; she was a character. She answered, saying, 'Sure, if I had my way, I would rather he met a girl and got married.' Because she was very direct, people laughed. She kept going, 'But my husband and I feel that if Bruce is happy, we're happy. We're glad he found this congregation, because we were worried that he was going with the wrong crowd.' The audience went wild. There was a huge round of applause."

Knowledgeable members, some of them gifted professional educators, eagerly shared their skills. Hebrew and Yiddish classes were offered as early as 1973. In December 1974, Pinchas ben Aharon, along with Carl Bennett and Murray Lichtenstein, established a Talmud class that still meets regularly almost forty years later.

In Westbeth CBST expanded its education program, creating an Education Committee in 1975 and launching its first roster of classes that fall, including three levels of Hebrew language; in December, Isaac Bashevis Singer visited a Yiddish class taught by Pesach Fiszman. The newsletter reported that Singer "spent a few hours of the afternoon talking with a dozen students, about Yiddish, homosexuals, and *Yiddishe* homosexuals. It was a mutually

David Carey, a talented Yiddish singer, performing at an *oneg* in the mid 70s

Mel Heuman, Ron Kohn, Jeff Scheckner, and their friends at a latke-making class, 1991

instructive experience. Singer, who consistently dealt with subjects previously ignored or taboo in Yiddish literature, was eager to expand his contact with homosexual Jews." Singer had published two stories on gay themes, one of which he reportedly decided to publish only after meeting with a member of CBST. According to the article in the newsletter, "Singer assured us that our conversation would percolate through to his creative source, eventually emerging in some form in his writings. To think that CBST is already so close to putting its mark on the Jewish consciousness!"

The November 1976 newsletter boasted over fifty participants in that fall's classes, a significant percentage of the congregation. Under the leadership of such members as Roy Doliner and Steve Siegel, an editor of the CBST newsletter and archivist at the 92nd Street Y, the shul's educational programs developed further over the following years. New offerings drew on members' expertise, featuring a Zionist *chug*, a film series, and cultural outings to New York museums and historical neighborhoods.

During the 1980s, Education Committee chairs included Ron Weiss, Ron Kohn, Harris Goldstein, and Mel Rosen, each of whom developed the program in their own way. Enhancing the education program was part of Mel's vision for hiring a rabbi for CBST; he maintained that a rabbi would provide critical "direction, guidance, and continuity."

Ron Weiss, 1989

## CONGREGANTS AS TEACHERS

My first encounter with education at CBST was in June 1981, just a month after I moved to New Jersey from California to start a new life and relationship with my partner Jack Greenberg. This was the first time Jack taught a class anywhere, and it was to be the first of many classes he was to teach— and continues to teach to this day— at CBST. This first class was Torah Cantillation, and there were three students: Sherry Fyman, Roy Doliner, and me. The class culminated with each of us reading an *aliyah* of Torah from *Parshat Mattot–Massei* at a Saturday morning service that summer.

The class had a profound effect on all three of us: We enjoyed it, had a celebratory meal afterwards, and learned to be proficient Torah readers. Sherry went on to become the regular *baalat korei* at an east side Manhattan synagogue and occasionally taught Torah as well. Roy—who was a professional Jewish educator—became the principal of a Hebrew School and in 1982-1983 put together a regular group of classes at CBST and led the Education *Chug*, of which I was a member. After having begun to teach Hebrew school in New Jersey in the fall of 1982 (as well as a class in Jewish Genealogy), I taught my first class at the synagogue, Beginning Hebrew, in the spring of 1983. This began my teaching career, with adults and children, which continues to this day. As a Board member, I became Education Coordinator in 1984 and put together an Education committee that included Steve Siegel and Marilyn Mishaan.

The rich tradition of education at CBST has allowed many congregants to teach, enriching the lives of others and providing the whole congregation with a variety of learning experiences.

RON WEISS, MEMBER SINCE 1981

## Studying with the Rabbi

In her first year at CBST Rabbi Kleinbaum initiated a weekly *parshat hashavuah* class, which for several years anchored the adult education program. Members flocked to study with the rabbi in a more intimate context. Under her guidance, the Education Committee created a Tuesday night *beit midrash*, concentrating most classes on one lively evening. The March 1993 newsletter reported, "One of the students tells us she has 'made a commitment to *push* myself as a Jew (to use a phrase the Rabbi has emphasized) in making a space in my week for as long as it takes to prepare for and attend the class.' In the process, she has improved her Hebrew, and has begun to 'think in fundamental ways about issues like Jewish identity and spirituality.'"

### SPRING 1993 CLASSES

- Parshat Hashavuah
- Service Leading Workshop (required for leaders)
- Gemorah shiur
- Understanding the Friday Night Service
- Torah Cantillation
- Basic Hebrew
- Hebrew Reading and Conversation
- Gay Literature Discussion Group
- Yiddish Conversation
- Naomi and Ruth
- Mah Jongg

LEFT: Rabbi Kleinbaurm (center) teaching text to (clockwise from left) Michael Levine, Nancy Mertzel, Yolanda Potasinski, Glenn Mones, Marilyn Mishaan, Ron Kohn, Richard Connolly, and Hanna Gafni

BELOW LEFT: Nachum Niv, John Bliss, and Steve Kotick studying together, 1998

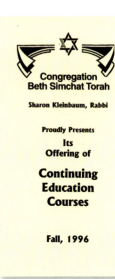

Congregation Beth Simchat Torah

Sharon Kleinbaum, Rabbi

Proudly Presents Its Offering of

**Continuing Education Courses**

Fall, 1996

# A GIFT OF TORAH

## THOUGHTS ON THE RABBI'S WEEKLY PARSHAH CLASS

I had studied the Bible before. But, as an adult, I had never studied Torah in a Jewish setting, let alone in a gay and lesbian synagogue, with the idea that a particular text could have a spiritual significance... Even though (or perhaps especially because?) we are all at different places, I feel an immense caring for the students in the class. It is an amazing gift for a professional scholar to feel joyful respect for every class participant, to feel the freedom to ask even the most basic and frustrating questions, to have my hunger to learn and the impassioned confusion I bring to this text received so well.

LISA BRUSH, MARCH 1994 NEWSLETTER

## Lehrhaus Judaica

In 1998 CBST received a four-year Jewish Continuity grant from UJA-Federation to implement a comprehensive adult education program and design programming for children of Jewish gay men and lesbians. With the grant, written by Regina Linder and David Flohr, and with the guidance of Rabbi Kleinbaum and the support of board president Yolanda Potasinski, CBST was able to hire its first part-time education director, Rabbi Benay Lappe, a gifted teacher of text and the first openly lesbian Conservative rabbi.

Rabbi Lappe worked with Rabbi Kleinbaum, Roderick Young (who was then a Cooperberg-Rittmaster Rabbinical Intern), the Education Task Force (chaired by Yael Bat-Chava and Robert Eppenstein), and education subcommittee co-chairs Bob Christensen and Leslie Deutsch, to create the CBST Lehrhaus Judaica Program. They drew the title from the *Freies Jüdisches Lehrhaus*, an experimental adult Jewish education institution founded by Martin Buber and Franz Rosenzweig in Frankfurt, Germany in 1920, and designed as a radical experience of intellectual challenge and Jewish integration.

Rabbi Roderick Young, who became education director and assistant rabbi upon his ordination the following year, and later Rabbi Cohen strove to meet that standard. Working closely with the Education Committee, long chaired by Laurie Hanin and Neal Hoffman, they expanded the offerings to produce an extensive Lehrhaus catalogue each semester.

Regina Linder wrote the original grant proposal with David Flohr for the Lehrhaus, 1998.

In addition to classes at CBST, the Lehrhaus included cultural explorations of New York City museums, theater, and opera, often preceded by preparatory classes and including opportunities to meet renowned writers and artists like Moises Kaufman and Frédéric Brenner. Member Andrew Ingall, for many years an assistant curator at the Jewish Museum, organized several special tours. The Lehrhaus also included day trips to the Reconstructionist Rabbinical College, the Jewish Theological Seminary, and the National Yiddish Book Center.

## New Programs

Always aiming to provide members with the opportunity to study with an array of noted scholars, Rabbi Kleinbaum, along with Joanne Jacobson and the Education Committee, created the Scholar-in-Residence Program in 1997. Rabbi Nancy Fuchs-Kreimer was the first scholar in residence, joining CBST for a full Shabbaton. In 2003 Ruth Berman and Connie Kurtz endowed the Ruthie and Connie Scholar-in-Residence Program. The Education Committee chose scholars and artists who could share their work with CBST, often linking the program to the congregation's annual educational theme.

ABOVE: Marsha Melnick, Mike Vine, Susan Meyer, and Rabbi Kleinbaum at the National Yiddish Book Center, 2001

RIGHT: Walking tour of Lower Manhattan with Rabbi Kleinbaum

An even more immersive Shabbat and learning experience was the annual congregational weekend retreat, which Rabbi Kleinbaum created in 1995 with committee co-chairs Mike Finesilver and Yolanda Potasinski. The first retreat was held in December at the Elat Chayyim Center. Although the experience convinced the community that retreats should take place in the spring and not during the winter, all agreed that the weekend would become a highlight of the year, which it has. For many congregants, the retreat continues to be a rare opportunity for members to celebrate an entire Shabbat together, to leave the bustle of the city, and dine and daven together, spending the weekend learning, relaxing, and getting to know one another in a convivial environment. Jill Weiss, reflects, "Going to retreats has been very powerful for me. Even going to synagogue and to chorus rehearsals every week, you don't get to know people the same way. On the retreat I really get to know deeply about people's lives and they get to know about mine."

## GLBT LEHRHAUS JUDAICA

### A GUIDE TO JEWISH LEARNING AT CONGREGATION BETH SIMCHAT TORAH

Welcome to Congregation Beth Simchat Torah's GLBT Lehrhaus Judaica. We welcome everyone, to a center of learning that integrates lesbian, gay, bisexual, and transgender studies and Jewish studies, regardless of your background.

This spring, we turn our attention to questions which are deeply resonant to the GLBT Jewish community: how do we, so accustomed to the feeling of being strangers in a land not our own, create a sense of home? How do we explore and assert our identities when we do not know if our true selves will be welcomed? How do we fulfill the commandment to welcome the stranger?

Our study delves into various interweaving elements of Jewish life: sacred text, the arts, creating community, and *tikkun olam*. At CBST we strive to include our whole selves in our study, asking the questions that are our own. During our Connie and Ruthie Scholar-in-Residence weekend we will look at Brazil, the place of departure of those first Jews who arrived in North America. At a program studying the experience of transgender Jews, we will look inward at the inclusiveness of the GLBT community. In a course examining Jewish attitudes on Deafness, we will look at the inclusiveness of the Jewish world....

RABBI AYELET S. COHEN, 3 SH'VAT 5765

# SAMPLING OF LEHRHAUS CLASSES 1998–2012

**The Book of Shmot/Exodus**, Rabbi Sharon Kleinbaum

**Welcoming Shabbat: An Introduction to the Friday Night Service**, Rabbi Ayelet S. Cohen

**Great Composers Sing the Psalms**, Professor Art Leonard

**Raising a Jewish Child in a GLBT family**, Rabbi Sharon Kleinbaum and Rabbi Ayelet S. Cohen

**Beginners Quilting: A New CBST AIDS Quilt**, Larry Gifford

**Jews of Color Speak-Out**, at JCC

**Diaspora in Action: A Trip to the Brooklyn Museum**, Frédéric Brenner, Marsha Melnick, and Rabbi Ayelet S. Cohen

**The Body in Jewish Thought and Legend**, Cooperberg-Rittmaster Rabbinical Intern Lauren Grabelle

**The Land of Israel, Yesterday and Today**, Rabbi Sharon Kleinbaum and Rabbi Ayelet S. Cohen

**Sounds of Silence: The Jewish Deaf Experience**, Cooperberg-Rittmaster Rabbinical Intern Darby Jared Leigh

**High Holiday Cantillation**, Jack Greenberg

**What's In a Name? A Learning Program about the Process of Naming and Choosing One's Name**, Rabbi Ayelet S. Cohen, sponsored by the Trans Working Group

**New Israeli Music with Old Jewish Roots: A Musical Celebration on Yom Ha'atsmaut**, Cantor David Berger

**Text and Music: Bringing the Machzor to Life**, Rabbi Ayelet S. Cohen and Cantor David Berger

**Cellulite on Celluloid: An Evening of Films about Jewish Women and Their Bodies**, With Maya Orli Cohen and Faye Lederman

**The Jews of Iran**, Houman Sharshar

**Tall Tales from the Talmud: An Introduction to Rabbinic Judaism**, Rabbi Ayelet S. Cohen

**Haftarah Cantillation**, Jack Greenberg

**Text Study for Interfaith Families at CBST**, Cooperberg-Rittmaster Rabbinical Intern Rachel Kahn-Troster

**Torah Cantillation**, Jack Greenberg

**Peddlers and Pioneers: American Jewish History Before 1900**, Rabbi Sharon Kleinbaum

**Shehechiyanu, Vekiymanu, V'higiyanu Lazman Hazeh – Where Are We and How Did We Get Here: Creating a Spiritual Autobiography**, Rabbi Ayelet S. Cohen

**Megillat Esther Cantillation**, Jack Greenberg

**Before Torch Song Trilogy: Queer Jewish Culture in the 20th Century**, Warren D. Hoffman

**Beginner's Hebrew**, Ron Weiss

**Intermediate Prayerbook Hebrew**, Larry Kay

**Embracing Life, Facing Death**, Cooperberg-Rittmaster Rabbinical Intern Rachel Weiss and Dr. Nathan Goldstein

**Jewish Influences on Broadway Musicals II, The Musicals of Harold Arlen, Harold Rome, and Jule Styne**, Kenn Harris

**How It All Began: An Introduction to Biblical Literature, History and Culture**, Rabbi Sharon Kleinbaum

**CBST Oral History Project**, Gerry Albarelli

**Hazan et Hakol – Who Provides Food For All: Judaism and Hunger**, Rabbi Ayelet S. Cohen

**Guarding Our Speech: Lashon HaRa and Shmirat HaLashon**, Cooperberg-Rittmaster Rabbinical Intern Michael Rothbaum

**Introduction to Yiddish Song**, Henry Carrey

## SCHOLARS/ARTISTS IN RESIDENCE

**Rabbi Nancy Fuchs-Kreimer:** Exploring Jewish Theology (1997)

**Rabbi Burton Visotzky:** Making the Bible a Timeless Text: How Do We Read the Book (1998)

**Rabbi Shefa Gold:** A Contemplative Shabbat of Chanting and Meditation (1999)

**Dr. Ernest Rubenstein:** Franz Rosenzweig (2000)

A Conversation with **Grace Paley** (2002)

**Rabbi Jacob Staub:** Medieval Jews in Arab Lands (2002)

**Rabbi David Forman:** Israel, Human Rights and the Jewish Tradition (2003)

**Rabbi Rebecca Alpert and Rabbi Steve Greenberg:** Sexual Ethics in the GLBT Community (2004)

**Professor Nelson Vieira:** Jewish Voices in Latin American Literature (2005)

**Professor Marla Brettschneider and Performance Artist Danielle Abrams:** Racial Diversity in the Jewish and Queer Communities: Lessons for CBST (2006)

**Rabbi Simkha Weintraub:** Facing Illness Jewishly (2007)

**Writer Daniel Mendelsohn:** The Art of Memoir (2007)

**Professor Joy Ladin:** Exploring the Torah as LGBT Jews (2008)

**StorahTelling** Comes to CBST (2010)

**Jay Michaelson,** God vs. Gay? How to Make the Religious Case FOR Equality (2012)

Rabbi Nancy Fuchs-Kreimer

### Building Community

From its inception, the education program has enabled the community to explore issues facing the LGBT community, whether pastoral, political, or internal. Classes have addressed AIDS, halachic positions on homosexuality, and *bikkur cholim*. In 2003 Rabbi Cohen created the *Talmud U'Ma'aseh* initiative, integrating Jewish study with social justice work. Eager to deepen its commitment to transgender members, in 2005 CBST hosted a major trans education program, featuring Rabbi Margaret Moers Wenig who had pioneered trans education at HUC since 2002, and a panel of two transgender activists and scholars: Donna Cartwright, convener of the Transgender Caucus of Pride at Work, AFL-CIO, and Paisley Currah, executive director of the Center for Lesbian and Gay Studies (CLAGS) and Associate Professor of political science at Brooklyn College of the City University of New York. When Reuben Zellman served as Cooperberg-Rittmaster Rabbinical Intern, he developed materials for CBST that became the foundation for TransTorah's guide for all trans-inclusive congregations.

In 2008, seeking to deepen the community-building aspect of learning, Rabbi Cohen and the Education Committee created the Neighborhood Chevruta Program, encouraging study in intimate groups at members' homes, guided by materials prepared by Rabbi Cohen or on topics of the group's own design. One group started meeting weekly at the home of Stan Moldovan, with Yehuda Berger, Saul Zalkin, Harriet Beckman, and Judy Hollander comprising its core. Neal Hoffman and Andrew Ingall formed a Washington Heights group, and George Perlov coordinated a Park Slope group.

## THE PHASES OF MY JEWISH LIFE

Like many LGBT Jews, I experienced three phases in my life: my early life, attending yeshiva schools, when I was a "good Jew." Second, coming out and abandoning Judaism, feeling like the religion was totally incompatible with who I was becoming. Third, meeting my now-husband, Daniel, who introduced me to CBST, and understanding that it was actually possible to integrate all of who I was.

Rabbi Kleinbaum had connected me with Rabbi Roderick Young, who gave me all of the responsa from the Conservative Movement's Committee on Jewish Law and Standards. I devoured the *teshuvot*, reading all the literature to educate myself. But it was the *Tikkun Leil Shavuot* [night of study] in 1998 led by Rabbi Benay Lappe and Rabbi Kleinbaum that brought me into the next phase of my Jewish life. Rabbi Lappe taught a Talmud class at the *tikkun*. It was the first time I had studied Talmud since graduating from yeshiva high school in 1987. Something about her style, and studying *gemara* for the first time in twenty years, was a wakeup call for me. I love studying *gemara* and *limudei kodesh*. Although I had recently been studying the contemporary *teshuvot*, the Talmud class showed me that I needed to go back and study the primary sources on my own. I couldn't just rely on what other people were telling me; I needed to go to it myself. That's when I came to phase four, realizing I wanted to become a rabbi and a teacher. Rabbi Kleinbaum took us to the water for our *hashkamah minyan*, which was such a powerful experience, davening at dawn after that transformative night of learning.

A few years later, after I had collected and organized hundreds of primary sources on sexuality, I taught them in the Lehrhaus. It was the first time I taught Torah and the first time I was studying with other LGBT Jews to wrestle with the texts, and connect them to God. For ten weeks I taught with Benay. The first week we had a group of twenty-five or thirty students. There they were, sitting around studying queer Talmud together. I was so grateful that CBST gave me the platform to teach. I felt so empowered and so blessed to live at a time when something like that was really possible.

IAN CHESIR-TERAN

Ian with his son Eliezer at a protest, 2009

### Adult B'nai Mitzvah Program

The early adult b'nai mitzvah classes were taught by Cooperberg-Rittmaster Rabbinical interns, starting with David Steinberg, Lina Zerbarini, and Sara Paasche–Orlow, each bringing their own traditions to the classes. As Rabbi Kleinbaum initially designed it, the Adult B'nai Mitzvah Program included one night of study a week for two years, but at the request of students the time was extended to a three-year cycle. Rabbis Young, Cohen, and Weiss each led adult b'nai mitzvah cohorts through years of study and moving celebrations that have become milestones for the entire community. Students forged deep connections with the rabbis, Cooperberg-Rittmaster Rabbinical Interns, and other teachers. As of this writing, nearly seventy congregants have had a bat or bar mitzvah at CBST. Jack Greenberg, CBST's most prolific Torah cantillation teacher, has taught more than one hundred students to chant from the Torah over the years.

The students are as diverse as the synagogue itself, and include members of every sexual orientation and gender identity with a wide range of ages and Jewish experiences: Jews by choice who wanted to continue their Jewish educations; Jews by birth who had limited or no Jewish education as children; women who came of age when girls were not allowed substantive b'not mitzvah; men who had a rote or even traumatic experience at thirteen and wanted to repeat it on their own terms; transgender people who wanted to complete the ritual as the Jews they had become.

According to Judy Hollander, it was because of "Rabbi Kleinbaum and Rabbi Cohen, who make Jewish learning so delicious, that I enrolled in the bat mitzvah class in the first place." Fifty years after her 1955 group bat

## FINDING MY JEWISH IDENTITY

Born to a Jewish mother and a Calvinist Protestant father, I received no religious education based on the belief from both parents that religion meant only hypocrisy, persecution, and death.

At thirteen, I asked my mother if I could have a bar mitzvah, but she declined, asserting that I was only interested in the gifts. At eighteen, I went to meet with the Rabbi of the Reform synagogue where my uncle took us for the High Holidays.

I stated the same request and he replied that I would be wasting my time and advised me to learn English instead, since I was a musician!

Spiritually though, there was always a yearning in me and so I went on to explore on my own. I studied Zen, then went to India to study and practice Buddhist Vipassana, then, in New York, converted into the Episcopalian Church, to finally arrive at CBST one Open Door Yom Kippur day in 2001, looking for answers.

I found my Jewish identity at CBST. Together with my partner Eric Rosenbaum, I completed the study for my bar mitzvah. I was elevated spiritually with the incredible teaching and insights of Rabbi Kleinbaum and Rabbi Cohen. This core knowledge now strengthens me and helps me in my interaction with singers and orchestras and with all the challenges of this very difficult profession. I can say I carry CBST around the world. And as I walk to the podium or the stage, I have CBST in my heart.

PIERRE VALLET, BAR MITZVAH, JUNE, 2005

## THE FIRST MILE

Studying with others in the bat/bar mitzvah class pretty well allayed my fears of looking like a total jerk, and I've discovered that the Jewish God is not an old man sitting in judgment of my performance. In fact, the transcendent can be found anywhere—nature, in loving relationships, in community, and yes in ritual, too. Feeling more comfortable with Jewish ritual, I've also begun to adopt a more personal approach to its practice. I've come to see that Judaism is not doctrinaire, that it provides room for interpretation and revision. Some traditions move me more than others. For example, I feel an overwhelming joy in reading directly from the Torah, chanting from a text in much the same way Jews have done for 2,000 years! I confess some practices still feel foreign to me, and maybe always will, but a bat mitzvah does not represent the end of the learning process by any means. A milestone, perhaps, but only the first mile: the journey continues.

SUSAN MEYER, BAT MITZVAH, JUNE 7, 1997

TOP: Judy Hollander (right) and Bonnie Marty

ABOVE: George Perlov inscribing the Torah with *soferet* Jen Taylor Friedman

mitzvah at a Conservative synagogue, where she hadn't been allowed to get near the Torah, Judy learned to chant Torah and haftarah for her CBST bat mitzvah. Many were grateful for the opportunity to go through the process as adults. Marcy Kahn, a New York State supreme court judge, and Rafael Cortes, a pianist from Puerto Rico, became close through their b'nai mitzvah preparations. Marcy Kahn wrote, "In our Reform Jewish household of the 1950s–60s, my parents thought the ceremony unnecessary for girls, and I thank them for allowing me to wait to undertake the bat mitzvah until I was old enough to truly enjoy and appreciate it. Although my mother warned me never to sing in public, I believe she would forgive me, given the joy I have experienced in the course of my study and preparation for this day."

At his 2012 bar mitzvah, George Perlov declared, "Today I am a…a…a…middle-aged man—an even fifty to be exact. I initially became a bar mitzvah on December 21, 1974, at the Van Cortlandt Jewish Center on Sedgwick Avenue in the Bronx, an experience I can hardly remember. I've been referring to today's event as my 'once-more-with-feeling' bar mitzvah, since I feel that much of what I did in 1974 was a parroting of what I was told to say and do, without really understanding or caring much about what I was doing. Today I am proud and excited to celebrate my *Yiddishkeit* with my family, friends, and my chosen congregation.

### Neighborhood Partnerships

While CBST was an oasis for LGBT Jews in a hostile world, it always sought to be a part of the larger Jewish community as well. The "Gay Jewish Omnibus," an early iteration of CBST's Education Committee, ran one of CBST's first collaborative programs with neighborhood synagogues in 1981, joining forces with the Reform Village Temple, the Conservative Fifth Avenue Synagogue, and the Town and Village Synagogue, as well as the Orthodox Derech Emuno. In 1986 CBST participated in a symposium on Judaism and homosexuality at the Stephen Wise Free Synagogue on the Upper West Side and joined in AIDS programs both there and at Congregation B'nai Jeshurun. Rabbi Young and Rabbi Cohen served on the board of the Downtown Kehillah, a consortium of downtown synagogues and organizations that sponsored various programs, including an annual Yom Hashoah Commemoration. CBST participated in this community partnership long before it was common for Conservative and even Orthodox rabbis to sit in a room as colleagues with a woman, let alone an openly gay rabbi, to collaborate on community events.

### Educating the Next Generation

The October 1988 newsletter reported that Sha'ar Zahav in San Francisco had established a Hebrew school; two years later, Mel Rosen predicted that creating a CBST Hebrew school was around the corner. In fact, while it would soon offer

## HAVING A SEAT AT THE TABLE

I learned so much through the B'nai Mitzvah program. Even though I was born Jewish, I really only felt I became a part of the Jewish people after my bar mitzvah. I felt much more comfortable going places and knowing that even though I'm not the most learned person, I still can have a seat at the table. It was such a moving experience—one of the best experiences of my life.

Reading from the Torah was challenging. It felt like the rite of passage. Not that I was an adult, but that I had become a Jewish adult. I came from a much more gendered Jewish tradition in Brazil, and the things that I was doing were things that only men did. Women don't even wear *kippot* there. If I had grown up here I may have felt differently because I would have seen women wearing them, but like a lot of other things during my transition, this felt really natural. The first time I put on a *tallit* felt totally natural.

As a child I was very envious of the boys who had bar mitzvahs. I was conflicted, because I really didn't like the treatment of women in the synagogue, but I wanted to have a bar mitzvah. It felt like something I missed out on.
MIKE WALDMAN,
BAR MITZVAH, 2005

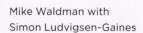

Mike Waldman with Simon Ludvigsen-Gaines

children's programming for Shabbat and holidays, CBST was still a decade away from establishing its own school. Families with young children were a very small minority. Until there was a critical mass of children in any age group, CBST members needed to enroll their children in other Jewish schools.

Gabrielle Weinstein, Jessica Petrow-Cohen, Katie Victor-Marlowe, and Emma Sennett-Kuzin were the first group of CBST children who were all named at the synagogue, went through its education program, and celebrated their b'not mitzvah there.

Judy Ribnick recalls that she and her partner Diane felt very welcomed by CBST when their daughter was born in 1990. Still, she reflects, "We were ahead of the curve among our friends in terms of having kids." Like most CBST members with children at the time, Judy and Diane sought support and a parenting community at Center Kids, a program of the Gay and Lesbian Community Services Center, and looked for a synagogue in their neighborhood to give their daughter a Jewish education.

In 1990 the education programming began to address the concerns of families with children. The announcement for a program on "Legal Ramifications of Life Partnerships," with legal expert panelists Art Leonard, Paula Ettelbrick, and Judith Turkel, emphasized that the topic was relevant to all couples considering parenting: "Family planning, usually a heterosexual concern, can also have major significance for same-sex couples. That's only in part because more couples are raising children." Following this program, in May 1990 the Education Committee organized a Jewish parenting seminar run by Wayne Steinman of Center Kids, attended by twenty-five people. That year was the first CBST offered to provide childcare during High Holiday services.

CBST's first event designed specifically for children was a Chanukah Party in 1991. Aware that few children were visible at CBST, the newsletter announcement promised the party would be "publicized with help from Center Kids, a project of the Lesbian and Gay Community Services Center, so lots of kids should be there." In fact, the party was such a success that a Purim party was planned the following March. While these successful events generated great excitement among only a few members, the children's program expanded very slowly.

## Overcoming Obstacles

In her first year, Rabbi Kleinbaum and Irving Cooperberg joined Center Kids' Wayne Steinman to facilitate a conversation on the future of children's programming at CBST. One new parent, Ron Kohn, reported: "We determined that many exciting and important events with children indeed can be a part of the wide range of services CBST provides, such as: Creating a 'child friendly' atmosphere in our congregation as a whole, providing 'child centered' activities, family education programs, and trips of interest to children."

By the mid 1990s, Rabbi Kleinbaum established the monthly Alef Bet Shabbat service for children and their families. It was led each year by a Cooperberg-Rittmaster Rabbinical Intern and was highly successful, yet it lacked the critical mass to warrant a more comprehensive children's education program. In addition, there remained considerable resistance to devoting the limited congregational resources to expanding children's programming.

In 1999 children's services were held for three age groups on Rosh Hashanah. In her Rosh Hashanah *drash*, "Plant a Tree for Those Who Come After Us," Rabbi Kleinbaum took up the complex issue of CBST's children. She began by addressing the phenomenon of members as "closeted parents," acknowledging the pain of many "invisible" parents and grandparents who had children from previous straight relationships. "We have a member of our community whose children will not allow her to come to the birthday parties of her grandchildren because she's a lesbian. We have a member of our community who cannot be out to her Orthodox children for fear they will reject her. We have many in our community who once feared losing their children, many who accepted unfair separation agreements because they were afraid that, in court, they would have lost custody altogether."

Rabbi Kleinbaum addressed the complexities of the many issues facing CBST, as she continued, "We have people in our community who don't want CBST, the GLBT synagogue of New York, to have a children's program, because 'Well, that's what every other straight synagogue has, and why should we become like them? And after all I'm gay, I'm a lesbian, and part of that means not having little kids around.'

For many years before she had children of her own, Laurie Hanin was one of the most significant figures in the lives of Yael Bat-Chava and Lisa Green's children. Laurie is pictured here with Jonathan Green.

"That is the place we must begin. For we know that a person can be single and live within a rich and deep family of friends. We know that a person can have a partner and no children and have a rich family life. So let us start at that place, by saying we will never believe there is only *one* form of human relationship, only *one* structure that constitutes a 'real' family. That argument has been used against us far too many times. We *must not* imitate the larger society by saying there is only *one* legitimate form of family, that *only* straight people have children, *only* straight people like children, only straight synagogues educate children and raise new generations of Jews."

Acknowledging the range of members—people without children, gay people with children from previous straight

## REFLECTIONS FROM MY YEAR AT CBST: GROWING PAINS

As I began my internship in 1999, I was tasked with formulating how a Hebrew school would look at CBST. More and more families with children were joining the synagogue, and they didn't want to leave in order to educate their kids Jewishly. I led Alef Bet Shabbat services with Gwynn Kessler, and we got to know the families, their stories, their needs. I remember feeling awed by a lesbian couple bringing their baby every month. The infant was obviously too young to take it in, but his parents wanted him to feel like CBST was his home and hear the melodies they hoped he would grow up with.

I was unprepared for the immense backlash against the project I was embarking upon. A few of the older men, some who were founders of the synagogue, expressed to me how heavily laden this endeavor was. When they had come out, fifty or so years prior, they were largely abandoned by their families, and what many of them heard as they were being disowned was, "Oy, there won't be any children," which was the worst fate imaginable for a Jew. They found each other, they founded CBST, and carved out a uniquely Jewish space that was mostly free of children; free of the Jewish pressure to procreate. Here, they could create a different sort of community. As the years passed, technology advanced and with that development also arrived "the lesbians," and eventually men, who were finding ways to procreate. The response of the elder members was riddled with pain. How dare these newcomers become so mainstream? How dare they reclaim what had been rejected by necessity? I recall people hushing children during services, as they do in many synagogues, but for different reasons. Here, the sound of kids threatened to take from them the sacred, Jewish space they had fought so hard to attain.

RABBI MYCHAL COPELAND (NÉE ROSENBAUM),
COOPERBERG-RITTMASTER RABBINICAL INTERN 1999-2000

CRRI Mychal Copeland (left) with Gwynn Kessler leading Purim services for children

marriages, gay and lesbian couples choosing to become parents together, straight couples, single parents—Rabbi Kleinbaum declared, "We do not discriminate. We will be an open community that embraces the broad range of what it is to be human. This community will model the kind of Judaism I believe Judaism is meant to be. The world out there doesn't know it yet. But we know it."

Rabbi Kleinbaum urged the congregation to value the significant roles many lesbians and gay men play in the lives of nieces, nephews, and other children and to honor those relationships. She also stressed the responsibility of the LGBT community to lesbian and gay children, to show them that there are gay people leading happy and productive lives. "We at CBST have a role to play that is not being played elsewhere in our world," she maintained. "As a synagogue, we have a moral responsibility to children. We don't all have to become parents to fulfill that responsibility. We don't all have to become biological parents to fulfill that responsibility. But I believe we have a moral responsibility to make sure that Jewish young people, children, young adults, know there is a community in which it is possible to be deeply Jewish and openly gay." Invoking the Talmudic story about planting trees for the next generation, Rabbi Kleinbaum called on the community to embody the values of CBST's pioneers, like Mel Rosen and Irving Cooperberg. They understood deeply that they were building CBST to be an institution larger than themselves, to exist for the next generation of gay and lesbian Jews, even if those lives looked radically different from their own. She concluded the *drash* by declaring her intention to create a Hebrew school at CBST.

### *Limmud Mishpachah:* **Education for Families with Children**

Over the next ten years, CBST hired several part-time children's educators who, along with various interns, oversaw and implemented the children's education program: JTS graduate student Gwynn Kessler, JTS education program graduate Josh Krakoff, educator Monique Spivak, and CBST Cooperberg-Rittmaster Rabbinical Interns and Rabbis Ayelet Cohen, Reuben Zellman, Melissa Simon, and Rachel Weiss. Cantor David Berger was also instrumental in the program.

Educators at CBST quickly realized that a traditional Hebrew school model wouldn't work for a population as geographically diverse as CBST. This issue intensified as more families with children were priced out of downtown Manhattan and moved elsewhere. Building a substantial group of any age range remained a challenge. Rabbi Melissa Simon, CBST's children's educator from 2007–2010, reflects, "There was a bit of a chicken and egg problem: there was a small program and therefore few children; there were few children so there was a small program." Even facing the obstacles, many families were committed to educating their children at CBST.

In 2006, under the leadership of Rabbi Cohen, CBST embarked on RE-IMAGINE, a visioning project guided by a consultant funded by UJA-Federation. Together with co-chairs Yolanda Potasinksi, former board president, and Laurie Hanin, long-serving board member, leader of the Education Committee, and advocate for childrens' education, they built a diverse task force of lay leaders. The RE-IMAGINE team included parents and non-parents and newer members, who came to the project of Jewish education from a variety of perspectives. In 2008,

Family portraits created by an early *Limmud Mishpachah* class.

TOP LEFT: CRRI Melissa Simon and Lauren Winter working on a Chanukah project, 2007

ABOVE: Micheale Taylor and Cheryl Prince with their daughter Maya at a retreat

LEFT: Cantor Berger leading Alef Bet Shabbat

recognizing that Shabbat morning services had become the center of CBST life for families with children, the group launched a Shabbat-based education program that developed into a new Children's Education Committee, led by Cooperberg-Rittmaster Rabbinical Intern Melissa Simon and co-chaired by Andrew Ingall and Lisa Springer. Celebrating the diversity of Jewish children and their families—issues the rest of the Jewish world was just learning to address—had long been at the forefront of CBST's education program. The program became a laboratory for exploring this diversity through Jewish education and curriculum. Rabbi Kleinbaum, Rabbi Cohen, and, later, Rabbi Weiss facilitated parenting groups to discuss the many issues parents faced.

By 2010, when Rabbi Weiss was hired as assistant rabbi to shepherd the expanding children's education program into its next phase, 150 children were already attending High Holy Day services.

ABOVE: Leslie Bernstein, Fran Dunkel, and Emily Bernstein-Dunkel at a retreat

ABOVE RIGHT: (left to right) Rabbi Weiss, Derek Frank-Lerner, (Asher Frank-Lerner not pictured), Mark Lerner, Steven Frank, and Rabbi Kleinbaum

The resistance to children's presence at CBST has receded over time, and many nonparents take great pleasure in seeing CBST's children flourish. The annual Rosh Hashanah children's blessing has become an inspiring moment for the entire community. Mark Lerner and Steven Frank, parents of two young sons, remarked on their wedding day in the summer of 2011, shortly after marriage equality passed in New York, "We never thought we'd get to have these things in our lives, getting married, having kids. Never in our wildest dreams would we have thought it could happen. We can't believe this is really our life."

## LIMMUD MISHPACHAH: EDUCATION FOR FAMILIES WITH CHILDREN

The rainbow is the symbol of God's covenant with Noah after the flood. It represents hope for the future, a commitment to the great diversity of creation, and the tremendous responsibility of all humanity who are now partners with God in creating and sustaining the earth. CBST envisions a dynamic, inclusive, and multifaceted Jewish education program for our children and their families. Our program strives to build and strengthen a contemporary, learned, relevant, ethical, and deeply rooted sense of *Yiddishkeit* through learning and doing: the study and practice of Torah, social justice, liturgy, Hebrew, music and arts, which make us the Jews we are. Just as our congregation serves a rainbow of members and participants of all ages, sexual orientations, gender identities, and Jewish experiences, our children's education program strives to include children and their families and friends and GLBT youth with a thirst for Jewish knowledge and a desire to be part of our sacred community. Like the varied colors of the rainbow, our program will offer varied models of participation to best serve our diverse congregation. We strive to provide a program that enables experiential and cooperative, multi-generational learning, stressing Shabbat/holiday-centered activities that integrate spirituality with study.

VISION STATMENT, DEVELOPED BY THE RE-IMAGINE: TASK FORCE

## REFLECTIONS FROM MY YEARS AT CBST: QUEER JEWISH FAMILIES

One thing I love about CBST families with young children is that you can never assume which child goes with which parent, a true embodiment of the concept that "love makes a family," and that biology isn't necessarily relevant. Children join families at CBST in all different ways: at birth, in childhood, through adoption, surrogacy, alternative insemination, in vitro fertilization, foster care, and beyond. Our kids and our parents are of all sorts of races, ethnicities, cultures, sexual orientations, and gender identities. Many of our parents of young children are now in their 40s, 50s, and 60s, having had children later in life as culture changed, with challenges of parenting toddlers while thinking about nearing retirement. CBST adults become part of the lives of these kids in all different ways too, as parents, as special grownups, aunts/uncles, honorary grandparents, teachers, and friends.

Families with young children experience Judaism at CBST like many other toddlers and school kids—learning rituals, prayers, *bim bam* and the Dinosaur Song. But they also experience community in a profoundly necessary way. For many of our kids, in their secular school classes, they're the only one with a family that looks like theirs. At CBST we're explicit: *Avinu malkeinu* teaches that God is like our parent. What kind of parents do you have? A Mommy and an Ima? A Daddy and a Papa? Mommy and Mama? One mom? Three parents? There are other families that look like yours here, and that is *kadosh*, that is the way we are created *b'tselem elohim*. And we also see the next generation of kids and their assumptions. One preschooler asks another: What do you call your moms? She responds, "Well, I call my Dads Abba and Tateh." We model all different kinds of families, and we teach Torah through a lens that is both Queer and diverse. Moses has two mommies? Absolutely. Just read the Bible.

RABBI RACHEL WEISS, COOPERBERG-RITTMASTER RABBINICAL INTERN 2006-07, 2007-2008, CBST ASSISTANT RABBI, 2010-PRESENT

By 2009 High Holiday services for families with children were full to overflowing.

OVERLEAF: The annual retreat has become a highlight for many members to celebrate an entire Shabbat together, and to deepen their connections to community within beautiful surroundings.

# 11. TRANSFORMING OUR WORLD

CBST HAS BEEN A REFUGE FOR ITS MEMBERS, but it was never an escape. Congregants have always been fully engaged in the world, committed to righting the injustices they witnessed or experienced both in the Jewish world and in the world at large. While never politically homogeneous, the community has always demonstrated concern for world Jewry, a deep commitment to Israel, and a profound dedication to achieving equality and justice for LGBT people.

Rabbi Kleinbaum brought her background of political activism to CBST and helped the synagogue articulate its commitment to social justice, advance its goal of LGBTQ visibility in Jewish life, and transform, on a large scale, the American religious landscape.

## CBST's Origins as an Activist Community

From its founding, CBST members organized contingents to march at LGBT Pride, originally called the Christopher Street Liberation Day Parade (CSLD) and in Soviet Jewry demonstrations.

A number of members shared the values of mainstream Jewish organizations and wanted CBST to join the rest of New York's Jews at the same events. Others keenly connected their own forced silence as gay men and lesbians to the refuseniks who were compelled to practice Judaism secretly in the oppressive Soviet Union of the 1970s and 1980s.

Established by 1975, CBST's Jewish Affairs Committee, coordinated efforts on behalf of Soviet Jews and other oppressed Jewish populations (such as Syrian and, later, Ethiopian Jews), volunteered as pen pals for gay Jews from around the country and the world, and coordinated outreach programs within the Jewish community. Created at the same time, the Social Action Committee was responsible for promoting CBST's participation in Gay Pride and the CSLD march. This committee also closely monitored the progress of local and national gay rights legislation and discrimination.

CBST members felt the sting of Jewish hostility toward LGBT people, particularly obvious when the ultra-Orthodox community formed a coalition with the Catholic Church to effectively block New York City's gay anti-discrimination bill for a full fifteen years before it finally passed in 1986.

The New York *Jewish Week*, March 9, 1984

Within the gay community, a number of CBST members sought ways to become actively visible as a Jewish presence, its members reaching out to people like themselves who may have been alienated from Jewish life since coming out. They refused to accept the idea that all religion was necessarily homophobic. In 1975 a forum organized by the Gay Activist Alliance addressed the question "Is Religion Compatible with Gay Liberation?" David Krause represented CBST, along with representatives of Metropolitan Community Church, Dignity (the gay Catholic organization), and the atheist Society of Separationists. Chuck Tyson was already active in the CLSD Committee when he attended CBST's first Friday night service in 1973. Chuck served as co-grand marshal of the CLSD first in 1978 and again the following year, leading all the religious groups marching.

Early banners revealed the prevailing culture of hiddenness. The bottom of the congregational banner, reading "the Gay Synagogue," could be detached for Soviet Jewry marches or other Jewish communal events, avoiding the risk of being outed where members were likely to run into colleagues or friends from the mainstream Jewish communal organizations with which many of them were affiliated.

Throughout the years CBST and its social justice activists have been featured frequently in the media: even early on many members participated in radio and print interviews discussing CBST, LGBT rights, and LGBT Jewish life, understanding the synagogue's essential role in promoting the visibility of gay Jews. The community documented this media attention. The October 1975 newsletter proudly reported on a radio interview with Michael Levine, Elenore Lester, and Barry Youngerman. The newsletter also noted the congregation in the *Advocate* as well as an interview with Arnold Mandlebaum in the Jewish periodical *Sh'ma*. "Slowly," the newsletter declared, "the closet door creaks open."

## CBST and the LGBT Rights Movement

New York City was the epicenter of both the gay rights movement and the AIDS crisis, and CBST members played key roles in both, founding many GLBT legal and advocacy organizations, serving as volunteers, board members, and professional staff. While some CBST members preferred the social aspects of the gay community, many—having grown up in activist families or involved in other civil rights struggles—were politically motivated. They had been radicalized by the times and by their personal experiences, often serving as the first openly gay or lesbian person in their professional circles, and feeling a responsibility to the gay people who were less comfortable being out.

One of the longest-standing LGBT organizations in New York—and one of the first with a large meeting space—CBST's physical plant played a significant role in the city's gay history. In 1977 after Anita Bryant's successful campaign to repeal a sexual orientation anti-discrimination ordinance in Dade County, Florida, many New Yorkers clamored for a national march on Washington. Grassroots town hall meetings were planned around the country to decide if and how a march should be organized. At Rick Landman's suggestion, the meeting in New York City was held at CBST, where the vast majority voted to march. Rick was elected one of New York's representatives for the first National March on Washington for Lesbian and Gay Rights, held on October 14, 1979.

In his living room in 1978, Art Leonard, then an associate in a law firm, founded a social organization that would become the Bar Association for Human Rights, one of the first lesbian and gay bar associations in the country. CBST hosted several key meetings and a number of continuing legal education seminars

BELOW: CBST members at the 1979 National March on Washington. (second row from left to right) Sy Robins, Arthur Strickler, Saul Mizrahi, Tim Nenno, Art Leonard, Victor Appel (front row) Jonathan Harwayne, Ian Loebel

INSET: Button worn by marchers

> **CHRISTOPHER STREET LIBERATION DAY**
>
> How does one define "gay pride?" Is it recovering a heritage, or perhaps creating one? Is it satisfaction in the efforts that have repealed the sodomy laws in fifteen states, or frustration and anger at the recent 3-1 defeat of a gay rights bill in the New York State Assembly? Is it living one's life openly, while protecting those of our sisters and brothers who cannot yet do so?
>
> NEWSLETTER, JUNE 1978

during the association's formation in the early '80s. Art Leonard served as the first president of the Bar Association for Human Rights (now called LeGaL or the LGBT Law Association of Greater New York), followed by CBST member Morty Newburgh; several other members have served in that role over the years. Art launched a newsletter on gay and lesbian legal developments, which evolved into *Lesbian/Gay Law Notes*, the nation's most comprehensive monthly publication covering LGBT and HIV/AIDS-related legal news, for which he still serves as chief editor and writer.

Before the existence of the LGBT Community Center, CBST opened its sanctuary to many community groups. SAGE (originally Senior Action in a Gay Environment and now Services and Advocacy for GLBT Elders) frequently used CBST's space. Even after being able to rent office space, SAGE needed a larger venue for social events and continued to use CBST until the community center space became available.

Similarly, when it was difficult to find a rehearsal space, the New York City Gay Men's Chorus often met at CBST, a connection facilitated by Sheldon Post, an active CBST member and board member and an early board chair of the Gay Men's Chorus. Several other CBST members, including Jack Nieman, have been active in the Gay Men's Chorus, which has performed at CBST events. As Rick Landman recalls, appearance at a Pride Shabbat service was among their earliest public performances.

In the early 1980s Irving Cooperberg complained that a gay organization could only be as big as someone's living room, because there was no other meeting space, a point that illustrated the obvious need for a significant gay and lesbian community center. CBST member Marcy Kahn spearheaded the legal research and negotiations that led to the purchase of the city-owned former Food and Maritime High School on West 13th Street. After a period of stormy negotiations, the city offered the organizers a short window to raise $200,000 to rescue the building from an impending auction. Lou Rittmaster recalls the events: "We went home and called 200 people (a lot of them CBST people), and asked them each for $1,000. We said, 'Lend us the money or give it to us, but we need it within a week.' We got more than 200 people to volunteer that $1,000, even from many who couldn't really afford it. The City knew we meant business when we came back to them, and that's when the tone of the negotiations changed." With the purchase, the LGBT Center was founded in 1983.

CBST celebrated the role played in the landmark case by (left to right) Ruth Berman, Connie Kurtz, Janet Blair, and Amy Chasanoff at a special *oneg*.

## Domestic Partnership Bill

Several CBST members played a critical role in the passage of New York City's domestic partnership legislation. In 1998 longtime CBST member, Ruth Berman, a guidance counselor at Sheepshead Bay High School, applied for health insurance benefits for Connie Kurtz, her partner of thirteen years, and was denied. Ruth and Connie, along with two other couples, including Amy Chasanoff, were the lead plaintiffs in the New York Lesbian and Gay Teachers Association suit against the city's Board of Education. Paula Ettelbrick, then Lambda Legal Defense attorney, litigated the case and Randi Weingarten, then United Federation of Teachers lawyer, negotiated and settled the case as part of the Municipal Labor Committee-Dinkins' administration agreement, making domestic partner benefits a reality for all New York City employees.

Art Leonard organized a major public program on family diversity and domestic partnership at the New York City Bar Association that helped launch the campaign for domestic partnership in New York. Meanwhile, Rick Landman was active in the Coalition for Lesbian and Gay Rights (CLGR), which had been instrumental in passing the city's anti-discrimination legislation. He drafted a domestic partnership bill with three other members of CLGR, using materials and model legislation designed by Art Leonard. Council member (now U.S. Representative) Carolyn Maloney convened a working group of community representatives to create a domestic partnership bill. A memorandum by Art

Art Leonard receiving the Lambda Legal Defense and Education Fund "Liberty Award" in 1995

Leonard defending the bill's constitutionality was attached to the bill Maloney introduced in 1990 to the City Council. That bill laid the foundation for an executive order issued by Mayor Dinkins in October 1993 as part of the settlement of the New York Lesbian and Gay Teachers Association lawsuit, providing domestic partnership benefits for New York City public school teachers and all city employees.

### Litigation and Legislation

Many CBST members have played key roles in LGBT civil rights litigation and legislation on the city, state, and national level. As a staff attorney at Lambda Legal, Suzanne Goldberg was co-counsel on the 1996 landmark case *Romer v. Evans*, the first major gay rights victory at the United States Supreme Court overturning Colorado Amendment 2, which would have prohibited the state from ever adopting sexual orientation nondiscrimination legislation.

CBST member Evan Wolfson, staff attorney and later director of the marriage project at Lambda Legal, served as trial co-counsel on the 1996 Hawaii case, the first court decision anywhere to uphold same-sex couples' constitutional right to marry. In 2000 Evan also argued the case of *Boy Scouts of America v. Dale* in the United States Supreme Court and later founded Freedom to Marry, one of the major national advocates for marriage equality remaining to this day.

Rabbi Kleinbaum began her rabbinical career at the Religious Action Center, the Reform Movement's social action organization. In January 1993 shortly after arriving at CBST, she published an open letter to newly inaugurated President Clinton in *Tikkun* magazine expressing the gay community's hopes for the issues he might address in office, including civil rights and increased visibility for gay men and lesbians and for AIDS. At least 125 CBST members joined the March on Washington for Lesbian, Gay, and Bisexual Equal Rights and Liberation for Lesbian, Gay, and

### CHANGING AIRLINE REWARDS POLICY

In 1988 CBST member Bill Johnson, having accumulated enough mileage for two free airline tickets, sought a frequent flyer ticket from T.W.A. for his partner Bill Hibsher. T.W.A. refused because its policy precluded transfer beyond immediate family and married spouses. The couple asked Lambda Legal Defense to threaten the airline with suit, and Lambda did so, charging discrimination. In settling the threatened suit, T.W.A. changed its policy to allow "nontraditional" companions to benefit from the bonus program, and most airlines quickly followed, allowing same-sex couples to transfer their mileage credit to their partners.

Bisexual Equal Rights and Liberation on April 25, 1993; Rabbi Kleinbaum addressed a premarch interfaith service the previous day. Quickly emerging as a national leader, Rabbi Kleinbaum became a prominent religious voice on issues of LGBT civil rights and a queer voice on issues of justice and equality within the Jewish world. She has also stressed CBST's obligations beyond its immediate community to other oppressed and disenfranchised populations.

"I deeply and fundamentally believe that every day our door is open, we as a congregation are engaged in social justice," she has said. "The fact that we started as a community focused on gay people in 1973 was an act of social justice; the fact that we continue to be a vital presence in the lives of many individuals at CBST and beyond, changing the very landscape of New York, of America, and the religious community of Judaism on the issue of LGBT rights, is a profound expression of our commitment to social justice.

"We begin with ourselves: *Im eyn ani li mi li?* 'If I am not for myself, who will be for me?' If we don't take care of our own, who will care? We start with ourselves but it doesn't end there. *V'im ani rak l'atzmi, ma ani.* 'If we're only for ourselves, what are we?' Ultimately, if we only care about ourselves, what kind of community are we? And of course the final line in that famous saying is, *Im lo achshav eimatai?* 'If not now, when?'"

ABOVE: Francis Dubois, Leah Trachten, Regina Linder, and Paul Jeselsohn at the March on Washington, 1993

RIGHT: CBST members at the 1993 March on Washington for Lesbian, Gay, and Bisexual Equal Rights and Liberation

## YOUNG ACTIVISTS AT CBST

I was newly out of college, and my circle was very political. Our definition of feminism was about understanding the experience of being oppressed, which enabled us to take the next step of connecting to other justice issues. I remember going with a crowd to the police brutality protests in the Amadou Diallo case [in 1999] where Rabbi Kleinbaum was arrested. I remember doing social justice work through Jews for Racial and Economic Justice. It was a given that CBST was the place we all came to for ritual, services, and a sense of a larger community. I remember thinking at that time of it being JFREJ's synagogue. I knew that formally it wasn't, but a lot of Jewish things JFREJ ended up doing were hosted by CBST. All of my friends went to CBST for High Holiday or Shabbat services. It was the natural place for us to go. My social justice life and my spiritual life were fused.

ERICA KATSKE, MEMBER 1998–2004

ABOVE: Part of the CBST delegation at the 2004 March for Women's Lives in Washington, D.C.

ABOVE RIGHT: Rabbi Kleinbaum and her daughter Liba Wenig Rubenstein at the march.

RIGHT: Israeli dancer Danny Pollock leading a CBST contingent at a Pride March, 1990s

### Changing the Jewish Community

A large number of CBST members who came from deeply connected Jewish backgrounds, have worked to move the mainstream Jewish community toward greater acceptance and inclusion of LGBT people. In the early days, when gay life was barely on the radar of the Jewish world, this effort was primarily a matter of increasing gay visibility. These members reached out and welcomed the rare supportive rabbis who had stepped forward: Conservative Rabbi Hershel Matt, who wrote an influential article in *Judaism* in 1978; Rabbi Dennis Math of Village Temple in the 1970s; Rabbi Margaret Moers Wenig of Beth Am, the People's Temple, in the 1980s; Rabbis Marshall Meyer and Rolando Matalon of B'nai Jeshurun; and Rabbis Balfour Brickner and Helene Ferris of Stephen Wise Free Synagogue in the 1980s.

Occasionally the encounters within the Jewish community were met with hostility; at other times the exchanges were more open than expected. In the spring of 1975, shortly after LA's gay synagogue Beth Chayim Chadashim was admitted to the Reform movement's Union of American Hebrew Congregations, Carl Bennett and Arnold Mandelbaum spoke at a regional convention of Reform high school students. Carl and Arnold recalled that "Most of the questions showed a positive attitude to the idea of a gay synagogue, and the few expressions of hostility were rejected by the group." A straw poll on whether a gay synagogue should be accepted as a member of the UAHC resulted in an overwhelmingly favorable vote. CBST's Community Relations Committee coordinated so many requests for members to speak at New York area synagogues and Jewish organizations that, in the 1980s, the board created a speakers' bureau to handle the volume of invitations.

In June 1980 CBST operated a booth at the West Side Jewish Peoplehood Week Fair, participating for the first time in a Jewish community-wide event as an openly gay organization. The newsletter reported that the booth attracted hundreds of visitors, including Mayor Koch, who stopped by the booth and "wished us well." Volunteers coordinated by CBST's Community Relations chair David Krause "answered questions regarding who we are, what we do, and how we view ourselves in the light of Jewish law and tradition. . . .There were some hecklers, but they were a tiny minority. One particularly obnoxious heckler was chastised by the general public, which persuaded him to leave. A robust 175 people came to services the following Friday night, with dozens of new faces reportedly recognized as people who had visited the booth.

The shul's leadership viewed such efforts as crucial for increasing visibility and establishing relationships with other Jewish organizations and leaders. However, some members in the Jewish community tried to quash that visibility: when CBST applied for booth space in 1982 for a third consecutive year, the West Side Jewish Community Council demanded the synagogue sign a statement agreeing to omit any mention in its banner that it was a gay synagogue. Some member organizations threatened to withdraw from both the fair and the council if CBST participated at all. Fearing that a crisis would be blamed on CBST further inflaming anti-gay sentiments, CBST withdrew its application.

*Letter to Charles Lieber, Chairman of the West Side Jewish Community Council, read at a meeting of the Council on June 1, 1980.*

Dear Mr. Lieber:

We stood at the base of Mount Sinai as one Jewish people. We endured together at Auschwitz as one Jewish people. We rallied, fought, and won the land of Israel for all Jewish people as one Jewish people. Sadly, the concept of one Jewish people, which has sustained us through thousands of years, is in peril within the ranks of the West Side Jewish Community Council. Your project, the Jewish Peoplehood Fair, is being used as a staffing ground by a bigoted and vocal minority to divide rather than to unite.

We of Congregation Beth Simchat Torah, New York's Gay Synagogue, sought in good faith and with the best motives to participate in the Fair, but our participation was blocked by a segment of the Council that believes one part of the Jewish community has the right to deny another part the full enjoyment of Jewish life.

Although we stand firm in our position that we are well within our rights to demand participation in the fair, although numerous members of the council have backed us in this, although governmental agencies concerned with Human Rights have assured us that our participation cannot be denied us, the members, congregants, and friends of the Gay Synagogue of New York have chosen not to press for inclusion in the Fair at this time. Our decision stems, in part, from an awareness that we have become a focal point for infighting and intrigues that seem to be the order of the day at the West Side Jewish Community Council. Should we continue to press for our rights, and should serious division occur within the ranks of the Council, it is inevitable that gay Jews would be used as scapegoats to take the blame for all the troubles of the Council, just as all Jews have been used throughout history as scapegoats for the troubles of others.

In spite of the injury that has been perpetrated upon us because of this matter, the larger issue of human rights and dignity for all Jewish people remains our uppermost concern. We choose to take the lead in easing above petty prejudice and squabbles. Therefore, we have come to our decision for *Shalom Bayis*, and for our deep commitment to the principles of *Am Israel*, One Jewish People. But, let it be noted, we are withdrawing our application *only* for the 1982 Fair.

We hope that those in the Council who have the true feeling of community in their hearts and minds can comprehend the sadness and bitterness within our congregation. Be assured that we will continue to strive toward the day when the term "One Jewish People" can be more to us than an empty slogan.

IRVING COOPERBERG, CHAIRMAN, BOARD OF TRUSTEES

ABOVE RIGHT: Conference attendees streaming up the ramp into CBST.

ABOVE: The conference schedule from the April 1977 newsletter

## The World Congress of Gay and Lesbian Jewish Organizations

The desire to create a community of other gay Jewish institutions was driven as much by the value of *klal yisrael* (the global Jewish community) as the gay liberation movement itself. In the wake of the November 1975 UN declaration equating Zionism with racism, many American Jews experienced a new sense of vulnerability and isolation in the face of a palpable anti-Semitism. CBST responded by hosting an emergency gathering of North American gay Jewish organizations that December, a program coordinated by Lyn Kneiter, Barrett Brick, Jerry (Ya'akov) Gladstone, and David Krause. "The Jewish community, and this synagogue in particular, will not sit helplessly by to watch the aftermath of this event unfold," the newsletter opined. "We will not allow 'anti-Zionism' to become a respectable slogan for those who would harm us for whatever reason."

The following February 1976, board member Michael Levine represented CBST at a follow-up conference hosted at what was then called MCT—Mishpocheh of Washington, DC–Baltimore—with representatives attending from the Miami and Philadelphia synagogues, to explore the possibility of establishing a network of the gay Jewish organizations around the world. The formal decision to establish what became known as the World Congress of GLBT Jewish Organizations was made in Washington, DC, during the summer of 1976. CBST members Michael Levine, Arnold Mandlebaum, Jeff Katz, and

Barry Youngerman were among the thirty participants attending, a number that also included members of the Chicago, Los Angeles, Montreal, and Toronto communities, as well as the first overseas delegate from London, making this the first International Conference of Gay Jews.

The second international conference, organized and hosted by CBST in April 1977, represented a milestone in the congregation's history. Members took great pride in hosting over two hundred attendees from ten other gay synagogues and organizations.

The World Congress became a meaningful point of connection for the members who traveled over the next three decades to conferences around the country and the world. For many years, CBST anchored the World Congress of GLBT Jewish Organizations, with members Michael Levine, Mark Bieber, Bill Wahler, and Barrett Brick all serving as president. Bill Wahler was the primary organizer of the 1995 conference, hosted again by CBST.

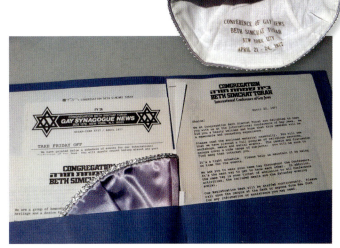

TOP: The packet for the 1977 conference at CBST

ABOVE: Flyer for 14th International Conference of Gay and Lesbian Jews hosted by CBST, 1995

LEFT: CBST members at a World Congress conference in the 1980s

TOP RIGHT: A plaque for CBST was placed in the American Bicentennial National Park in Israel.

TOP LEFT: Letter from JNF to Ya'akov Gladstone at CBST, April 22, 1977

ABOVE: CBST requested the wording on the certificate they received from JNF's New York Office.

## The JNF Forest

Shortly after its founding, the International Conference of Gay Jews undertook the ambitious plan of planting a grove of twenty-five hundred trees in Israel working through the Jewish National Fund. CBST had begun raising money for JNF very early in its history; it was a popular and concrete way for American Jews to show support for Israel, for which there was much enthusiasm after the Yom Kippur War. By 1978 CBST's annual Tu Bish'vat tree planting drive had planted one thousand trees in Israel. In March 1979 JNF hosted a brunch at its Manhattan headquarters thanking CBST and member Ya'akov Gladstone for their commitment to planting trees through their fund.

That month, the New York *Jewish Week* reported on the "woodland of 2,500 'Gay' trees" to be dedicated during the summer, timed to coincide with the fourth international conference in Tel Aviv. CBST was by far the biggest contributor to the grove. The article quoted a synagogue spokesperson, "We all contribute to various Jewish organizations and funds, but we want to have something concrete we can point to with pride to express our solidarity as homosexual Jews with our people." Instead, the grove became the source of a protracted and bitter controversy when JNF, which marks every donated tree and grove acknowledging the community that raises the funds, refused to install a plaque including the words *gay and lesbian*.

The following year the Israeli Society for the Protection of Personal Rights hosted the July 1979 international conference, followed by a tour of Israel and the scheduled dedication of the grove in Lahav in the northern Negev, which by then had grown to three thousand trees. Just weeks before the conference, the venue, Kibbutz Ma'ale Ha'hamisha, which owned a food processing plant as well as a guesthouse, canceled because the Ultra-Orthodox rabbinate—

The September 1979 newsletter included an account of the International Conference of Gay Jews with photos, (above left) the first gay rights demonstration in Israel, held in Tel Aviv, and (above right) the tree grove dedication ceremony in Lahav.

alerted by a group of American Orthodox rabbis—threatened to revoke the kashrut certification of the kibbutz and its factory if it hosted the conference. As a result, the conference managed to regroup in a Tel Aviv banquet hall secured just fifteen hours before its start. More than fifty CBST members attended, proudly participating in the first-ever public gay rights demonstration in Israel and outdoor Friday night services, led by CBST's Carl Bennett and Ira Jay Rosen. The group faced another blow when JNF canceled the grove's dedication, refusing to create a plaque reading "4th International Conference of Gay and Lesbian Jews," claiming that the conference was using them to propagandize for gay rights in Israel.

Back in New York, CBST began extensive negotiations with JNF. Ya'akov Gladstone, Dick Radvon, Art Strickler, and Art Leonard met with the senior leadership of JNF's New York office. The director, an Orthodox rabbi, said the Israeli JNF board decision was dictated by pressure from other sources, probably including the Chief Rabbinate himself. The only fault the director acknowledged was in the New York office processing the order without questioning the wording for the plaque. The negotiations, led by Art Leonard, became contentious, with the JNF rabbi saying that he had instructions from Israel to return the money. When Dick Radvon invited JNF to send a representative to CBST, the rabbi said he would be crucified by his Orthodox colleagues if he set foot in a gay synagogue. Finally, an agreement was made to install a blank plaque, the members of the conference feeling it was more effective to install a plaque demonstrating that the gay community was being silenced, which in turn might elicit questions, than install a plaque that would simply cover up the situation. The same dispute wore on for thirteen years, until 1992—under sustained pressure from the mainstream Jewish community—when the JNF finally installed the plaque acknowledging the World Congress.

## Salute to Israel Parade

In 1993 CBST was banned from the Salute to Israel Parade, New York City's major Jewish visibility event, echoing the incident with the West Side Jewish Community Council ten years earlier. Emboldened by a decade of progress in gay rights achievements, the empowerment that came from AIDS activism, and a new rabbi who did not back down from confrontation, the synagogue took a very different position.

Rabbi Kleinbaum was the first openly gay rabbi admitted to the New York Board of Rabbis. At age thirty-three in the midst of a highly eventful first year at CBST punctuated by numerous AIDS funerals, she spoke throughout the city and across the country as the openly lesbian rabbi of New York's gay and lesbian synagogue. Yet it was the Salute to Israel Parade that catapulted her and CBST into national attention.

After CBST applied to march, the parade's sponsor, the American Zionist Youth Foundation, denied permission under pressure from Orthodox groups threatening to boycott. The controversy immediately attracted the attention of the *New York Times*, which had previously reported on the exclusion of gay groups from the St. Patrick's Day Parade. When ARZA, the Reform Movement's Zionist association, invited CBST to march with them under a joint banner, the controversy escalated further. After weeks of protracted negotiations about the wording of the banner (the words *gay and lesbian* were forbidden, and even a banner reading "ARZA and CBST proudly support Israel" was deemed too flagrantly gay), AZYF tentatively approved the compromise. Just two days before the parade, AZYF banned CBST from participating on any level, falsely claiming that Rabbi Kleinbaum had violated a confidentiality agreement barring communication with the press. In fact, Rabbi Kleinbaum had carefully upheld the agreement, which was limited only to discussing the wording of the banner. The media attention was enormous. Numerous articles appeared in the Jewish press, and five articles in the *New York Times*, among them an in-depth profile of Rabbi Kleinbaum. The press coverage and the outcry from many of its Orthodox constituencies proved too great for the parade's sponsor organization.

Scrambling to react to its last-minute expulsion, and under pressure from all sides, CBST organized an alternative event near the parade route at Central Synagogue. Hundreds of supporters, including many New York officials (such as Governor Mario Cuomo, Mayor David Dinkins, and former Mayor Ed Koch), rabbis, and representatives of Jewish

For a few years CBST members attended from the sidelines, before finally marching in 1999.

## ON THE SALUTE TO ISRAEL PARADE

As a Zionist, I am here to salute the State of Israel on its forty-fifth birthday. Congregation Beth Simchat Torah is a community of deeply committed Jews whose love of Torah transcends political differences. Today we stand here to say to Israel that, despite the hatred shown towards us, despite the bigotry, we will fight for our right to stand up proudly, openly, and declare that Israel should be safe and peace should prosper in her gates.

Today is a victory for Israel, even while here in New York our Jewish community struggles over who's "in" and who's "out." Today is a victory for CBST because we are making clear that though we have been excluded from the parade, we are not silenced . . .

We were excluded from the parade because the constituencies of the American Zionist Youth Foundation realized that no matter what words appeared on or were excluded from the banner everyone would know we were there. For CBST has ceased to be an invisible part of the New York Jewish community. Lesbian and gay Jews have ceased to be an invisible part of our families, schools, and synagogues. Lesbian and gay people of all religions and races have ceased to be an invisible part of the American people.

The conflict was about visibility. For generations lesbian and gay Jews have lived like Marranos, the hidden Jews of Inquisition Spain who were forced to live closeted Jewish lives. Elements in the Jewish community want us to remain hidden. CBST made compromise after compromise with AZYF. Ultimately no compromise was acceptable—only our complete invisibility. Neither anti-Semitism nor antigay attitudes will render invisible our support for the State of Israel.

We are grateful to the many individuals and organizations, especially ARZA, who supported our inclusion in the parade. CBST received many hate calls and frightening threats of bloodshed. But the hate calls were far outnumbered by the calls of support from non-Jews and Jews, Reform, Reconstructionist, Conservative, and yes, even Orthodox.

And so Israel—we, the gay and lesbian Jews of New York join our voices with the rest of the Jewish community in New York in wishing you a mazel tov on your 45th birthday. We at Congregation Beth Simchat Torah, whose members' political views range from right of Likud to left of Labor, join in fervent prayer for peace in Eretz Yisrael and in New York. All we want is "l'hiyot am chofshi b'artzaynu," to be free people in our land.

RABBI SHARON KLEINBAUM,
STATEMENT AT CENTRAL SYNAGOGUE, MAY 9, 1993

CLOCKWISE FROM BELOW LEFT: The Israel Tribute Committee presented the synagogue with this certificate of participation, 1999.

CBST members proudly carry the synagogue banner in 1999.

Rick Landman wore a rainbow shirt over a shirt with the 1992 *New York Post* front page headline about the Parade, "Oy Gay!"

It wasn't until 2012, with the parade under the auspices of the Jewish Community Relations Council, that LBGT groups were allowed to march openly.

organizations attended the parallel event. Some critics felt CBST hadn't gone far enough, and should have disrupted the parade; others, worried the controversy was taking the focus away from the celebration of Israel, wished CBST had stepped away quietly. Members of Jewish Activist Gays and Lesbians (JAGL), a group of young Jews, many of whom attended the CBST event, protested the parade from the sidelines. Daniel Chesir-Teran recalls, "It wasn't JAGL vs. CBST." Many of the marchers, including students from the Yeshivah of Flatbush, Daniel's alma mater, indicated their support for both CBST and the JAGL protest. Tamara Cohen, then a student at Barnard College, agrees. "Many of us had grown up marching in the parade, and we felt it was ours. We wanted to be out there on the street, visible to everyone walking by." The event marked a watershed moment in local Jewish public opinion: even individuals and organizations ambivalent about the religious Jewish stance on gay men and lesbians were offended at the exclusion of CBST from a Jewish communal event.

# STATEMENTS FROM OUR SUPPORTERS

This day is about solidarity, about love and affection for the state of Israel. If you could not come to the parade, the parade has come to you.
**COLETTE AVITAL, CONSUL GENERAL OF ISRAEL IN NEW YORK**

The state of Israel has been a beacon for Jews everywhere. It was born of the ashes of the Holocaust . . . During the Holocaust, whether you wore a yellow star or a pink triangle, you were oppressed and brutalized. The fates of Jews and gays then, as now, were inextricably linked. For Jews who are also lesbian or gay, the State of Israel has special meaning . . . I hope that next year all New Yorkers who wish to honor the State of Israel, Jew and gentile, Black, white, Asian, or Latino, straight or gay, can all join together in one massive celebration of Israel's glory.
**DAVID DINKINS, MAYOR OF NEW YORK**

Mayor David Dinkins and Rabbi Kleinbaum at the Central Synagogue counter-protest

I would like to affirm that the State of Israel is not a halakhic state, and its state secular law forbids any discrimination based on sexual orientation. Gays are equally drafted to the Israel Defense Forces, are equal in the labor market, and discriminating against them is punishable by law. It will be most unfortunate if an archaic Jewish notion overcomes a liberal Israeli position in a Salute to Israel parade, which is meant to exhibit unity to support Israel the way it really is.
**YAEL DAYAN, MEMBER OF THE KNESSET, LETTER TO COLETTE AVITAL, MAY 7, 1993**

We are not out of Egypt yet. We look forward to the day when we will all go out from Egypt together.
**GREATER NEW YORK REGION FEDERATION OF RECONSTRUCTIONIST CONGREGATIONS AND HAVUROT**

We deplore the unconscionable decision of the American Zionist Youth Foundation to renege on its agreement with us in inviting Congregation Beth Simchat Torah to participate in the Salute to Israel Parade. Suddenly, a secular event, a parade whose purpose is to bring together Jews and all others who support Israel, has been turned into a divisive religious issue.
**MARCIA CAYNE, PRESIDENT, ASSOCIATION FOR REFORM ZIONISTS IN AMERICA**

The [Salute to Israel Parade] exists as a celebration of the State of Israel, and we feel that all who wish to participate in this celebration should be welcome. While it is well known that the Conservative Movement has serious halakhic problems with homosexuality, we deem that totally irrelevant in this context. It is deplorable that one congregation's desire to participate in this joyous occasion has diverted attention from what should have been a united support for the Jewish State.
**ALAN TICHNOR, PRESIDENT OF THE UNITED SYNAGOGUE OF CONSERVATIVE JUDAISM**

## CBST and the Movements

Since the 1970s CBST members have closely monitored American Jewish movements, advocating for progress in their positions and attitudes toward LGBT people. The synagogue's members and its clergy have actively worked to alter the perceptions and policies of the movements. In the late 1980s, knowing that both the Reform and Conservative Movements were reviewing their policies on gay and lesbian Jews, CBST stepped up its outreach. The CBST members who grew up in the Conservative Movement followed its public positions on homosexuality with great personal interest. Frustrated by the Conservative Movement's refusal to prioritize the issue of gay and lesbian inclusion, Mel Rosen complained in the April 1989 newsletter that, while there may have been glimmers of progress, the Conservative Movement was far more "occupied with the problem of ordaining women. They've relegated the gay issue to the back burner. As far as the Orthodox, well, forget that. As long as they continue to view gays as violating halachah, there'll be no change."

That month in 1989, longtime member Judith Tax—one of the most active members of the CBST speakers' bureau—broke new ground by addressing a group of rabbis, cantors, and rabbinical students at JTS, in an event initiated by the students, which the school permitted them to publicize, and for which both students and faculty requested and received samples of the CBST liturgy.

Both the Reform and Conservative Movements addressed their policies on homosexuality at their spring 1990 rabbinical conventions. In a front page article in the September 1990 *Gay and Lesbian Synagogue News*, Mel Rosen emphasized CBST's role in the progress that had been achieved: "In the past year we became

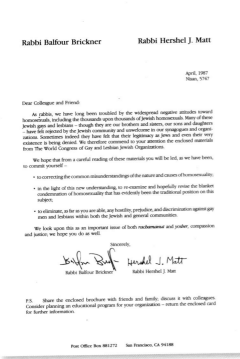

A 1987 letter from Rabbis Balfour Brickner and Herschel Matt appealing to colleagues to change their views and treatment of gay and lesbian Jews, which they sent with a brochure created by the World Congress of Gay and Lesbian Jewish Organizations

involved in efforts to change the attitudes and perceptions of the mainstream movements towards gays and lesbians. Our congregants met with movement leaders in groups and individually in order to educate these branches of Judaism. We're very proud that significant changes came out in two of these movements." The Reconstructionist Movement was the first to decide to ordain, admit to the Central Conference of American Rabbis, and place openly lesbian and gay rabbis. The Rabbinical Assembly of the Conservative Movement adopted a resolution condemning violence against lesbians and gays, calling for civil rights for lesbians and gay men on a national level, and encouraging synagogues to welcome gay and lesbian members. Rabbi J. B. Sacks, Mel's partner, helped author that resolution and build support among straight allies within the Rabbinical Assembly.

CBST had long been a sanctuary for rabbinical students and rabbis who could not be openly gay in their seminaries or communities. *Gay Synagogue News* served as an important communication tool for that largely underground network, announcing initiatives like Ameinu, the first ever national conference for gay and lesbian rabbis and rabbinical students in 1986. Rabbi Kleinbaum recalls the

## CBST CHANGING THE CONVERSATION

It was especially bitter when organizations supported by CBST members rejected the interests of gay people. In 1988, for example, the B'nai Brith Anti Defamation League launched "World of Difference," a major educational project confronting bigotry in American society, that wholly ignored homophobia. In response, the Gay and Lesbian Alliance Against Defamation (now GLAAD), enlisted CBST to help petition the ADL; even Mayor Ed Koch intervened, asking ADL President Abraham Foxman to correct the omission. The ADL National Board declined. The following year, under pressure from gay and lesbian organizations and New York politicians, the ADL finally reversed its position. CBST member Barrett Brick, then executive director of the World Congress of Gay and Lesbian Jewish Organizations, joined representatives from the National Gay and Lesbian Task Force, Gay and Lesbian Alliance Against Defamation, as well as Mayor Koch and Governor Mario Cuomo's offices to meet with ADL's associate director. As Barrett reported to the CBST newsletter, although ADL refused to change the content of the program, they did agree to acknowledge to educators and media outlets that "'World of Difference' is not an all-inclusive campaign against prejudice" and that gay and lesbian organizations would be included in its bibliography and in ADL's Community Resource Listing. ADL also agreed to have gay and lesbian organizations participate in the implementation of 'World of Difference,' promising to help gay and lesbian organizations develop other anti-hate campaigns. Similarly, in 1993 the Jewish War Veterans of America strongly opposed repealing the ban on gay men and lesbians serving in the military, a debate that rose to the forefront of national attention in the wake of President Clinton's inauguration, and resulting in the compromise policy of "Don't Ask, Don't Tell." CBST members joined progressive Jewish organizations supporting the repeal of "Don't Ask, Don't Tell," which finally succeeded in 2011.

# MANHATTAN

## Out Of The Closet, Into The Classroom

*With recent grant from UJA-Federation, gay synagogue in West Village launches ambitious education program.*

**SUSAN JOSEPHS**
STAFF WRITER

Although replete with course offerings such as Hebrew ulpan, intermediate Talmud, and "An Introduction to Jewish Prayer," the new education program at Congregation Beth Simchat Torah can hardly be classified as just another center for Jewish study. In fact, it may be the only place in town to get the latest scoop on gay-friendly kosher caterers for commitment ceremonies, explore biblical perspectives on coming out and pore over the details of raising Jewish children in gay and lesbian families.

Starting next week, CBST — New York's only gay and lesbian synagogue, located in the West Village — will launch its most ambitious and comprehensive educational series in its 25-year history: a Gay and Lesbian Lehrhaus Judaica.

Funded by a four-year $168,000 grant from UJA-Federation's Jewish Continuity Commission, CBST's Lehrhaus features an 18-member faculty, course offerings for adults from all levels of Jewish background and a small children's program that the synagogue hopes will expand into a permanent Hebrew school. The concept of a Lehrhaus — literally, house of learning — dates back to 1920, when the theologian Franz Rosenzweig founded the first one in Frankfurt, Germany.

At CBST, the Lehrhaus reflects both an evolution in spiritual maturity and demographics in the gay and lesbian Jewish community. "There's been a baby boom and an increase in families in the gay and lesbian Jewish world," says Rabbi Sharon Kleinbaum, CBST's spiritual leader. "As the only gay and lesbian synagogue in New York, we are here to provide for these families. [Currently,] a lot of parents wind up enrolling their children in Hebrew schools worrying about whether their kid will be harassed for having two fathers."

Although the educational institute's director, Rabbi Benay Lappe — a recent graduate of the Jewish Theological Seminary — had dreamt for years of starting "a gay and lesbian yeshiva, the Lehrhaus could not have happened 10 years ago."

"We were not ready for it. Only now do we have gay and lesbian rabbis and scholars who can teach us our tradition and help us realize we're agents for change, and not just passive recipients of our tradition," says the rabbi, who's also a senior teaching fellow at CLAL - The National Center for Learning and Leadership. "Our overall goal is to give a gay or lesbian Jewish person a sense that his or her own personal story is part of a larger Jewish story."

In other words, the Lehrhaus offers adults the opportunity to enroll in trade Jewish education classes that they could take elsewhere but would rather do so in a gay and lesbian environment," explains Yael Bat-Chava, who co-chairs CBST's education task force committee. "But it also offers courses specific to being gay and lesbian ... courses that are not offered anywhere else."

One of 13 projects selected to receive funding from 80 submitted applications, CBST's proposal "was exceptional," says Dana Rawitch, a program associate for the Jewish Continuity Commission. "It reflected a tremendous amount of work in planning and thinking of what they [CBST] wanted education to look like in their synagogue."

Rawitch adds that while the Commission has awarded grant money to projects that have "served the gay and lesbian community, this is the first grant for an institution specifically for gays and lesbians."

The grant money serves as a clear indication "that the Jewish world is in a different place today," observes Rabbi Kleinbaum of the greater Jewish community's increasing recognition and support of gay and lesbian Jews. "We still have a long way to go but [the grant demonstrates] a radical shift."

Rabbi Lappe also uses the term "a long way to go" — in relation to the numbers of gay and lesbian Jews "who remain alienated and estranged from Judaism. The biases against us are so insidious and inherent in our tradition," she observes. "We have felt so alienated from our tradition, so we have believed the fallacy that only one group of people has the right to interpret what the Torah means. That is not historically or philosophically accurate. We know that generations before have made Midrash [re-interpreted tradition] when their reality no longer matched the reality of the previous generation. What we're doing in fact, is deeply traditional."

"Yet," we can't make changes until we understand what we're changing," Rabbi Lappe adds. "From learning comes the authority to interpret. This is a big job. When you've been told your entire life that you don't belong in this tradition, it's difficult to say that 'this tradition is mine.'"

A course in intermediate Talmud on "The Politics of Passing" for example, requires that students explore original source material that on the surface, might not resonate with their contemporary lives. But "the issue of going undercover for different reasons is relevant to us, even though the Talmud does not say that [this issue] is about gay people," Rabbi Lappe says. "We are not making the Torah a queer Torah but we can look at it from the lens of our own lives."

While the Lehrhaus remains physically confined to New York, Rabbi Lappe can "see it affecting people all over the world. I think it represents a quantum jump in gay-Jewish consciousness," she says. "If someone visiting New York sees our brochure, he or she might be inspired to start something in their own communities."

From the buzz that is heard among the 3,000 people who attended her congregation's Yom Kippur services at the Javitz Center, Yael Bat-Chava feels that "people are really excited about the program. We've never done something on this kind of scale and for now, we're just hoping for successful registration."

Whatever the future brings, the Lehrhaus, without a doubt, attests to substantial "psychic evolution," in the gay and lesbian Jewish community, according to Rabbi Lappe, who observes that at the turn of the century, newly arrived immigrants could not imagine "being both Jewish and American. It's the same thing with being Jewish and gay ... two worlds coming together that hadn't been together before," she says. "We first had to feel good about being gay and to say we're not an abomination. Now, we're in the next phase. As gays and lesbians, we will love Judaism enough to struggle with it, shape it and pass it down."

*Jewish Week,*
*October 16, 1998*

---

conference being held under such a cloak of secrecy that participants were only given the name of the city and airport to fly into and the number to call upon arrival for further instructions. A few years later, twenty-nine North American lesbian and gay rabbis signed a statement which was sent to every major Jewish organization and periodical in North America calling on all religious movements to affirm their right to function as rabbis while being fully out of the closet. Only eight of those rabbis released their names publicly: Rabbis Rebecca Alpert and Linda Holtzman, both faculty at RRC; the three rabbis of gay and lesbian synagogues, Allen Bennett, Yoel Kahn, and Denise Eger, and Rabbis Julie Greenberg, Sanford Lowe, and Eric Weiss. The others remained anonymous.

Rabbis Nancy Wiener and David Edelson completed their studies at a time when gay rabbinical students inhabited a strange no-man's land at HUC, tacitly tolerated as students and ordained just as the Central Conference of American Rabbis voted to admit openly gay and lesbian rabbis as members. David wrote, "I can't say how important it was to me to have CBST for support and sustenance. It is hard to imagine my years as a rabbinical student without the synagogue." In 1991 the Incognito Club was formed at the Jewish Theological Seminary, a confidential lesbian and gay support, networking, and educational group. One of its coordinators, Dawn Rose (later a CBST member with her partner Marla Brettschneider and their children), was forced to leave the rabbinical school when it was discovered she was a lesbian. She completed her PhD at JTS and later received rabbinic ordination from the Academy of Jewish Religion. Rabbi Benay Lappe, in the anthology *Lesbian Rabbis*, writes that she was so fearful of being outed as a lesbian while she was a student at JTS that although she davened at CBST she was closeted there about being a rabbinical student. An anonymous phone call to the rabbinical school dean on the eve of Benay's ordination led to a two-hour interrogation during which she was told she would not be ordained unless she denied the claim (in violation of the movement's policy against "instigating witch hunts"). Benay Lappe turned to Rabbi Kleinbaum for support. "She was outraged and helped me find my own rage. She talked me out of as much shame as I was willing to let go

### Role of gays still limited
*No change in policy on homosexuality, say Conservatives*

By Debra Nussbaum Cohen, Jewish Telegraphic Agency

### Conservatives reject bid to grant religious equality to gay Jews
By STEWART AIN

### CONSERVATIVE JEWS TO GAYS: 'NO!'
By Yosef I. Abramowitz

of." After an article about Rabbi Lappe and the new Gay and Lesbian Lehrhaus Judaica appeared in the *Jewish Week*, Rabbi Lappe received a call from the head of the Rabbinical Assembly demanding to know if she was "a homosexual" and stating that if so she would likely be expelled by the Rabbinical Assembly. Rabbi Lappe fought back, refusing to allow them to expel her quietly. With the support of Rabbi Kleinbaum, a number of her Conservative colleagues, and many feminist and gay and lesbian supporters, she faced down charges from the RA's Ethics Committee and its expulsion threats until they finally withdrew the charges against her. Rabbi Lappe celebrated her ordination at CBST and became its first part-time education director a year later. "At CLAL (the National Jewish Center for Learning and Leadership) I healed intellectually from my Seminary experience, and it was at CBST that I healed emotionally."

Frédéric Brenner's photo of CBST with students and friends of The Jewish Theological Seminary, 1994

Sara Paasche-Orlow was the first JTS student to serve as a Cooperberg-Rittmaster Rabbinical Intern. Each time a JTS student served as an intern, it furthered the goal of LGBT visibility at JTS, as both students and faculty heard about CBST, its services and its community, and the significant work the interns were doing there. Ayelet Cohen entered JTS only a few months after Rabbi Lappe's ordination. She founded Keshet, a student organization agitating for change in the admissions policy of the rabbinical and cantorial school and its treatment of LGBT rabbis in the field, and spoke publicly about her displeasure with the status quo. As a straight woman, Ayelet knew she was safe from the scrutiny and discrimination that others, like Rabbi Lappe had suffered, and was determined to use her privilege to help change the policies and attitudes of the Movement and its institutions. Many CBST members attended her ordination, wearing the rainbow ribbons a small number of students had chosen to wear to protest the Seminary's discriminatory ordination policy.

After withstanding an effort to expel her from the Rabbinical Assembly, Rabbi Cohen became one of the most outspoken advocates for LGBT rights within the Conservative Movement. She and the JTS students who followed her—notably Rabbis Tracy Nathan and Rachel Kahn-Troster—continued the fight until the policy against ordaining gay and lesbian rabbis was finally reversed in 2008. During their required year of study in Israel in 2009-10, JTS students and future Cooperberg-Rittmaster Rabbinical Interns Yosef Goldman and Guy Izhak Austrian refused to study at the Schechter Institute—the Conservative rabbinical seminary in Jerusalem—in solidarity with their gay classmates, including Ian Chesir-Teran, who were precluded from enrolling there. They were determined to put pressure on both JTS and Schechter, compelling both institutions to address Schechter's antigay policy. Cooperberg-Rittmaster Rabbinical Interns and alumni Conservative rabbis have played a huge role in pushing the Movement's policies and institutions toward full inclusion and celebration of LGBT Jews and families.

**The Relationship with Israel**

While Rabbi Kleinbaum began her CBST career passionately defending CBST's right to march in the Salute to Israel Parade, she later came under even greater fire for criticizing Israel's actions in the West Bank and Gaza and its treatment of Palestinians. CBST members have always run the gamut of political beliefs with regard to Israel and the Palestinians. CBST's rabbis struggled to present an intelligent and nuanced picture of the political situation and to cultivate a deep connection to Israel among its members, organizing trips to Israel even during the most tumultuous political periods. A lecture series the rabbis organized at CBST during the second Intifada that included a conscientious objector from the Israeli army and Israel's consul general elicited protests from both the right and the left sides of the political spectrum. Through a UJA-Federation Partnership 2000 grant, one of CBST's most meaningful connections to Israel flourished with the Jerusalem Open House (Jerusalem's LGBT community center), serving both Jewish and Palestinian Israelis. The grant was initiated by Amos Gil, CBST's first executive director, and Hagai El-Ad, then executive director of the Open House, and later coordinated by Rabbi Cohen and Ilene Sameth, with JOH executive director Noa Sattath.

Through the grant, which was extended for more than a decade, CBST members built lasting relationships with the Open House and its members and have been exchanging numerous visits and developing close personal relationships ever since. Four official CBST trips to Israel have taken place since the partnership's beginnings, and, by the time of this writing, nine delegations of young activists from JOH have traveled to New York. For several years, young activists from the Open House have observed Yom Kippur with CBST, sharing their experiences with those assembled at the Javits Center. Additionally, when individual members of either group travel to the other city, they are welcome to enjoy the hospitality of the home community.

CBST stood with the JOH when, as hosts of WorldPride—an international LGBT visibility event—JOH and WorldPride were condemned by antigay religious leaders across the faiths. Rabbi Kleinbaum, who

ABOVE: Israeli Consul Alon Pinkas at the Center with the JOH delegation

LEFT: CBST rabbis and staff on the Brooklyn Bridge with the JOH *mishlachat,* (delegation), (front row, left to right): Tsila Zalt, Nethanel Lipshitz, Haneen Maikey, Noa Sattath, Ronen Hady, Rabbi Kleinbaum; (back row, left to right): Avi Rose, Rina Shapiro, Aviad Doron, Rabbi Cohen, Danny Savich, Maya Orli Cohen

TOP: Group photo from Chanukah 2003 trip to Israel

ABOVE: Josephine Kleinbaum and Seymour Krasney

RIGHT: During the trip Jack Nieman and Rick Reder had a Jewish wedding ceremony. Rabbis Kleinbaum and Cohen, assisted by cantorial student David Berger, officiated at the King David Hotel. The wedding party (top row, left to right): Rabbi Kleinbaum, Neal Hoffman, Hagai El-Ad, David Berger, Lisa Kartzman, Pierre Vallet, Eric Rosenbaum, Rabbi Cohen; (bottom row) Andrew Ingall, Jack Nieman, Rick Reder, Dylan Nieman

served as North American co-chair of the event, originally scheduled for 2005 but postponed until 2006 because of the Lebanon War, was called "the greatest living moral terrorist in the world" by one New York ultra-Orthodox rabbi. Co-chairs of Jerusalem WorldPride, Noa Sattath and Hagai El-Ad, were the targets of vicious death threats. The event proceeded despite numerous political obstacles and nasty vitriol, attracting thousands of participants from around the world for a distinctly "Jerusalemite" event that embraced the religious and political nature of the city. A centerpiece was the WorldPride Interfaith Conference, organized in part by Cantor David Berger, which featured LGBT religious leaders including Rabbis Kleinbaum and Cohen, the Reverend Pat Bumgardner of MCC in New York, and Bishop Zachary Jones of Unity Fellowship Church, who accompanied CBST as it explored Jerusalem.

TOP LEFT: Thousands of Satmar Chasidim were bussed to the Israeli Consulate in New York City in protest to holding WorldPride in Jerusalem. CBST organized a multi-faith counter-protest where Rabbi Kleinbaum was arrested.

LEFT: Rabbi Kleinbaum, Elder Joseph W. Tolton (Rehoboth Temple Christ Conscious Church in Harlem), Rev. Pat Bumgardner (Metropolitan Community Church, New York), Bishop Zachary Jones (Unity Fellowship Church), and Rabbi Cohen at the Multi-Faith Conference at WorldPride.

BOTTOM LEFT: CBST at the WorldPride demonstration

BOTTOM RIGHT: CBST members joined by Amos Gil (third from right) at a pre-WorldPride demonstration at the Jerusalem separation wall

TOP RIGHT: Members of the New York Jewish and LGBT communities gather at a memorial vigil for the antigay shooting at a Tel Aviv LGBT Youth Center in the summer of 2009

TOP LEFT: A makeshift memorial at the vigil

RIGHT: Rabbi Kleinbaum addressing the crowd

After the antigay shooting at a Tel Aviv LGBT youth center in August 2009 resulting in the deaths of twenty-six-year old counselor Nir Katz and sixteen-year old Liz Trobishi and many others wounded, CBST mobilized the New York Jewish and LGBT communities for a memorial vigil. That fall, a delegation of remarkable young LGBT leaders from the JOH, selected among numerous applicants, came to New York for a mission of healing and activist training.

### AIDS in the Age of Antiretrovirals

CBST lost a quarter of its men to AIDS. Thanks to AIDS activists and increased awareness, education, and testing, new HIV diagnoses slowed in the 1990s, and by the late 1990s there were many fewer deaths from the disease. The development of AIDS treatments meant that more people are living long lives with HIV and AIDS. The new CBST siddur includes an extensive AIDS section, with writings from CBST members and others that reflect not only the losses but the lessons of AIDS, to express the full range of emotions and experiences that are meaningful for anyone facing illness. CBST prayers for healing have become less specifically about AIDS. Other illnesses, including those primarily impacting women and lesbians, such as breast cancer, have overtaken the center of concern. Nevertheless, CBST still participates in the GMHC AIDS Walk every year, with "Mamacita" Rita Fischer leading its contingent, having raised a total of nearly $850,000 by 2013.

Over time, World AIDS Day commemorations at CBST have begun to focus less on AIDS at home and more on the AIDS crisis internationally, particularly in Africa, inviting such guest speakers as Ruth Messinger of American Jewish World Service. For many years Dick Radvon coordinated the World AIDS Day Shabbat service. Overwhelmed for over twenty years with survivor's guilt, Dick concealed from all but his closest friends the fact that he was living with HIV and requested that his HIV status be disclosed only at his funeral. "All of my pre-synagogue friends, Jewish and non-Jewish, are gone. All of them. As well as many, many, many of my synagogue friends. They're all gone," Dick lamented.

By 2000, a worrisome new silence was developing around HIV and AIDS. Many men living with HIV chose not to disclose their status. Some younger men came of age without knowing anyone who had died from AIDS. The perception that AIDS was no longer fatal gave rise to club drugs that led to unsafe sex and new infections. Some younger men were ashamed to have contracted HIV in an age of greater information and kept their status hidden.

CBST's AIDS Walk Team, 1994

Rita Fischer began participating in the AIDS walk in memory of her husband, Alex Fischer, and is one of the largest individual fund-raisers in the walk's history.

BELOW RIGHT: Rita's team in 1997

BELOW: As of 2013, Rita raised a total of $848,699, of which $63,024 was raised just in 2013.

Trying to break the silence, one young CBST member who is HIV positive has made a point of giving a *drash* each year to disclose his status. Some men who had been living with the virus for decades continue to mentor younger men learning to cope with their diagnosis. Still, newer members are unfamiliar with the names on the AIDS quilt or the names on the Yizkor list read aloud each year. In his legendary appeal speeches and Yizkor talks, Irving Cooperberg mentioned specific members who had been lost, reflecting on their gifts to CBST and to the world. Since 2007, that spirit has been revived in the World AIDS Day tradition conceived by members Scott Fried, an AIDS educator, and Karen Benezra, featuring members who share their remembrances of CBST members who died from AIDS. These moving presentations invite newer congregants of the synagogue to share in the sacred responsibility of remembering its dead.

CBST has continued to support AIDS organizations and education, believing that the synagogue is an essential place for honest conversations about sex and sexuality. As soon as New York City started a safer-sex initiative by offering free condoms, CBST placed a basket of condoms on the counter in the synagogue alongside other information brochures.

"When I first came to CBST," Rabbi Kleinbaum recalls, "I knew if we survived AIDS as a community and found our footing, it would be time for us to take what we knew as Jews, as oppressed people, as GLBT people, and as sensitive straight people to transform our community into being leaders in expressing a vision of Judaism with social justice at its core."

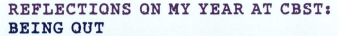

## REFLECTIONS ON MY YEAR AT CBST: BEING OUT

The summer before beginning my work at CBST, I worked at a "Conservative-ish" yet unaffiliated synagogue in New Jersey. I was just filling in, so I didn't feel the need to be out as a lesbian. They were still dealing with the fact that I was a woman; I decided they weren't ready. Congregants tried to set me up with their grandsons and embraced my partner (I was lucky to have such a good girlfriend who accompanied me to my services). It just didn't seem relevant or necessary to tell them the truth. I took advantage of how well I passed as straight. So I finished my time there and began my internship at CBST.

I had never thought of myself as closeted—I had come out as a lesbian about seven years earlier. But I really came out at CBST. I can't tell you how uncomfortable I was when I learned in one of our first meetings that interns had to come out to the congregation, regardless of our identity. Before that moment I didn't know how loud I was going to be about my identity, but now I had no choice. So I did, and I never kept quiet again.

The time came for my last Shabbat service at CBST. I proudly sat where my previous chair sign used to say "Cooperberg-Rittmaster Rabbinical Intern," and now it read "Rabbi."

After graduation from RRC, I was asked to return to that same "Conservative-ish" synagogue as a full-time assistant rabbi. This time, I knew I had to come out. So I told them in the interview what I had kept to myself the summer before. It was a surprise to them; they had never contemplated this question. After some discussion with the board, they decided to hire me. In the end, my partner and I were fully embraced by this community and they would have kept me on longer than one year if I hadn't chosen to return to my native California. They hired women rabbis after me, and I know now they would have no qualms about hiring another gay or lesbian rabbi. I realized that by being out I could help change the way a synagogue related to LGBT people. I could effect change simply by being myself. That knowledge has helped shape my rabbinate, my activism, my voice, and the way I work with the LGBTQ students I now serve on the college campus. Students of all faiths come to me because there aren't many models of how to live a spiritually authentic life and be out. I often repeat to my students a teaching I internalized at CBST that helped me come out publicly: the root of the word "shalom" is wholeness, so we cannot be at peace until we are whole. As long as there is brokenness and disintegration in our own spiritual lives, there cannot be peace in the world.

RABBI MYCHAL COPELAND (NÉE ROSENBAUM),
COOPERBERG-RITTMASTER RABBINICAL INTERN, 1999–2000

# REFLECTIONS ON MY YEAR AT CBST: TIKKUN OLAM

It was 1999, so of course we all knew it—we knew all along there was nothing wrong, shameful, or impossible about being LGBTQI. In fact, the opposite was true, and the community walked proudly and joyfully.

Despite public proclamations of pride, the grip of internalized homophobia left deep bruises on people's souls, causing a spiritual pain surpassed only, perhaps, by the rejection from their Jewish families. People expressed deep insecurities about how they could stand proudly as what I might call spiritually legitimate or kosher Queer Jews. Like superheroes, these folks armored up and repelled all the negative messages hurled at them over the years. But as human beings, they could not shield themselves completely from the toxicity in their environment. For some, corrosive messages had gotten under their skin and reconstituted themselves as subtle but enduring spiritual unease.

Thank God they had a place like CBST where they could bring their spiritual questions and come into fuller spiritual wholeness.

I saw it most intimately through pastoral care at CBST. Again and again I found myself marveling at the resilience of the Queer spirit, the Jewish spirit, the human spirit. In these encounters I came closest to experiencing God in action in life.

What a blessing to witness the transformative, healing power that sitting with a rabbi, in a synagogue, and engaging with Jewish texts in a personal and honest way can have for those who have been hurt so badly by all of those.

When I came to CBST, I told Rabbi Kleinbaum that I was looking forward to doing *tikkun olam* work. She replied, "Your care for the community will be *tikkun olam* work. You'll see." At CBST, I came to appreciate the many ways we can help usher more healing and joy into the world, and the varied parts each of us has to play in that process. I came to appreciate the dazzling resilience and insight of those I served. I will never recite the prayer *"Elohai, neshamah she natata bi, tehora hi"* the same way again. I will never be the same person or the same rabbi I was before my time at CBST. The impact the CBST community had on me is beautiful, enduring, and without measure. For this, I am forever grateful.

RABBI RACHEL GARTNER, COOPERBERG-RITTMASTER RABBINICAL INTERN, 1999–2000

TOP LEFT: On June 5, 2012, Rabbi Kleinbaum participated in a press conference with LGBT and African American community leaders against the NYPD's stop and frisk policy.

TOP RIGHT: Sisters Liz (left) and Leslie Deutsch proudly wearing their U.S. Army uniforms

RIGHT: In 2007 Matt Foreman, executive director of the National Gay and Lesbian Task Force, and Rabbi Kleinbaum were arrested outside the Armed Forces Recruiting Station in Times Square, as they were protesting the "Don't Ask, Don't Tell" policy and General Peter Pace's comments that homosexuality is "immoral."

## Mobilizing for Change

CBST and the rabbis have consistently participated in community partnerships for organizing around social justice issues and advocated for New York State LGBT rights legislation: SONDA, the New York State Sexual Orientation Non-discrimination Act, passed in December 2002, nearly twenty-two years after it was first introduced; the anti-bullying Dignity for All Students Act, enacted in 2010; and the Gender Expression Non-Discrimination Act, which, as of this writing, still has not been enacted.

The Cooperberg-Rittmaster Rabbinical interns and CBST staff members—some not Jewish or gay themselves—have played key roles in rallies and demonstrations. Many former interns have continued to work for LGBT social justice in their careers. For example, alumnus Rabbi Dan Judson, a straight Reform rabbi, led the Massachusetts Religious Coalition to legalize marriage for same-sex couples, and Rabbi Melissa Simon was a leader of the faith coalition in the Minnesota movement for marriage equality.

### REFLECTIONS ON MY YEARS AT CBST: THE WESTBORO BAPTIST CHURCH PROTEST

By accident, I discovered that there was going to be a protest by the Westboro Baptist Church against CBST. I had already heard Westboro was protesting the ordination of the first African American woman rabbi at HUC–JIR, and knew they were making the rounds protesting Jewish institutions in New York City. But CBST responded very differently from other organizations targeted for protest. While others chose to ignore Westboro, CBST planned a prayer vigil and turned the protest into a counter-protest and fund-raiser. People from around the country donated money for each minute CBST was being targeted by the hate group. Members and hundreds of people showed up to rally in support of CBST. On Sunday, June 21, 2009, we gathered together to express a message of love, hope, and respect. When the few church representatives showed up, shouting hateful messages and treading on Israeli and American flags, 150 prayerful counter-protesters greeted them with songs, including Psalm 150 and "Hinei Mah Tov." The Westboro protestors stayed for 47 minutes, raising $12,315 for CBST's building fund. I love to think about how, one day soon, CBST will be in a home of its own, thanks in small part to the members of Westboro Baptist Church!

RABBI MELISSA SIMON, COOPERBERG-RITTMASTER RABBINICAL INTERN, 2008–09, 2009–10

CBST and its supporters, including New York City Council Speaker Christine Quinn, gathered in prayer and song to counter-protest the Westboro Baptist Church demonstrators.

## REFLECTIONS ON MY YEARS AT CBST: RALLYING AGAINST ISLAMOPHOBIA

I turned to the group of Muslim Americans facing me, seated on the prayer carpet in the makeshift mosque, and said, "Our tradition teaches that the Torah has 70 facets—or really, faces. And some of those faces are yours."

On my first day of work as CBST's Social Justice Rabbinical Intern, Rabbi Kleinbaum charged me with coordinating CBST's response to the controversy then raging about the proposed Muslim community center in Lower Manhattan, not far from the former World Trade Center site. A few days later, she devoted a Rosh Hashanah sermon to the message that Muslim Americans are welcome as part of the fabric of our city and our nation. Hundreds of congregants signed a poster of welcome from CBST to the organizers of the community center. And on September 12, 2010, I joined about twenty-five CBST members filling three pews in a packed St. Peter's Church downtown for an interfaith rally against islamophobia.

Several weeks later, the coalition invited CBST to represent Judaism at an interfaith text study in the prayer space slated to become Park51, the community center maligned by opponents as the "Ground Zero mosque." I taught alongside an imam and a minister to a mixed crowd that included a number of CBST members. One of the Muslim participants was extremely excited by the Jewish fascination with the number seventy. His joyful, surprised smile was the same I've seen on Jews who realize that our ancient tradition resonates with their modern lives. I don't know whether CBST's queer identity was relevant that evening, but diversifying the faces that encounter Torah is our queer mission, and I felt proud to be holding the looking glass that night.

RABBI GUY IZHAK AUSTRIAN, SOCIAL JUSTICE RABBINICAL INTERN, 2010–11, COOPERBERG-RITTMASTER RABBINICAL INTERN, 2011–12

### The Soup Kitchen

The Church of the Holy Apostles runs one of the largest soup kitchens in the country, serving well over twelve hundred meals each day. After a devastating fire in 1990, Holy Apostles rebuilt its historic sanctuary without fixed pews in order to accommodate more guests, capable of turning the entire sanctuary into a dining room. Many CBST members, including Steven Fruh, Paul Marsolini, and Rick Landman, volunteer regularly at the soup kitchen. The Rabbis and the volunteers have commented that praying in the sanctuary seems to gain an additional dimension of holiness after serving what for many guests is their only hot meal of the day.

Barbara Gaines, Aari Ludvigsen, Simon Ludvigsen–Gaines, and Rabbi Cohen with the compact fluorescent Chanukah menorah Barbara created.

### The Green Team

Initiated by members Liz Galst and Aari Ludvigsen, the Green Team—teaching CBST members to make environmentally responsible choices in their own lives—was most active in 2005–07. The team led initiatives to switch to green power using compact fluorescent lightbulbs, when these were little-known. Inspiring social justice initiatives in other synagogues and churches, the Green Team worked with the Coalition on the Environment and Jewish Life. The Shalom Center awarded CBST its first Green Menorah Award for its environmental efforts in 2006.

### *Koleinu*

In 2008 a group of CBST members embarked on a Congregation-Based Community Organizing social justice initiative named *Koleinu* "our voice." Through a community-building process relying on the principles of grassroots organizing, and one-to-one listening campaigns conducted with hundreds of members, CBST members determined to focus their energies on a variety of pressing LGBT social justice issues, including over time: marriage equality, healthcare and eldercare, and the need for safe shelter of runaway and homeless youth on the streets of New York City, a large number of whom identify as LGBTQ. In Rabbi Kleinbaum's September 2008 Shabbat sermon on *Shoftim*, which contains the oft-quoted passage, *Tzedek, tzedek tirdof* (Justice, justice shall thou pursue), she made the following observation:

> The prophets of our Bible are quoted over and over as great orators. They were great at giving sermons but, in fact, they weren't so great at community organizing. In their lifetime none of them saw an impact of their word on the community in which they lived. Their words have continued to inspire us thousands of years later, but I would argue if they had some good community organizers among them there would

## KOLEINU: INITIATIVE

Over the past few months, I've been meeting with a group of CBST members and staff, to help launch an exciting new Congregation-Based Community Organizing (CBCO) initiative. This grassroots model of social justice advocacy, relying on the principles of community organizing, is active in more than 100 synagogues of all denominations across North America, spearheaded by the Jewish Funds for Justice.

This initiative will create opportunities for us to set our Jewish values into action and strengthen our bonds of community through telling our stories, building relationships, and identifying issues of common concern. Ultimately, this process will make us stronger leaders in our community and in the larger world and empower us to effect real change in the lives of others through our collective efforts. Social advocacy work, which is aimed at influencing public policy, laws, and resource allocations within political, economic, and social institutions, depends on the strength and collective efforts of a community—it depends on us.

I've been energized by the one-to-one conversations I've had so far, and feel that I've just begun to tap into the richness of the people around me and, not surprisingly, to sense the value of sharing our stories.

*Koleinu* not only captures the spirit of gathering our voices and listening to each other, it also expresses our aspirations and dreams for amplifying our voice in the public arena. It is my hope that *Koleinu* will grow and blossom in our community and that it will be a significant force for contributing to positive social change in our world.

MARSHA MELNICK,
APRIL/MAY 2008 NEWSLETTER

have been more change in society at that time. If you could combine great oration, words that really inspire us to want to change, and to imagine the possibility of hoping for change, along with somebody who knows how to organize communities to make that change happen, I think we would see a fulfillment of the Jewish Bible.

In 2009 a grant from the Arcus Foundation enabled CBST to hire Alex Weissman as its first social justice coordinator, while rabbinical students Guy Austrian and Cecelia Beyer served as Social Justice Rabbinical Interns.

Alex Weissman

### Strength Through Community

In the fall of 2010, in the wake of the "It Gets Better" internet campaign, CBST quickly created the "Strength Through Community" Project, an online Jewish community response to anti-LGBTQ bullying and suicide among LGBTQ youth. Rabbi Kleinbaum and Rabbi Weiss, Social Justice Coordinator Alex Weissman, and other staff and members of CBST, under the direction of Gabriel Blau, contributed personal video statements, reaching out to those in crisis and need of support.

### Shelter of Peace

In July 2011, under the leadership of RoseAnn Hermann and George Hermann, CBST launched Shelter of Peace, a multi-faith coalition advocating for the support of LGBTQ homeless youth in New York. The initiative has organized collective actions with congregations across New York City, including rallies, petitions, letter-writing campaigns and advocacy at City Hall and in Albany to ensure sufficient funding for LGBTQ homeless youth shelters.

RIGHT: Lea Rizack and other CBST members at a Shelter of Peace demonstration

BELOW: Carl Siciliano (left), founder and executive director of the Ali Forney Center, with George and RoseAnn Hermann

## Marriage Equality

Together with Empire State Pride Agenda and other organizations, CBST advocated for marriage equality in New York State for many years. When the law finally passed in June 2011 after weeks of lobbying and delay, the dramatic eleventh-hour vote at the end of the legislative session unfolded during an overflowing Pride Shabbat service. Activist and actor Cynthia Nixon, the evening's speaker, came prepared with speeches for any outcome. More than a few congregants followed the vote on their smart phones, sending updates to Rabbi Kleinbaum on the bimah. A cheer went up as soon as the news of the majority vote came through in favor of the bill.

TOP LEFT: CBST organized clergy for a marriage rally at One Police Plaza on March 11, 2004.

TOP RIGHT: Rabbi Kleinbaum at the State House in Albany days before the New York State legislature legalized marriage for same-sex couples

RIGHT: The LGBT Rights Action Team in Albany on Equality and Justice Day, advocating for marriage equality, 2010

ABOVE: Cynthia Nixon speaking at Pride Shabbat, 2011

### Striking Down DOMA

The statewide victories for marriage equality were exciting and momentum was building. CBST members closely monitored progress around the country, following the marriage equality movement in nearby New Jersey, the Proposition 8 case in California, and everything in between. But none of these state-sanctioned marriages would have federal standing as long as the Defense of Marriage Act, voted into law and signed by President Clinton in 1996, was in force.

On December 7, 2012 the Supreme Court agreed to hear the case now referred to as *Windsor v. United States.* Hundreds of *amicus* briefs came to the court in support

## THEA AND EDIE

Edie Windsor and Thea Spyer were very much in love when they took an apartment together in 1967. Thea, a Clinical Psychologist in private practice, proposed to Edie, a Corporate Senior Systems Programmer Strategist at IBM; they settled into an apartment on lower Fifth Avenue, made a second home in Southampton, and built a large circle of friends. They drove everywhere in their cream-colored Cadillac convertible and traveled widely. Their life began to change in 1977, when Thea, at the age of forty-five, was diagnosed with Multiple Sclerosis. As the MS progressed, Thea never lost her passion for living and Edie did everything possible to help Thea maintain her professional and intellectual practice. "Even when Thea was in a wheelchair," Edie reflects, "she'd dance from the chair, and after she lost motion in her arms and was unable to hold a book, she read on the computer. I remember her staying up late one night because she was so engrossed in *Madame Bovary*."

In 2007 Thea and Edie flew to Ontario, Canada, where they were legally married. Their story prompted filmmakers Susan Muska and Gréta

Olafsdóttir to create a documentary called "Edie and Thea: A Very Long Engagement," released in 2009, just a few months before Thea died.

Thea willed her entire estate to Edie. According to federal tax code, married couples can transfer money or property from spouse to spouse at death without triggering estate taxes. Edie was barred from doing so because, according to Section 3 of DOMA, the term "spouse" only applied to a marriage between a man and woman. Edie was compelled to pay $363,053 in estate taxes. She was indignant. Already in her eighties, Edie was determined to challenge the ruling.

At first she found that several gay rights and advocacy groups were unwilling to represent her, until she was referred to Roberta Kaplan, a partner at the law firm of Paul, Weiss, Rifkind, Wharton & Garrison. "When I heard her story," Roberta reported, "it took me about five seconds, maybe less" to agree to represent her. In November 2010, Roberta Kaplan, in conjunction with the ACLU, filed the case in the U.S. District Court of New York and later with the U.S. Second Circuit Court of Appeals. Both courts ruled that Section 3 of DOMA was unconstitutional.

of Edith Windsor as plaintiff, including one by CBST, the only brief submitted by a synagogue. One of the more remarkable briefs was filed by JTS, an acknowledgement of how far the Conservative Movement and the gay rights cause had come.

Skeptics declared that the conservative Supreme Court was destined to reject Edie's claim; optimists were more confident that the time had come. Tensions rose steadily as the Supreme Court session drew to a close. On June 26th—the last day of the session and ten years to the day after striking down the sodomy laws in *Lawrence v. Texas*—the Supreme Court declared DOMA unconstitutional.

## Celebrating the Demise of DOMA

Crowds gathered throughout the country to celebrate the Pride week 5 to 4 decision. President Obama telephoned Edie Windsor to offer his congratulations. In New York City, a rally in front of Stonewall attracted hundreds. Edie was hailed as the Rosa Parks of the LGBT movement.

More than six hundred people came to celebrate Edie and her attorney, Roberta Kaplan, both members of CBST, at the synagogue's Pride service that Friday night. To accommodate those unable to get a seat in the sanctuary, amplifiers were set up in the annex adjacent to the sanctuary and on the sidewalk outside, where dozens of people stood in the rain listening to the service. The mood was euphoric. Rabbi Kleinbaum opened quietly by dedicating the service to Thea, whose father had brought his family to the United States before the Nazis occupied Holland. She cited Thea's commitment to Edie, "to never postpone joy," which was at the core of their relationship. Thunderous applause erupted after the speeches of Roberta and Edie, and Rabbi Kleinbaum laughed, "You see, it took two Jewish lesbians from New York to bring down DOMA."

CLOCKWISE FROM TOP LEFT: Speakers Roberta Kaplan, Edie Windsor, and Rabbi Kleinbaum address the ecstatic crowd at the Stonewall rally.

Edie being honored at CBST's Pride Service

# 12. BUILDING FOR THE FUTURE

Nearing its third decade, CBST entered a time of unprecedented organizational sophistication and communal readiness to look into a future made possible by the visionary leadership that had governed the synagogue up to the end of the century. The board presidents who followed—Yolanda Potasinksi, Mike Vine, Lisa Kartzman, Eric Rosenbaum, Steve Frank, and Bill Hibsher—have each played a major role in leading CBST to become a thriving twenty-first century synagogue, embracing the challenges and the opportunities of Jewish life in New York in the new millennium.

By the time Yolanda Potasinski was elected President in 1996, the synagogue was already on its way to becoming a more mature institution. With the help of consultant Beth Appelgate, CBST undertook a new strategic plan. Over the next five years the synagogue celebrated its twenty-fifth anniversary, organized board retreats, established its own cemetery, and expanded its language to include bisexual and transgender members. During the time Yolanda served as president, CBST constructed a cabinet for the Holocaust Torah, the arks for home and travel, and commissioned new Torah covers. The board approved the purchase of 3,600 *machzors* for the High Holiday services, transferred Friday night services to The Church of the Holy Apostles, scheduled the first trip to Israel, and hired the first assistant rabbi and a music director. It also adopted a new "Fair Share" dues policy, assessing membership dues based on income, meeting the growing synagogue budget through increased fundraising efforts while maintaining its affordability for all.

Poster announcing the party celebrating CBST's twenty-fifth anniversary, 1998

CBST members at a telephone fundraising drive made possible by UJA-Federation (left to right) Chuck Tyson, Rhoda Zimet, Michael Ekman

## LOOKING BACK IN GRATITUDE

I will never forget the first time I stepped foot into the sanctuary at 57 Bethune Street in August 1987 for a Friday night service. I was thirty-one and I landed there by the invitation of a long-time friend who wasn't even Jewish. I remember vividly the camaraderie of the people, the prayers, and being invited to the bimah for the *motzi*, which was the *minhag* at that time: anyone who was a first-timer was welcomed into the congregation in this way.

Being so easily invited to the bimah for a traditional and familiar ritual was the beginning of the answer to a question I had been grappling with since I was a teenager exploring my sexuality. As a child of Holocaust survivors, I was completely comfortable with my Jewish identity, but I asked myself how and where was I ever going to belong and participate in a shul as an adult Jewish lesbian. I am grateful to CBST for offering a spiritual place where I could bring my entire self as a Jew and as a lesbian.

It has been an honor and a privilege to serve on every imaginable committee, giving back where I could, learning, growing, laughing, crying, celebrating, and at times exhausted and overwhelmed by responding to the complex controversies about change and growth in the congregation.

I still have my notebook from 1995, when Mark Bieber—already a past president of the congregation—invited me to dinner at one of his favorite places in Hell's Kitchen. This felt like a rite of passage: he encouraged me to step up and take the reins, which I did in 1996.

I am grateful to all the men and women at CBST who came before me, and to the rabbis and teachers, my friends and fellow congregants whose dedication, love, and creative energy have provided and still provide room for everyone to find their path and who help this special community continue to thrive.

YOLANDA POTASINSKI, PRESIDENT, 1996-2001

Shep Wahnon, Yolanda Potasinski, Dick Radvon, and Liz Deutsch at work at the second board retreat in 1999.

### The New Century

When Mike Vine became board president in 2001, he brought his unique experiences to the role, working to prepare CBST for the future. Mike's Jewish commitment stemmed in part from his father, a Holocaust survivor and dedicated lay leader in his home synagogue. Mike enthusiastically supported the synagogue's Solidarity Mission to Israel in early 2001 at the height of the second intifada, joining the trip along with his father. Mike helped guide the synagogue in the uncertain months following September 11, although temporarily displaced from his home in Battery Park City. Along with Rabbi Kleinbaum, he presided over the installation of Rabbi Ayelet Cohen in 2002.

## 9/11/2001

On the morning of September 11, 2001, Rabbi Roderick Young was walking to the Christopher Street subway station when he noticed an unusually low flying plane over the Village. Descending to the subway, he looked up at one of the World Trade Towers and saw smoke coming out of one of the towers.

Ayelet Cohen heard on NPR that a small plane had hit the World Trade Center as she left to meet Rabbi Young and her fellow Cooperberg-Rittmaster Rabbinical Intern Tracy Nathan at the Upper West Side Mikvah for the conversion of a new baby. Moments later Rabbi Kleinbaum called her from Washington Street while watching the North Tower burn. As they talked, Rabbi Kleinbaum saw the second plane hit the South Tower. Much of the CBST staff watched, standing on the street, steps away from the synagogue.

"I saw the strangest thing as I was getting into the train," Rabbi Young told the interns. "It looked like a plane flew into the World Trade Center." "There was another one," Cohen told him. Shaken, Rabbi Young asked his interns to put their own fears aside and be present for the conversion.

When Michael Nelson arrived at the mikvah with his baby, he was out of breath. He had emerged from the PATH train to a scene of chaos, debris falling everywhere and people running and screaming. He knew the area—his son attended day care in the World Trade Center. Michael's only thought was, "I have to meet the rabbi," and he ducked into the subway, boarding one of the last uptown trains.

On Bethune Street, CBST was directly in the path of the thousands of people streaming uptown to escape. One member to stop by for respite was Michael Reichbach, manager of the New Balance store in the World Trade Center concourse. Following emergency protocol, he initially secured his staff inside the store before receiving a warning to evacuate.

CBST was in the frozen zone below 14th Street, sealed for days to anyone who didn't live or work there. On September 12, CBST held a service of prayer and healing at its Chelsea sanctuary. In the days that followed, the rabbis and interns reached out to members to see how they had been affected by the tragedy. Ian Chesir-Teran had stayed home from his office in Tower 2 because his infant son was sick. Diane Burhenne was in a subway car stopped under the Fulton Street station, filling with smoke.

You could still smell the burning outside of the Metropolitan Pavilion on the first night of Rosh Hashanah. When Rabbi Kleinbaum invited all those who had been near the World Trade Center to come to the bimah to *bench gomel*, throngs of people streamed forward.

The New York State Troopers were stationed in the windowed hall of the Javits Center where CBST usually holds Yom Kippur services. Javits offered a larger, windowless space on a lower level instead. So many people had attended

## MILESTONES

My installation as CBST's president in March 2001 coincided with the hiring of the synagogue's first executive director, Amos Gil. The board of directors had begun a new strategic planning process, which included significant leadership development. How would a paid executive director establish their leadership role in overseeing the administration of the synagogue and at the same time support the rabbis, the board, and the membership? The trial and error phase that continued over the next two years led to the "triangle" leadership model (rabbi, board, executive director) still in use today.

During this period, Rabbi Roderick Young returned to England and a search committee formed to find a successor, selecting Rabbi Ayelet Cohen as the second assistant rabbi in 2002. Her presence at CBST extended for ten years.

In the fall of 2001, just days before the High Holidays, we all experienced the horror of the destruction of the World Trade Towers on September 11. CBST held a special gathering at the Church of the Holy Apostles to bring the community together during this difficult time. More than 6,000 people attended *Kol Nidrei* services at the Jacob Javits Center that year, the largest attendance at any CBST event or service in history.

Happy and memorable milestones were celebrated in 2002 and 2003, with Rabbi Kleinbaum's tenth anniversary and the synagogue's thirtieth anniversary celebrations. In addition to the traditional lifecycle events (commitment ceremonies, conversions, and funerals), we celebrated one of the largest groups of adult b'nai mitzvah students to complete the program. The growth spurt of children at this time signaled the beginning of a baby boom at CBST.

I am honored to have been a part of these milestones during my term.

MIKE VINE, PRESIDENT, 2001-2003

---

Rosh Hashanah services that it was decided to set up 4,000 chairs for *Kol Nidrei*, to accommodate almost a thousand more people than had attended the year before. As it turned out, six thousand people came for *Kol Nidrei*. That year the light came from inside the room.

Rabbi Tracy Nathan reflects on the way September 11 and its aftermath informed her year at CBST, "In the days that followed, we gathered the congregation together for moments of stability in a city where the ground had given way beneath our feet. We came together to embrace, grieve, and remember that as a Jewish and a gay community, we had encountered catastrophe before; we would learn to make sense of our changed world and re-commit ourselves to the choice of life and love. Over the year I learned countless times of the importance of ritual, community, and laughter in carrying us through fear and tragedy, and was startled to realize that even while dealing with my own post-traumatic stress and that of so many others, I also experienced many moments of deep joy."

### Building Infrastructure

Mike Vine worked closely with Rabbi Kleinbaum to hire CBST's first executive director in 2001, with the leadership of Barbara Dolgin, chair of the executive director search committee. They selected Amos Gil, whose background in progressive and social justice nonprofit leadership in Israel, qualified him for the position.

The hiring of an executive director was one of the infrastructure projects made possible by a $250,000 grant from the Ford Foundation, awarded in 1999. This unprecedented support recognized CBST and Rabbi Kleinbaum's transformational work in the progressive religious world. Ford Foundation religion program officer Constance Buchanan had a profound interest in progressive and women's religious leadership and considered Rabbi Kleinbaum an essential voice in contemporary American religious life. She frequently included her, and occasionally Rabbi Cohen, in roundtables of cutting-edge religious thinkers, and she wrote the foreword to Rabbi Kleinbaum's 2005 book of *drashot*, *Listening for the Oboe*. Renewing the grant, the Ford Foundation continued its support of CBST for ten years.

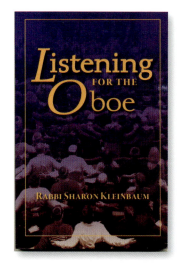

*Listening for the Oboe*, a collection of *drashot*, was published in honor of Rabbi Kleinbaum's tenth anniversary.

Lisa Kartzman became president in 2003. Under her tenure, the inaugural cantorial intern was hired and a new, streamlined board prepared itself for the next phase of the synagogue's life. When Amos Gil returned to Israel in 2004, Lisa participated in the hiring of Ilene Sameth to succeed him. Ilene was a former opera singer who had developed an expertise in synagogue administration at two other Manhattan synagogues. She served as executive director at CBST for nearly nine years.

When Lisa became a volunteer soon after she first attended High Holiday services in 1990, the board leadership was still almost exclusively male. By the time she became president, there were two female rabbis and, with Ilene Sameth's hiring, a female executive director. While the board had equal numbers of male and female members and all hiring was done at the recommendation of gender-balanced search committees, some men grew anxious with the perception that they were no longer adequately represented in the leadership. Lisa worked to address those concerns while remaining focused on the goals of strengthening and developing the board and staff. Responsibilities for day-to-day operations were shifting away from the board so that lay leaders could focus on long-term planning, and ensure that CBST was fulfilling its vision.

TOP: Amos Gil
ABOVE: Ilene Sameth

## CHANGE IN THE AIR

Three years as president of CBST seems like a long time. The reality is that the weeks and months pass very quickly. Now, years later, the moments of difficulty have disappeared into the mist of the past, and what remains are memories of the people who comprised the leadership at that time. We were in a passage of the synagogue's history when change was in the air. It was time for the bylaws and election rules to be overhauled again; we hired a new executive director and expanded the office support staff; we reviewed and revised the structure of volunteer committees; we initiated and completed a new strategic plan; we negotiated the rabbinic contracts to keep our spiritual leadership intact; we shrunk the number of board members; and, as always, we balanced a tight budget each year. These are highlights of thirty-six months in the life of a board, president, rabbinic leadership, and staff. In the end, looking back, I glean joy from the accomplishment of fulfilling my role in keeping our community moving forward, living within our yearly budget, and continuing to grow. The success was not my own; it was a function of those who worked tirelessly alongside me. When I enter a CBST service now as a quieter and older volunteer, I always take a few moments to look around the room at the expanse of people and I *shep* a bit of *naches*, knowing that I played a role in the strength of this community we all so love. CBST is a home for so many. We feed and nurture souls who are often lost Jewishly before they find us. We create incredible music and liturgy that will fill our home for the next generation. We work as activists and help improve the larger world around us for everyone, not just those who look like us. Finally, we have given our rabbis the space to learn and stretch their knowledge and to teach us to revel in Torah values as befits our community. We are a special community and continue to stand proudly on the shoulders of those who came before us.

LISA KARTZMAN, PRESIDENT, 2003-2006

What began as a very part-time administrative staff has grown into a full-time professional team. When Rabbi Kleinbaum was hired, Saul Zalkin was taking in the mail and answering phone calls a few hours a week. In 1994 CBST hired Tasha Calhoun, Rabbi Kleinbaum's assistant, and next to her the longest-serving staff member. A trusted and beloved presence in the synagogue office, Tasha functions as an extension of the rabbis. She has provided essential support for many of CBST's major projects, including Rabbi Kleinbaum's *Listening for the Oboe*, the 2007 edition of CBST's siddur, the rabbi's twentieth anniversary tribute video, as well as this book.

The expanding infrastructure included administrative, operations, development, and programming personnel. Because CBST attracts those who incorporate its values into their personal and professional lives, some members later served on the synagogue's staff and vice versa, including Maya Orli Cohen, Jacob Lieberman,

The CBST staff at the LGBT Center's Women's Event honoring Rabbi Kleinbaum in 2009. (left to right) Joyce Rosenzweig, Amy Lessler, Jason Kaufman, Rabbi Kleinbaum, Katie Naughton, Rabbi Cohen, Scott Robertson, Tasha Calhoun, Ariel Kates-Harris, Chet Roijce, Alex Weissman

Gabriel Blau, Assaf Astrinsky, and Yolanda Potasinski (who became executive director in 2013). Many staff members, several of whom are neither LGBTQ nor Jewish, have been devoted to CBST, and built close relationships with congregants. They have prepared for rallies, attended CBST anniversary celebrations, and participated in life events of volunteers with whom they worked closely, such as the funerals of Marc Janover and Dick Radvon and a milestone birthday celebration for Annette Miller.

### Claiming Identities

In CBST's early days, many members remained closeted in their professional or extended family lives, fearing the consequences of being publically outed. Membership lists were kept in strictest confidence. Even lay leaders were not always privy to that information. When Art Leonard first joined as a member and started leading services, Mark Bieber objected that a non-member was on the bimah; despite his role as chair of the Religious Committee, he had no access to the membership list. Photography at synagogue events was limited and permission carefully obtained to print members' names in the newsletter. Throughout the 1980s and 1990s the newsletter reminded members to make their confidentiality preferences clear. Newsletters and other correspondence were mailed in nondescript sealed envelopes, with no identifying information and a PO box return address. It wasn't until the 2000s that mail from CBST began to bear the synagogue's name on the envelope, a change that some members found startling even then.

As times changed, standards shifted—being out became a community value and a point of pride, and more members were able to be open about their sexual orientation and gender identity at work and in their extended personal lives without repercussions, with most members choosing to use their full names. Rich Greenberg, who had been known by a pseudonym at CBST for decades, held a ritual when he retired from the military in 2005 and was finally able to use his real name.

With this new standard of openness, synagogue members—especially those of younger generations, although not exclusively so—felt freer to push the boundaries of binary gender definitions and categories of sexual orientation. What had first been a gay, and then gay and lesbian community, was now LGBTQ and beyond, as more people identified as queer, intersex, straight, cisgender, and transgender. A new vocabulary developed challenging the idea of what is normative. While some in the community struggled to catch up, the new terminologies provided opportunities for the community as a whole to explore gender, sexual orientation, and identity. This new vocabulary was created in no small part by CBST alumni: Rabbi Reuben Zellman is the co-founder of the Jewish transgender resource guide *TransTorah*, using materials he first developed for CBST; Rabbi David Dunn Bauer is a leading teacher of queer men's sexuality; Rabbi Tracy Nathan was project editor of Keshet's LGBTQ marriage resource guide; Rabbi Joshua Lesser is co-editor of the queer Torah commentary *Torah Queeries* (several CBST rabbis and alumni are contributors) and a national LGBT religious leader.

## BEYOND THE BINARY

Kate Bornstein's *drash* in June, 2012 was so beautiful that it nearly moved me to tears. She elegantly reminded us of the wonders of the world which lie between and beyond the binary. For far too long we have been stuck in a black/white, gay/straight, trans/cis, women/men type of world, which is like looking at a rainbow and only seeing two colors. Kate reminded all of us of to look for and embrace the parts of ourselves that are more complex and wondrous than what a binary approach has to offer. Rabbi Kleinbaum introduced Kate as "Queer Royalty" because of how Kate has blazed the trail on queer issues, especially when it comes to gender. Kate wasn't invited to speak just because she is trans. She was invited because we are proud that Kate Bornstein, Queer Royalty, is part of our LGBTQIA Jewish community. Some people may think that CBST is "sensitive" to the trans and/or gender non-conforming communities, when in reality we aren't just "sensitive," for we know that trans Jewish people and Jewish people who don't fall into the traditional ways we are taught to be "men" and "women" make up exactly what CBST is. We recognize the importance of seamlessly integrating the different parts of our entire CBST community. We also acknowledge the struggle inherent in embracing our diversity and complexity and must see challenges as opportunities for growth and dialogue. To quote from the Mishnah, "It is not up to us to finish the work but neither are we free to desist from it."

JASE SCHWARTZ, MEMBER SINCE 2008

## WHO IS QUEER?

In 2008, when I was Vice President, I attended a board retreat. One of the major topics on the agenda was the current usage of the word "queer," which by then no longer carried the pejorative connotation it did in previous generations. "Quite the contrary," Rabbi Kleinbaum said, "Many younger people embrace and prefer the word queer, which encompasses a much broader understanding of sexual orientation and gender identity, and transcends binary definitions of sexuality, challenging the assumption that heterosexuality is normative. The word describes a set of attitudes and political commitments that may or may not refer to the gender of the people you are attracted to."

Taryn Higashi and Ivan Zimmerman at their wedding officiated by Rabbi Roderick Young

"Ivan," the Rabbi said, "is queer." Not something I had realized. It was nice to be called out, but I couldn't resist asking, "I wonder how Taryn [my wife] will take this?" Then I stopped for a moment and added, "You know, I am really flattered to be called queer and I'm sure Taryn will be proud too."

IVAN ZIMMERMAN, 2012

"I was once asked why my wife Sherri and I are members of a gay synagogue. That's an easy question to answer: Because CBST is how the world should be." SIMON DRATFIELD

### Telling Our Story

Even in the days when more LGBT people were in the closet than in the open, members of CBST have been eager to have a public voice, to educate the community and record their history. Members appeared on radio shows, wrote letters in the Jewish press, and participated in CBST's speakers' bureau.

When Israeli anthropologist Moshe Shokeid chose CBST as the subject of his major anthropological fieldwork study between 1989–1990, many members were thrilled to participate, feeling validated by the interest in CBST and hopeful that the world would learn about the synagogue. Shokeid's book, *A Gay Synagogue in New York*, published in 1995—one of the few academic texts on a gay Jewish community—is still assigned in college courses, and students continue to reach out to CBST for help researching their papers. The book effectively captures the moment when the synagogue was staggering under the impact of AIDS and debating the hiring of a rabbi. The book also expresses Shokeid's own sense of risk at choosing a gay subject for his research. True to its time, certain that no one interviewed would want their names published, Shokeid's publisher insisted he use pseudonyms for all CBST members. Only Jack Greenberg and Ron Weiss, who saw the proofs of the book and asked Shokeid *not* to use pseudonyms, are identified by their real names. Shokeid built many relationships in the community and returned on several occasions to follow up on his research and visit CBST.

Still, members longed to tell CBST's story from their own perspective. In 2009, during a one-to-one conversation for the Koleinu project, Marsha Melnick asked Harriet Beckman what aspect of the CBST community most inspired her. "Recording our history," Harriet replied. After that meeting, Harriet approached StoryCorps, the oral history organization collecting and archiving interviews at the American Folklife Center at the Library of Congress. Harriet reached Veronica Ordaz from the StoryCorps staff, and described the project she had in mind. "That's good timing, Veronica responded, "we received funding to record the story of Stonewall. Do you happen to know anyone who was there that night?" At Harriet's suggestion, StoryCorps contacted Michael Levine for an interview. On the anniversary of Stonewall, Michael's interview was broadcast nationally on NPR.

As part of an initiative to record stories from LGBT communities, StoryCorps invited CBST members to record their stories. To help plan interviews and engage participants, Harriet put together a committee—Yehuda Berger, Joanne Jacobson, Jay Fischer, Judy Hollander, Maryann King, Michael Levine, Stan Moldovan, and Beth Rosen. Thanks to StoryCorps, CBST's history now has a permanent presence in the Library of Congress.

*A Gay Synagogue in New York* by Moshe Shokeid, (above) 1995

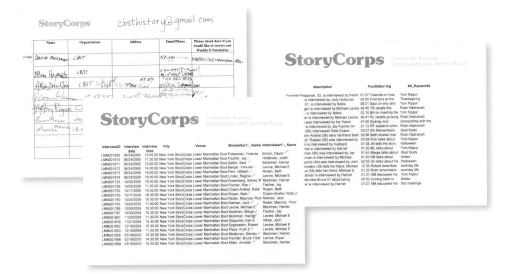

Harriet Beckman coordinated CBST's participation in StoryCorps, recruiting interviewers and interviewees.

The evolution of the CBST logotypes

## Modernizing the Communication

In 2008 a communications committee was created, chaired by Karen Benezra with members Andy Austin, Susan Meyer, Simon Dratfield, George Perlov, and Aari Ludvigsen. They overhauled the website, which had become the primary portal for information. The CBST newsletter—for decades, lovingly created by its members—was mailed for the last time in 2008.

The committee worked with a communications firm to recast the synagogue's visual identity and mission statement in 2010. As a part of that process the spelling of the synagogue's name was updated—"Beth" became "Beit" to accurately reflect its Hebrew pronunciation.

> Our Mission
>
> Congregation Beit Simchat Torah (CBST) is a vibrant spiritual community and a progressive voice within Judaism. Founded in 1973, CBST attracts and welcomes gay men, lesbians, bisexuals, transgender, queer, and straight individuals and families who share common values. Passionate, provocative, and deeply Jewish, CBST champions a Judaism that rejoices in diversity, denounces social injustice wherever it exists, and strives for human rights for all people.
>
> * We are a house of prayer, offering both traditional and liberal services and lifecycle events.
>
> * We are a house of learning, continually expanding our knowledge and deepening our understanding of our religious and cultural heritage.
>
> * We are a house of refuge and healing, offering community support and pastoral care.
>
> * We are a house of conscience, fighting for the full equality of LGBTQ people locally, nationally, and internationally.
>
> * We are committed to Israel and engaged in supporting efforts to secure peace, justice, and equality for all.

## A Home of Our Own

Westbeth was never intended as CBST's long-term home. In October 1976, when the lease on the 57 Bethune Street space was first secured, the newsletter reported its success in an article called "Gimme Shelter":

> The continuing saga of Beth Simchat Torah, a tender young congregation roaming in the cruel cold streets of the big city in search of a warm hearth and a friendly smile from a real estate broker, continues. In the last episode, CBST had been rescued from the streets in the nick of time by a six-month rental agreement, with a 30-day cancellation clause, for a suite of rooms tucked away in a forgotten corner of Westbeth, a huge, faceless building on the seamy western fringes of Greenwich Village.

Irving Cooperberg knew the time would come when the synagogue would outgrow its rented Bethune Street accommodations. During his first term as chair of the

Sydney Rosenberg in 2013

## HOW I GOT TO CBST

It was 1974. I was at a party and someone said he had been to a gay synagogue. I just couldn't believe there was such a place. It seemed like an oxymoron. I was going on a trip to Israel, and I said as soon as I come back, the first Friday night, I'm going to go to see what this place is all about. The synagogue was meeting on Ninth Avenue and 28th Street in the Church of the Holy Apostles in the community room. I remember walking in, and there were perhaps twenty-five or thirty people sitting around in a circle. I recognized one of the people by his voice; I knew him from my childhood in Brooklyn. His parents owned the corner grocery store. His name was Irving Cooperberg. I told him, "I know you from Kosciuszko Street." I hadn't seen him in twenty-five years.

When I was growing up, we never went to shul on Friday night. We went on the holidays. When I was in the army, I went to synagogue during basic training. To be frank, I went to get out of the barracks and be in a more civilian atmosphere. Everybody was my age, and the services were basically in English so I could understand what was going on. I had a very warm feeling.

When I got to CBST, I had the same feeling. People were more or less the same age, the service was a little bit in Hebrew but mostly in English, there was a warm atmosphere, and I started to go every Friday night. I enjoyed it. I gradually got to see that it was a serious undertaking to provide a spiritual and religious service to gays and lesbians. Then I got more involved.

SYDNEY ROSENBERG, MEMBER SINCE 1974

The Premises Trust Fund Committee reported the financial status to the board at every meeting.

board, he suggested establishing a fund for CBST to have reserves for a future home, at a time when there was very little money and no need for a building. Sydney Rosenberg recalls, "In my apartment in April 1981, Paul Jeselsohn, Steve Hochberg, and I (all three of us attorneys), wrote up the resolution to present to the board establishing the Premises Trust Fund, with seven trustees. I joined the committee in about 1988, and around 1990 I became chair." For more than twenty years, Sydney served as chair.

Knowing that the possibility of a permanent home was still a long way off, the Bethune street space was renovated several times to meet the requirements of the community: remodeling the sanctuary, removing a number of smaller offices to enlarge the community space to accommodate the crowds for High Holiday services, building the rabbi's office, all with the help of architect Ann Macklin, and later rebuilding the offices to accommodate the growing staff. Despite these efforts, the space never fully met CBST's needs. The community longed for a home that could hold all of CBST's offices, classrooms, Shabbat services, and lifecycle events in a single, comfortable space.

With a hidden, poorly marked entrance that you had to know how to find, some members complained that the location felt closeted, even though the neighborhood had become fashionable and expensive. Rabbi Kleinbaum frequently joked that the shul felt more like an underground lesbian bar from the 70s than the proud locus of community life and political activism that it had become. Bill Hibsher reflects that "while Rabbi Kleinbaum had long criticized mainstream synagogues for suffering from an 'Edifice Complex' decrying a permanent home for CBST, her view changed as our needs grew, and as we became aware of the significance of having a prominent visible street presence."

The Mishkan Committee was formed in 1995 with Bill Hibsher and Marcy Kahn as co-chairs to investigate real estate possibilities. As Bill remembers, "At the beginning of this phase, the market was quite hot, and every time we saw a space that looked interesting, it went into contract as a residential condominium almost immediately. As we viewed available spaces, we were overwhelmed by the asking prices and increasingly aware of our lack of sophistication in evaluating potential spaces."

## MY THREE YEARS AS PRESIDENT

CBST has changed the trajectory of my life, and I have seen how it has changed the lives of many others. I can't think of any greater purpose for a synagogue than this. We get consumed with the details of budgets and liturgy and committees and music and buildings and contracts, but it is remarkable what happens when an individual and an institution come together with complementary purposes for a period of time, and both are uplifted by their interaction. That is how I feel about my past three years as CBST's president.

On a personal note: Being CBST's president was an opportunity for me to dive more deeply into Judaism than ever before in my life. Coming to services each week was a privilege that grounded me in the Jewish calendar, seeing Jewish life at the granular level of days and weeks. I read the weekly *parshiot* not just once but three times, each in a different frame of mind. I don't pretend to be an expert in anything Jewish, but I understand the basic structure of a Friday night and Saturday morning service and High Holy Day liturgy. I know something about how different music affects prayer, and I have some feeling for what a rabbi really does and for the details of how a Jewish community really works. I've sounded the shofar and given *drashot* and gone to classes and once I even kashered part of my kitchen to have some friends for a Shabbat meal. I could have done most of this without being CBST's president, but somehow I don't think it would have happened. So I am grateful to all for creating and leading and supporting and loving and kibitzing and kvetching with me about this wonderful institution that is our own true creation.

ERIC ROSENBAUM,
PRESIDENT, 2006–2009

Eric Rosenbaum recalls a critical turning point in CBST's search for a permanent home when, as board vice president, he and Bill Hibsher attended a meeting with two young gay men in the City Planning Department. After the meeting, Bill shared some of his frustrations with CBST's inability to make serious progress in finding a permanent home. As Eric recalled, "It had become clear that just looking at property wasn't an effective approach—anything we liked would require the funds to negotiate a contract and yet, without a site in hand, no one was going to make any financial commitments. Bill asked me what I thought it would take to make it happen 'for real.' I said we had to take a strategic approach, recognizing that doing so could take a very long time to bear fruit. Instead of just looking for property, we had to build an infrastructure capable of raising the money needed. This required a cadre of lay leaders knowledgeable and networked in real estate, a few key major donors to step forward and to make early commitments that would give us enough evidence to believe that the long-term goal was possible."

Inspired by this conversation, Bill and Eric began to assemble a team, with the support of Executive Director Ilene Sameth, that included David Wine, Heymi Kuriel, Jonathan Sheffer, and Aari Ludvigsen, each of whom brought professional expertise and deep personal commitment. They found the first viable site, hired a fund-raising consultant and secured commitments of over $5 million in three months. Although that site fell through, CBST had proved capable of mobilizing quickly, making it possible to successfully engage in serious fund-raising. Strategic planning and capacity building were the hallmarks of Eric's presidency, as the synagogue's leadership focused on readying the institution for fulfillment of the long-held dream to find CBST a home of its own.

In 2007 a new design committee was formed, which led to the decision to retain an architect. Bill Hibsher recalls:

> Jonathan Sheffer took the lead in soliciting candidates, and, much to our surprise, most of the nation's recognized 'Starchitects' sought our project. We decided to retain Architecture Research Office, led at that time by two principals who both taught architecture at Harvard and who, we felt, spoke our language. Stephen Cassell began working with us in evaluating potential sites—warehouses, dance theaters, churches, firehouses—more than thirty sites were subject to analysis.

Even with a changed economy and a few disappointments when promising sites fell through, CBST kept focused on its goal as Steve Frank became president in 2009. All told, the Mishkan Committee had looked at roughly one hundred sites over the years. In June 2011 CBST finally succeeded in purchasing a home of its own in the heart of Manhattan. The total cost was $7.1 million. The Premises Trust Fund was able to contribute $1.16 million to the purchase of the new site.

ABOVE: David Wine, Ilene Sameth, Bill Hibsher, Heymi Kuriel, and Rabbi Kleinbaum can barely contain their excitement as Steve Frank signs the paperwork for the purchase of 130 West 30th Street.

ABOVE RIGHT: Steve Frank and Erika Karp discuss the terms of the deal.

### From Dream to Reality

"From the beginning," Steve Frank explains, "because we weren't sure how much money we'd be able to raise, we approached the transaction very conservatively. Many board meetings took place to discuss the funding strategies We didn't put it to a vote of the congregation before we had pledges equal to the purchase price. We knew that if we failed in raising the rest of the money needed for the renovation, we could always rent out the space as retail space, or sell it."

By the time of the closing thirty-four pledges had been secured which, when added to the Premises Trust Fund, totaled almost precisely the purchase price. The thirty-four pledges—including lead gifts from David Wine, Bill Fern, Jonathan Sheffer, Erika Karp, and Heymi Kuriel—came from each of the eighteen members of the board, as well as several past presidents, and a handful of members who were approached during the silent phase of the capital campaign.

> "One of the things you hear at CBST is about changing the world. For me, CBST's new home will surely change the world and its perception of LGBT Jews as we emerge into a new-found light and grow in new and incalculable ways." DAVID WINE

"The premises were previously owned by a fur store and a knockoff handbag store. The fur store vacated and we were able to freshen up the space a bit with lights and paint so that CBST could use it for events and meetings. The handbag store agreed to rent the space from CBST for two years while the funds were raised for the renovation."

With the property secured, the capital campaign was formally underway.

## MY FAMILY AT CBST

CBST was born in February 1973. A few months later, so was I. I became president of CBST in April 2009, around the time the congregation and I celebrated our thirty-sixth birthdays. I was the first president of CBST never to have known anyone who died of AIDS—as well as the first to have a child while president. These twin facts speak remarkably to the LGBT experience in the United States at the start of the twenty-first century.

My partner Adam Berger and I celebrated the naming of our son, Ethan, at CBST's Family and Friends service in June 2009. New York City Mayor Michael Bloomberg was our guest speaker that evening, marking what may well have been the first naming ceremony for the child of a same-sex couple he had ever attended. Over the next two years, Mayor Bloomberg campaigned actively for marriage equality in New York State, and I would like to think that seeing our family on the bimah that evening contributed to his passion for the cause.

CBST's principal focus during my three years as president was finding a home of our own. In June 2011, on the eve of Pride Shabbat, we purchased nearly 17,000 square feet of space in a landmark Cass Gilbert-designed building at 130 West 30th Street. The deal marked a leap of faith by CBST's board that our community would be able to raise the funds for the purchase and renovation.

Even as we achieved that long-held dream, we were also marking other milestones as a community, signing a long-term contract with Rabbi Sharon Kleinbaum, bidding farewell to our remarkable rabbi, Ayelet Cohen, and welcoming Rabbi Rachel Weiss as the third assistant rabbi in CBST's history. We continued to focus on the professionalization of CBST's staff, hiring our first full-time director of development and communications, and retaining consultants to analyze and improve our staffing structure. It was a period of growth for the community, with membership surging more than 20 percent.

It was also a remarkable time for LGBT rights nationally. On Pride Shabbat 2011, just one day after we signed the contract to buy our new home, the New York state legislature legalized same-sex marriage. By the end of that year, Don't Ask Don't Tell had been repealed, and Secretary of State Hillary Clinton had announced at the United Nations that advancing LGBT civil rights was part of the official foreign policy of the United States.

Yet, as a new parent juggling work and family with my CBST responsibilities, the moments that resonated most for me were those tied up with family—like the Friday night when I brought a two-year-old Ethan up to the bimah for announcements after services and he said "Shabbat Shalom" into the microphone or the Rosh Hashanah when we had to bless the children of our congregation in the aisles of Town Hall because there was not enough space for them all to fit onstage. These, in particular, are magical memories I will forever cherish.

STEVE FRANK, PRESIDENT 2009-2012

Steve Frank (second from left under the tallit) and his partner Adam Berger, holding their son Ethan, surrounded by their family, June 2009

The design process proceeded almost immediately, becoming the focus of countless meetings as well as open evening sessions for congregants to share their ideas for the new space. Every idea was considered and presented to Stephen Cassell. Over the months that followed, Stephen and his team at ARO presented plans visualizing how the entrance, sanctuary, chapel, classrooms, and staff offices would be organized to best accommodate the community's needs.

ABOVE: Stephen Cassell of ARO

LEFT: The community gathers to view the architects' schematic model for the new building.

## The Capital Campaign

A Capital Project Steering Committee, consisting of Steve Frank, Eric Rosenbaum, Aari Ludvigsen, and Bill Hibsher as chair, began weekly meetings to oversee design, fund-raising, and preparations for the new space. At every stage, CBST's rabbis and staff have played an integral role. Member Aari Ludvigsen took the lead on design and construction with help from civil engineer Heymi Kuriel and Joseph Cunin. Eric and David Wine co-chaired the fund-raising campaign, and Sherri Dratfield, Lisa Kartzman, and Janet Pavloff co-chaired the Community Campaign, along with scores of volunteers, who realized contributions from more than 700 donors. Affinity group and neighborhood parties were also held, encouraging members to have their names inscribed on the community wall planned for the entrance foyer of the new home by donating $1,800 or more. Eric and

Renderings of CBST's New Home at Completion of Design Development

CLOCKWISE FROM LEFT: Bill Hibsher; Richard Orient; members and friends; David Wine and Aari Ludvigsen

Nate Goldstein took on the task of leading a strategic planning initiative and board treasurer Rosalba Messina of overseeing all aspects of the finances as the project moved forward.

A fund-raising event, at which Bill Hibsher reluctantly agreed to be honored, was held in the new space. Invitations and a celebratory wall display were designed by artist Richard Orient, Bill's partner. The assembled crowd and a matching grant by David Wine and Heymi Kuriel raised $760,000 for the capital campaign that evening.

This event was followed by Rabbi Kleinbaum's twentieth anniversary celebration which raised $1.3 million toward the capital campaign, including a matching grant from David Wine. And late in the campaign, when Jonathan Sheffer committed to doubling his own pledge, he hosted an event at his home, encouraging others to follow his lead. The pledges that evening from major donors, including matching grants made by Jonathan and David Wine, contributed $2.2 million to the capital campaign.

# ARCHITECTURAL RENDERINGS

Working with ideas suggested by CBST staff and members, ARO produced plans and renderings envisioning how the synagogue's new home would accommodate the community's various programs. From the entry to the sanctuary, the offices to the classrooms and chapel, ARO focused on creating transparency, intimacy, warmth, and flexibility.

SANCTUARY/ GROUND LEVEL

CHILDREN'S CLASSROOM/LOWER LEVEL

LOBBY/LOWER LEVEL

## The Fortieth Anniversary Year

Celebrations marked CBST's fortieth year, beginning in late December, 2012. The congregation honored Rabbi Kleinbaum on her twentieth anniversary with a major fund-raising event at the Gerald W. Lynch Theater at John Jay College, moderated by actress and activist Cynthia Nixon, who read the full text of Rabbi Kleinbaum's installation sermon. The afternoon featured an interview of Rabbi Kleinbaum by Frank Rich, Rabbi Cohen, and Cynthia Nixon and a special video tribute by member David I. Sigal. The celebration, planned to every detail by a committee chaired by Marsha Melnick and Bill Hibsher and produced by Barbara Gaines, attracted a full house of 600 people. The special journal marking the day gathered tributes and letters to the rabbi, including ones from Governor Andrew Cuomo, Senator Kirsten Gillibrand, Mayor Michael Bloomberg, and countless members and friends of the synagogue.

ABOVE CLOCKWISE: Cynthia Nixon; the interviewers with Rabbi Kleinbaum; co-chairs Marsha Melnick and Bill Hibsher presenting a model of the bimah, which will be named in her honor.

The celebration coincided with the second night of Chanukah and candle-lighting led by Rabbi Weiss, with Joyce and the community chorus. Rabbi Kleinbaum's daughters Molly and Liba joined her on stage for their family rendition of "Candles Burning," a CBST Chanukah favorite.

The fortieth anniversary party

In June 2013 the synagogue celebrated its fortieth anniversary at a party in the Ramscale event space in Westbeth with breathtaking views of the transformed West Village. Honoring its history, the synagogue offered the celebration as a gift to its members.

Later that summer, after a heady Pride season capped by the defeat of DOMA, CBST cleared the final hurdle to achieving its dream of a new home. Just as the board resolved the synagogue would not close on the sale until they had cash and pledges in hand to pay for the property, they committed to the congregation not to break ground on construction before they knew how they would pay for it. "We have held firm to that pledge," says Steve Frank. "By the time the board voted to proceed with construction, we had pledges nearly equal to the hard costs of construction."

A note to the community on the website announced the momentous decision to proceed:

We write to let you know that CBST's Board of Directors voted unanimously on July 18 to proceed with renovation of our New Home. . . . Our designs are complete and construction bids have been received, and with the Board's vote, work can start this fall. This historic milestone comes in the middle of our 40th Anniversary year and is testimony to how far we have come. We owe gratitude to our leaders, donors, clergy, staff, and members. And we remember all who came before us who helped make this important step possible.

## OUR MISHKAN

It has been my privilege to chair CBST's board as the long-term dream of having a home of our own is closer to reality.

Prior to recommending the acquisition of 130 West 30th Street to the congregation, we reached out to two dozen congregants who had been CBST's major supporters, quietly asking if they would support this project. Every response was a resounding "Yes." In the Spring of 2011, the congregation approved the acquisition, and we publicly launched our campaign. An army of volunteers mobilized to solicit once-in-a-lifetime gifts from members and others for this project. At the time of this writing, more than 700 donors have contributed to our capital campaign, and we are in sight of our new *mishkan*.

So as I perform the duties of CBST's 17th board president, I am humbled by the fact that my tenure coincides with: the ground-breaking on the renovation project for our new home; the twentieth anniversary of Sharon Kleinbaum's installation as CBST's first rabbi; and the 40th anniversary of this amazing congregation. How privileged am I?

BILL HIBSHER, PRESIDENT 2012-2014

## The Next Forty Years

Finding a permanent home for CBST was an exciting triumph; a physical manifestation of that which the synagogue had come to represent in its first four decades. Many people ask if an LGBT synagogue is still relevant in a world that has seen so much progress on LGBT civil and religious equality. Certainly in New York City, in 2013, there are more than a handful of progressive synagogues in which LGBT people are integrated and celebrated. Many progressive synagogues and organizations in major cities now have a gay and lesbian *chavurah* or an LGBT program area.

Those changes have been achieved in no small part because of CBST. For forty years CBST's members and rabbis have been advocating and agitating, building alliances and reaching out to transform the world for LGBT Jews. The gay synagogue movement, with CBST as its largest and most powerful voice, set the stage for the proliferation of Jewish LGBT organizations in existence today. CBST's rabbis and Cooperberg-Rittmaster Rabbinical Intern alumni are some of the greatest religious activists for LGBTQ rights; they play essential roles in queer Jewish organizations; they have created some of the most valuable resources in the field. Their work at CBST provided the foundation for their continuing creativity and grassroots activism.

CBST remains a rare community whose spiritual leaders and worshippers proudly and openly identify across the spectrum of sexual orientation and gender identity; sex and gender are discussed without shame in terms of holiness. CBST's influence was present in the defeat of DOMA; doubtless it will be in the coming victories for LGBT rights in the United States and globally. In its next forty years, CBST will continue to work toward a time when the radical religious right has no dominance over religious life or political influence in the United States, or anywhere else in the world, until equality and justice for people of all sexual orientations, gender identities and expressions, and religious affiliation are understood as a basic civil right. At forty, CBST is more relevant than ever. It both serves as spiritual home for its members and, at the same time, serves as a beacon of progress beyond its membership. The joy, spirituality, and connectedness of CBST's community translates into a profound commitment to achieving justice and transforming the world.

# GLOSSARY

**Achot k'tanah** "Little Sister," a Sephardic liturgical poem traditionally sung on the first night of Rosh Hashanah

**adult bat/bar mitzvah** culmination of adult Jewish learning or reaffirming acceptance of religious responsibility

**alav hashalom** May he rest in peace

**Al hanisim** prayer of thanksgiving recited at CBST on Jewish holidays of Chanukah, Purim, Yom Ha'atsmaut, and GLBT Pride

**aliyah** 1: honor of blessing the Torah  2: chanted Torah portion  3: permanent residence in Israel (lit. "going up")

**Amidah** central prayer in each Jewish liturgical service (lit. "standing")

**atzei chayim** wooden Torah rollers (lit. "trees of life")

**aufruf** blessing or *aliyah* for a couple before their wedding (Yid.)

**Avinu malkeinu** prayer in the liturgy for High Holidays and fast days (lit. "our parent, our sovereign")

**ba'al, ba'alat korei** (m., f.) Torah reader

**ba'al, ba'alat, ba'alei tefillah** (m., f., pl.) prayer leader

**bar/bat mitzvah** (m., f.) ceremony at which a Jewish twelve- or thirteen-year-old child enters the age of religious responsibility (lit. "age of obligation")

**bashert** meant to be (Yid.)

**beit din** religious court, consisting of at least three rabbis or knowledgeable, observant Jews

**beit midrash** house of study

**bench gomel** pray for thanksgiving upon surviving a life-threatening experience (Yid.-Heb.)

**Bereishit** Genesis (also the first *parashah* of Genesis)

**bikkur cholim** visiting the sick

**bimah** raised platform in a synagogue from which services are led and Torah is read

**Birkat hachamah** blessing of the sun

**b'nai mitzvah/b'not mitzvah** (m. pl., f. pl.) *See also* bar/bat mitzvah

**brachah** blessing

**brit ahavah** commitment ceremony (lit. "covenant of love")

**b'tselem elohim** in the image of God

**Chasid, Chasidic** (n., adj.) a member of a religious Jewish sect founded in 18th-century Poland by the Baal Shem-Tov, characterized by its emphasis on mysticism, prayer, strict ritual observance, and joyful religious ardor

**Chasidishe rebbe** Chasidic rabbi (Yid.)

**chasonim** grooms (Yid.)

**chaverim** friends/comrades

**chavurah, chavurot** (s., pl.) lay-led prayer community

**chazzanut** cantorial singing

**chazzan** cantor

**chesed** lovingkindness

**chug** club

**chuppah** wedding canopy

**darshan, darshanit, darshanim, darshaniot** (m., f., m. pl., f. pl.) one who gives the sermon

**daven** pray (Yid.)

**drash, drashot** (s., pl.) sermon

**ein kamohu** There is no one like him

**Ein keloheinu** prayer from the Shabbat and festival liturgy (lit. "there is none like our God")

**frumkeit** religiosity, religious observance (Yid.)

**ga'aguim** Chasidic melodies of longing

**Gemara** the part of the Talmud comprising rabbinic commentary on the Mishnah

**get** writ of divorce

**g'lilah** wrapping the Torah after it has been lifted and shown to the community

**hachnasat orchim** welcoming guests

**haftarah** the reading from the Prophets that complements the Torah reading

**hagbah** lifting the partially unscrolled Torah for the community to see (lit. "raising")

**Haggadah** the book of text and liturgy recited at the Passover seder (lit. "the telling")

**hakadosh baruch hu** the Holy One of Blessing

**halachah, halachic** (n., adj.) Jewish law, pertaining to Jewish law

**hashkamah minyan** early morning prayer service

**Hashkiveinu** prayer for peace from the evening liturgy (lit. "lay us down")

**Havdalah** ritual at the end of Shabbat or a festival (lit. "separation")

**heimish** homey, informal (Yid.)

***Kabbalat Shabbat*** service to welcome Shabbat (lit. "welcoming Shabbat")

**Kaddish** prayer that punctuates synagogue services, a version of which is recited by mourners

*kadosh* sacred

*kahal* congregation

*kavod* respect

*kehillah* community

*kehillah kedoshah* a holy congregation

*keter* crown (in context, adornment for the Torah)

*ketubah* marriage contract

*kiddush* blessing over wine on Shabbat and festivals (lit. "sanctification")

*kippah, kippot* (s., pl.) skullcap

*klal yisrael* broad Jewish community (lit. "all of Israel")

*klei kodesh* spiritual objects (lit. "sacred vessels")

***Kol Nidrei*** liturgical introduction to the Yom Kippur service (lit. "all my vows")

*koreen* full prostration (as performed during the Yom Kippur service)

***L'chah dodi*** liturgical song in the *Kabbalat Shabbat* service (lit. "come my love")

***Lech Lecha*** go forth (from Gen. 12)

*l'dor vador* from generation to generation

*lih'yot am chofshi b'artzeinu* to be a free people in our land (from *Hatikvah*, lit. "The Hope," Israel's national anthem)

***Limmud Mishpachah*** CBST education program for families with children (lit. "family learning")

*limudei kodesh* religious studies

***Ma'ariv*** evening service

*machzor* High Holiday prayer book

***Magen avot*** blessing from the *Amidah* in the Friday night service (lit. "shield of our ancestors")

*makom* 1. place 2. God

*matbeya* structure

*mechitzah* partition separating men and women in a prayer service

*megillah* scroll, most commonly the scroll of Esther

*menschlichkeit* the qualities of integrity and honor that make one a mensch (Yid.)

*meshugeneh alte kaker* crazy old man (Yid.)

***Mevarchim Minyan*** a CBST minyan that met monthly on *Shabbat mevarchim*, when the blessing for the new month is recited

*mikvah* ritual bath

***Minchah*** afternoon service

*minhag* custom

**minyan, minyanim** (s., pl.) prayer quorum of ten Jewish adults

**Minyan Chadash** the New Minyan

***Mi shebeirach*** prayer for healing (lit. "the One who blessed")

*mishpachah* family

**mitzvah, mitzvot** (s., pl.) commandment

**mohel, mohelet** (m., f.) one who conducts ritual circumcisions

*motzi* shorthand for the blessing over bread (lit. "who brings forth")

**Mourner's Kaddish** mourner's prayer

***Musaf*** additional service included in the morning liturgy on Shabbat and festivals

***N'ilah* or *Neilah*** the final service at the end of Yom Kippur (lit. "locking")

*neirot* candles

**nekudah, nekudot** (s., pl.) vowel, (lit. "point")

*neshamah* soul

**niggun, niggunim** (s., pl.) wordless melody

*nusach* prayer melody

*oneg* the social and cultural hour after services (lit. "enjoyment")

*or lagoyim* a light unto the nations

**Orthopractic Minyan** the prayer service at CBST that tried to adhere to Orthodox ritual practice

*parashah, parshat hashavua* the weekly Torah portion

*pasuk* verse (usually from Torah)

*piyyut* liturgical poem

**responsum, responsa** (s., pl.) written decision(s) from a rabbinic authority responding to Jewish legal questions

**Rosh Chodesh** new Jewish month (lit. "head of the month")

**Rosh Hashanah** Jewish New Year (lit. "head of the year")

**seder, sedarim** (s., pl.) Passover home ritual guided by the Haggadah (lit. "order")

**Shabbat Mevarchim** the Shabbat before Rosh Chodesh, when the blessing of the new month is recited (lit. "Shabbat of blessing")

*shabbatot* plural of Shabbat

**Shabbes** Sabbath (Yid.)

**Shacharit** morning service

***Shalom aleichem*** a Friday evening song originating in the home ritual, sung at the start of Friday night services at CBST (lit. "welcome")

***Shehechiyanu*** blessing recited upon a new or notable occasion (lit. "who has given us life")

*shep naches* get pleasure (Yid.)

***Sheva brachot*** seven wedding blessings

***Shir hashirim*** Song of Songs

**shiva** seven days of mourning, where customarily Jewish mourners sit at home and receive visitors offering consolation

***shlepper*** an uneducated manual laborer (Yid.)

***Sh'ma*** central prayer and declaration of faith in Jewish liturgy, from Deuteronomy 6:4 (lit. "hear")

***shmatte*** rag (Yid.)

**Sh'mini Atseret** the festival immediately following Sukkot (lit. "the eighth day of assembly")

***shmirah*** watching over a body until burial

***Sh'moneh esreh*** the *Amidah* prayer (lit. "eighteen," referring to the eighteen blessings that originally formed the *Amidah*)

***shmooze*** to chat; at CBST, a program or discussion after services

***shofar*** ram's horn

***shomer, shomeret*** (m., f.) one who watches over a body until burial (lit. "guard")

***shpiel*** a humorous show or performance (Yid.)

***shtiebel*** small, intimate synagogue (Yid.)

**shul** synagogue (Yid.)

***siddur, siddurim*** (s., pl.) prayer book

***simchah*** joy

**Simchat Torah** festival of rejoicing in the Torah

***sofer, soferet, sof'rim*** (m., f., pl.) scribe

***streimel*** fur hat worn by Chasidic men (Yid.)

***sukkah*** temporary booth built for the festival of Sukkot

***taharah*** ritual of purifying a body before burial

***tallit, tallitot*** (s., pl.) prayer shawl

***talmud u'ma'aseh*** study and action

**Tanach** Bible

***tefillah, tefillot*** (s., pl.) prayer

***teshuvot*** responsa

**Tikkun Leil Shavuot** all-night Torah study on the festival of Shavuot

***tikkun olam*** repairing the world

***tisches*** festive gatherings usually consisting of teaching and singing (lit. "tables," Yid.)

***Tov lehodot*** Psalm 92, the Psalm for Shabbat (lit. "it is good to give thanks")

**Tu Bish'vat** the new year of the trees

***tzedakah*** acts of justice and charity

**Unetaneh tokef** significant passage from the High Holiday liturgy

***V'ahavta*** the first paragraph of the *Sh'ma* (lit. "and you shall love")

***yamim tovim*** festivals

***V'shamru*** biblical passage announcing Shabbat, used in the Friday night liturgy and in the Shabbat day kiddush (lit. "and you shall observe")

***yarmulke*** *kippah* or skull cap (Yid.)

***yeshiva, yeshivot*** (s., pl.) seminary of religious study

**Yiddishkeit** Jewishness (Yid.)

**Yizkor** memorial prayer recited on festivals

**Yom Ha'atsmaut** Israeli Independence Day

**Yom Hashoah** Holocaust Remembrance Day

**Yom Hazikaron** Israeli Remembrance Day

***yontif*** festival (Yid.)

***z"l*** abbreviation for *zichrono or zichronah livrachah,* may his or her memory be a blessing

# ABBREVIATIONS

| | |
|---|---|
| **ACT UP** | AIDS Coalition to Unleash Power |
| **ADL** | Anti Defamation League |
| **AIDS** | Acquired Immune Deficiency Syndrome |
| **ARZA** | Association of Reform Zionists of America |
| **AZT** | Zidovudine, medication for AIDS |
| **AZYF** | American Zionist Youth Foundation |
| **AZYF** | Reform Movement's Zionist Association |
| **BCC** | Beth Chayim Chadashim |
| **CA** | Cantors Assembly (Conservative) |
| **CBCO** | Congregation-Based Community Organizing |
| **CCAR** | Central Conference of American Rabbis (Reform) |
| **CLAL** | National Jewish Center for Learning and Leadership |
| **CLGR** | Coalition for Lesbian and Gay Rights |
| **CRRI** | Cooperberg-Rittmaster Rabinnical Internship |
| **CSLD** | Christopher Street Liberation Day |
| **DOMA** | Defense of Marriage Act |
| **GLAAD** | Gay and Lesbian Alliance Against Defamation |
| **GLYDSA** | Gay and Lesbian Yeshiva Day School Alumni Association |
| **GMHC** | Gay Mens' Heath Crisis |
| **HIV** | Human Immunodeficiency Virus |
| **HUC-JIR** | Hebrew Union College-Jewish Institute of Religion (Reform) |
| **JAGL** | Jewish Activist Gays and Lesbians |
| **JBFCS** | Jewish Board of Family and Children's Services |
| **JFREJ** | Jews for Racial and Economic Justice |
| **JOH** | Jerusalem Open House |
| **JTS** | Jewish Theological Seminary |
| **LeGAL** | LGBT Law Association of Greater New York |
| **MCC** | Metropolitan Community Church |
| **NACOEJ** | North American Conference on Ethiopian Jewry |
| **NGHEF** | National Gay Health Education Foundation |
| **NGLTF** | National Gay and Lesbian Task Force |
| **PWAs** | People with AIDS |
| **RA** | Rabbinical Assembly (Conservative) |
| **RRC** | Reconstructionist Rabbinical College (Reconstructionist) |
| **SAGE** | Originally Senior Action in a Gay Environment Currently Services and Advocacy of GLBT Elders |
| **SONDA** | New York State Sexual Orientation Non-discrimination Act |
| **UAHC** | Union of American Hebrew Congregations |
| **WCGLJO** | World Congress of Gay and Lesbian Jewish Organizations |

# INDEX

Note: bold indicates a sidebar on this person or topic

*A Gay Synagogue in New York*, 294-95
Achuff, Charles, 150
ACT UP, 67
Aderman, Shelli, 124, 125, 149, 151, 214
Aderman-Alcorn, Malka, 125, 151
Adler, Gary, 67, 112, 118, 150, 214
Affiliation Committee, 51, 86-87
AIDS, 51-52, 56-81, *see also* Gay Men's Health Crisis (GMHC), World AIDS Day
  AIDS Walk, 66, 273-74
  and Bikkur Cholim Committee, 63-64
  CBST's education and activism, 58-60, 66-67, 174-75, 273-74
  first mention of in CBST newsletter, 57-58
  pastoral care from CBST rabbinical staff, 111-15
  and rabbi search, 84-85, 87, 92, 95, 99, 101, 102
  ritual resources and services for, 62, 68-72, 75, 138, 236, 272-73
  quilt, 73-75, 135, 231
AIDS Institute, New York State, 59, 67, 92
AIDS Quilt, 73-75
Alcorn, Narda, **214**
Alef Bet Shabbat, 124-25, 238-39, 241
Alliance for Judaism and Social Justice, 218
Alpert, Nancy, 93-94, 102
Alpert, Rabbi Rebecca, 266
Alter, David, 45, 50
Ameinu, 265-66
American Jewish Committee, 17
American Zionist Youth Foundation (AZYF), 260, 261
Ames, Jessica, 162
Anshel, Rafaela, 46, 151, 181, 184
Appel, Victor, 49, 248
Applegate, Beth, 286
Architecture Research Office (ARO), 299, 302, 304-05
Arden, Sheldon, 112
Artson, Rabbi Bradley Shavit, 89, 140
Asch, David, 42, 166, 180
Association of Reform Zionists of America (ARZA), 260, 261
Astrinsky, Assaf, 192, **193**, 292
Austin, Andrew (Andy), 151, 296
Austrian, Rabbi Guy, 116, 268, **279**, 281
Avital, Colette, 263
Axelrod, Dr. David, 62, 164
Azneer, Jay, 80, 166, 180

Bank, David, 62
Barbakoff, Jordan, 51

Barkan, Herman, 23
Barnett, Allen, 66
Bat-Chava, Yael, 125, 228, 238
Bauer, Rabbi David Dunn, 116, **127**, 293
Beckenstein, Sariel, 155, 166, 184
Beckman, Harriet, 48, 52, 139, 232, 295
Beebe, Dr. Peter, 47
Bender, Adam, 150
Benezra, Karen, 274, 296
Benjamin, Adria, 176, 189, 192, 195
Bennett, Rabbi Allen, 266
Bennett, Carl
  and Bikkur Cholim Committee, 112
  early days at CBST, 28, 33, 36, 132, 225
  gay rights demonstration in Israel, 259
  service leadership, 36
  speaker at Reform convention, 254
  as teacher, 45, 78, 225
  on Walter Schwartz, 81
Ben-Ze'ev, cantorial soloist Re'ut, 176, 191, 194, 196
Berger, Adam, 221, 301
Berger, Andrew, 150, 151
Berger, Cantor David, 121, 139, 162, 176, 179, 194-96, 231, 240, 270, 271
Berger, Ira, 58, 69
Berger, Pinchas, 67, 84
Berger, Yehuda (Howard), 136, 144, 151, 157
  and CBST's traditionalism, 32
  early days at CBST, 15, 28, 37, 42, 132
  and Religious Committee, 35
  ritual observance and liturgy, 45-46, 50, 54, 69-70, 136-39, 160
Berman, Debbi, 151
Berman, Eugene, 216
Berman, Ruth, 153, 222, 229, 250
Bernstein, Leslie, 147, 242
Bernstein-Dunkel, Emily, 242
Beth Am, The People's Temple, 254
Beth Chayim Chadashim (BCC), 254
Bethune Minyan, 130
Bethune Street sanctuary *see* Westbeth
Beyer, Rabbi Cecelia, 116, 160, 281
Bieber, Ethel, 37, 225
Bieber, Mark, **37**
  and Bill Amplo, 37
  and Art Leonard, 43
  board and committee involvement, 35, 39, 48, 51, 68, 169, 256, 257, 287, 292
  ritual involvement, 136, 143, 166, 169, 184
  and Robert Mark Dennet, 79
Bikkur Cholim Committee, 63-64, 66, 76, 112, 214-15
Binder, Ken, 211
*Birkat hachamah*, 160, 310

Blair, Janet, 250
Blake, Louis, 64
Blau, Gabriel, 281, 292
Bliss, John, 227
Block, Ilene, 130, 167, **188**
Bloomberg, Mayor Michael, 163, 165, 301, 306
Blumenthal, Marc, 63
B'nai Brith Anti-Defamation League, 265
b'nai mitzvah, 124, 134, 209-11, 213, 217-18, 233-37
board elections, 35, 40, 48, 87, 110, 286-87, 291
Bonder, Jason, 116
Boone, Laural, 149
Boone, Owen, 125, 149
Bornstein, Allan, 76
Bornstein, Kate, 165, 293
Brenner, Frédéric, 229, 267
Brettschneider, Marla, 266
Brick, Barbara, 225
Brick, Barrett, 225, 256, 257, 265
Brickner, Rabbi Balfour, 254, 264
*brit ahavah*, 92, 201, 203, 205, 310 *see also* weddings
Brush, Lisa, **228**
Buchanan, Constance, 290
Bumgardner, Reverend Pat, 271
Burhenne, Diane, 49, 51, 212, 288

Calhoun, Tasha, 11, 115, 139, 140, 148, 223, 291, 292
cantorial internship, 122, 162, 176, 193-94, 196, 290 *see also* names of individual cantorial interns
Capital Campaign, 300, 302-03, 308
Capital Project Steering Committee, 302
Carey, David, 157
Carrey, Henry, 231
Cartwright, Donna, 232
Cassell, Stephen, 299, 302
Caul, Shayna, 93-94, 181
Cayne, Marcia, 263
Cecilio, Gustavo, 11
Cemetery, Cedar Park, 37, 216, 286
Central Conference of American Rabbis (CCAR), 88-89 *see also* Reform Movement
Chaiken, Shami, 86, 166, 181
Chaikin, Ora, 46, 201, 203
Charles, Ronn, 68
Chasanoff, Amy, 250
Chelsea sanctuary *see* Church of the Holy Apostles
Cheren, Mel, 59
Chesir-Teran, Daniel, 129, 154, 193, 204-05, 220, 221, **233**, 262

Chesir-Teran, Eliezer, 233
Chesir-Teran, Ian, 129, 193, 204-05, 224, **233**, 268, 288
children at CBST, 56, 113-14, 124-26, 211-13, 236-43, 289 *see also Limmud Mishpachah*
Children's Education Committee, 241
Chorus, CBST Community, 162, 165, 176, 182-91, 193, 197, 208, 307
Christensen, Bob, 183, 228
Chung, Roger, 78, 112
Church of the Holy Apostles, 14-15, 18, 23, 29, 128-30, 170, 279, 286, 289
Citro, Ron, 184
Clein, Ed, 71
Cohen, Rabbi Ayelet, 117, 163, 221, 269, 271, 292, 306
 and CBST siddur, 139
 and children's education, 240-41
 creating new rituals, 207
 *drash* on transgender inclusion, 218
 hiring and installation of, 114-15, **120-21**, 287
 on coming out, **115**
 and the Conservative Movement, **119**, 268
 and holidays, 158-59, 177, 179, 280
 and the Liberal Minyan, 124
 and September 11, 2001, 288
 as teacher, 211, 231-33
Cohen, Maya Orli, 11, 231, 269, 291
Cohen, Tamara, 120, 126, 262
Cohen-Margolius, Galia, 223
Comerchero, Melissa, 221
commitment ceremonies, 200-05 *see also brit ahavah*
Community Campaign, 302
Community Development Committee, 47-48
concerts *see* Shabbat Shirah concert
Congregation Ansche Chesed, 170, 190
Congregation Bet Haverim, 99
Congregation Beth Chayim Chadashim (BCC), 18, 88, 254
Congregation B'nai Jeshurun, 85, 92, 164, 236, 254
Congregation B'nai Olam, 40
Congregation Sha'ar Zahav, 88, 164, 236
Connolly, Richard, 212, 227
Conservative Movement
 and CBST affiliation, **88-89**, 95, 264
 CBST members' identification with, 32, 36, 38, 51, 181, 235
 and Mel Rosen, 92, 95,
 position on homosexuality, 101-102, 233, 263-65, 268
 and Rabbi Cohen, **119**, 120
 and rabbi search and hire, 96, 98, 102
conversion, 105, 124, 208-10, 288
Cooperberg, Irving, 58, 65, 105, 141, **174-75**, **255**
 AIDS activism, 67-68, 175, 274
 and children's programming, 237
 early days at CBST, 15, 25, 40-41, 47

and High Holiday services, 166-67, 171, **172**, 177-78
 internship program *see* Cooperberg-Rittmaster Rabbinical Intern Program
 and Lou Rittmaster, 113, 174-175
 and rabbi search and hire, 94, 101-02
Cooperberg-Rittmaster Rabbinical Intern Program, 113-16, 207, 233-34, 268, 309 *see also* names of individual interns
Copeland, Rabbi Mychal, 116, **239**, 275
Cortes, Rafael, 235
Cortman, Michael, 59
Croland, Jeffery, 58
Cunin, Joseph, 151, 221-22, 302
Cunningham, Jerome, 20, 32
Cuomo, Governor Mario, 59, 65, 260-61, 265, 306
Currah, Paisley, 232

Dachinger, Penny, 46, 61
Davis, Ben, 116
Davis, Mitchell, 206
Dayan, MK Yael, 164, 165, 263
Defense of Marriage Act (DOMA), 204, 284-85, 308, 309
Deibach, Alfred, 43
Dennet, Robert Mark, 79
Derech Emuno (synagogue), 236
Deutsch, Elizabeth (Liz), 75, 128, 213, 277, 287
Deutsch, Leslie, 75, 128, 228, 277
Diamant, Anita, 201
Dinkins, Mayor David, 260, 263
Dolgin, Barbara, 149, 211, 290
Doliner, Ray, 226
Domestic Partnership Bill, 250
Dorman, Yosef, 78
Dornfeld, Liz, 128, 213
Doron, Aviad, 221, 269
Downtown Kehillah, 161, 236
Dratfield, Sherri, 146, 148, 294, 302
Dratfield, Simon, 148, 192, 294, 296
Dressler, Dean, 153
Druin, *sofer* Gedalia, 146, 148, 212
Dubois, Francis, 252
Dulkin, Rabbi Ryan, 116
Dunkel, Fran, 242

Ebersole, Christine, 191
Edelson, Rabbi David, 53, 88, 266
Education Committee, 85, 91, 224, 225-27, 228, 229, 232, 236-37, 240, 241
Edwards, Rabbi Lisa, 126
egalitarianism, 26, 33, 41, 48-49, 123, 131
Eger, Rabbi Denise, 266
Ehrich, David, 171
Ekman, Michael, 286
El-Ad, Hagai, 270, 271
Ellenson, Rabbi David, 140
Englund, Janet, 184, 210
Eppenstein, Robert, 135, 173, 193, **222**, 228
Epstein, Rabbi Gilbert M., 95
Ettelbrick, Paula, 237, 250

Faddis, Sandy, 173
Faier, Gerry, 148, 223
Falk, Marcia, 123, 125, 127
Feinberg, David, 123
Feldman, Dean, 189
Feminist Minyan, 53-55, 99, 108, 125-27, 160, 217
Feminist Voices, 126-127 *see also* Lesbian Voices
Fern, William (Bill), **15**, 58, 141, 156, 174
 early days at CBST, 18-20, 29-30, 40-41
 and High Holiday services, 166
 leadership and philanthropy, 47, 113, 300
 and rabbi search and hire, 91-94, 96, 98
Ferris, Rabbi Helene, 202, 254
Fifth Avenue Synagogue, 236
Finesilver, Mike, 159, 214, 230
Finn, William (Bill), 164, 189-90
Fischer, Jay, 205, 295
Fischer, Rita, 273-74
 and Alex, 205, 274
Fishman, Cantor Magda, 176, 194, 196
Fiszman, Pesach, 225
Fix, Nicole, 146, **177**
Flohr, David, 117, 228
Ford Foundation, 290
Foreman, Matt, 277
Fornari, Ari Lev, 116
Frank, Stephen E. (Steve), 147, 221, 286, 299, 300, **301**, 302, 308
Frank, Steven, 125, 242
Frank-Lerner, Derek, 125, 149, 242
Freedman, Barbara, 192
Freitag, Joe, 23
Fried, Scott, 274
Friedkin, Ruth, 154
Friedman, Bruce, 11, 44, 50, 91, 141, 225
Friedman, Debbie, 138, 181, 189-90
Friedman, *soferet* Jen Taylor, 146, 148, 235
Friedman, Rabbi Joan, 88, 212
Friedman, Michael, 112
Friedman, Selma, 225
Fruh, Steve, 159, 194, 208, 279
Fuchs-Kreimer, Rabbi Nancy, 140, 229, 232
Fyman, Sherry, 226

Gafni, Hanna, 11, 38, 75, 128, 144, 149, 227
Gaines, Barbara, 280, 306
Galst, Liz, 124-25, 146, 208, 280
Ganz, Jerry, 38, 155
Gartner, Rabbi Rachel, 116, **276**
Gay Activists Alliance, 16, 67
Gay and Lesbian Alliance Against Defamation (GLAAD), 265
Gay and Lesbian Community Services Center, 80, 212, 237
Gay and Lesbian Yeshiva Day School Alum Association (GLYDSA), 218
Gay Men's Health Crisis (GMHC), 58-61, 63, 66-67, 69, 92, 165
Geitner, Kate, **210**
Gelfarb, Rabbi Ruth, 116

315

Giaquinto, Earl Anthony, 152, 159
Gifford, Larry, 75, 231
Gil, Amos, 269, 271, 289-90
Gillibrand, Senator Kirstin, 165, 306
Gindi, Mort, 68
Gladstone, Ya'akov, 58, 180, 256, 258-59
Glick, Assembly Member Deborah, 165
God's Love We Deliver, 63
Goldberg, Rabbi Elisa, 116
Goldberg, Geoffrey, 184
Goldberg, Suzanne, 251
Goldman, Ari, 95
Goldman, Jesse, 58
Goldman, Rabbi Yosef, 116, 268
Goldstein, Harris, 226
Goldstein, Nathan (Nate), 206, 231, 303
Goltsman, Yelena, 217
Goodman, Arthur, 79
Gore, Matthew, 149
Green, Jonathan, 151, 238
Green, Lisa, 151, 238
Green, Talia, 125
Greenberg, Jack, **38**, 149, 150, 155
   cantorial intern search, 194
   early days at CBST, 15, 32, 39, 49, 54-55, 84
   and *A Gay Synagogue in New York*, 295
   and rabbi search and hire, 85, 90, 93-94, 96, 102, 108, 110
   and Religious (later Ritual) Committee, 39, 56, 108, 126, 131, 143, 146, 203
   ritual leadership and liturgy, 69, 139-40, 166, 177
   as teacher, 209, 231-32, 234
Greenberg, Rabbi Julie, 266
Greenberg, Rich, 293
Greenlaw, Father William, 129
Gubbay, Jacob, 14, 18, 20, 30
Gursky, Ruth, 135, 150

Hady, Ronen, 269
Hammerstein Ballroom, 168, 170, 178
Handler, Rabbi Howard, 89
Hanin, Laurie, 151, 228, 238, 240
Harris, Stacey, 151
Harrison, David, 217
Harwayne, Jonathan, 248
Hebrew classes, 225-27, 231
Heldeman, Marvin, 93-94
Heller, Bob, 74
Hermann, George, 282
Hermann, RoseAnn, 282
Herrmann, Rabbi Lauren Grabelle, 116, 231
Hertz, Herbert, 79
Heuman, Mel, 225
Hibsher, William (Bill), 164
   and AIDS discrimination case, 59
   and Changing Airlines Reward Policy, **251**
   and Rabbi Kleinbaum's twentieth anniversary celebration, **306**
   leadership of, 128-29, 164, 286, 298, 299, 300, 302, 303, 306, **308**
Higashi, Taryn, 294
High Holidays, 14, 26, 70-71, 91, 141, 166-79, 219, 288
Hirschmann, Rabbi Jo, 125
Hirschmann, Shoshana, 125
Hochberg, Steve, 297
Hoffman, Neal, 124, 228, 232, 270
Hoffman-Ingall, Shirley, 125
Hollander, Judy, 146, 173, 211, 232, 234-35, 295
Holtzman, Rabbi Linda, 266
Holub, Rabbi Margaret, 88
Honig, Herbert, 41
Howe, Richard, 11, 162
Hruska, Peter, 79

Iacullo, Sal, 212
Ingall, Andrew, 124, 125, 229, 232, 241, 270
Ingerman, Susan, 151
Irving, John, 112
Ismond, Reny, 77, 80
Israel and Zionism
   CBST commitment to, 246
   CBST education on, 231-32
   CBST guest speakers from, 164-65
   CBST members' trips to, 80, 112, 205, 209, 270-71, 287
   Israel bonds, 69
   Israeli dancing, 29, 157, 253
   Israeli holidays, 141, 190 *see also* Yom Hazikaron *and* Yom Ha'atsmaut
   Israeli media, announcement of Rabbi Kleinbaum's hire in, 103
   Israeli music, 43, 186
   Jerusalem Open House, 165, 221, 269
   Jewish National Fund (JNF), 77, 258-59
   Salute to Israel Parade, 260-63
   Zionist *chug*, 217, 226

Jacob Javits Center, 121, 167-68, 170-73, 177, 179, 183, 220, 269, 289
Jacobs, Danny, 112, 214
Jacobson, Joanne, 121, 229, 295
Jaffe, Harold, 64
James, Marisa, 221
Janover, Marc, 114, 187, 214, 292
Jerusalem Open House, 165, 221, 269
Jeselsohn, Paul, 252, 297
Jewish Activist Gays and Lesbians (JAGL), 218, 262
Jewish Board of Family and Children's Services (JBFCS), 66-67, 84
Johnson, Bill, 251
Jones, Bishop Zachary, 271
Judson, Rabbi Daniel, 116, 277
Julius, Ralph, 79

Kabakov, Miryam, 218
*Kabbalat Shabbat*, 14, 28, 48, 53-54, 126, 130
Kahn, Marcy, 128, 235, 249, 298
Kahn, Rabbi Yoel, 88, 266
Kahn-Troster, Rabbi Rachel, 116, 231, 268
Kaplan, Roberta (Robbie), 165, 285
Karger, Murray, 38, 86
Karle, Margot, 86
Karp, Erika, 205, 300
   and Hanna, Molly, and Ruby Kessler-Karp, 205
Kartzman, Lisa, 270
   and High Holidays, 167, 179
   leadership, 214, 286, 290, **291**
   volunteerism, 128, 153, 167, 168, 173, 302
Kates-Harris, Ariel, 11, 292
Katske, Erica, 253
Katz, Jeff, 53, 58, 256
Katz, Nir, 272
Katz, Phil, 158
Kaufman, Don, 77
Kaufman, Cantor Jason, 176, 194, **196**, 292
Kaufman, Moises, 229
Kaufman, Rachel, 184
Kay, Lawrence (Larry), 121, 195, **183**
   and Orthopractic Minyan, 53
   service leadership, 153, 166, 176-78, 181, 184
   as teacher, 231
   volunteerism, 130
Kessler, Gwynn, 11, 239-40
Kessler, Sari, 194, 205
King, Maryann, 148, 208, 295
Klein, Peter, 146
Klein, Tova, 124
Kleinbaum, Josephine, 148, 173, 270
Kleinbaum, Rabbi Sharon, 270-72, 292
   activism, 246, 251-53, 260, 263, 265, 277, 281, 283
   and AIDS crisis, 111-13, 274
   and the CBST siddur, 139-40
   and the Church of the Holy Apostles, 129
   and the Conservative Movement, 89, 119, 267
   *drashot*, **177**, 280, 290-91
   and gay marriage, 283, 285
   and gender issues, 25, 109, 217
   and holidays, 153, 157, 159, 162, 167, 171, 178-79, 220
   hiring of, 99-103, 174-75
   installation of, 102, **104-05**, 126
   and lifecycle rituals, 203, 205, 210-11, 213, 233
   *Listening for the Oboe*, 290-91
   and music, 182-85, **186**
   and pastoral care, 111-13
   and queer identity, 294
   and the Reform Movement, 118
   ritual leadership, 108-10, 115-17, 124-25, 129-31, 153, 207, 233
   and September 11, 2001, 288
   and speakers at CBST, 164-65
   as teacher, 227, 229, 231, 233-34

and transgender issues, 218-19
twentieth anniversary celebration, 292, 303, 306
and WorldPride, 269-71
Klotz, Jeffry, 62
Klugman, Shari, 151
Knieter, Lyn, 23, 256
Knox, Gary, 66
Koch, Mayor Edward, 59, 184, 254, 260-61, 265
Kohn, Ron, 124, 184, 212, 216, 225-27, 237-38
*Koleinu*, 280-81, 295
Korenfield, Irene, 123
Korn, Danielle, 147, 173
Kotick, Steve, 227
Krakoff, Josh, 240
Kramer, Larry, 58, 67
Krasney, Seymour, 270
Krause, David, 35, 37, 47, 136, 247, 254, 256
Krim, Dr. Mathilde, 164
Krop, Karen, 176, 192
Krulwich, Sara, 71, **213**
Krulwich, Theodore, 71
Kuriel, Heymi, 299, 300, 302, 303
Kurtz, Connie, 222, 229, 250
Kushner, Tony, 164

Lambda Legal, 16, 59, 61, 65, 67, 77, 164-65, 251
Landman, Richard (Rick), 128, **145**, 158-59, 161, 248, 249-50, 262, 279
Lappe, Rabbi Benay, 228, 233, 266-67, 268
*Lawrence v. Texas*, 285
Lehrhaus Judaica Program, 228-29, 231, 233, 267
Lehrman, Michael, 184, 205
Leigh, Rabbi Darby Jared, 116, 159, **178**, 221, 231
Leipzig, Rosanne, **86**
*brit ahavah*, 201, 203
and rabbi search and hire, 87, 90-94
and Religious Committee, 49, 84
service leadership, 42-44, 46, 49, 53, 70, 126, 166, 184
Leonard, Arthur (Art), **43**
activism, 249, 251-51
and AIDS crisis, 59-60, 66-67
and the Conservative Movement, 89
and Howard Schwartz, 78
and Jewish National Fund, 259
on legal ramifications of families with children, 237
and rabbi search and hire, 91, 93-96, 98, 102, 207
service leadership, 42, 292
as teacher, 231
Lercher, Lawrence, 65
Lerner, Mark, 242
Lesbian, Gay, Bisexual, & Transgender Community Center, 144, 174-75, 249
Lesbian Voices (minyan), 126 *see also* Feminist Minyan *and* Feminist Voices

Lesiger, Jay, 202
Lesser, Rabbi Joshua, 116, 218, 293
Lessler, Amy, 292
Lester, Elenore, 16-17, 21, 25, **27**, 31, 33, 157, 224, 248
Levien, Michael, 56-57
Levin, David, 221
Levin, Lee, 73, 75, 77, 80, 167
Levine, Rabbi Darren, 116
Levine, Michael, 52, 109, 128, 173, 227
and the AIDS crisis, 63
and Dick Radvon, 134-35
early days at CBST, 14-15, 18, 32, 35-37
on coming out, 16
leadership, 35-37, 40-41, 109
and rabbi search and hire, 97, 102
radio interviews, 248, 295
volunteerism, 173
and World Congress of GLBT Jewish Organizations, 256-57
Levine, Sam, 144
Levitz, Cindy, 153
Liberal Minyan, 117, 123-24
Lichtenstein, Murray, 28, **30**, 32-33, 36, 47, 166, 180, 225
Lieberman, Jacob, 218, 291
*Limmud Mishpachah*, 240-41, **242**, 311
Linder, Regina, 126, 131, 150, 217, 252
and AIDS crisis, 112
and adult education grant, 228
early days at CBST, 17, 25-27, 33
leadership, 102, 126
on misogyny following hire of Rabbi Kleinbaum, 109
on service leadership, 131
on transgender inclusion, 217
*Listening for the Oboe*, 290-91
Loebel, Irwin (Ian), 66, 248
Lopez, Johnny, 78
Lowe, Nancy, 20, 25
Lowe, Rabbi Sanford, 266
Ludvigsen, Aari, 6, 125, 146, 208, 280, 296, 299, 303
Ludvigsen-Gaines, Simon, 125, 159, 236, 280
Lutrin, Harry, 49, 148, 216
Lutvak, Mark, 72

Mable, Judy *see* Ora Chaikin
Macklin, Ann, 221, 297
Maikey, Haneen, 269
Malick, Jack, 144
Mandelbaum, Arnold, 20, 134, 248, 254
March, Stan, 79
Margolius, Rabbi Marc, 11, 119
marriage *see* weddings
Marsolini, Paul, 159, 208, 279
Martin Luther King Day, 161, 188
Martinez, Patricia, **161**
Marty, Bonnie, 235
Maseng, Danny, 189
Masur, Allan, 23, 40
Matalon, Rabbi Rolando, 88, 92, 254

Matesky, Jared, 144
Math, Rabbi Dennis, 254
Matt, Rabbi Hershel, 254, 264
Mazon, a Jewish Response to Hunger, 160
McFarlane, Roger, 92
Meitner, Margot, 116
Melnick, Marsha, 11, 139-40, 206, 215, 229, 231, **281**, 295, 306
membership dues, 40, 47, 51, 97, 132, 286
Mencher, Rabbi Edythe Held (Edie), 116, **129**
Mendel, Tom, 150
Mendelson, Henry, 20
Mercado, Ricardo, 69
Mertzel, Nancy, 11, 125-26, 203-04, 227
Messinger, Ruth, 164, 273
Metropolitan Community Church, 18, 247, 271
Metropolian Pavilion, 167, 170, 177, 288
Metz, Zachary, 161
Mevarchim Minyan, 45-46, 117, 123
Meyer, Rabbi Marshall, 92, 164, 254
Meyer, Nancy, 148, 218, **220**
Meyer, Susan, 11, 206, 214-15, 224, 229, **235**, 296
*Mi shebeirach* (prayer for the sick), 138
Michaels, Sheila, 75, 91, 108
Miller, Annette, 11, 26, 73, 75, 117-18, 154, 211, 292
Miller, Gilbert, 68
minyanim
Bethune, 130
Feminist, 53-55, 99, 108, 125-27, 160, 217
Liberal, 117, 123-24
Mevarchim/Traditional, 45-46, 117, 123
Minyan Chadash, 46
Orthopractic, 53-55, 99, 108, 123
Shabbat Morning, 34, 45-46, 146, 153, 194
shiva, 214
Mishaan, Albert Shemmy, 212
Mishaan, Marilyn, 211-12, 226-27
Mishkan Committee, 128, 298, 299
Mishpachah, The, 221-22
Mizrahi, Saul, 20, 29, 40, 45, 132, 156, **158**, 202, 248
Moldovan, Stanley (Stan), 148, 221, 232, 295
Mones, Glenn, 128, 227
Mooy, George, 42
Morellet, Florent, 163
Motzkin, *soferet* Rabbi Linda, 146-47
movement affiliation, 86-89 *see also* Affiliation Committee
music, 26, 29, 32, 43, 86, 176-77, 180-197

Nachemin, Robert, 72
Nacianceno, Ray, 135
Nadler, US Representative Jerrold, 165
Nathan, Rabbi Tracy, 116, 268, 288-89, 293
National Gay and Lesbian Task Force (NGLTF), 16, 265, 277

Naughton, Katie, 292
Neighborhood Chevruta Program, 232
Nelson, Michael, 288
Nenno, Tim, 248
Newburgh, Morty, 249
Nieman, Dylan, 270
Nieman, Jack, 146, 148, 208, **209**, 215, 249, 270
    as Jacqueline Jonée, 159
Niv, Nachum, 227
Nixon, Cynthia, 283, 306
NY AIDS Action Committee, 66

Offner, Rabbi Stacy, 201
Ofrane, Avi, 218
Orensanz Synagogue, 189
Orient, Richard, 206, 303
Orthodoxy, 174, 200-01, 218
    Anti-gay action, 258-61
    CBST members with Orthodox background, 25, 32, 38, 46, 71, 112, 120, 129, 174, 238
    CBST partnerships with Orthodox synagogues, 236
    LGBT Groups, 218
    and Pinchas ben Aharon, 31-35, 91, 200
    and Purim, 157-58
    religious practice at CBST, 49, 53-54, 109, 123, 127
Orthodykes, 217-18
Orthopractic Minyan, 53-55, 99, 108, 123

Paasche-Orlow, Rabbi Sara, 114, 116-17, 233, 268
Pack, Sheila, 150
Paley, Grace, 100
Paltrow, Lynn, **213**
Paltrow-Krulwich, Samantha and Allen, **213**
Parker, Graham, 192
Passover, 18, 70, 80, 135, 152, 156, 208
pastoral care
    during AIDS crisis, 62, 69, 76, 84, 91, 99, 105, 111-13
    early days at CBST, 56
    Rabbi Rachel Gartner on, **276**
Pavloff, Janet, frontispiece, 150, 302
Perlov, George, 149, 232, 235, 296
Perry, Reverend Troy, 18
Petrow-Cohen, Jessica, 237
Pilshaw, Elliot, 181
Pinchas ben Aharon, 152, 225
    background, 31
    and lifecycle rituals, 200, 215-16
    as member of Board of Trustees, 20
    return to Orthodoxy, 34-35
    and rabbi search and hire, 91, 110
    spiritual leadership and vision, 16, 28, 31, 33, 42, 45, 49, 132-33, 136, 177, 180
    and women's leadership, 27, 33-34, 43
Pinkas, Alon, 269
Plastock, Pam, 66
Plave, Ruth, 48, 181

Pollock, Danny, 157, 253
Post, Sheldon (Shelly), 57-59, 76, 202, 249
Potasinski, Lee, 161
Potasinski, Yolanda, 109, 128, 164, 227
    leadership, 53, 110, 125-26, 173, 215-16, 228, 230, 286, **287**, 292
    wedding of, 203-04
Potasinski-Mertzel, Shari, 125
Press, Harve, 61
Pride Shabbat, 120, 128, 162-63, 165, 170, 249, 283, 301
Prince, Cheryl, 241
Proposition 8, 184
Purim, 157-60

queer (identity), 134, 219-20, 294
Quell, Asher, 174
Quinn, New York City Council Speaker Christine, 165, 278

Rabbi Liaison Committee, 102
Rabbi Search Committee, 91, 93-94, 97, 98-99
Rabbinical Assembly, 89, 95-96, 119, 265, 267-68
Rabbis for Human Rights, 160
Radvon, Richard (Dick), 73, 128, 156, **134-35**, 273, 287
    early days at CBST, 15, 55, 132
    and Jewish National Fund, 259
    on open door policy, 166
    volunteerism, 173, 273
Rapoport, Paul, 58, 72
Reconstructionist Movement, 86-87, 88-89, 95-96, 98-99, 156, 177, 265
Reconstructionist Rabbinical College (RRC), 99, 114, 116, 229
Reder, Rick, 209, 215, 270
Reform Movement
    CBST affiliation with, 32, 86-89, 95
    policies on homosexuality, 118, 264
    and Rabbi Roderick Young, 118
    and rabbi search, 95-96, 98-99
    Religious Action Center, 99-100, 112, 165, 251
    Union of American Hebrew Congregations (UAHC), 87-89, 102, 254
Regelson, Roslyn (Ros), 25, **27**, 224
Reich, Myrna, 146, 147
Reichbach, Michael, 288
Religious Action Center of Reform Judaism (RAC), 99-100, 112, 165, 251
Religious Committee 99, 131, 138, 143, 177, 201, 292 *see also* Ritual Committee
    and AIDS crisis, 62-63, 66, 70, 75, 84
    and alternative minyanim, 52-55
    creation of, 35-36
    expansion of in 1980s, 49-50
    and lifecycle needs, 56, 201-02
    and purchase of cemetery plot, 68
    and purchase of a Torah, 143
    and rabbi search and hire, 93-94, 97, 99, 131

religious backgrounds of first members, 38-39
    and service structure, 42-46
    and siddur project, 136, 138, 177
retreat, annual, 221, 230, 242, 244-45
Ribnick, Judy, **51, 162, 176-77, 181, 192, 195, 202, 212, 237**
Rich, Frank, 164, 306
Riegner, Irene, 147
Rittmaster, Lou, 37, 58, 94, 102, 142, 157, 174-75, 249 *see also* Cooperberg-Rittmaster Rabbinical Intern Program
Ritual Committee, 131, 139, 166 *see also* Religious Committee
Rizack, Lea, 150, 161, 282
Robertson, Scott, 292
Robins, Sy, 248
Roijce, Chet, 11, 292
Rosansky, Sue, 130
Rose, Avi, 269
Rose, Rabbi Dawn, 266
Rosen, Beth, 208, 295
Rosen, Ira Jay, 259
Rosen, Melvin (Mel)
    and AIDS crisis, 59, **60**, 66-68, 76, 80, 92, 101-02
    leadership, 51, 52, 53, 85, 110, 226, 240
    on Movements, 264-65
    on new minyanim, 55
    and rabbi search and hire, 85, 87, 95, 101-02, 105, 175
    on Yom Kippur services, 168-69
Rosenbaum, Eric, 215, 234, 270, 286, **298**, 299, 302
Rosenbaum, Rabbi Mychal *see* Rabbi Mychal Copeland
Rosenberg, Sydney, 75, 154, 213, 297
Rosenbloom, Bill, 130, 184
Rosenzweig, Joyce, 139, 153, 161, 176, 182-89, 193-97, 292
Rosh Hashanah
    early days at CBST, 28, 80, 174
    services in later years, 166-68, 170, 178-79, 238, 288-89
Roth, Mark, 85
Rothbaum, Rabbi Michael, 116, 231
Rotstein, Miya, 221
Rubenstein, Liba Wenig, 155, 253, 307
Rubenstein, Molly Wenig, 155, 162, 307
Russian group, 217

Sabin, Michael, 69
Sacks, Rabbi J.B., 80, 88-89, 92, 265
Sadowsky, Harold, 77
Sager, Daniel, 79
Sameth, Ilene, 146, 269, 290, 299-300
Sand, Jonathan, 68
Sattath, Noa, 165, 221, 269, 271
Savage, Danny, 269
Schatell-Prince, Emmet Nathan, 122
Scheckner, Jeff, 225
Schindler, Rabbi Alexander, 102, 105, 164
Schoenholtz, Howard, 77

Schumer, Senator Charles E., 165
Schwartz, Howard, 78
Schwartz, Jase, 218, **293**
Schwartz, Stuart, 64
Schwartz, Walter, 81, 112
Selden, Rob, 85
Sennett-Kuzin, Emma, 237
September 11, 2001, 173, 287, 288-89
Services and Advocacy for GLBT Elders (SAGE), 165, 222, 249
Shabbat Morning Minyan, 34, 45-46, 146, 153, 194
Shabbat Shirah concert, 189-91
Shapiro, Rina, 269
Shavuot, 142-43, 146, 153, 157, 233
Shaw, Evelyn, 222
Shear, Spencer, 151
Sheffer, Jonathan, 150, 191-92, 210, 299-300, 303
Shelter of Peace, 282
shiva, 111, 214-16
Shokeid, Moshe, 294-95
Shuman, Jeffrey, 77
Siciliano, Carl, 282
siddurim, 123
   *Blue Shmatte*, 132-33, 137
   *Book of Blessings*, 125, 127
   Orthodox, 45, 54
   *Siddur B'chol L'vav'cha* (1981 edition), 37, 42, 136-38, 162, 183
   *Siddur B'chol L'vav'cha* (2007 edition), 123, 139-41, 162, 207, 272-73, 291
Siegel, Laurie, 146, 148, **197**, **211**
Siegel, Steve, 38, 146, 226
Sigal, David I., 306
Silver, Dr. Larry, 79
Silver, Michael, 80
Silverstein, Susie, 205
Simchat Torah, 153, 212
Simon, Rabbi Melissa, 116, 219, 240-41, 277, **278**
Sinacore, Rob, 73
Singer, Cantor Daniel, 162, 194, 196
Singer, Isaac Bashevis, 225-26
Sklamberg, Lorin, 181
Slomack, Judy, 135
*sofrim* and *sofrot*, 146, 148, 212, 235
Sonnenstein, Janet *see* Shayna Caul
Sotolongo, Jose, 78
Spegal, David, 66, 184
Spencer Memorial Church, 166
Spivak, Monique, 240
Springer, Lisa, 208, 241
Springer-Galst, Aviv, 208
Springer-Galst, Naomi, 125, 208
Spyer, Thea, 284-85
Steinberg, David Rabbi, 116, 233
Steinman, Wayne, 212, 237
Stephen Wise Free Synagogue, 57, 164, 170, 191, 202, 236, 254
Stonewall riots, 16, 115, 295
Strickler, Arthur (Art), 48, 52, 63, 66, 80, 130, 216, 248, 259

Sukkot, 152-53
Sull, Catherine, 53, 110, 126, 184
Sussholtz, Michael, 77

Tashlich, 167
Tauber, Julia, 122
Tax, Judith, 49, 88, 264
Taylor, Micheale, 241
Temkin, Diane, 184
Terr, Elliot, 20
Tessler, Marilyn, 221, **223**
Thomasson, Ruby, 221
Tichnor, Alan, 263
Torah acquisition and dedication, 141-47, 150-51
Torah, Holocaust, 144-45
Torah, member written, 146-51
Tot Shabbat, 124 *see also* Aleph Bet Shabbat
Town and Village Synagogue, 236
Town Hall, 168, 170, 301
Trachten, Leah, 112, 150, 252
Traditional Evening Minyan, 123, 127
Traditional Morning Minyan, 123 *see also* Mevarchim Minyan
Trainin, Rabbi Isaac, 63
Trans Empowerment Committee, **219**
Trans Working Group, 219, 231
Transgender Day of Remembrance, 152, 161
transgender inclusion, 217-19
Trester, Mickie, 221
Trobishi, Liz, 272
Troum, Carol, 73
Tu Bish'vat, 160, 258
Turkel, Judith, 237
Turkel, Mark, 65, 67, 171
20s and 30s group, 220-21
Tyson, Chuck, 247, 286
*tzedakah*, 160

Union of American Hebrew Congregations (UAHC), 87-89, 102, 254
Urban, Louis, 216

Vallet, Pierre, 191-92, **234**, 270
Vexler, Jill, 189
Vexler, Tibarek, 151
Victor-Marlowe, Katie, 237
Village Temple, 236, 254
Vine, George, 161
Vine, Mike, 128, 161, 229, 286-87, **289**, 290
Vogel, Linda, 173
Vogel, Peter, 59, 65

Wahler, William (Bill), 51-52, 85, 87, 93-94, 144, 257
Wahnon, Shep, 151, 217, 287
Waldman, Mike, 217-18, **219**, **236**
Warshaw, Sandy, 109, 125, **126**, 127, 128, 146, 150, 211
Weber, Fred, 20
weddings, 121, 138, 193, 200-06, 242, 294
   *see also brit ahavah*
Weiner, Gloria, 156

Weingarten, Randi, 165, 250
Weinstein, Gabrielle, 237
Weintraub, Rabbi Simkha, 88, 232
Weiss, Rabbi Eric, 266
Weiss, Jillian (Jill), **138**, **187**, 217-18, 230
Weiss, Marc, 218
Weiss, Rabbi Rachel, 11, 114, 116, **122**, 231, 240-42, **243**
Weiss, Ron, 38, 61-62, 71, 75, 150, 162, **226**, 231, 295
Weissman, Alex, 150, 281, 292
Wells, Lloyd, 76
Wenig, Rabbi Margaret Moers, 88, 182, 232, 254
Wertheim, Ellen, 121, 146, 149, 153
Westbeth, 23-25, 41, 43, 128-30, 153-54, 166-69, 170, 296
Westboro Baptist Church Protest, 278
Westside Discussion Group, 18
Wiener, Rabbi Nancy, 49, 88, 266
Windsor, Edith (Edie), 165, 284-85
Wine, David, 299-300, 302-03
Winter, Lauren, 241
Wolf, Felix, 146, 150
Wolfson, Evan, 251
Wolfson, Ron, 111
Women's Outreach Committee, 25
World AIDS Day, 141, 152, 161, 273-74
World Congress of GLBT Jewish Organizations, 256-57
WorldPride, 269-71

Yiddish classes, 27, 225-26
Yom Ha'atsmaut, 188, 231
Yom Hashoah, 161, 188, 236
Yom Kippur, 43, 121, 166-72, 177-79, 288
Yom Kippur War, 18, 40, 78, 152, 174, 258
Young, Rabbi Roderick, 114, 116, **118**, 139, 159, 228, 233, 288, 289, 294
Youngerman, Barry, 53-54, 248, 257

Zaleon, Janet, 150, 184
Zalkin, Michele, 151
Zalkin, Saul, **36**, 117, 151
   and AIDS counseling, 84
   early days at CBST, 36-39, 42, 44-45, 47, 52
   on High Holiday services, 179
   and Neighborhood Chevruta Program, 232
   office work, 85, 291
   recital in memory of Shelly Post, 76
   and Religious Committee, 52, 56, 63-64, 66, 68, 70, 138, 143, 202-03
   service leadership, 166, 177, 180
Zellman, Rabbi Reuben, 218, 219, 232, 240, 293
Zenzel, Bill, 213
Zerbarini, Rabbi Lina, 114, 116, 233
Zimet, Rhoda, 286
Zimmerman, Ivan, 159, 218, 294
Zionism *see* Israel and Zionism

# PHOTO CREDITS

Credits are listed by page number and t (top), b (bottom), c (center), l (left), r (right).

Joan Abrams 284 t
*AIDS DEMO GRAPHICS*, Douglas Crimp with Adam Rolston, Bay Press, Seattle (1990) 67
Nancy Alpert (courtesy of) 94 t c
AP Photo/Tina Fineberg 205 b
Harriet Beckman (courtesy of) 295 b
Karen Benezra 300 all
Yehuda Berger (courtesy of) 56
Gabriel Blau 283 t r, 302 c
Diane Bondareff 263
Jay Brady 273
Frédéric Brenner 267 b
Bruce J. Brumberg 154 b
Lisa Abbott Canfield 161 b
CBST Archives 12-13, 14 all, 15, 16, 17 all, 18 b, 19, 20-21 all, 22-23 all, 24-25 all, 26-27 all, 28-29 all, 30, 32, 33, 37 t, b, 40-41 all, 42 all, 44 b, 45 all, 46-47 all, 49 all, 50, 53, 54, 57, 58, 66 b, 70, 73 all, 74, 75 inset, 78 inset, 84-85, 86 t, 88-89, 92 t, 94 t l, t r, b l, b c, b l, b r, 95, 99, 101 all, 103 all, 104, 112 all, 117 t, 118 b, 119 all, 120, 124, 129 b, 132, 133 b, 135 t, b, 136 r, 137, 138, 139, 140 t, l, r c, 141 all, 142-143 all, 146, 147 b, 152 all, 154 l, c, r, 155 t r, b, 156 c, 157 t, r, 158 all, 159 r b, 161 t, 162 b, 164 all, 165 t, c, 166-167 all, 168-169 all, 171, 172, 174, 175 b, 177 all, 180, 181 all, 182, 184, 188 l, 189 t r, 190, 191 l, 193, 194, 200, 204 b, 207 all, 215, 216 t l, 217, 221 t r, b r, l, 224, 225 t, 227 t r, l r, b, 231, 232, 239, 240, 244-245 all, 246-247 all, 248 all, 250 all, 253 all, 255, 256 all, 257 all, 258 t l, b l, 259, 260, 262 t r, t l, b l, 264 all, 266, 267 t, 269 t, 274 b r, 277 t, r, 280, 281 b, 282 all, 283 t l, b, 289, 290 t, 291, 296 all

Maya Orli Cohen (courtesy of) 269 b
Ralph DiBart 206 b
Barbara Dolgin 121 t
Sharon Dressler (courtesy of Andrew Ingall & Neal Hoffman) 118 t
James Estrin (courtesy of Sara Krulwich and Lynn Paltrow) 213 r
Hugo Fernandes 106-107, 303 all, 308 all
Jay Fischer and Michael Lehrman (courtesy of) 205 t
Randi Friedman 223 b
Hanna Gafni 153 all, (courtesy of) 144 b l
Barbara Gaines 92 b, 122 t, 124-125 all, 144 r t, r b, 159 t l, c, r c, r b, 198-199, 208 l b, r, 219, 221 t l, 229 b, 230, 236, 238, 241 all, 242 r, 243, 244-245, 270 b, 272
Jerry Ganz 44, 66 t
Ya'akov Gladstone 18 t, 157 l b, 258 t r
Martha Gorfein 191 t, b, 196 b, 197 r, 283 c, 307 t r
Donna Gray 242 l
Jack Greenberg (courtesy of) 140 b, 226
Hartsdale Camera & Portrait Studio 129 t
Joan Heller and Ellen Tickner (courtesy of Rosanne Leipzig) 51, 201, 202
Judy Hollander (courtesy of) 211, 270 t, c
Richard Howe for CBST White Paper 113
Rabbi Sharon Kleinbaum (courtesy of) 98, 100 all, 105, 162 t
Daniel Kohanski 31, 58, 133 t, 136 c, 256 t
Sara Krulwich (courtesy of) 71
Rick Landman (courtesy of) 145, 262 b r
LGBT Center Archive 65 l, 248 c
Jicky Leidicke 75 top, 83, 121, 156 t r, b, 173 all, 176 all, 178, 183, 185, 186 all, 188 t, b, 190 c, b, 192 t r, 194-195 all, 196 t, 197 b, 208 t l, 233, 278 b l, b r, 306 t l, t r, b l, b r, 307 t l, b l, b r
Rosanne Leipzig (courtesy of) 86, 94 t c
Art Leonard (courtesy of) 43 t
Michael Levine (courtesy of) 134, 135 c, 136 l

Regina Linder (courtesy of) 228 all, 252 all
Marla S. Maritzer 222
Amy Meadow (courtesy of Sara Krulwich and Lynn Paltrow) 213 l
Meryl Meisler 285 b l, r
Marsha Melnick 165 b, 257 t, 271 t
Susan E. Meyer 43 b, 59, 65 r, 72 all, 75 b, 82 all, 122 b, 123, 126, 127, 135 t, 140 c t, r, 155 t l, 159 t r, l c, b c, 189 c r, 190 t, 220, 244-45, 285 t l r, c, 290 b, 297
Annette Miller 114, 117 t, 128 all, 213 t, 223 t, 244-245, 274 b, 287
Jennie Miller 237
Saul Mizrahi (courtesy of) 257 b
Virginia Morawerk 284 b
New York Public Library 18 t
Jack Nieman 6, 147 t, 148-149 all, 150-151 all, 154 t, 192 l, bl, bc, 197 t r, 212 t, 234-235 all
Jack Nieman (courtesy of) 270 b
Tina Paul 109, 155 r c, 189 b, 227 t
Yolanda Potasinski 160 b
Yolanda Potasinski and Nancy Mertzel (courtesy of) 204 t
Laurie Rhodes (courtesy of Nathan Goldstein & Mitchell Davis) 206 t
Lou Rittmaster (courtesy of) 157 l, b, 174
Gabriel Rosenberg 160 t
Miya Rotstein 271 b, l, r
Jase Schwartz (courtesy of) 293
Larry Selzer 52, 155 b, 212 b, 225 b
Laurie Siegel 229 t
Roberta Sklar 257, 277 b
Bill Wahler (courtesy of) 144 t l
Ron Weiss (courtesy of) 38
Ellen Wertheim 216 c l, c r, b
Saul Zalkin (courtesy of) 36
Ivan Zimmerman and Taryn Higashi (courtesy of) 294